IN AND OUT OF
MENTAL RETARDATION

320-1
20

IN AND OUT OF MENTAL RETARDATION

Essays on Educability, Disability, and Human Policy

Burton Blatt, Ed.D.
Dean, School of Education
Syracuse University

University Park Press
Baltimore

UNIVERSITY PARK PRESS
International Publishers in Science, Medicine, and Education
300 North Charles Street
Baltimore, Maryland 21201

Typeset by Maryland Composition Co.
Manufactured in the United States of America by The Maple Press
Company.

Library of Congress Cataloging in Publication Data

Blatt, Burton, 1927–
In and out of mental retardation.

Includes index.
Contents: Educability: Toward an understanding of people with special needs. A
concept of educability and the correlates of mental illness, mental retardation, and
cultural deprivation. Teaching the mentally retarded. Poems and aphorisms. How
to destroy lives by telling stories—Disability: Purgatory. Exodus from pandemonium. This crazy business. From institution to community, a conversion model.
The family papers, a return to purgatory—[etc.]
1. Mentally handicapped—United States—Addresses, essays, lectures. 2. Mentally
handicapped—Education—United States—Addresses, essays, lectures.
3. Mentally handicapped—Government policy—United States—Addresses, essays,
lectures. I. Title.
[DNLM: 1. Education of mentally retarded—Collected works. 2. Mental
retardation—Collected works.
WM 300 B644i]
HV3006.A4B567   362.3'0973   81-1652
ISBN 0-8391-1664-0   AACR2

Contents

Foreword

If there has been a revolution in the field of mental retardation over the past two or three decades, it has been not in the solution of its fundamental problems but in their perception. From a seemingly universal faith that technical and scientific progress would ameliorate and even eliminate the problems of mentally retarded people, we have come to a realization that the most fundamental of those problems are not even addressed by such an approach. It has become increasingly evident that the segregation, dehumanization, and even physical abuse that mentally retarded people were subjected to was not caused by a breakdown of the technology of treatment, but by the application of that technology.

It is true that the technology *had* broken down—no one can defend what was happening in America's institutions as treatment or therapy. But the revolution was in the perception that, even if institutions were put in the best working order, they would be intrinsically abusive at their best and their best would be virtually impossible to sustain. At best, institutions segregate people, deprive them of their civil rights and civil liberties. As was forcefully brought to our awareness by the civil rights movement, separate is never equal. Worse still, studies of the nature and history of segregated institutions have shown that they inevitably produce dehumanization and abuse in spite of the intentions and best precautions of their managers. For a hundred years, institution after institution has slipped from the noble ideals of its planners into a warehouse of hopelessness and despair. Even the history of the language of those ideals cautions us against repeating the institutional experiment: where once the offer of "asylum" meant a refuge of security and kindness, it quickly came to be known as a euphemism for imprisonment and torture.

The collection of writings in this volume represents one of the most influential voices in reformulating the problem of mental retardation from technical-scientific to essentially human terms. The alternative to the "institutional monolith" emerges from the premise that mentally retarded people are *people*; and that, as people, we are all valuable, capable of growth, and entitled to fundamental rights, regardless of the level of our intellectual abilities. If the professionals in mental retardation are to offer help to mentally retarded people, it cannot be at the sacrifice of those principles. Incarceration does not contribute to the development of intellectual potential; segregation is not a cure for the lack of adaptive social skills. However, in ordinary homes in ordinary communities, such services *can* be provided, even to the most seriously disabled people. Indeed, such services can be more effective within the framework of the community than they were in "special" and isolated settings: factors such as a sense of dignity, self-esteem, and mutual respect provide meaning and motivation in the lives of mentally retarded people as much as in the lives of anyone else.

Twenty years ago, hardly anyone would have found such a position intelligible, much less plausible. It was a time when not only the rights of mentally retarded people but the rights of blacks, women, and many other groups could still be dismissed with paternalistic amusement. The change has been enormous and probably irreversible.

Yet, although the fundamental changes of attitude and legal status have produced substantial practical gains for such formerly devalued groups as women and black people, progress in the field of mental retardation has not been comparable. There are success stories, to be sure, but on the whole we seem to be in a period of contradictions and frustrations. Issues that seemed nearly settled ten years ago smolder on unresolved. Group homes for mentally retarded people are well integrated and welcomed in some communities, whereas in others vitriolic opposition seeks to exclude them, sometimes even by violence. The rights of handicapped people have been established in legislation, but court battles threaten to vitiate their implementation. And, although hardly anyone can be found to defend custodial institutions, leading professionals emerge to oppose the closing of such institutions.

In some ways these difficulties are neither surprising nor disturbing. That is, although it is very disturbing that some people continue to suffer abusive and debilitating treatment, in the longer run these things are sure to change. One of the reasons that human rights are difficult to obtain is the fact that, once established, they are even more difficult to take away. It is not surprising that the newly established rights of mentally retarded people should be subjected to challenges and tests; the trials will ultimately only strengthen them. Nor is it surprising that the public attitude in many communities is still antagonistic toward mentally retarded people. It is an attitude that only recently was endorsed by the most enlightened professionals. In time, the change of professional and legal viewpoint will spread and become established.

However, there is something else in the dynamics of the field of mental retardation that may not be resolved by the momentum of social change alone. That momentum, based on the human and civil rights of mentally retarded people, began with the realization that some problems do not have technical solutions. Today, we are faced with the even more difficult realization that there are problems that do not have a solution at all—at least not in the ordinary sense of the word. There are problems that present genuine dilemmas.

As a nation we have historically been impatient with such problems and our characteristic response to a dilemma has been to simply overwhelm it. "The difficult we do immediately; the impossible takes a little longer." Because we have been rich enough to sustain the illusion that our resources and resourcefulness are unlimited, we have indeed accomplished much that was "impossible." But, even in the technological sphere, which has been our greatest strength, it is becoming obvious that some dilemmas are beyond our power to overwhelm. We must after all choose between a clean environment and maximized industrialization, between the unrestricted enjoyment of private automobiles and a viable balance of trade, between the need for guns and the needs of ghettos. Not everyone recognizes these choices as problematic and certainly only a minority of people today recognize them as dilemmas. The habit of mind persists that, in America, *everything* is possible. Many people interpret the problem as the work of some culprit, such as big government, oil cartels, or welfare chiselers. Others trust that yet another technical innovation–a new tax scheme, fusion power–is all we need to dissolve the dilemmas. Yet, despite the rhetoric and denial, our national policy is more and more coming to reflect the reality that some goods can only be maximized at the expense of others.

The dilemmas of mental retardation, and of the human services generally, however, are even more troublesome. They arise not from a shortage of resources (although resources are necessary and limited here as elsewhere), but from the very nature of the context. No new energy source or administrative design or service delivery system can resolve such intrinsic dilemmas.

Much of the controversy in the field of mental retardation today centers on the intrinsic dilemma that we simultaneously recognize the rights of mentally retarded people and the obligation to provide them with needed services. This is not a problem that arises with the thousands of people with little or no disability who were locked up in institutions on specious pretexts—because they were "different." Theirs was simply a case of gross injustice to be corrected by setting them free and allowing them access to whatever services they both need and want. But, for more seriously disabled people, especially if they are children, the dilemma comes into play and becomes serious. These are people for whom, on whose behalf, in whose interests decisions must be made, and every such decision to some extent compromises the autonomy and rights of the person whose life it affects.

In the ordinary course of events, we do not dwell on such compromises or take them seriously. Parents make decisions for their children, surgeons for their patients, policemen for motorists in a traffic jam. The casuistry of such events is so functional and commonly accepted that we are usually quite unaware of the compromise. But what is harmless in ordinary circumstances has had devastating consequences in the lives of handicapped people. For a century, we failed to question whether the efficiency of institutional treatment could justify or excuse the loss of liberty it demanded. The decision was made for mentally retarded people under one or another rubric of ordinary life—their rights could be suspended as though they were children, criminals, or (perhaps most damagingly) medical patients. We were unconscious of the dilemma that the very forces that presumably would help them lead better lives took away the preconditions of a meaningful life—their freedom, their dignity, even their status as human beings.

If it seems somewhat artificial to dwell on the conflict between the nature of treatment and the rights of the treated, I suspect it is only because we are still unable to envision a human service model that could take the dilemma seriously. The thrust of all current efforts is to create objective, measurable, foolproof, and unambiguous mechanisms of service delivery. Monitoring bodies, redundant safeguards, and other devices are intended to make sure nothing goes wrong. These efforts are based on a denial of the dilemma, on a belief that there exists a "right answer" that does not sacrifice some competing value. In Burton Blatt's phrase in the concluding essay of this volume, it is an attempt at "bureaucratizing values"—an attempt to reduce the richness and complexity of life to a rulebook. But life will not be reduced; the dilemma will reemerge to demand the exercise of human judgment, to strain our wisdom and test our conscience.

In dwelling on the uncertainties and contradictions, the metaphors and dilemmas of the field of mental retardation, Burton Blatt may be moving toward the next "revolution" in our perception of its problems. But, although it might be a revolution, it is hardly new. Much of what we have to struggle with—and of what we have struggled with for a century—was foreshadowed at the birth of the field of mental retardation. The work of Jean-Marc-Gaspard Itard can illuminate much of what is best as well as worst in the field.

As the "founding father," Itard has received ample praise for the best in his work with Victor, the "Wild Boy of Aveyron." Indeed, in all honesty, perhaps we should confess more freely that there is little the profession of today can do that Itard did not do for his "client." But there is a side of his story that is not so generally noticed: a side that, at least in principle, embodies the most reprehensible practices of the institutional era. To read the story through the viewpoint of modern advocacy is to read a tale of atrocities.

At the outset, Victor was captured and incarcerated against his will. For several years he continued to attempt escapes only to be recaptured. For a considerable time he was not even given a human name, but exhibited as an animal-like scientific curiosity under the label of "Wild Boy" ("*sauvage*"). In the course of his "special education," Victor was subjected to various coercive manipulations and cruel experiments. To test whether Victor had a sense of justice, Itard heaped unjust abuse on him; Victor's hysterical distress earned a passing mark. In the most commonly recalled such episode, Itard used the shock of dangling Victor out of a fourth-story window to improve his concentration.

Just as institutions have tended to certify their subjects ineducable and give up the effort, Itard "abandoned my pupil to incurable dumbness." He decided to withhold sex education because it would have led to "acts of revolting indecency," thus anticipating the segregation and confinement of the sexes in institutions.

Through these and innumerable other examples we can trace the all too familiar pattern of institutionalization. A vital and, in many ways, viable individual is subjected to remedial programs with the result that he loses what strengths he had and acquires none of the intended compensations. Victor sank into a "dull apathy," became subject to diseases, lost his tolerance of extreme temperatures and became totally dependent on his caretakers. In return he gained very little—no useful speech, an interesting but useless ability to spell some words, somewhat improved manners, and the habit of wearing clothes.

The important point here is not to establish that Itard set in motion all the evils of subsequent institutions—he may inadvertently have done so, but that is a subject that should be examined elsewhere. Nor is it that he was a bad or unethical teacher. On the contrary, he was exceptionally skillful and scrupulous. The point is that in his work we see the full force of the dilemma: the clinical service Itard offered Victor was *inseparable* from the compromises of Victor's rights and autonomy. At every point of the story, Itard had to choose between incompatible alternatives. Victor wanted to be free in the countryside; his education demanded that he be confined. He was content to eat with his hands, go without clothes, communicate with no one; Itard undertook to "civilize" each of these characteristics out of him. What is extraordinary about Itard is that he maintained a clear awareness of the implications of each step in his work, conscious of each as a dilemma. It is only because he hoped that the benefits would outweigh the cost to Victor that he undertook to impose those costs.

Although, in a technical sense, Itard failed—Victor did not become "normal"—we recognize his work as one of the most brilliant examples of special education. What made his work great? What is the lesson to be learned from him? The tragedy of the institutional era was launched by taking the lesson to be in Itard's pedagogical methods. That era dismissed the moral struggles and misgivings, the continual concern for Victor's happiness and appreciation of his singular qualities as irrelevant to the process. In fact, it became a point of pride that such subjectivity was banished from the scientific technology of treatment. But it was the wrong lesson, and it unleashed a century of torment for mentally retarded people. Even the treatment perished in the process.

Today we are resolved to restore to mentally retarded people everything the institutional monolith took away. And, predictably, there have already occurred cases in which the formerly imprisoned have been "dumped" into the freedom to be abandoned and helpless. Clearly, to deny all help is as destructive as to deny all freedom.

The dispute today is between those who argue that we should provide good service in good institutions and those who argue that every person is entitled to both good service and the full rights of citizenship. The first position reflects a belief that there can be such a thing as a good institution, that the historical inevitability of abuse can somehow be overcome. The basis for such belief is weak at best and getting weaker, but the second position, too, has its problems. As long as we measure our success at affording full rights and the best service to mentally retarded people living in ordinary communities against what was possible in institutions, we may be very satisifed. But once the contrast ceases to be a justification, we will find ourselves doing what Itard did. We will make decisions about those whose interests we have at heart—decisions that they cannot or will not support—in the hope of improving their lives. We will need to recognize the dilemmas inherent in such decisionmaking, lest we repeat the institutional mistake.

The important lesson of Itard was not in his techniques. More important was his sense of the responsibility he undertook in interfering in the life of another person. It was a responsibility Itard met even after his work was ended; he provided Victor with a place to live and a governess—an arrangement which would probably qualify as a community placement today. Itard never lost sight of Victor as a human being, someone with preferences, moods, feeling, a history and a claim to our respect. And this is a lesson running throughout this volume by Burton Blatt.

Andrejs Ozolins
Syracuse University

Preface

It seems that in America and other affluent cultures one is honored to be dishonored. A few weeks ago, a dear friend and a scholar of national reputation came to tell me that Senator Proxmire wanted to award him his Golden Fleece. Notwithstanding that my friend thinks his work is good, and that the Senator obviously doesn't, notwithstanding the dubious honor, it was honor enough! My friend was delighted with the prospect. Unfortunately, Proxmire's cynical recognition had to be withheld, for my friend accomplished his work without the necessary government sponsorship to qualify for the Senator's coveted ridicule.

What does that story have to do with my life In and Out of Mental Retardation? Nothing, but it's the analogue to almost everything. Picture a field that prides itself on the number of clients it *doesn't* serve. If you can't entertain so strange a prospect, you're normal; after all, I'd call the college president a lunatic if he boasted to his Board of Trustees that, while last year the school attracted a thousand freshmen, this year it would attract 500 freshmen, and if the word gets out even further and they were lucky, it might attract only 200 freshmen next year. If that sort of behavior doesn't appear strange to you, then you understand better than I why superintendents of mental hospitals and assorted other bughouses boast of reductions in their censuses, not only boast but indicate that such reductions are proof positive that they're doing good works, that they're responsive to the needs of the people, the state, their profession, everyone here and in heaven. That's why one of the essays in this collection is titled, "This Crazy Business." That's why three others speak about Purgatory and Pandemonium, and that's why another one, "Life With the Decision Makers," deals with people who are dedicated to the crazy business of looking after crazy people. A long time ago, someone once created a now-famous motto for an institution for the mentally retarded, "Happiness First, All Else Will Follow." The dishonor in our society is that, while that motto may have once been honest, even if naive and misguided, an accurate motto for today might be, "Business First, and What Else is There?" Business first. Crazy business. Funny business. Craziness and Business. These are recurring themes in this collection.

There are other themes, each laid out in the first chapter, "Toward an Understanding of People with Special Needs." People underestimate their potential for learning, but under proper conditions capability is educable, is a function of practice and training and motivation. The idea that people can change—learn—is the idea I've pursued for 30 years. This book recounts my quest to unravel the "educability puzzle." And beginning with the first chapter, imbedded in almost every chapter here, is the story of what happened to that idea through the years, a story punctuated mainly by research failures, with the idea rescued only by my repugnance to the alternative—the other idea—the belief that capability is fixed at birth, that development is linear and predictable, that people don't change very much, that retardation is permanent, that institutions are necessary for certain people and will always be necessary, that what is will be.

And so, I begin this book with remarks about my good fortune with family and teachers. And I then explain what I mean by educability, not leaving out my own educability, how I changed. And I also write about the monolith, that impenetrable slab of a system that offers few options, needs no defenses, envelops all who are snared by its enticements or commandments. Throughout this book are descriptions and analyses, complaints and worries connected to the mental health-mental retardation monolith and the education monolith. Throughout this book, sometimes through repetition of earlier commentary, sometimes by argument with earlier commentary, sometimes by allusion and indirection and sometimes as plainly as a pen could write, I enlist your support of the belief that monoliths do more mischief than good, and their adherents inflict damage even when they are binding wounds. The chapters are as they were when originally published, except for corrections of a few of the more glaring typographical errors and the deletions of a few unnecessarily repetitive passages.

In this volume, I tell stories that illustrate how lives are destroyed by telling certain stories, and I ask you to be careful about the stories you tell because even made-up stories have a way of becoming the truth. Cassandra told true stories, and she was disregarded only on order from one of the gods. But it seems that there are made-up stories these days which have the force of true stories. However, while ordinary mortals have the power to tell false stories, God chooses not to interfere with whether or how we react to them. Cassandra had an Apollo to prevent the harm of her true stories—we have no one but ourselves. So we had better be careful about the stories *we* tell, especially the made-up ones.

I write here about magnanimity, that when reason fails and we have to decide whom to support, whom to anoint, whom to trust, we should place our faith in those of our leaders and colleagues who are magnanimous, who would bend over backward to avoid hurting and insulting another human being, who would look everywhere to find good in a person and in the world. And while I write again and again about educability, I also write that it's a two-edged sword, that human miracles occur not from among those whom we expect to change, but from among those whom we don't expect to change. I remind us, especially myself, that by definition a miracle must be unexpected, that by definition Anne Sullivan didn't expect Helen Keller to eventually attend Radcliffe College and become a world-famous author and social reformer. The miracle had the chance to occur because she believed with all her soul that Helen Keller had a right to learn, to grow, because *all* people have that right.

This book has many themes, but one major theme—the idea that people can change, that society can change. Throughout, there are stories (and sometimes data) to attempt to illuminate that central theme, stories that examine: the idea that people are people—fragile, mortal, interdependent, just people; the idea that everything worthwhile is mainstreamed, connected to normal soceity, to ordinary people, to the ebb and tide of the human experience, not to the state contrivance that substitutes a "Russian Village" for the real thing; the idea that the disease of mental retardation is an invention, and our treatments were invented as if there were actually something "real" to treat, and now we have invented new treatments to be the antidotes for the side effects of the old treatments; the idea that the ancient Greeks knew their punishments better than we know ours, knew that banishment—not execution—is the ultimate punishment, that banishment is the supreme, the "capital punishment," and that we inflict here more "capital punishment" than elsewhere on earth.

This book comes to a few connected conclusions: that *all* people are equally valuable and deserve to be part of a normal world; that the world isn't now, but *can* be, hospitable and normal; so we must try to change the world, else we contribute to its evil. This book took 30 years to write, and I hope it will teach someone that what we can learn from the life of Helen Keller isn't only that she was educable but that all people are educable. I hope this book will teach someone that to have known Dick Hungerford and Margaret Neuber is to know that not only were those people noble but that all people can be noble. And I hope this book will teach someone that the life of Seymour Sarason is a lesson not only about genius but also about humility, and that the second is the more important lesson to learn.

Burton Blatt
Jamesville, New York

*With love and admiration,
this book is for Ethel.*

IN AND OUT OF
MENTAL RETARDATION

PART I
EDUCABILITY

CHAPTER 1

Toward an Understanding of People with Special Needs

THREE TEACHERS

Antecedents

It's difficult to feel confident about how and where to begin, so I'll just begin. A book of mine was published in 1967 by the Massachusetts Department of Mental Health (*The Intellectually Disfranchised: Impoverished Learners and Their Teachers*). Parts of it were personal and, during the subsequent years, my books became more reflective than critical and more autobiographical than scientific. I somehow found all of this to be important for me while, surely, others were less impressed. Yet, even before that time and until today, I've learned to resist explaining or reinterpreting what I had written, for I have felt that it hardly matters what one intends to say, only what is said or seems to be said. However, for whatever the reason now, permit me to do what I have just implied is fruitless—explain myself.

Although many who read a lot seem to believe that the writers they most admire usually inform them more about the writer than the presumed substance of his work, and although those who write a lot hope that the work itself will lead to the author, nevertheless they are people who write essentially for themselves, to think through their lives, not merely to describe life. And that's what I believe; the writer writes and the reader reads. And, while the writer is as lucky to find a good reader as vice versa, the manner in which my work is evaluated is a matter that I try to keep from intruding into what I do with my life. Yet I now seem to want to explain myself, and even while I fight the continuous battle with those three universal human traits—self-justification, a sense of embarrassment, and a need for privacy—I now set down on paper these recollections and thoughts about my life and some of the people who have influenced me. For although I write alone, and write essentially for myself,

This essay was originally published in J. F. Kauffman & J. S. Payne (Eds.), *Mental retardation: Introduction and personal perspectives*. Columbus, Ohio: Charles E. Merrill, 1975. Reprinted by permission.

and live at times in a private world, I also write to share with others and to be included in some of their experiences. Now the story, almost from the beginning.

In 1949, I was teaching school, finishing a Master's degree at Columbia, trying to understand what teaching was all about, not yet able to comprehend what I was all about. The school had, among other features—including the basketball team, which I coached—a unit of several special classes for the mentally retarded. It was in this school where I met Horace Mann, now director of the Division of Exceptional Children Education at the State University College in Buffalo, New York. He was one of the school's special class teachers. His encouragement led me to this field and sustained me, especially during some difficult beginning years. He also led me to Dick Hungerford. Will I ever again meet a person with such dazzling brilliance and such zeal to do good for people as Dick Hungerford?

It had happened to others, now to me. I put aside what I had thought were primary goals. Instead, I became a special class teacher in the Coney Island section of Brooklyn, working with Dick, Horace, and others, each believing in our special mission and in the Occupational Education curriculum for the mentally retarded.

I met Ethel in 1950. We were married eighteen months later, and for that, I will always be grateful for my good fortune; she is my blessing. By 1956, I had completed doctoral work with Margaret Neuber at Penn State, we had our first of three sons, who is currently a sophomore at Alfred University, and I was beginning professorial life at what was then New Haven State Teachers' College and is now Southern Connecticut State College. I also published papers on my dissertation concerned with the effectiveness of special classes for the educable mentally retarded. That research may have been the first of the post-war so-called efficacy studies and, consequently, it was less neglected than is the fate of most dissertations in our field. But all of that is in *The Intellectually Disfranchised*, and most of the rest of this personal history is found in *Exodus from Pandemonium* (1970) and *Souls in Extremis* (1973).

Suffice to say here, I found Seymour Sarason in New Haven. We began work on the development of a psychoeducational clinic, which was described in our book, coauthored with Ken Davidson, *The Preparation of Teachers* (Sarason, Davidson, & Blatt, 1962). Those collaborations with Sarason led to the design of research with young culturally disadvantaged children and, because of the need for graduate student involvement in that study, precipitated my move to Boston University. At Boston, we continued the preschool research for several years and, as part of that original project, developed what became known as the Boston

University Psycho-Educational Clinic. In Boston, my collaborations with Frank Garfunkel, originating in Connecticut a few years earlier, deepened. It was in Boston where I met Albert Murphy, who is one of the most eloquent and poetic thinkers in our field. It was also in Boston where I began a new research collaboration which included Frank Garfunkel and Fred Finn, superintendent of the Seaside Regional Center, a state facility for the mentally retarded located in Waterford, Connecticut. The results of that collaboration, our demographic study, my decision to visit state institutions and photograph back wards, and the subsequent *Look* article (Blatt & Mangel, 1967) are discussed in the three books I wrote for Allyn and Bacon, the two previously mentioned and the photographic essay co-authored with Fred Kaplan, *Christmas in Purgatory* (1966). I suspect that, if one were interested, widely varying evaluations of those institutional studies can be obtained, especially from some directors of residential facilities who may never forgive me for what I had written and said.

I am in my twenty-fifth year of teaching, the last five at Syracuse University. I have interacted with many groups of students; I have known some of those people as well as most teachers know their students; I think I have influenced my share, and they have influenced me. The truth of the matter is that I'm proud of my students and of my teaching. But what is truth?

And what is self-justification? Why does it appear as if immodesty usually follows "truth"? I hope that you are not offended by the immodesty. I didn't find a better way to prepare you for what I want to communicate. I was unable to summarize the antecedents without, I'm fearful, giving the impression that my friends and anyone I admire are the best and the most talented. If these words appear that way to you, forgive me and please understand that it is no more possible to be objective about one's work than about one's values.

Now for three of my teachers. That is, now for more biography in autobiography, more immodest "truth."

Analysis

I sat at my desk for several hours, rereading old correspondence, books long out of print, and now-yellowed mimeographed plans and project proposals never implemented. And, as I tried to make judgments about these people I want to describe for you, I was reminded that they never seemed to need support or explanations of their works. It appears as if truly great people don't require journalists, academics, enemies, or apologists to judge their works; with precision and honesty, they are their most capable critics. What a joy it would have been to have them here with us today, speaking for themselves. How you would have loved being with them and arguing with them, as I once loved those times we had together. But we waited too long; and now, two have left us, and the third is a shy person whom one must know well to know at all. Therefore, I sat there trying to plan what to write, yet knowing that it's too complicated, and too personal, to plan in your head. I just wrote, realizing that by the act of writing itself I might learn about the bits and pieces that remained hidden away in my head.

There was a time in my life when everything was marvelous because I didn't know enough. I had owned the earth, but now it owns me. I had innocence once. I thought that goodness was always rewarded and evil was always punished, that society needed only uncover unjustice to rectify it. When I lost my innocence, I joined the mob who had lost theirs; yet amid their jaundices, I might someday recover it again. That is the way things are now. But there was a beginning, and, like all beginnings, it was filled with innocence and with hope.

Once, in my callowness, I knew that all people could respect me and I could respect them, if we would work to know one another. But then I experienced the world outside, and tried to see it as social scientists and politicians see it and, thus, I tried to confront it as the mob confronts it. What was lost was more than innocence, for nothing was gained. Since that time, when I realized what was squandered, I have been seeking to again feel the world as I remember it to have been. I have been searching for a life that I could understand again; if I find that life, it may be because there is wisdom even in the mob and I will have learned how to mind it. And if I do find that life, it will be because there were those outside of the mob who tried to teach me what they had learned, how they had escaped from the mundane, and how they had regained their lost innocence.

This is a selfish paper. How does it matter to me what the teachers tried to teach? I will concern myself with what I think I have learned. So, although there were other teachers before and after, I begin exactly where I should, with Richard Hungerford, who once thought my optimism refreshing and tested it to find me little more than merely optimistic. Without a direct word, Richard Hungerford taught me the difference between being happy and happiness, between honesty and honor, between what one should do for others and what one must do for himself, between ignorance and insensitivity, between untested innocence and innocence earned. He taught that goodness deprived of truth is more a liability than a virtue. I met that man on a winter's night in New York City, December, 1949. I was a teacher of English and social studies in a Brooklyn junior high school. He was the city's director of special education for the mentally retarded. I was twenty-two years old and thought him an old man (I wonder if my students now view me as an old man). We talked and talked, about many things, but mainly about me. I didn't understand all he said and, in retrospect, after we knew each other better, I hoped he didn't understand all that I said. He spoke about complex matters and, so it appeared to me, in ways that were almost deliberately evasive. A sentence begun wasn't finished with words, but with a nod or a smile or just the faintest movement of a hand. And all the while I was supposed to hear what was said and understand what was intended. Surely, as if he knew it would happen, I did hear and did understand.

Dick Hungerford taught me that any word has multiple meanings and that there isn't *truth* but many truths. He taught me that only the very young or the very insensitive deal with complex issues simply or believe that easy solutions to problems are as easy as they seem. He taught me about the law of the pendulum, and that the only thing we learn from history is that we don't learn from history—that a person is doomed to repeat his acts and problems and their solutions uncountable times during his life. As I can't avoid the law of the pendulum, neither does the larger society—as I don't learn from my experiences, neither do other people and groups.

Dick Hungerford taught me that, while truth is elusive and complex, it's the best that one can hope for in a human being; for while most people view honesty as a nuisance, for him it was no less important than his life. Yet I also learned from him that Don Quixote was a foolish loser, not because he fought windmills, but only because he didn't try to understand why others thought him the fool for the effort. He couldn't turn his battles to an advantage because he didn't "read" the minds of those with whom he needed to deal. He remained blissfully ignorant and, thus, his innocence was never put to the essential test of the mob.

Dick Hungerford instructed me as to the ways of the academy, which are to mistrust the abstract, the facile, the light, the generalist. He taught me why I should be wary of that of which academe is wary, and why I must learn to appreciate and value that which is often disdained. He taught me that learning—discovering, changing—can be a moving experience for its own sake. It's wondrous because one finds that there is power in discovery and in gaining competency. It's especially grand as one learns about his own educability; the more one learns, the more one comprehends that he can learn more, and more, and more. Dick Hungerford helped me to believe again in my own educability. I learned from him that, when one is right, he doesn't need a miracle to win. In the end, the opposition needs the miracle to defeat him. He was the first of my great teachers and my indebtedness to him has been a life-long affair, even though he is now gone.

What I learned from Dick Hungerford about my educability was widened by Margaret Neuber to encompass the educability of all people. Suddenly, too quickly some predicted, the time came for me to continue graduate studies. Dick Hungerford advised me to seek out Margaret Neuber, professor of special education at Penn State University. But was I ready for doctoral study? How will you know to answer that question if you don't seek informed and disinterested opinion? Why a doctorate? You are now capable of learning more elsewhere than you can here. And you need further graduate preparation to be ready for that time when you will be asked to assume greater responsibility. Why Penn State? Because Margaret Neuber is there. What is any place, any university, but its people?

I matriculated, studied, and tried to understand things better. I even completed what was required of me. Yet, at least so I now believe, the victory was not in the degree but in earning Margaret Neuber's friendship and respect. Miss Neuber taught me about the correctness of things, order, values, and priorities. She helped me to comprehend the essentialness of judgment, the difference between one who has judgment and one who cannot make decisions because he has no values. I also learned to believe, because she so fervently believed, that the future for all people holds nothing but good. Yet she wasn't only a fatalist, for she, more than anyone before or since, taught me that there would be times when I should take great risks, grasp the rod, or all that would remain would be the snake. I must not passively accept the world as it is, people as they are, or myself as I appear to be. I must try to change the world, and the beginning hurdle is always with oneself. I must change or nothing changes. I am at the center of conflict, at its origin, and at the solution. Miss Neuber lived a life that taught anyone who would understand that innocence and goodness aren't rewarded. They *are* the rewards, as honesty is the reward. Everything else is good fortune or bad fortune.

A degree was won and, in our culture, that signals the start of a different life. New Haven beckoned, not because I was special but more, I suppose, because someone special was needed and I was available. Why was I available? Not, in all honesty, because of New Haven's attractiveness at that time; more because no one else called or wrote. It was, as the saying goes, a marriage of convenience, and it turned out splendidly. There I met Seymour Sarason of Yale University, and the success of my first academic appointment and finding Seymour are not unrelated. I learned from that man. He offered a perspective that had been foreign to me, in spite of prior training and experiences. I learned about the clinical ethos. Describe the observation. Separate it from your interpretation of its meaning and significance. What is the presenting problem? What did you do about it? What happened? If you had to do it over again, what would you now do differently?

I also learned about settings and how they are created, about community, in its psychological as well as physical sense. But, most importantly I believe, Seymour Sarason influenced my method and style in analyzing and attempting to solve problems. He taught me how to think better. And he showed me that at least somewhere, there is a scholar with literary talent; it isn't altogether futile to hope for clear and interesting sentences from professors. And so I hoped for that event to occur more frequently, while I also hoped that something would rub off on me. Seymour Sarason encouraged me to commit my thinking to paper; he caused me to want to become a writer.

Once I had three teachers. The first, Dick Hungerford, helped me to believe in my own educability. The second, Margaret Neuber, encouraged me to better comprehend the educability of all people. The third, Seymour Sarason, guided and supported me as I groped to develop a more efficient and deeper way of thinking about things and expressing myself. The first teacher can no longer be called at midnight for advice. The second teacher has also passed on. And the third, although still productive and vigorous, is not any more in close geographic proximity to me. Once there was a period when I thought that the supports would last forever. Why is current reality so deceiving? Why does time run away, never to return? Why didn't I take better advantage of the wisdom and hours offered by those teachers? Once the days were longer and there was time to do everything and accomplish anything. Once I had three teachers, and now I teach. Once I disdained the clock and discipline as, inevitably, my students now disdain those restraints to their freedoms. Once I was given everything; now I am supposed to give everything. The surprise of it all is that nothing has changed, and nothing will change. I remain the learner as my teachers must surely have believed they were learners. I remain the teacher, as I once taught my teachers. Only the people change, some new ones coming, some old ones going—as I intrude into the lives of others, as I will leave them some day. Who is teacher? Who is learner? Does it matter? Does it matter when one mistakes the dusk for the dawn? Not immediately, but everything matters eventually, as it matters to me now that I wrote down who my teachers were and what they gave to me.

OVERVIEW

Summary

Now, how should I summarize what I think I have learned, and what should I attempt to convey to you on the subsequent pages?

1. People traditionally underestimate their potential for changing or, to use a more common term, for learning.

2. Pessimism concerning the conditions of change becomes a self-ful-filling prophecy. People—any people—do not learn when they become convinced that they cannot or should not.
3. Under proper conditions, it can be demonstrated that intelligence is plastic; i.e., intelligence is a function of practice and training. That we have not been able to accomplish such change in people is, I believe, less a defect in this hypothesis than it is of our practice.
4. There is a design of things, I believe. And I believe that the design for all of us holds nothing but good.

As I once remarked in an address before the Massachusetts legislature, there is a dark side of every mirror, a side beyond inspection (Blatt, 1970). And while the optimism and pride of our lives is for the gains made in civil rights, for our few achievements in mental retardation, for the concept of the Declaration of Independence and the Constitution, surely a dark side in the evolution of our civilization in this mid-twentieth century must be reserved for the deeply unremitting, unrewarding lives of drudgery and pain we inflict upon the institutionalized and all others who are needlessly segregated.

I said to the legislature, and I believe even more firmly today, that no resident of a state school needs to live in a denuded condition, needs to be a head banger, or needs to be locked in solitary confinement. Practically every resident can be taught to eat meals independently, can be taught to live among his fellows without being dangerous to himself or to others, and without the use of physical restraints. All building odors can be eliminated without the need for even more repugnant chemical treatments or electronic gadgets that mask the sources of these odors but do not eliminate the cause: filth and neglect. I even have some evidence that intelligence is educable; people can change—learn—and this concept applies both to the retarded and those who minister to their needs. It applies to us as well. We can change in our conception of human potential and thus promote change in others; ultimately, we can create a society that does not need closed institutions. The lives of Anne Sullivan and Helen Keller speak volumes about this concept, as do the lives of Jean Itard and Victor, the Wild Boy of Aveyron.

To begin our discussion, let us examine the term "monolith," which is central to some of the ideas in this chapter. I will be using it in a special way—to mean a closed, no-option system, as the monolith of mental health or the monolith of the educational establishment. Many in the field of special education identify the "monolith" as the special class, the segregated curriculum, or the mental institution. Certainly, one side of the disability monolith is the educational establishment, as the other side is the mental health establishment. But the monolith is not the teachers' college, not even the special class, the segregated curriculum, or the institution. The education monolith involves a network of seemingly open but actually closed systems that are not systems so much as integral parts of a larger whole. The mental health–mental retardation monolith is not the institution but the fact that there are no viable alternatives to the institution. The disability monolith—traditional special education and traditional mental health—is the one-way, narrow, total environment planned and implemented by the city, the state, the institution, or the school. The monolith is created and sustains itself because of an absence of *alternatives*. The problem is not with officialdom's good intentions but with a limited vision of human potential and what the world may yet become.

What are the consequences of such unitary approaches? What results from a system that has forgotten the difference between special education and special class? What is the price society must pay for a contemporary system that has too little vision and a fragile optimism, where the only hope is to expect a future that is little more than a larger mass of the past? In that culture, to know where one is going would require merely to look back in anguish. In that culture, a man would not learn from history; one would relive it and relive it again. It may be that such a culture is required not only to produce but also to sustain policies supposedly on behalf of children with special needs that, in reality, deprive them of basic developmental opportunities. Some may claim that we in this age are products of that culture.

There are two sides to the mental health–mental retardation monolith: the education–special education–school side and the medical–mental health–institution side; certainly not a clear-cut dichotomy, certainly overlapping, certainly not all-inclusive; nevertheless they have a relative logical distinctiveness and they also interact. Yet there is more distinction than interaction. Considering the fact that the two organizations are fundamentally and strikingly similar, deal with similar populations, and have similar values and objectives, special educators know precious little about institutional caretakers and vice versa. Obviously, grossly horrifying institutions that you have read about and some of us have seen are different from most conventional schools. But in several basic ways, the people are not different from other human beings—neither the caretaker nor the client, each a victim and each ultimately a victimizer. In the institution and in the school there are insufficient options for families, for children with special needs, and—of equal importance—for teachers and other staff. Possibly for that reason if for no other, in institutions and in too many schools, one generation's vipers are another's heroes; that which is one's disdain is another's enthusiasm. For, possibly, institutions and schools, more than open environments, are vulnerable to the fashions of the moment, fashions that dupe us into believing that we are the height of chic and enlightenment. Possibly, had it not been for the monolith, we would have kept our promises, our commitments to ourselves and others. Special education would have led to something more, something grander, than the creation of the largest and the most pervasive segregated special class and institutional system known to civilized people.

What is the "promise" that special education was to keep? It was to demonstrate to all people, and especially to those of us most intimately involved, that each person can contribute to the larger society; that all people are equally valuable; that a human being is entitled to developmental opportunities; and that development is plastic. We have been faithful; we have supported humanistic precepts and philosophies, and we have believed that there is "enrichment through difference." Thus the promise of special education has always been, and remains today, not a special curriculum, or special methods, or even special teachers. The gifts that this movement was to endow us with were the gifts of optimism and belief in the human ethos, charity and love for our brothers, and the conviction that our work is not to judge who can or cannot change but rather to fulfill the prophecy that all people can change; each person can learn. For the promise to be kept, for these things to occur beyond wish or fantasy, one must begin with oneself. Before I ask the world to change, I must change. I am the beginning step.

The Perspective

In the Old Testament, we are commanded to speak the truth and to so respect language as a reflection of truth that we must not take oaths. Even if one fulfills an oath, the responsibility—the risk of a failure—is too grave, and thus the oath itself is sinful. There is even the admonition not to engage in idle gossip, for all too often such "harmless" talk leads to slander or meanness. Silence is golden. There are lessons to be learned from such commentaries on our language as analogies of our total selves.

Those in academe, who supposedly live not by truth but by the pursuit of it, subscribe to the ancient precepts to beware the man who too often proclaims his integrity and promises to accomplish good deeds; beware those who have found the "truth" and reveal it to save us. In the Old Testament, the burden in merely making a promise is too awesome for ordinary people to contemplate. In the academy, one is cautioned to speak with care, or not to speak, and to write with a very special care, or not to write. In the academy, hypotheses are generated, then tested, then others generated, then retested; and all the while, otherwise brave men can do no more than test the null hypothesis (i.e., there is no difference), engaging in experiments or surveys that lead only to an acceptance or a rejection of it. We have neither the tools nor the traditions to test whether there had been a significant difference, for example, between those who received special Treatment A in contrast with those who received ordinary Treatment B. Only by indirection do we study the effects of special treatments, special environments, special opportunities, all kinds of special interventions.

And yet, within the nature of the writer-thinker is the belief that his work, his prose, rings true, and there is a faith that truth has its own beauty and conviction its own value. There is also a creed of the professor, which is to profess, and a creed of the active man, which requires the initiation of events, not merely a reaction to them. The writer, the thinker, the professor, the activist, all want more than anything else to have their works taken seriously—more than they want people to care for their words, their books, or even their behavior.

With admonitions from the past and the present realities of academe, too many scholars appear afraid of being wrong or wronged, appear intimidated by critics, colleagues, their shadows, and other ghosts. There is a joylessness in our literature, and it is suffocating us while advancing neither science nor mankind. How many books does a person remember? How many ideas change him, possibly change others because of him? Can we name that handful of human beings whose ideas so profoundly influenced us that our own works would have been different had those ideas not been part of the scene? The fascination of living through this period of American education and psychology is its own reward because, in spite of the pessimists and their arguments, we have had our share of unique human beings whose ideas and influence will remain long after their books and words are forgotten. This has not been a completely barren time, not a period of only despair. Therefore, admonitions notwithstanding, one who has participated might feel obligated to document the period, both for those who were not present and for those who were there but missed the excitement. I want to list some of the ideas and a few of the people and movements that still influence our lives, that see us through the dark nights and long days. I want to record the works that deserve an ear and maybe a few that deserve one's total attention. I want to synthesize, then analyze, then synthesize again, for as we read and write too much, it becomes apparent that few among us are synthesizing and analyzing; few educators are thinking about what we have become, what we have accomplished for people, what it all means for people, what the world has been, and what the world is about for the disabled, the sick, the "different," the frail, anyone in jeopardy.

Hence, this kit is for all those who seek to do battle with the mythical but real monolith and with what I call its Human Disposal Authority, especially its Department of Subnormal Affairs.[1] The kit may prepare you to think differently about people, their natures, their capacities to change and contribute and rise to new heights. The kit may help a little as a person gropes to comprehend himself, his mortality, his intelligence, his conception of his capability for change, and his unfolding. The kit discusses the works of people who share an optimism concerning the human potential. Since this is a basic kit, it is, I hope, uncontaminated by the conglomerate affairs of big business and institutional technologists; like all basic kits, it is stripped down. It has flaws, defects, weaknesses, holes. It will review the research neither exhaustively nor deeply. It will neither cover all aspects of educational programming and treatments for children with special needs nor feel the requirement for such coverage. Some of the holes and some of the flaws may be part of whatever is good about it. For example, children are, after all the polemics are voiced, just children; and there may be no need in a paper on special education to say something about each of the categorical disabilities which are, in reality, administrative rather than scientific designations. Possibly it may be more important to communicate that the world is dull for most people because our lives are made dull by the blandness, the sameness, of home and school and almost everything. Possibly it may be more important to tell about people who should belong to humanity but cannot find a way to join up. Possibly it may be more important for us to understand that the problem facing special educators is not just one of helping the unfortunate handful but also of bringing to so-called typical people opportunities to grow through their involvements with what Dick Hungerford (once the director of the largest public school special class system in the world) called "difference." What I have been trying to say (but I have been intimidated by those who I fear may misunderstand) is that this paper is less about the so-called "handicapped" and what we can do for them than it is about people and what we must do for each other. For example, our society will be more civilized when equality of educational opportunity becomes not only an individual's right and the group's responsibility, *but* the individual's responsibility and the group's right. Will there be a day when I will feel that not only am I entitled to an equal educational opportunity, but also I have the right to live in an educated society; and, therefore, that I am franchised only when you are franchised?

What is the trick? The trick is to both guarantee such entitlements and deliberately maximize human variance. The objective is to offer each human being opportunities to live in peaceful surroundings and engage

---

[1] From "A Basic Kit to Confront the Human Disposal Authority" (Blatt, 1974).

in his work and interests—within a community, included, not hidden away, in a land where no longer will there be special institutions to cage a human spirit.

SINS OF THE PROPHETS: A SHORT PREJUDICED HISTORY

Psychologists and sociologists have never helped a person understand why he creates madhouses and why he refuses to destroy them. This may be the proper time to turn to historians and poets for such help. Historians would describe the world as it is—the people, the places, the forces that brought them together and those which caused their alienation. Poets would describe the world as it should be, as it could become. Historians are unfettered by the constraints imposed on other social scientists, constraints that require computation of averages and normative models. Historians record and discuss real people, events, and places. Poets, uncluttered by the past, untarnished in the present, and uncowed with prospects of the mysterious, would study our history and lead us to new and better ways.

History is the basic science. From history flows more than knowledge, more than prescription, more than how it was—how we might try to make it become. Although the one thing we learn from history is that we do not learn from history, it is the basic science. Physics is a history. Mathematics is a history. Chemistry is a history. The way we express history is the ultimate utilization of those unique human gifts, language and creativity. If there were but a poet with such talents and interests to record the history of the care and education of people with special needs, much could be revealed; possibly, great discoveries would be made. While we await the contributions of more gifted historians, the following may temporarily fill the breach.

In the beginning, humans were created, and then humans created the criteria for being human. In the beginning, such criteria were simple, so simple that criteria were not important. When no person had language, humans needed no language. When no person had tools, humans needed no tools. In the beginning, the mere emergence from a woman's belly made one human.

Then humans discovered their hands and their fingers. Subsequent discoveries led to the invention of laws, books, print, civilization, science, and attempts to control the environment. During the interim, humans sought new understandings of themselves, their relationships with others and with a higher being. All the while, new criteria were invented and stipulated, first to classify, then to separate and set aside, eventually to defile, to dehumanize, to murder.

People with special characteristics—the blind, the deaf, the retarded, the special for a time, or the special irrespective of time or culture—

became consistent targets for those who would separate one human being from another. And with each separation, prophets would announce that solutions to problems were at hand; the light at the end of the tunnel would now shine brightly. Desperate and sick humans would now be saved.

The ancients had their solutions, not humane but honest and without sham. Go, mother, take your sick child to the mountaintop; there the gods will decide who should live, who should die, who will be inscribed in the Book of Life or the Book of Final Decree. So they went, some to the mountains, and the Hansels and Gretels to the forests. But our priests told us that God was not pleased. Go ye not to the mountains and the forests. Thou shalt not kill. We, the State, will take your child in our asylums. We will care for the sick, the mad, the idiot child that you have spawned and let loose in this cruel and hard world.

Give us your child to minister unto.
Give us this forsaken being whom you have loved.
Give us that progeny who has no future.
God and the State will serve all beings.

And so they came,
From the farms and the villages,
From the great and the weak,
Innocent of the ways of priests and prophets.

And the State kept its word,
If not its faith,
Kept its covenant,
If not with God, then with the Devil.

First hundreds,
Then thousands,
Then hundreds of thousands,
Tomorrow, millions may inhabit our hells on this earth.

Again, certain prophets told the people that the god-state was not pleased with the work of these faithful servants. We must design new homes, small homes, regional homes, halfway homes, group homes, normalized homes, unit homes, extended-care homes; but we must keep separate those who belong with us from those who do not. We must guarantee to families who have a child with special needs that the family will be here and the child will be there. This is a Great American Dream.

Consequently, it was nearly universally agreed that it would be good if special homes for mental defectives were created. The doctors believed that such homes would be healthier for eligible patients than the precariousness of community existence. The psychologists believed that such homes would prove more therapeutic than other arrangements. The educators believed that such homes would provide greater developmental opportunities than public community facilities. The economists believed that such homes would be less expensive. Public safety officials believed that such homes would be more protective of *both* the general society and the defectives themselves. The politicians believed that such homes were what the people wanted. The parents thought that they should be grateful for whatever was allocated to relieve their problems. The defectives, not expected to think, were never asked to comment on the matter.

Only poets—not the doctors, who proved to be wrong, or all the others who were also wrong—saw the world differently. Poets comprehend this life through eyes that see differently and souls that feel and dream differently. Therefore, poets—neither shackled by the past nor contaminated by the future, not trained as technicians and, therefore, not constricted by tradition—were the first to accurately describe what had been wrought for the so-called defectives; they were the first to envision a different promise, a different world for people—a world yet to be created.

HISTORIES, VANITIES, AND DELUSIONS

Research

History can be a strength of society or its anchor. We can learn from it or not. History can be the basis for science, for progress, for creativity— or it can justify our vanities with the games it plays and those we play. History can lead us to freedom, or it can continue to delude and thus enslave those who would, who could otherwise, be free.

In this field we call special education, history has not served us well. We have not learned from it. It has made us almost hopelessly vain when we should have been humble; satisfied, when we might have been constructively impatient. Examine the history of special education for the mentally retarded. Note well the discrepancy between the research and the practice; yet note, too, that research in the broader social sciences has neither prohibited poor practice nor stimulated good practice. Possibly some among you may then conclude that research is little more than something for scholars to do, and that probably its major value lies in the process of doing it rather than in the results or even the implementation.

Since the early 1930s, hundreds of researchers, involving millions of dollars, millions of hours, and thousands of children and their teachers, have attempted to study the effectiveness of curricula, methods, administrative designs, and other factors that contribute to variance among special education programs for disabled children. Using the field of mental retardation as one example, the dollars and the hours essentially have been wasted, and the products are generally useless. It is not that the research has been dishonest or even "untrue"; it has been merely trivial or irrelevant. For example, research on the efficacy of special classes for the so-called mentally retarded fails to indicate the superiority of special classes over more conventional classroom settings—although it should be noted that the regular grades as they now exist are not proper placements for the mentally retarded. The earliest studies comparing mildly mentally retarded children in regular and special classes found that special class children did poorly in physical, personality, and academic areas when compared with children in regular classes (Bennett, 1932; Pertsch, 1936). Research by this writer (Blatt, 1956) was the first postwar study roughly analogous to those of Bennett and Pertsch. I, too, found that special class placements did not appear to enhance the development of these so-called mentally retarded children. Cassidy and Stanton (1959) and Johnson (1961), among many others, also conducted projects that were basically isomorphic with the aforementioned studies, reporting similar results; i.e., it has yet to be demonstrated that placement of mildly mentally retarded children in conventional special classes meets their needs in ways that regular class placement cannot. Studies concerned with so-called trainable mentally retarded children have been no more successful in demonstrating the superiority of special class placements (Caine & Levine, 1961; Dunn & Hottel, 1958).

A more recent review (Blatt & Garfunkel, 1973) confirmed the continued popularity of these efficacy studies, as well as the continued profusion of research on curriculum and teaching methods. In one way, the abundance of research of this type is disconcerting and frustrating. However, we have learned important lessons from these efficacy and methodology studies—that is, if we remember those lessons well enough to take them seriously. The accumulation of evidence vis-à-vis special classes, special curricula, and special methodologies leads to the *clear rejection* of the special class–regular class dichotomy, special–nonspecial curricula, and special–nonspecial methodology as defensible independent research variables. Although there may be rare exceptions to this conclusion, the regularity of the findings suggests strongly that children's experiences are not systematically different if they are, for example, in one or another class. A child can have individual attention, warmth, support, friends, and an exciting program in either class. Furthermore, his home varies independently of the kind of class he is in; it contributes so potently to variance that the home may well drown out the effects of any differences connected with educational programming (Blatt & Garfunkel, 1969; Coleman, Campbell, Hobson, McPartland, Mood, Weinfeld, & York, 1966).

Why is it that there is a plethora of research activity dealing with the effectiveness of curricula and methods and, on the other hand, a virtual absence of studies concerned with the effects of the home and community on learning and achievement? In view of the enormous support to compensatory education and subsequent documentation during the past decade of a persistent and pervasive relationship between socioeconomic class and educational achievement (Coleman et al., 1966; Hurley, 1969), it should be apparent that families and communities have a great deal of influence on the education and development of young children. Not only is the dearth of research dealing specifically with the home and community discouraging, but when such variables are employed as part of an intervention design, they are usually trivial in nature; i.e., they do not have particular meaning or importance, nor are they expected to contribute very much to the researcher's general understanding of the problems. For example, asking parents of Head Start children questions about how they feel towards their children, towards Head Start, or towards their community does not deliver revealing data. It amounts to using a teaspoon to do the work of a steam shovel. Similarly, attention to socioeconomic status does not, in itself, attend to the relationship between poverty and the ways that poor families, families with mentally retarded children, or any families deal with schools.

Why? Why the disinterest in family–community studies and—in spite of a discouraging history of neither research payoffs nor program development—why the continued adherence to experimental and quasi-experimental efficacy–curricula–methods studies? An answer may lie in the widely held belief that when one gets into other than traditional research methodologies, many months of observation are usually required. Secondly, most researchers are loath to use the less well-established instruments, which have uncertain reliabilities, and the long and difficult data-collection procedures that characterize family–community studies. Probably, researchers take satisfaction in doing relatively "clean" research, even if it has neither meaning nor relevancy. Researchers, like other people, have needs to conceptualize and pursue problems in manageable terms. A covert factor may be related to whatever biases researchers have concerning the concept of change itself. To discover that others can change implies that the researcher too can change. He could be somebody other than who he is. Expectations for change are tied up with the lives of the expectors as much as with those for whom they have greater or lesser expectations. Designs, variables, procedures, and analyses are certainly influenced by these expectations.

However, although all of these are reasonable explanations for the continued interest that researchers exhibit in traditional research that attempts to study the effects of stipulated interventions, it is doubtful that those reasons—even collectively—could continue to persuade intelligent and educated professionals to devote themselves to an endeavor that fails to reinforce either the researchers or the public at large that sponsors them. Therefore, there must be additional reasons for this pollution of feeble research on trivial problems.

During the years, and to the present time, many well-reasoned theories and methods have been presented both to explain behavior and describe ways to modify it efficiently and beneficially. We may label and discuss these developments either in terms of methodological pronouncements or in their fuller contexts—the application of method derived from theory. For the sake of simplicity, I will refer to, for example, the Montessori method or Moore's responsive-environments method, knowing that they have rich and exciting theoretical histories that deserve discussion in their own rights.

An examination of the more spectacular methods that have been developed in pedagogy and psychology has led me to the following observation; it is based on a review of the lives and works of such early greats as Itard, Seguin, Sullivan, Freud, and Montessori, as well as the study of contemporary methodologists including Skinner, Frostig, Omar Moore, and others who have developed reading, mathematics, and special and general methodological approaches to teaching children. Each significant methodological contribution begins with an individual who is interacting with a child or a group of children in such a way as to promote extraordinary change. This change is noted and causes astonishment and excitement. Why are the children doing so well? Why are they learning to read so quickly? Why is mathematics no longer a horrendous puzzlement? Why is the sick person getting better? Closer attention is given to the interaction between the teacher (or therapist, or experimentor, or psychologist) and the child. A careful description of the interaction is reported. From this inductive approach, a recording of the educational or therapeutic presentation is prepared; a new "method" unfolds. The teacher is teaching in a certain way, using a certain style, and promoting certain desired responses. Various people develop collaborations with the methodologist, but around the method. They study it in its original natural setting. They experiment with it. They refine and modify it. They become infatuated with the notion that the gains they observe are dependent on the order, style, and materials of the presentation. They learn a good deal about this method, the responses it ordinarily generates, its frailties, its problems and how to overcome them, and its most efficient utilization. They train others to use the method. They write books about it and develop elaborate ways to present, test, and relate it to a host of other methods, treatments, and conditions. Hence, we have literally thousands of studies completed on how almost infinite varieties of individuals behave, for example, in psychoanalytic settings, what the behaviors mean in innumerable circumstances, what responses should be presumed to be pathological, and what responses are healthy.

There are several things that strike me about individuals who have been responsible for the development of spectacular methods. From an examination of the literature and from my own observations of the current scene, each appears to be a gifted teacher and interactor. Each appears to have a dynamic quality that attracts the attention of other individuals. Each appears to have a powerfully charismatic personality that brings droves of disciples into the fold. Each is a great teacher! An analysis of the research relating to spectacular methodologies produces other interesting conditions to speculate about. From the sensationalist method of Itard and Seguin to the present works of Doman and Delacato, Omar Moore, Bereiter and Engelmann, the new math, and the special reading programs, verification studies of special methodologies find less conclusive, less promising, less significant results than those found by the method's originator(s). For example, Omar Moore has demonstrated a good deal more with automated or nonautomated typewriters than have those who replicated his work. The most significant changes observed in children using the Doman-Delacato methodology can be observed at their Institute for the Development of Human Potential.

If a method has an integrity of its own, if it is not almost singularly dependent on the skill and interactive ability of the applicator and the social–psychological setting of its application, it should work when properly applied by other capable people. One would suppose that psychoanalysis, for example, after more than a half-century of the analytic model, would have advanced on methodological refinements alone beyond its current place in the psychological scheme of things. There is no doubt that some methods work well. There is no doubt that some methods work better for some people than do other methods. Further, there is no doubt that some methods are more logically conceived, implemented, and utilized than others. There is a great deal of doubt that any method is very far removed from those who employ it, understand it, have faith in it, and experiment with it. There is only assurance that great teachers have great methods and poor teachers have poor methods—irrespective of the methods the teachers employ, irrespective of the fact that, regularly, great teachers and poor teachers utilize similar methods in contiguous settings.

Yet, the vanity and delusion are sustained—the vanity that we have effective curricula and methods and the delusion that these contribute most to change in children. What does it matter if history could teach us that there are no especially superior theories and methods for studying and dealing with behavior, that there are only teachers and psychologists whose endeavors yield low productivity? What does it matter if precision and vigorous controls are just not available in the study of natural settings? What does it matter if we should have learned by now that only extreme changes in placement, procedure, or opportunity can possibly produce measurable effects on individuals? One hour each day for "enrichment," a summer Head Start program, even a special class, much less a special method or curriculum, will have about as much effect as what one should expect from a trivial intrusion into an enormously complicated human totality!

Then, what research should be done? And why? Let us set aside, for the moment, most educational research, which has used traditional designs such as efficacy studies, follow-up studies of children in special and regular classes, and studies of different methodological and curriculum approaches. There may be more appropriate ways to study teaching-learning environments. These ways utilize research perspectives that may be characterized as "process" and focus on human interactive concerns rather than methodological concerns. As methods do not exist outside unique psychological-educational settings, only a naive or cynical researcher could conclude that the superiority of his method has direct and specific transferability to other educational settings. Our strategy recommends the study of children and adults in different educational environments, generalizing about their interactions rather than the procedures utilized to promote their interactions. That is, we believe that independent variation in the classroom obtains more from interaction effects (what we now usually try to neutralize or ignore in most experiments) than from methodological or curricular effects (what we now usually design as "independent variables").

Why research? For that matter, why education? Do the products of research or education make people smarter, more moral, more mentally healthy, more physically able? Is our president today, or the next one to be, more intelligent than Jefferson? Is this pope or chief rabbi more spiritual, a greater leader than the first pope or the first rabbi? Is there a connection between research results and practices? And if there is not, should we be disturbed about the matter?

Research and education are activities that cannot be separated from values and prejudices about people. Because of that, the one who conducts the research is most affected by it, as the one who engages in his education is most influenced by the experience. Research is valuable because of its effects on the people who engage in it. If it is helpful to the greater society, or disabled children, or the child you teach, all to the good. However, as unpopular as this may be to many, the history of research in the social sciences suggests that its primary value is for those who do it, and the payoff to the larger community results as those researchers and their various colleagues, and *their* colleagues, influence us.

These considerations cause me to recommend that we should not promote studies that examine the effects of a special curriculum (or talking typewriters or open classrooms) on, for example, the intellectual development of mentally retarded children. Studies of this kind are literally doomed to demonstrate little and, more seriously, will hardly influence even the researchers. Better, we might study a group of children, their teachers, their schools, their families, and their community. We might better study how the effects of our intervention changed the "traffic patterns" of parents vis-à-vis the school than how the intervention stimulated IQ changes in the children. We might better study how the intervention influenced the community, the city leaders, and the media in directions related to such issues as equal educational opportunities, advocacy, options for people, and consumer rights and responsibilities. As long as we continue to study children developmentally, utilizing single-variable approaches, we will continue to exaggerate group differences as we attempt to minimize individual differences; we will continue to reinforce the position of those who claim that you can't make a silk purse out of a sow's ear, that dull children must always remain dull, that nothing is curable and hardly anything preventable. The dominant research strategy in our culture virtually guarantees the triviality of our research. However, maybe that is exactly what some political and class interests count on.

Teaching

The preparation of teachers in special education, regular education, you-name-it education has not suffered from a lack of discussion. However, the preparation of teachers remains essentially an unstudied problem in education (Sarason, Davidson, & Blatt, 1962). It is unstudied for the same reasons that research activities in our field are of little consequence. As researchers seek better methods and general solutions to pedagogical problems, professors in our teachers' colleges teach "best" methods and "best" curricula, hoping to fortify students with enough techniques for them to teach well—and, so it turns out, to teach without having to think independently. The relationship between educational research and teacher preparation is so direct as to hardly permit the separation of one from the other, each activity mobilized in search of universal, happy, and simple solutions to complex problems and issues.

Like the alchemists of the Middle Ages who limited their scientific and mystical pursuits to the search for the alkahest and the panacea, their modern counterparts make the extraordinarily puzzling extraordinarily simple in their quest for ways to educate the child. In their distrust of the unknown, they return to some simple life of order and design, of cherished theory and trusted method. The foolishness continues in the same way that young children maintain fantasy lives for long periods of time, and in the same way that escapist adults believe that by ignoring a problem it will go away. We continue to grind out teachers whose teaching reflects the conception that education is primarily what one puts into children rather than what one can get out of them, whose preparation has reinforced this conception, and who at best can claim that they are good technicians and implementors. Our competency-based efforts, our technologies, our new certifications or noncertifications are making matters worse rather than better. As one colleague recently remarked, there truly is a difference between the competent teacher and the teacher who can demonstrate stipulated competencies.

Yet, the educational enterprise endures its problems and critics with such stiff-necked forbearance that one might be tempted to believe that they are indifferent to the slings and arrows. There have been so many problems, so many critics, so many new laws and law suits, new programs, money allocated, banners hoisted; and still the problems continue, the critics multiply, but hardly anything changes. Why has the educational enterprise created franchised schools, on the one hand, and educational supermarkets to support them on the other? A better question is, "Could it be any other way?" Given the circumstances of our teachers and their training, given the world as it is and what it was, one must answer that it could not be any other way, and the future portends yesterday. The educational enterprise is a monolith, no more capable of dealing with revisionism than any other monolith, be it Soviet Communism or the International Business Machine Company. Although there is embedded in any monolith the possibilities for flexibility and change (or it crumbles), there is only such freedom as is contained within the confines of rigidly enforced rules, regulations, customs, and values. As I have said, not far from the surface of every educational argument is that single massive, uniform, no-alternative slot machine of one system. It is found in children's classrooms because their teachers found it in their classrooms, because their teachers' teachers found it in theirs. Within the flexibility of the system that encourages almost infinite varieties of methods and curricula, that fosters open schools which are contiguous to traditional schools, and supports both free schools and special schools, is an oppressive custom that demands allegiance to but one generalized commandment: *you will not create because you are what you are*. Let us seek the best way for all people, because one individual is incapable of finding it for himself; let us develop together and, thus, avoid my confrontation with myself as creator as well as user.

Hence, sameness of mind is the mortar that binds and strengthens the Monolith. In the elementary classroom, a child who remembers well scores well; in the education college, the student who consumes and implements is preparing for the Teacher of the Year award. We train technicians in our colleges who, from the beginning and to the present, seek technical competency. We train for technical skills as we train people to live apart from those who have lesser skills, who appear different, who think differently, or whose metaphors are different. Essentially, our technical consumer education promotes an invariance of life and spirit, both by the influence of the technology on us and by our subsequent behavior as consuming experience-bound beings.

Consequently, there is an apparent—and in a sense, real—flexibility and innovation to be found in our schools! We advertise segregated schools, open schools, free schools, and ungraded schools in the educational supermarket for the same reasons others advertise Chevrolets, Keds, and popsicles; we believe we have the best product or, at the very least, we wish to convince the consumer that our products offer the most value. As a result, our schools virtually have become franchised—duplicative in the same way General Motors and Howard Johnson's are duplicative—strengthened by our teachers' colleges, which have always been educational supermarkets: "You don't have to (we know you can't) think independently; see all the goodies we offer, choose within this wide array, and consume to your satiation level, beyond if you wish; buy, but do not create, do not struggle to understand the process from the product, do not go beyond the boundaries of the marketplace; be different but do not be different from any of the rest of us, be a part of this wonderful educational slot-machine world."

What does humanity receive for its educational investment? Without doubt, most children learn to read and write; some progress far beyond their teachers' hopes, some far beyond their teachers. It is not that consumerism prevents learning; it merely interferes with it. That is, to the degree that teachers do not discourage abstract behavior and classroom variance, learning (changing) is more likely to occur. To the degree that teachers—elementary and university teachers alike—impose a standard curriculum, method, school organization, even content (perhaps *especially* content), the educational monolith will thrive.

What we need more of are child and teacher independence (thus fostering their interdependence), learning towards greater generalizations, inductive models, options, and the maximization of heterogenous groupings of people. What we need less of are mandated curricula, lonely teachers and children, segregated classes and schools—for whatever the reasons—consumerism to the discouragement of creativeness, and program consolidation.

In education, as we have indicated, the monolith is not the teachers' college, or the segregated class, or even the pedantic curriculum. The monolith is created and held together from the rubble of destroyed options, from the absence of not so much the bricks and structures of alternative educational designs (for these, too, have been known to victimize those who hold minority views), but from the absence of alternative thinking and values. Yet, I must keep remembering what Henry Ford has taught us. It is far less efficient to service people individually than on an assembly line. I have been forgetting that the people I would want the schools to educate must "run" (function) efficiently and be "serviced" (satisfied) easily.

The franchised school and the educational supermarket—the fulcrum of the monolith—are the enemies of those who would seek an education for themselves, enemies not because of any deliberate wickedness but because they represent a limited view of human potential, of what the world can become, that the world is each person, not multiplied but singular, unique and valuable, and that each person can create to help himself and, possibly, to help others.

In essence, I am suggesting that educational models should be studied from historical rather than prescriptive perspectives. That is, curricula, methods, media, and school organizations might be understood best in the context of what was accomplished rather than what must be attempted. This strategy seems less restrictive and promises greater discovery and illumination than the traditional prescriptive "best method" strategy. The literature on pedagogy and psychology confirms this position; i.e., there is no consistent significant source of independent (treatment) variation obtaining from special methods, curricula strategies, or administrative organizations. Further, I believe that the process of creating educational environments contributes more to independent variation than the environments themselves, especially when these are artificially contrived from educational supermarkets.

Shakespeare said, "Though this be madness, yet there is method in it." To some educational researchers and those who utilize their products, I rebut, "Though this be your method, there is mindlessness in it."

Educability

Throughout my career, I have been engaged in but one general endeavor. I have written books and monographs, studied and interacted with children and their families, the nature of that work always concerning concepts relating to educability, plasticity of development, the potentials each person has for changing. During the years, my work has dealt with several recurring themes, each inevitably anchored to the hypothesis of mankind's educability. The first such theme deals with the nature-nurture question. Although there is little scientific evidence that permits definitive answers to this age-old issue, I have concluded that there is considerable clinical evidence that people can change. The work of Itard, the autobiography of Helen Keller, the works of Mae Seagoe, Harold Skeels, Samuel Kirk, Seymour Sarason, and my own experiences and research lend support to the educability hypothesis. However, evidence aside, for but one reason dealing with the historic responsibility of those in the helping professions, I believe that this hypothesis is our only defensible hypothesis.

The philosophical underpinnings of my research and other activities are strengthened by the belief that, as human beings, all people are equally valuable. Bengt Nirje enunciated this concept through the so-called normalization theory. However, the religious and ethical teachings of countless others since the beginning of our civilization provide us with varied expressions of this idea, and with a glimmer of hope that we will one day take it more seriously than heretofore.

Unfortunately, human beings have a penchant to segregate, to separate, to stigmatize, to make pariahs of other human beings; more than ever before, we seem to be engrossed in such activities. On the other hand, I am encouraged that people today seem to want to discuss these issues. Further, at long last, the myth of such terms as "mental retardation" appears to be partially understood. The efficacy studies, the nomenclature changes,[2] the black revolution, and other scientific and social movements have led us to a better comprehension that, for example, "mental retardation" is no more than an administrative term. The words "mental retardation" have little, if any, scientific integrity. We had to appreciate that idea before we could take seriously the concept of educability. Or, maybe, it's the other way around; before we were able to learn that mental retardation is a contrived administrative label, referring to a current functional condition, we had to admit to a notion of human educability.

We are learning. More than that, learning—changing—need not necessarily proceed at an invarient rate. Even more importantly, educability need not refer only to children, but to their teachers, and their teachers' teachers, to all people. Most importantly, learning and knowing are not enough. People are essentially what they do, not what they think or hope. Not only should we consider the possibility that people can change but, if we want to give that hypothesis a chance to prove itself, we must behave as if people *can* change.

Hence, my preoccupation with the hypothesis of educability of intelligence. The literature relevant to the research in this area is vast, partly because it deals with problems as old as man, and partly because

---

[2] The most recent, little appreciated but astonishing, revision of the American Association on Mental Deficiency definition of mental retardation to include theoretical eligibility—i.e., psychometric retardation—to from one to two standard deviations on the "wrong" side of the mean literally revolutionized the incidence, prevalence, and concept of mental retardation, all with the simple stroke of Herbert Grossman's pen (1973). We cannot redefine measles, or cancer, or pregnancy with so easy and such external procedures. The Grossman Committee, sitting around a conference table, reduced enormously the incidence of mental retardation, never having to "see," or "dose," or deal with a client, only having to say that, hereinafter, mental retardation is such and such, rather than this or that. What, then, is mental retardation?

the questions asked and the answers given remain, to this day, far from clear. Perhaps, for our purposes, it might be enough to suggest that the evidence is ambiguous, some of the evidence suggesting that man can change, while other research suggests the opposite; the jury is out— Jensen notwithstanding, Blatt notwithstanding.

For our purposes, it might be enough to conclude this section with a definition of what I mean by educating intelligence. Simply stated, educating intelligence may be thought of as referring to procedures and conditions that bring out or elicit capacities in an individual for changing, both in rate and complexity, his learning performance insofar as school-related and other problem-solving tasks are concerned (Blatt & Garfunkel, 1969). The emphasis here reflects the Latin origin of the word "education": to lead forth, to draw forth, bring out, elicit. Change may be measured through the use of intelligence and other standardized and informal tests. On the behavioral level, change is reflected in the child's ability to handle with increasing skill the variety of problems confronting him as a student and as a human being. It is our assumption that change becomes both significant and possible when the individual needs to change, aspires to change, and is optimistic about the possibility for change. Educating intelligence refers to more than hypothetical mental faculties or abilities. It also refers to attitudes about self, learning, and abilities, without which the phenomenon of the change cannot be comprehended.

Alfred Binet, whose concepts provided much of the inspiration for our research on educability, was unable to create an environment to promote intellectual development. Neither Binet's "Mental Orthopedics," Omar Moore's "Responsive Environments," our Early Education Program, nor *any* other known to us have been able to demonstrate convincingly that capability is educable. However, as long as one maintains a genuine interest in the concept of educability, or as long as one believes that the true vocation of the teacher is to help people learn, not make determinations about who can or can't learn, this is a type of research or clinical activity that demands continued involvement, regardless of the outcome of one's previous failures. Therefore, I continue to invest totally in an examination of the concept of educability. We still have much to learn about the nature-nurture interaction, about the most efficient period to begin intervention, about the varieties of possible intervention models that may have the most desired effects, about better ways to study interventions, about better ways to study groups of children interacting with teachers and how they affect families, communities, and cultures. It is all terribly complicated; and, for reasons brought out earlier, most research efforts, including research on educability, are doomed from the beginning to disappoint us. But isn't that the reason why at least some "nativists" support the funding of Head Start and other studies of educability, to illustrate by such failures the attractiveness of a rational racism? However, what has again and again been brought to us so clearly is that the "educability" hypothesis has a pervasive fascination that sustains the researcher, for the concept includes all people and so many things that it can easily intrude into every nook and cranny of our time and energy; the hypothesis refers not only to children, not only to the mentally retarded, not only to those in the inner city or those in the institution; but, to the degree it has relevance for those groups, it has relevance for all of us—not only for children, but for their teachers, not only for their teachers, but for the teachers of their teachers. For a child to change, his teacher has to change. For my students to have changed, I had to.

Epidemiology

Epidemiological research aims to define and describe conditions associated with specific disorders. It analyzes the incidence, characteristics, and distributions of such disorders, attempting to relate demographic variables to etiological factors. No careful epidemiologic study can be conducted without a great deal of effort and resources. And, further, epidemiological study of the so-called handicapped places yet greater burdens on the researcher. Review of our own study, *Mental Retardation in Southeastern Connecticut* (in Blatt, 1973), or any of the other serious investigations of the incidence, prevalence, distribution, and antecedents of disability (Tarjan, Wright, Eyman, & Keeran, 1973) reveal why there are relatively few comprehensive epidemiological reports in our literature, in contrast to the enormous contributions such studies might offer to the solution of both basic and applied problems. However, there is a sufficient body of work available for us to have learned that the incidence and, especially, the prevalence of mental retardation depend almost precisely on such influences as definition and criteria, age, program supports, community resiliency, broad cultural values, social class, and other factors that provide compelling support for the position that the label "mental retardation" has more to do with political and administrative than with biological–psychological–scientific matters. That is, to describe mental retardation as a condition which affects 2 percent or 3 percent (or, since the Grossman manual, 1 percent) of the total population is to be less than naive, is to camouflage reality, is to deny thought and reason with the hope that prayers to the Gaussian curve will bring happiness if not wisdom. After several years of intense involvement in our aforementioned study of the incidence and prevalence of retardation, we are persuaded that we are dealing with no more than 1 percent of the total population, and possibly no more than 0.75 percent of the total population, who at any one time need (or were known to have needed) special services because of their mental retardation. This is by way of saying that, although it is quite apparent that 3 percent of our population are psychometrically retarded (the test construction guarantees this in the exact manner it guarantees that 50 percent of our population have IQs below 100; half the population is below average; that's about what the word "average" means), no more than 1 percent of our population are in need of special services because they are mentally retarded. Further, one-half of that 1 percent are either in the public schools' special programs for the mentally retarded or do not need any special services at the present time. Further still, given an adequate community-based program of alternatives for families, there should never be a need for more than 0.1 percent of the total general population to require residential placements because of some situation associated with their retardation; and, it should be noted, such residential placements need never be in arrangements that include populations greater than eight. That is, our large, traditional institutions should be evacuated as speedily as possible. They neither help people, nor are they necessary; they persist only because they serve magnificently that portion of our society who are responsible for the creation and maintenance of human slot fillers, wherever they are and for whomever they are.

For purposes of program planning and service delivery, it is important to understand the difference between psychometric and administrative mental retardation, a concept that unfortunately has not reached most of our textbooks in the field. For example, on the one hand, we have psychometric mental retardation (essentially IQ less than 75) including approximately 3 percent of our total population. On the other hand, we find the incidence of known retardation to be approximately 1 percent. Further, prevalences among preschool and adult populations is somewhat less than 1 percent, while it is somewhat more than 1 percent among school-aged children. Stated another way, from group to group—depending on age, socioeconomic status, community values, etc.—prevalences of mental retardation range from much less than 1 percent to much more than 1 percent; nevertheless, the total population includes 3 percent who are psychometrically (but not necessarily mentally) retarded, and no more than 1 percent who are mentally (i.e., administratively) retarded.

This problem, vis-à-vis the incidence and prevalence of a particular condition, exists across all so-called disability groups and, consequently, estimates of the various categorical handicaps vary from study to study, from culture to culture, and from time to time. What should be stated, as plainly as possible, is that disability means no more or less than being placed in a special class, a special program, or a special setting as a consequence of that disability—or, not being placed as a consequence of that disability. That is, the most relevant definition of a disability must include reference to the fact that it is essentially administratively determined.

Developing incidence estimates, predictions of program needs, and cost-benefit analyses is extraordinarily hazardous when dealing with these diverse populations. For example, in one state, attempts are made to integrate so-called educable mentally retarded children in regular grades; in another state, such youngsters are in regular grades and are not thought of or called mentally retarded. In yet another state, every effort is made to place as many children as possible with IQs less than 75 in special classes for the mentally retarded. In Connecticut, for example, many blind children attend public schools, most in regular classes. In a contiguous state, Massachusetts, possibly because of the presence of a venerable and heavily endowed private school, most blind children do not attend the public schools. In some cities in New York State, deaf children attend public schools. In other cities, deaf children must attend residential schools if they are to be educated since, unfortunately, there are no classes or programs for the deaf in the public schools of those areas.

Therefore, estimating the incidence and prevalence of a disability is, at best, difficult and always error-ridden, even after arduous epidemiologic study. In one community, there may be as many as 30 percent or 40 percent of the public school population who are psychometrically retarded; in another community, within the same city or region, psychometric retardation may be as low as 0.5 percent of a school population. Similarly, estimating the incidence of behavioral disturbances is very difficult. Surprisingly, even estimates of such apparently objective disabilities as blindness, deafness, and physical handicap do not provide the clear-cut data some might expect (*Fleischmann Report*, 1972).

After all is counted and analyzed, the prepotent lesson one learns is that there is a difference—a political, pragmatic, legal, and scientific difference—yet a hardly understood difference, between psychometric and administrative mental retardation, or, as another example, between audiogrammatic and administrative deafness. In the last analysis, there is an irony which suggests that not until we appreciate this special difference between objective and administrative disability will we begin to understand that, basically, there is never a difference between people. That is, we will eventually understand that, as human beings, people are just people; and our shared heritage cuts through a veneer of potentially enriching variability which, although thin, causes us too much grief as one excludes the other from his "turf" and consciousness.

A Summary

Since the early 1950s, when I began study of public school special education programs, there have been a great many attempts to evaluate the effectiveness of those programs. And although state schools, being more secluded and more segregated, have been subjected to fewer formal evaluations in contrast with the numerous so-called special class efficacy studies, these too are now regularly examined.

Research on the effectiveness of special classes for so-called handicapped children, as mentioned earlier in this paper, has now grown to impressively large and depressingly hollow proportions. Again, as mentioned earlier, the conclusion is that there is little research to encourage the expansion of special classes as we now know them. And, from Dorothea Dix to Kraepelin, to the more recent observations of Wolfensberger, Klaber, Menolascino, Dybwad, and others, there is consistent confirmation that, by its very nature, the state institution is infinitely less able to offer its residents humane care, and completely incompetent to provide them with opportunities to contribute to society and live dignified and purposeful lives. Yet, in total disregard of the few, but powerful, reports of institutional life and the scientifically questionable, but numerous, reports of special class life, we continue to build more and more institutions and pass more and more mandatory, rather than permissive, special class (not education) laws—in spite of the well-known fact that we have yet to demonstrate either the efficacy or moral rectitude in continuing, much less encouraging, these segregated programs. To return to an earlier theme, such proliferation in the face of no evidence is but another illustration of the monolithic influence. There is an urge that we seem to have to segregate while we engage ourselves in a constant flirtation between order and disaster, humanism and barbarism, love and hate. Little wonder that we have lost sight of the distinction between human privileges and human rights.

The Promise

Why this discrepancy between what we know and what we do? Why the back wards of state institutions? Why have we moved so grudgingly from Dorothea Dix to the twentieth century? Why do we, in the United States, know more about and do less for disabled people than other Western cultures? Are we, in fact, a nation devoted to our young and our vulnerable? We speak as if we are; our proclamations are frequent and strident. Moreover, we enact child-labor laws and public education laws; we support treatment services for handicapped children. However, in spite of what some may consider our best efforts, there are more violence, more frustration, more alienated youth, more sick children in our culture than ever before. Consequently, we must think seriously about the notion that we are not a "child-centered society," that we use this term in an unexamined way. On the evidence of too many reports, I am forced to consider the possibility that we never had a child-centered society. We are for children to the degree that children are for us; but first, and sometimes only, in this adult-centered society, each person is for himself. At least, one would be hard put to find sufficient evidence to reject this characterization of us—not of "them" or even of "you," but of *us*.

While I wait for a better world, I reflect on those days of our youth and callowness when we thought that, if people only would "understand," mental retardation would be prevented. But while I wait, I must change. While I wait for the millenium, I painfully record our human frailties, our inabilities to face life for whatever it is and for whatever it has to offer, and I must, in spite of its vicissitudes and the unfairness of it all, respect living as the one thing we have in common; for better or worse, it is all we have to stay alive. And, if your retarded child is all you have, that child is part of the reality of your life. That human being is part of the enrichment of your life. Without her, your life would be less full, and you would have fewer opportunities to learn, and contribute, and love. She owns part of your world, as you must own part of hers.

And I, too, own a part of my family, a part of the university, a part of society, a part of the total "action." I, too, must think and do, not only for others, but for myself. But what I must do most urgently is change. For the world to change, I must change. If I blame an evil world, a stupid system, ineffective leaders, or man's obvious imperfections, I may be right. But if it means that I do not have to change, I contribute to the evil. Before we can change humanity, we must change ourselves. Before I attempt to solve the human puzzle, I must solve the riddle "I." I must think about my unfolding as the beginning of understanding civilization's evolution.

What is the promise for people? What are we, and what must we become? We have seen the views of monoliths from behind windows to nothing and we are not pleased. Therefore, we wonder what our people have become, what we have become—and what we must now do. The answer is as plain as it is complicated, clear as it is opaque. We must create a union of consumers, professionals, attendants, students, their professors, great people, ordinary people—each concerned with monoliths, with departments of mental health and education, with the inner city, with institutions and public schools, with the legislature, and united on behalf of all who have asked or wondered what we have become. We must join together on behalf of the inmates, the state school and hospital residents, the ghetto children, and—finally—on behalf of each of us living through these difficult times.

We must seek a society where leaders will not merely lead but will be led by greater visions and authority than they possess, a society where the people will be led because they are independent. We must envision a society that will be free of dehumanizing and debilitating state-sponsored domiciles, a society that will evacuate human beings from any facility that abuses or enslaves. We must create a society that has compassion for all those who are saddened, yet comprehends the difference between the man who regrets his own lost years and the man who worries for his brothers. We must think about a man who weeps, not for those for whom the world may suspect he weeps, but for his zealousness and for himself. And possibly today, each of us is that man.

We must create an organization that earlier reformers, were they here today, would join. We must unite, not about specific task orientations but about powerful ideologies, not about special means but about a consensus of humanistic ends, not about silly slogans thoughtlessly chanted but about the infinite perspectives of a complex dilemma. We must describe and understand the subtle as well as the flagrant, ennui as well as flailing arms and diffuse excrement, and pandemonium as an extension of the best-managed "model" institution. We must act as if Itard, Howe, Dorothea Dix, Helen Keller, and Emil Kraepelin are our judges. We must convince others—and ourselves—that the state does not own a man, that the state controls but may not buy or sell a human being, that *I* may destroy *myself* but the state has no right to my self or my corpse, nor to my feelings, nor mind, nor spirit; that freedom is more important than life itself. We must illuminate the irony of a state that is permitted, by law, to take or reduce my life while I—who should be the owner—may not, under penalty of fine or imprisonment, take my own life or cause myself bodily harm. The state may with (or sometimes without) provocation kill me, institutionalize me, seclude me, shock me, drug me, dirty me, animalize me. But I, who should be the owner, may not kill myself, scandalize myself, drug myself, dirty myself, or dehumanize myself. The state—as it substitutes pills for strait jackets and therapeutic isolation for solitary cells—does not change in the truly important dimensions, as it demands that each of us bend and twist, as we scrape low to say grace and pay homage to the state. Long live the state and to hell with man— even, exquisite irony, to hell with each man who represents the state. Man once manufactured the state and now the state manufactures man; the state is now the apotheosis of man! Possibly, Hemingway thought of the state when he remarked, "All things truly wicked start from innocence."

Are there not some informed people who share these concerns? Certainly, there have been many who tried to reshape our styles of living and thinking. There are some among us who understand the difference between feeding and eating, and between eating and dining. But all their concerns seem to have led to such meager accomplishment, to so trivial a common good; and so our involvement, and a small hope, and these words. For, in spite of some claims that it is darkest before the dawn, one may yet encounter terror at high noon; and one may thus conclude that man's days can be as black as his nights.

Therefore, we must band together, as each makes his special commitment to change. We must become a new people, no longer underestimating the potentials we have for changing, no longer pessimistic concerning the conditions of change, and thus no longer fulfilling the prophecy of no-change, finally convinced that development is a function of opportunity and training. We must believe that our inability to have better stipulated the conditions of learning is less a defect of the educability hypothesis than of our practices. Finally, for me to change and thus for the world to change, I must believe in a design of things, and that the design for all of us holds nothing but good. I must become a new man. But how, the final question? And, after the question, not an answer but a hypothetical dialogue, a speculation; and then there remains only you and only me. But possibly, at least today, we are brothers and sisters.

What is Man?
One who knows he exists.
That's Descartes.
Descartes is Man.

Can Man endure?
First, he must think, so he can be.
Is that enough?
No, to endure, Man must feel.

How can he improve?
He must invent.
What is his most important invention?
Ideas.

But, Man has so few ideas.
Because he is violated.
Then, how should Man meet violence?
With other than violence.

How will I know what I am?
When you know what you are not.
And, then will I know?
Yes, if you don't fool yourself.

How will I know of the Cosmos?
When you cease the struggle to understand.
How can I know without understanding?
That is the only way to know of the Cosmos.

What must I resist?
What everyone else seems to do.
What, then, would I learn?
What no one else knows.

When everything is gone, what is left?
You.

Then, what do I have?
Everything, or nothing.

But, there is an interconnection.
Are you asking if a man is alone?
No, I am saying he is not.
Then, you are wrong.

A person is not unrelated!
But he is unique.
He is not an island!
But he is even less a carbon.

I sense an unfriendliness.
No, it is independence you feel.
Whose?
Yours, if you seize it.

But, there are paradoxes and contradictions.
Where aren't there?
Why make them manifest?
So we may deal with them.

Independence risks everything.
Dependence nothing, for there is nothing.
Too many problems.
And many solutions.

How do I begin?
Analyze things.
To learn about them?
To learn about yourself.

What should I look for?
Your vulnerability.
Which is?
What you will try to overlook.

How will I know when my path is honest?
When you walk alone.
What is the danger then?
That others may follow you.

Who will our leaders be?
Those who have learned to listen.
Then, how will they lead?
By following their people.

What will it require?
Independence.
The leaders'?
And the peoples'.

Who will follow this kind of leader?
Those who will be free not to.
Who will obey?
Those who are independent.

Then, what is the world?
Each person.
All people together?

No, each one counted separately.

Where is the world going?
Look at its past.
What will we learn from it?
That we learn nothing from it.

Don't we learn from history?
Only that we have not learned from history.
Then, we are doomed to relive it again and again.
Or, to begin to learn from history.

How, then, have we planned?
Poorly.
One hears that there is virtue in not planning.
False virtue, for any road will take you to your goal.

You are too negative about the past.
Or too optimistic for our future.
But you find so little that has been good.
Because I feel it can become better.

When will it?
When the enslaved are freed.
Why?
So I will be free.

Whom do you mean?
Anyone who does not harm, yet remains enchained.
Possibly for his protection?
Possibly merely to enslave him.

Who are some examples?
All those whom we separate without cause.
Name some.
All those whom we have segregated thoughtlessly.

You would set them free?
So we can be free.
Where will they go?
Where we go.

But they will need help.
Who doesn't?
But you said each man is alone.
And you said he isn't.

Then, what is the riddle?
First, let's find the answer.
Which is?
Only a free person can be responsible for other free people.
And the riddle?
Why does being free cause one to give up freedom,
To ensure his freedom,
And, enlarge his respect for freedom?
Eureka!

Those who are enslaved cannot contribute to others.
And, no one is completely free until all who should be are free.
That's why leaders must follow their people.

And the people must be free to choose leaders.
And, to be free, a man must have self-respect,
Which requires relationships with others,
That reinforce his freedom and dependence,
Which again answers the riddle.
Therefore, you call for a New Man.
Is there another way?
From where will he arise?
Obviously, from the ranks of the enslaved.

REFERENCES

Bennett, A. A comparative study of sub-normal children in the elementary grades. *Contributions to Education*. Teachers' College, 1932.

Blatt, B. *The physical, personality, and academic status of children who are mentally retarded attending special classes as compared with children who are mentally retarded attending regular classes.* (Doctoral dissertation, Pennsylvania State University). Ann Arbor, Mich.: University Microfilms, 1956.

Blatt, B. *The intellectually disfranchised: Impoverished learners and their teachers.* Boston: Massachusetts Department of Mental Health, Community Mental Health Monograph Series, 1967.

Blatt, B. *Exodus from pandemonium: Human abuse and a reformation of public policy.* Boston: Allyn & Bacon, 1970.

Blatt, B. *Souls in extremis: An anthology on victims and victimizers.* Boston: Allyn & Bacon, 1973.

Blatt, B. A basic kit to confront the human disposal authority, department of subnormal affairs of the monolith, in this land of opportunity. *Journal of Education*, 1974, 156:70–104.

Blatt, B., & Garfunkel, F. *The educability of intelligence.* Washington, D.C.: Council for Exceptional Children, 1969.

Blatt, B., & Garfunkel, F. Teaching the mentally retarded. In N. L. Gage (Ed.), *Handbook of research on teaching.* Chicago: Rand McNally, 1973.

Blatt, B. & Kaplan, F. *Christmas in purgatory: A photographic essay on mental retardation.* Boston: Allyn and Bacon, 1966.

Blatt, B. & Mangel, C. "The Tragedy and Hope of Retarded Children," *Look*, October 31, 1967, 31:96–103.

Caine, L. F., Levine, S., and others. *A study of the effects of community and institutional school classes for trainable mentally retarded children.* San Francisco: San Francisco State College, 1961.

Cassidy, V. M., & Stanton, J. *An investigation of factors involved in the educational placement of mentally retarded children.* Columbus: Ohio State University Press, 1959.

Coleman, J. S., Campbell, E. Q., Hobson, C. J., McPartland, J., Mood, A. M., Weinfeld, F. B., & York, R. L. *Equality of educational opportunity.* Washington, D.C.: U.S. Government Printing Office, 1966.

Dunn, L. M., & Hottel, J. V. *The effectiveness of special day class training programs for severely (trainable) mentally retarded children.* Nashville: George Peabody College, 1958.

Fleischmann report on the quality, cost and financing of elementary and secondary education in New York State. Vol. 1. New York: Viking Press, 1972.

Grossman, H. J. (Ed.). *Manual on terminology and classification in mental retardation.* Washington, D.C.: American Association on Mental Deficiency, 1973.

Hurley, R. *Poverty and mental retardation: A causal relationship.* New York: Random House, 1969.

Johnson, G. O. *A comparative study of the personal and social adjustment of mentally handicapped children placed in special classes with mentally handicapped children who remain in regular classes.* Syracuse, N.Y.: Syracuse University Research Institute, 1961.

Pertsch, C. F. A comparative study of the progress of subnormal pupils in the grades and in special classes. *Teachers' College Contributions to Education,* 1936.

Sarason, S. B., Davidson, K., & Blatt, B. *The preparation of teachers: An unstudied problem in education.* New York: John Wiley, 1962.

Tarjan, G., Wright, S. U., Eyman, R. R., & Keeran, C. U. Natural history of mental retardation: Some aspects of epidemiology. *American Journal of Mental Deficiency,* 1973, 77:369–79.

CHAPTER 2

A Concept of Educability and the Correlates of Mental Illness, Mental Retardation, and Cultural Deprivation

On February 5, 1963, President Kennedy delivered his now famous message to the Eighty-eighth Congress [23] that called for a massive national effort to deal with the "twin problems" of mental illness and mental retardation. Of critical importance to us are his remarks concerning the relationship between cultural deprivation and mental retardation, and possibilities for amelioration or prevention of the latter.

> Cultural and educational deprivation resulting in mental retardation can also be prevented. Studies have demonstrated that large numbers of children in urban and rural slums, including pre-school children, lack the stimulus necessary for proper development in their intelligence. Even when there is no organic impairment, prolonged neglect and the lack of stimulus and opportunity for learning can result in the failure of young minds to develop. Other studies have shown that, if proper opportunities for learning are provided early enough, many of these deprived children can and will learn and achieve as much as children from more favored neighborhoods.[1] This self-perpetuating intellectual blight should not be allowed to continue.

The President's complete text provoked, at that time, puzzlement among a number of professional workers involved in treating the mentally ill, the mentally retarded, and the culturally deprived. Their most serious disagreements with his message concerned the pooling of mental illness and mental retardation as twin problems, his assertion that a cause-and-

---

This essay was originally published in N. R. Bernstein (Ed.), *Diminished people: The problems and care of the retarded*. Boston: Little Brown, 1970. Reprinted by permission.

[1] The recent Jensen report [21] and those reactions of its many adherents and detractors (please see especially "How Much Can We Boost I.Q. and Scholastic Achievement? A Discussion" by Kagan et al. [22]) said it all—all that should have been said and all that should not have been said about "nature-nurture," the relationship of social class and intelligence, and the hypothesis that intelligence is educable or plastic. This chapter will explore, in addition to some of Jensen's major concerns, less visible facets of the global problem confronting disfranchised poor children.

effect relationship exists between cultural deprivation and mental retardation, and his prediction that improvements in preschool, elementary, and secondary education—particularly in distressed areas—would help prevent mental retardation. I am in full agreement with what must have been a carefully planned strategy of President Kennedy and his advisors and, upon reflection, must add that the wisdom of his message is literally astonishing. Not only was it the ideational progenitor of the Economic Opportunity Act of 1964 and the basis for the War on Poverty, but the Kennedy document can also be considered an important statement concerning a set of related and complex problems.

What is the relationship between mental illness and mental retardation? As we discussed elsewhere [7], even before the turn of this century a distinction was made between *dementia* and *amentia*. Dementia (mental illness) was described as a sickness during which the individual lost his ability to function normally. The term means literally "a loss of mentality." Amentia (mental retardation) was described as a condition of intellectual subnormality. The term means literally "without mentality," implying that the individual never had normal mentality. Today, in textbooks and in scholarly journals this distinction is often maintained. Mental illness is described as a sickness that deprives a "normal" person of his abilities to use his intelligence and emotions appropriately. The prognosis of mental illness, although not particularly encouraging in certain cases, never categorically precludes the possibility of either prevention or cure. In fact, practically all programs for treatment of the mentally ill focus on what Caplan [9] termed *secondary* or *tertiary preventions*.

The distinction between *illness* and *condition* is very important. Although some notable scholars within the field maintain that mental retardation can be prevented or cured, even they generally agree that retardation is a condition and not a sickness.[2] In the vernacular we use the word *illness* to denote a state that is the opposite of *wellness*. However,

---

[2] For a full discussion of classification and terminological problems in mental retardation, see Blatt [3, 4] and Heber [19]. Traditionally, mental retardation was defined as a constitutional condition of the central nervous system, existing from birth or early age, incurable and irremediable, often resulting in the inability of the individual to profit from ordinary schooling. This traditional definition was joined to a classification system that utilized arbitrarily determined IQ scores to categorize levels of intellectual capacity; e.g., 25–50 IQ was the "trainable category; 50–75 IQ was the "educable" category. More recently a new (and widely used) definition and classification manual [19] was developed by a committee of the American Association on Mental Deficiency. This new manual defines mental retardation as subaverage general intellectual functioning, originating during the developmental period and associated with impairment in adaptive behavior. This definition does not assume a constitutional condition as a necessary requirement for mental retardation (see "cultural-familial mental retardation," pp. 39–40). It refers to function rather than, as is traditional, to capacity, and it does not preclude possibilities for prevention, cure, or amelioration of mental retardation and its associated consequences.

we imply more. When we speak about sickness, we make certain assumptions about prior conditions of health, and, depending on our optimism and the specific nature of the illness concerned, we arrive at a prognosis and a plan of treatment for eventual cure. The term *condition* refers to a more static state in which we do not imply that health is attainable.

In this respect the term *condition* is not logical if one believes that mental retardation is curable. Why, then, are the many professionals in the field of mental retardation who view mental retardation more optimistically, and who may even be involved in programs designed to prevent or reverse retardation, reluctant to use the terms *illness* or *sickness* in discussing retardation? Their reluctance may be derived from similar sources that prevented earlier workers with the insane from calling their patients ill or sick. In the vernacular, sickness implies that an individual shows certain symptoms. Only relatively recently have the fields of psychiatry and psychology been able to devise sufficient diagnostic procedures to identify symptoms of emotional disturbance or mental illness. Only within the last few years have interrelationships between physical and emotional factors (psychosomatic effects) been even partly understood.

Therefore, in view of the well-known presumption that 75 to 85 percent of all known mental retardates have no measurable physiological abnormalities or pathological central nervous system impairments, some workers in retardation feel it necessary to make a distinction between physical normality and intellectual subnormality. Further, although an important distinction is made between retarded children who are presumed to be physiologically intact—the cultural-familial mentally retarded[3]—and those who have central nervous system impairments, both the cultural-familial and the organically impaired retarded are considered to be intellectually subnormal or weak or defective, but not sick.

I believe it may add perspective to the problem if we consider any child who has serious learning or behavior disorders to be a sick child. I would include all the mentally retarded and many of the culturally disadvantaged in this category of "sick children." In spite of the fact that their sickness may not be considered physical in origin, we cannot discount the consequences of what we presently term their "condition." These children have severe cognitive restrictions and deficits and are

---

[3] Although the "technical" definition of cultural-familial mental retardation is stated somewhat differently [19], substantively it suggests at least five characteristics which have long been descriptive of certain individuals: 1) by traditional methods of evaluation their intelligence is subnormal, 2) the intellectual level and social adequacy of at least one parent and one sibling appear also to be subnormal, 3) there is no discernible central nervous system pathology giving rise to the subnormality, 4) they were born into and reared in a cultural milieu which is "inferior" to other strata of our society, and 5) they represent a disproportionately large part of the case load of many social agencies.

faced with global intellectual discontinuities and difficulties. During the school years further consequences of such an "illness" may result in academic retardation and character disorders which may lead, in turn, to problems of illiteracy, school dropouts, social maladjustments, and economic dependency on society. This chapter is concerned with children who are prone to this illness, with the hope that, for many, it may be prevented and, for most, it will be treated and subsequently ameliorated or cured.

What is the relationship between mental retardation and cultural deprivation? It would distort the history of several scholarly fields to suggest that President Kennedy raised a new controversy. The relationship between retardation and social class has been a long-standing concern of sociologists, anthropologists, and political scientists and, more recently, of psychologists and teachers. Our earlier review of the literature [6] (condensed here) bearing on this relationship, and upon attempts to prevent or reverse intellectual inadequacy, disclosed the following:

1. At present there appears to be a marked resurgence of interest in mental retardation generally and in the cultural-familial type of case in particular [1, 11, 16, 20, 26, 29]. Whereas in earlier decades the cultural-familial cases (variously labeled "Kallikak," garden-variety, subcultural) were viewed as a distinct etiological grouping of genetic origin, they tend today to be viewed as part of that much larger problem group of our society given the label "culturally deprived."

2. There seems to be general agreement that genetic processes represent an important source of influence on the biological foundations of intelligence. There also seems to be increasing recognition that far too little is known about the nature of intelligence (except, perhaps, that it is vastly more complex than is indicated by the usual IQ score) to justify drawing anything resembling specific hypotheses about the role played by genetic factors [10, 12, 13, 19, 25, 28, 34, 36]. Put another way, the heated nature-nurture controversies of the past have been superseded by the recognition that earlier formulations were oversimplifications which served the participants' personal opinions far better than they did clarification of the problem.

3. The above change in viewing the nature-nurture controversy, together with the emergence of cultural deprivation as a major problem in our society, seemed to set the stage for systematic research and social action on ways of bringing about environmental changes that might prevent intellectual deficits. Put more positively, the aim seems to be to invade and change environments in order to determine the degree to which the intelligence of these individuals could be educated, i.e., to evaluate what one "could bring out" under changed conditions [8, 33, 35].

4. Relatively few systematic studies bear directly on the effects of planned intervention on the intellectual development of culturally deprived or cultural-familial mentally retarded children. The studies which have been done vary greatly in methodological sophistication, quality and quantity of descriptive detail about such important variables as selection of cases, differences in contrasting environments, and control of bias in collection of data [14, 15, 24, 33, 35]. The findings tend to suggest—more or less mildly—that planned interventions have the predicted effect of increasing intelligence test scores, although it is by no means clear what aspects of the environment are the most important ones. Perhaps the wisest conclusion one should draw is that available studies do not allow one to infer that the problem is solved.

5. It is possible that a major difficulty encountered by recent studies may in itself turn out to be one of the most illuminating aspects of the development of children from culturally deprived or cultural-familial backgrounds. Although they can be found in great numbers in the school setting, mildly mentally retarded children of preschool age without central nervous system defect were extremely difficult to locate, even when special case-finding efforts were made in neighborhoods where one would expect to find them in fair number [14, 15, 24]. One possibility, of course, is that the intelligence tests measure different abilities or behaviors in the preschool period than in the school years. However, there is no evidence that this possibility could account for more than a part of the difficulty in case finding. Another possibility is that, in as yet undetermined ways, introducing these children into the school setting maximizes a conflict between the home and school cultures, producing attitudes toward learning and self that negatively affect test performance. In any event, if the difficulty in case finding is a real one, its explanation becomes of major significance in future theorizing and research.

To summarize, there are strong suggestions that the so-called cultural-familial mentally retarded are found almost exclusively among the culturally disadvantaged portion of our population. Secondly, efforts to prevent and reverse school failures and retardation among children who are in the cultural-familial group have been encouraging, although the problem is by no means "laid by the heels." As Sarason [31] stated, although we are not in a position to deny the possibility that heredity is a powerful factor in the development of so-called cultural-familial retardation, we should set that possibility aside until there is clearer evidence to support it. Essentially, it is not a very useful hypothesis for purposes of research or program development. If we conceptualize such retardation as arising from some multiple genetic etiology, we may assume that there is scarcely anything that can be accomplished in preventing or remedying the disorder. Certainly, if such were the case there would be little left in this group to interest educational researchers or program planners.

On the other hand, the optimistic viewpoint that intelligence is educable (i.e., intelligence is a function of practice and training) permits exploration into the possibilities for prevention and cure of learning disorders associated with retardation or cultural deprivation or both. The central hypothesis of this chapter is the assumption that any child is capable of better performance. This assumption is equally valid for a child with visible psychological or physiological pathology, but it is especially directed toward the child who comes from an intellectually disadvantaged environment and who may be helped, early in his life, in a variety of ways calculated to stimulate his cognitive development and his motivation to succeed.

IMPOVERISHED LEARNERS AND THEIR FAMILIES

In the sixties several major works describing the plight of the culturally disadvantaged in the United States were published. Four of the more important ones are Harrington's *The Other America* [17], May's *The Wasted Americans* [27], Riessman's *The Culturally Deprived Child* [29], and Riessman, Cohen, and Pearl's *Mental Health of the Poor* [30]. However, no one states the problem more simply or more effectively than Sargent Shriver in *The War on Poverty* [32], a Congressional presentation prepared for the Select Subcommittee on Poverty of the Committee of Labor and Public Welfare of the United States Senate.

> . . . there remains an unseen America, a land of limited opportunity and restricted choice. In it live nearly 10 million families who try to find shelter, feed and clothe their children, stave off disease and malnutrition, and somehow build a better life on less than $60 a week. Almost two-thirds of these families struggle to get along on less than $40 a week.
>
> These are the people behind the American looking glass. There are nearly 35 million of them. Being poor is not a choice for these millions; it is a rigid way of life. It is handed down from generation to generation in a cycle of inadequate education, inadequate homes, inadequate jobs, and stunted ambitions. It is a peculiar axiom of poverty that the poor are poor because they earn little, and they also earn little because they are poor. For the rebel who seeks a way out of this closed circle, there is little help. The communities of the poor generally have the poorest schools, the scarcest opportunities for training. The poor citizen lacks organization, endures sometimes arbitrary impingement on his rights by courts and law enforcement agencies; cannot make his protest heard or has stopped protesting. . . .
>
> Patterns of poverty are established early in life. Thousands of children grow up in homes where education, ambition, and hope are as scarce as money. Many of these children attend school with little incentive or guidance

from home to get them through. They drop out as soon as the law permits, or sooner. Others fail to attend school at all.

By the time such children reach 16, they begin a lifelong drift through a series of low-skill or no-skill jobs that grow increasingly harder to find as automation spreads through business and industry. Some who can't find jobs at all turn to drug addiction, petty crime, then major crime.

But most simply find a niche of minimum usefulness to themselves and society, where they may cling for the rest of their lives. They need opportunities for escape, but first, their attitudes have to be rebuilt, in a sense, from the ground up. For poverty can be a state of mind, and many of these young people feel already defeated.

Another group falls in this youthful army of the poor who form ranks in the city slums and the rural backwaters across the nation. These are the children of poor families who grow up with the motivation and the ambition, but not the opportunities. If they get through high school they are unable to find part-time work to help them to meet college expenses, or to help them contribute to needed support at home.

How should one describe disadvantaged children for the purposes of classification? Havighurst [18] recommends evaluation of the child in terms of certain family characteristics which are related directly to the child, in terms of the social group characteristics of families, and in terms of the child's personal characteristics. With this recommendation in mind, we will make a number of generalizations from the literature on disadvantaged children.

Hard-core deprived families have been reported to have certain characteristics that relate directly to and act as a negative reinforcement on the development of their children. Often parents have been found to have low intelligence and to be socially inadequate. Consequently, many show low educational attainments and have been early school dropouts. As adults they may also be having difficulty in adjusting socially. Their children, likewise, are generally found to experience a high degree of reading and learning disabilities, school failures, and problems of social adjustment. The parent-child relationship is often characterized by extremes of parental overprotection or rejection. In such families the status goals are highly restricted by inferior self-image and by self-derogating and self-defeating outlooks.

Case studies suggest that these families have moral standards which are unacceptable to middle-class society, and as a result of their standards the disadvantaged find themselves in frequent conflict with the legal codes and mores of affluent America. Disadvantaged families are oftentimes dependent on social agencies for continual financial and other support. Frequently there is no male adult living in the home, and when there is one, he may not be the father of the children.

In the homes of disadvantaged families there is a scarcity of furniture and appliances of all types. There is an absence of educational materials such as toys, puzzles, scissors, and books. The families are often non-verbal, i.e., there is little meaningful language used, and the language that is used is frequently unacceptable in nondeprived settings, such as the school. In general, the home and the contiguous neighborhood provide children with a limited range of stimuli and encouragement for exploration and discovery in worlds other than the one in which they live.

Generally, children raised in such environments have been found to suffer from two overlapping groups of deficits, cognitive and motivational. Of crucial importance to a discussion of educability are the environmental influences—other than the school—that operate before the child is born and that seem to continue to have profound effects throughout the formative years. In order to understand them, we must discuss the variability that exists between and within families. We have completed a study [6] in which we dealt with some aspects of the very broad, complex, and significant problem of the relationship among social class, family characteristics, and intellectual and academic growth. We were concerned specifically with testing some methods of intervention with preschool children from disadvantaged homes—procedures that might reduce the likelihood that they would develop intellectual and academic deficits so frequently found in youngsters from such environments. The following case descriptions, which are from data collected in that study, demonstrate our contention vis-à-vis variability *between* families and *within* a family in populations of the culturally deprived.

These three cases in the aforementioned study [6] illustrate problems that are encountered in attempting to categorize the disadvantaged in neat, unequivocal ways. Obviously, all names of families and places are fictitious.

Case 1. The Marcellino family lives in a congested section of the city comprising two large low-income housing projects and severely run-down tenement dwellings. Their block contains four four-story apartments houses, all connected. The family lives in a building that was condemned several years ago but never demolished. Many families move to this block as a last resort when they are evicted from the housing project. In this neighborhood it is considered degrading to have to live on this block.

The Marcellinos live in a building that is in deplorable physical condition, dirty, and an apparent firetrap. Stairways are broken and garbage is strewn on all floors. Stairways and hallways are dark, their only light coming through a skylight during the day. Obscene messages are written on the walls of the hallways. The entire house smells of kerosene, which is the only type of heating available. The ceilings are cracked and plaster is falling down. The house is infested with rats, which seem to be a continuous problem to the tenants. No door has a name or number on it and mail boxes do not indicate which apartment contains which family. Most people in the house pick up their mail at the Post Office, as most mail is in the form of relief or other dependency checks and it is not a good idea to rely upon the broken boxes from which mail can be easily stolen. It was pointed out that this obscurity helps in avoiding creditors as well as other unwanted visitors.

The Marcellino apartment has no name on the front door. It is dirty and smells much worse than the hallways. There are three bedrooms, a combination bedroom-living room, a kitchen, and a bathroom. All the furniture is in disrepair and the physical surroundings appear to be grossly neglected.

The family is known to eleven social agencies in the Greater Boston area, including Public Welfare, Catholic Charities, and Family Service.

The father, who is 40 years old, reported that he had completed seven grades of school, is not working, and presently is being treated at the Veterans Administration Hospital for asthma. Prior to his hospitalization he was an odd-job worker. He is said to be an alcoholic. The mother, who is 37 years old, reported that she stayed back a lot in school and did not like school but completed seven grades. There are eight children in this family, six of school age, none in the special class. However, the 14-year-old son is in fifth grade, the 12-year-old daughter is in sixth grade, the 11-year-old daughter is in third grade, the 8-year-old daughter is in first grade, and the 7-year-old daughter and 6-year-old son are in kindergarten. There is evidence here of general and multiple grade repetition among siblings.

Bobby Marcellino, the 3½-year-old boy who was one of the 60 children participating in the aforementioned preschool research project, is one of two preschoolers in the family. He was delivered after a normal pregnancy. The mother reported an uneventful early rearing of Bobby. He ate well, was weaned without difficulty, walked at about 1 year, and talked at about 1 year. His toilet training began at about 6 months of age, and by 1 year he attended to his toilet needs independently and regularly. On psychological evaluation upon entrance to the study, Bobby was evaluated as somewhat mildly mentally retarded. Psychometrically, he scored the lowest of any child entering the study.

Case 2.   The Gomez family lives in a five-room apartment in one of the two housing projects located in the neighborhood where our research was conducted. The interior of the apartment is neat and clean, although sparsely and poorly furnished. There is some semblance of an attempt to keep the apartment in good order.

The family is known to nine social agencies, including Public Welfare, Family Service, State Division of Child Guardianship, and the Society for the Prevention of Cruelty to Children. Mr. Gomez is 38 years old. He completed six grades of school and repeated at least three grades prior to leaving school at age 16. He has always worked as a fisherman. During the fishing season he leaves his family for long periods of time, and when he is home he spends his evenings drinking, gambling, and "running around." He is reported to be ill-tempered, easily angered, and unconcerned with the financial and emotional support of his family.

Mrs. Gomez is 30 years old and attended Latin High School through part of the second year of high school. She left school at the age of 16 in order to get out of an unhappy home situation, married at that time, and is presently suing for divorce. Since her separation she has been receiving Aid to Dependent Children funds. Because her husband was frequently away from home, child-rearing was left almost entirely to her. She feels that she is too easy on the children and that, as a result, the children get what they want.

The oldest sibling, a daughter, has just completed the eighth grade and has never repeated any grades. The son, age 9, repeated the first grade and is now attending special class at the elementary school. He is a "fire setter," who was sent by the courts to a residential guidance center and is presently awaiting treatment. A son, age 8, has completed the second grade at the elementary school and has not repeated any grades. A daughter, age 5, just completed kindergarten and is going into the first grade.

Johnny Gomez, one of two preschool children in the family and the child in whom we were most interested, had an uneventful early childhood. He talked at about the same age as the other children in the family and walked by the time he was 1 year old. He was toilet-trained by the time he was 2½; however, he still has "accidents" at night. He is a pleasant little boy, minds his mother well, responds to her discipline, rarely has to be spanked, is good-natured, and mixes well, both with other children in the neighborhood and with his siblings.

Case 3. The Brown family lives in one of the two aforementioned housing projects. The apartment is dirty, barren of furniture, extremely crowded (although it is a five-room apartment) and, in general, very dilapidated.

The family is known to eleven social agencies in the Greater Boston area, including Public Welfare, Family Service, and Legal Aid Society.

The father, whose age in unknown, is rarely home, and the mother had little idea what his educational attainment was. The mother described him as "drunk all the time and there's no point in interviewing him."

The mother is 39 years old, toothless, and has just returned from the hospital where she gave birth to her eighth child. She completed three years of high school in a small Massachusetts town.

The oldest sibling, 18 years of age, was a special class graduate who went one year to vocational high school and is now "away." A 17-year-old son is in the first year of trade school. A 13-year-old daughter is in a special class at the elementary school. A 9-year-old son is in the first grade. A 6-year-old daughter is in kindergarten. Larry Brown, one of three preschool children in the family and the boy in whom our study was interested, is 4 years of age. He is an appealing child, inhibited and largely nonverbal. He is average in size and does not have any noticeable physical disorders.

Originally, in our research we intended to select preschool children whose siblings were classified as cultural-familial retarded school-age children. We hoped to determine whether a variety of preschool experiences would significantly affect their academic efficiency when they entered school. In order to meet criteria for cultural-familial retardation as defined in the American Association on Mental Deficiency's *A Manual on Terminology and Classification in Mental Retardation* [19], we stipulated that each child selected must have a mentally retarded older sibling who had no organic involvement and at least one mentally retarded parent who had no organic involvement. By this method we hoped to select children who would likely be classified eventually as mildly mentally retarded without central nervous system involvement. We used this method of selection because we assumed that, without outside special intervention, the preschool children could be expected to develop in patterns somewhat similar to those of their older siblings and their parents.

In brief, then, our original criteria were that subjects 1) come from a lower class, 2) be of preschool age, 3) have at least one older retarded sibling, and 4) have at least one retarded parent. We were interested in finding cultural-familial retarded families, which the literature reputes to be a distinct and identifiable subpopulation of the much larger total population of disadvantaged families. We soon realized that, despite several sampling strategies, our criteria were essentially unworkable (see Blatt and Garfunkel [6] for a detailed discussion of this problem). We found that children in special classes do not, in general, have retarded parents—although a fair percentage of these parents were once in special classes or were early school dropouts. Further, we found that we could not make any sound judgment about the current level of intellectual functioning of the parents. Whether there is a strong relationship between retardation in parents and in their children is a moot point, but our experiences suggest that if it exists at all, such a relationship is a weak one. Obviously, the three families just described can be categorized as culturally deprived and do exhibit high incidences of school failure in both parents and children. However, even with the availability of certain school records and cooperation from local school officials, we found it very difficult to verify the intellectual level of the parents. Further, records of children currently enrolled in school did not always enable us to understand the significance of their attainments.

These families could be designated as culturally deprived and as cultural-familial mentally retarded in view of multiple school failures of parents and children and the apparently low level of current intellectual functioning of many of the parents. On the other hand, several of the siblings were reported to be doing well in school. In addition, we were aware that what we were judging as inferior school adjustment of certain parents might have been less a function of their intellect and more a function of their realistic attempts to cope with an overwhelming socioeconomic situation. As a result, we were forced to conclude that in spite of the multiple school failures of certain siblings and their parents, there was sufficient contraevidence to suggest the hypothesis that the occurrence of mental retardation in a so-called cultural-familial retarded parent is relatively independent of its occurrence in his child.

I believe that a quotation from our monograph [6] brings into focus some critical questions that workers involved with retarded or disadvantaged children must now begin to study more seriously:

> It may be that for reasons now poorly understood, or not even yet stated, the cultural-familial family exists in far fewer numbers than in earlier decades. [*Author's note:* Cultural-familial mental retardation is estimated as

accounting for 75–85% of all cases of mild mental retardation. Supposedly, it is due either to some multiple genetic mechanism or as yet unknown etiology. It occurs mainly among disadvantaged populations and is not associated with evidence of central nervous system pathology or other physiological conditions that could explain the subnormal behavior of family members.] This is not to say that there are not certain neighborhoods and, in fact, particular families that breed large numbers of so-called familial mentally retarded children. Nor do we imply that these neighborhoods are decreasing in size. The point we are emphasizing is that it is becoming more apparent that the clear-cut, easily categorized familial family is less and less available for study and more and more difficult to explain. For example, if one were to review some of the earlier family studies presented by Goddard (1912) [*Author's note:* Goddard was the research director at the Vineland Training School in New Jersey who was responsible for "The Kallikak Study"] and other workers, it would have been fairly easy to categorize certain families as familial, based on currently accepted criteria. In those families it was usual for both mother and father to be in special classes or to be early school dropouts or school failures. It was also quite usual to find several of the children either in special classes, institutional programs, or school failures. Our experiences have disclosed that those families that are now found often present such confusing discrepancies with the stereotype "cultural-familial mental retardation" that it is very difficult to designate them as familial, even though they meet the minimum criteria. When one considers the dramatic changes which have occurred in our society since the early decades of this century, it is by no means far-fetched to assume that they have operated to reduce the number of such families. Acceleration of urbanization of our society, the great advances in transportation and communication, the increase in special education facilities, the ever-increasing number and quality of social agencies—these and other changes conceivably may have had the consequence of reducing the number of cultural-familial families.

Although the nature of our subject population restricts us from generalizing directly to a population of cultural-familial mentally retarded children, it does seem that we can generalize, however cautiously, to a much larger population. It will be remembered that the basic consideration in selecting subjects was that they come from an environment which had a history of producing a high percentage of school failures. [*Author's note:* The aforementioned became, in substance, the dominant criterion for our subject selection.] This kind of environment has come to be referred to as a culturally deprived environment. There is good reason to believe that such environments exist throughout the United States in cities and in rural areas. They are characterized by low incomes, high unemployment, high delinquency rates, a great dependency on social welfare agencies, and a high incidence of school failure in the local schools. Not only is there assumed to be a great similarity in the symptomatic social behavior within these neighborhoods, but it is also assumed that the deprivation that is operating upon individual children is more or less homogeneous from area to area.

It is, of course, plausible to entertain the question of different kinds of cultural deprivation that exist within different kinds of communities. However, for the purposes of this study, it seems reasonable to assume that, within the variety of circumstances that exist in lower-class environments, there is a substantial core of communality which is more a function of the conditions that exist within the environment than it is a function of the biological characteristics of the children within these environments. Without making any judgment as to how much weight can be given to the environmental characteristics, on one hand, and the biological characteristics, on the other, it is assumed that the weighting of the environmental characteristics is sufficient to make programs such as will be described in this volume generally applicable.[4]

DISCUSSION

To recapitulate, several conclusions are offered concerning our case-finding activities in our now completed study of preschool disadvantaged children and their families. To begin, it appears indefensible to continue support for the notion that there exist large numbers of so-called cultural-familial retarded families except, possibly, in very isolated rural areas. The levels of attainment of children within disadvantaged families has been shown to be relatively independent of the levels of the parents' or siblings' attainments. The level of attainment of any disadvantaged child is a function of both the disadvantaged community in which the child lives and his family. Perhaps one should ponder that when dealing with defective families we are, in reality, also dealing with defective communities. We think this to be an important distinction, important enough to consider its implications. Professional workers usually have assumed that within deprived communities there exist families who cope well with the environment and rear relatively typical children. They assumed that other families are defective and because of either genetically weakened endowments or extremely impoverished family conditions, produce retarded and otherwise disordered children. By this reasoning they explain why certain slum-dwelling families are successful—often to the point of leaving the slum and sometimes contributing a talented or gifted son or daughter to society—and why other slum-dwelling families are unsuccessful.

Frankly, I am somewhat skeptical about this explanation. Our observations suggest the possibility that there are communities that Woolman [38] labels "culturally asynchronic." Within their own ghetto subculture the people of such a community move from infancy to maturity with demonstrated adaptability across language, emotive, and social-interaction dimensions. However, as they enter the "other world" of the schools and middle-class society, they are unprepared and unable to interact on a multidimensional level. In those new settings they are failures. Because such failures are so frequent in these communities, a great many

---

[4] From B. Blatt and F. Garfunkel, *A Field Demonstration of the Effects of Nonautomated Responsive Environments on the Intellectual and Social Competence of Educable Mentally Retarded Children*. Washington, D.C.: U.S. Office of Education, Cooperative Research Project No. D-014, 1965, pp. 57–59.

families appear to be "defective families" rather than disadvantaged individuals living in "defective communities."

To structure the above proposition another way, we cite Thomas Szasz [37], who writes about "the manufacture of madness," his hypothesis being that the kind and quality of treatment facilities and programs for mental patients in our culture cause such individuals to become sicker, not healthier—such people enter institutions as patients and remain as inmates. In the case of the so-called culturally disadvanted, we manufacture their madness and their retardation and whatever other evils are attributed to them. We manufacture these conditions as we continue to permit the existence of—and, in fact, as we continue to actively support and encourage—sick and debilitating communities that disfranchise those who are forced to live there and degrade all of us who contribute to their growth and ever-increasing permanence.

For reasons that we cannot now clearly explain, other families who also live in these communities but contribute few, if any, disordered children could be said to be "normal." I speculate that, since variability within families (that is, some children doing well and others doing poorly, one parent literate and the other seemingly retarded) is approximately similar to the variability among families in such a community, it would be fruitful to qualify the notions of "defective" and "nondefective" families and, further, to reject the strategy of attempting to deal with the effects of deprivation by treating defective families.

I prefer a more global strategy. I would select certain communities that are likely to produce children with severe learning and motivational disorders. This approach would compel us to design interventions to prevent or reverse these disorders and then to provide these programs for all children in such communities, whether they live in cultural-familial homes or apparently more adequate homes. Until we learn a great deal more about the genesis and conditions of cultural deprivation, we must assume that any family living under such severely debilitating circumstances is apt to rear children who develop any one of a number of learning and behavioral disorders.

Last, although I believe that the relationship between mental retardation and cultural deprivation is provocative, the traditional concept of cultural-familial mental retardation appears to be meaningless—especially for those of us in teaching or therapeutic work who are dedicated to helping people change, not to explaining why or certifying that they haven't changed.

REFERENCES

1. Benda, C. E., Squires, W. D., Ogonik, J., and Wise, R. Personality factors in mild mental retardation. I: Family background and sociocultural patterns. *Amer. J. Ment. Defic.* 68:24, 1963.

2. Benne, K. D., Birnbaum, M., and Klein, D. C. *Conference on Training Programs for Personnel Who Work with Educationally Disadvantaged Students.* Boston: Boston University Human Relations Center, 1964.

3. Blatt, B. Some persistently recurring assumptions concerning the mentally subnormal. *Train. Sch. Bull.* (Vineland) 57:48, 1960.

4. Blatt, B. Toward a more acceptable terminology in mental retardation. *Train. Sch. Bull.* (Vineland) 58:47, 1961.

5. Blatt, B. *The Intellectually Disfranchised: Impoverished Learners and Their Teachers.* Boston: Massachusetts Department of Mental Health, 1966.

6. Blatt, B., and Garfunkel, F. *A Field Demonstration of the Effects of Nonautomated Responsive Environments on the Intellectual and Social Competence of Educable Mentally Retarded Children.* Washington, D.C.: U.S. Office of Education, Cooperative Research Project No. D-014, 1965.

7. Blatt, B., and Garfunkel, F. Dissonant notions concerning disordered children and their educability. *J. Educ. Ment. Retard.* 1:11, 1966.

8. Callet, A., Gatchell, M., and Hamilton, D. A Pilot Study on Increasing Reading Readiness of Young Children from an Inner-City Area. Unpublished manuscript, University of Chicago, 1961.

9. Caplan, G. *Concepts of Mental Health and Consultation.* (Children's Bureau Publication No. 373.) Washington, D.C.: U.S. Government Printing Office, 1959.

10. Charles, D. C. Ability and accomplishment of persons earlier judged mentally deficient. *Genet. Psychol. Monogr.* 47:3, 1953.

11. Clarke, A. D. B., and Clarke, A. M. Pseudo-feeblemindedness: Some implications. *Amer. J. Ment. Defic.* 59:507, 1955.

12. Coffey, H. S., and Wellman, B. L. The role of cultural status in intelligence changes of pre-school children. *J. Exp. Educ.* 3:191, 1936.

13. DeGroot, A. D. The effects of war upon the intelligence of youth. *J. Abnorm. Soc. Psychol.* 43:311, 1948.

14. Fouracre, M. H., Connor, F. P., and Goldberg, I. I. *The Effects of a Preschool Program upon Young Educable Mentally Retarded Children. I: Measurable Growth and Development.* New York: Teachers College, Columbia University, 1962.

15. Fouracre, M. H., Connor, F. P., and Goldberg, I. I. *The Effects of a Preschool Program upon Young Educable Mentally Retarded Children. II: The Experimental Pre-school Curriculum.* New York: Teachers College, Columbia University, 1962.

16. Ginzberg, E., and Bray, D. W. *The Uneducated.* New York: Columbia University Press, 1953.

17. Harrington, M. *The Other America.* New York: Macmillan, 1964.

18. Havighurst, R. J. Educationally difficult student: What can the schools do? *Nat. Ass. Second. Sch. Princip. Bull.* 49:110, 1965.

19. Heber, R. (Ed.). A Manual on Terminology and Classification in Mental Retardation. *Amer. J. Ment. Defic.* 64 (monogr. suppl.), 1959.

20. Jenkins, J. J., and Paterson, D. G. (Eds.), *Studies in Individual Differences.* New York: Appleton-Century-Crofts, 1961.

21. Jensen, A. R. How much can be boost I.Q. and scholastic achievement? *Harvard Educ. Rev.* 39:1, 1969.

22. Kagan, J. S., et al. How much can we boost I.Q. and scholastic achievement? A discussion. *Harvard Educ. Rev.* 39:273, 1969.

23. Kennedy, J. F. Mental Illness and Mental Retardation. Message to 88th Congress, House of Representatives, 58, Feb. 5, 1963.

24. Kirk, S. A. *Early Education of the Mentally Retarded*. Urbana: University of Illinois Press, 1958.
25. McCandless, B. Environment and intelligence. *Amer. J. Ment. Defic.* 56:674, 1952.
26. Masland, R. L., Sarason, S. B., and Gladwin, T. *Mental Subnormality*. New York: Basic Books, 1958.
27. May, E. *The Wasted Americans: Cost of Our Welfare Dilemma*. New York: Harper & Row, 1964.
28. Pinneau, S. R. *Changes in Intelligence Quotient*. Boston: Houghton Mifflin, 1961.
29. Riessman, F. *The Culturally Deprived Child*. New York: Harper, 1962.
30. Riessman, F., Cohen, J., and Pearl, A. (Eds.). *Mental Health of the Poor*. New York: Free Press of Glencoe, 1964.
31. Sarason, S. B. *Psychological Problems in Mental Deficiency* (3d ed.). New York: Harper, 1959.
32. Shriver, S. *The War on Poverty: The Economic Opportunity Act of 1964*. (Committee on Labor and Public Welfare, United States Senate.) Washington, D.C.: U.S. Government Printing Office, 1964.
33. Skeels, H. M., and Dye, H. B. A study of the effects of differential stimulation on mentally retarded children. *Proc. Amer. Ass. Ment. Defic.* 44:114, 1939.
34. Skeels, H. M., and Harms, I. Children with inferior social histories: Their mental development in adoptive homes. *J. Genet. Psychol.* 72:283, 1948.
35. Skeels, H. M., Updegraff, R., Wellman, B. L., and Williams, H. M. A Study of Environmental Stimulation: An Orphanage Preschool Project. In *University of Iowa Studies in Child Welfare*, Vol. 15. Iowa City: University of Iowa, 1938.
36. Skodak, M., and Skeels, H. M. A final follow-up study of one hundred adopted children. *J. Genet. Psychol.* 75:85, 1949.
37. Szasz, T. *The Myth of Mental Illness*. New York: Dell, 1967.
38. Woolman, M. Cultural Asynchrony and Contingency in Learning Disorders. Unpublished paper. Washington, D.C.: Institute of Educational Research, 1965.

CHAPTER 3

Teaching the
Mentally Retarded[1]

INTRODUCTION

Focus of this Chapter

Our central focus is concerned with research on teaching the mentally retarded. For reasons to be discussed in the next section, we adhere to a broad operational definition of empirical study that includes formal experimentation as well as other types of observational systems. Frankly, we have viewed with concern an almost total commitment to experimental and quasi-experimental approaches applied even to very complex and "dirty" field problems that cannot be studied satisfactorily in the laboratory—i.e., outside the natural setting. As Shulman (1970) remarked:

> If the object of such research [educational] is the development of co-herent and workable theories, researchers are nearly as far from that goal today as they are from controlling the weather. If the goal of educational research is significant improvement in the daily functioning of educational programs, I know of little evidence that researchers have made discernible strides in that direction (p. 371).

The problem of relevancy has been particularly troublesome in the field of mental retardation. With some rare exceptions—few of which might be called research on teaching (e.g., Edgerton, 1967; Goffman, 1961)—research in mental retardation has followed traditional lines of experimentation, survey analysis, and test construction and validation. With rare exceptions participant observation procedures and other phenomenological approaches to systematic data collection and analysis have

This article, co-authored with Frank Garfunkel, was originally published in R. M. W. Travers (Ed.), *Second handbook of research on teaching*. Chicago: Rand McNally, 1973. Reprinted by permission.

[1] The authors are grateful to Dr. Harriett Blank and Professors Arthur Blumberg, Thomas Green, Samuel Guskin, Samuel A. Kirk, Horace Mann, James J. McCarthy, Maynard Reynolds, Seymour B. Sarason, Paul R. Salamone and Howard Spicker for reading earlier drafts of this chapter and offering us valuable and constructive comments and suggestions. We are also indebted to Mrs. Virginia Andrews, Mrs. Mary Kishman, and Mrs. Nancy Spekman for their generous assistance in typing various manuscript drafts of this chapter.

not been applied to the general study of mentally retarded children or, specifically, to their school lives.

The above remarks are not meant to suggest antagonism to the value and promotion of formal experimentation in the field. Our concern is with the extent to which traditional models have determined the kind of research that is being conducted rather than, conversely, models determined by the nature of problems studied. Further, we are concerned that such traditional research models also determine the kinds of independent variables that are selected for study and influence the scaling of independent variations.[2] To state this another way, researchers are confronted by problems connected with the assignment of children to treatments and, to further complicate this, of teachers to treatments. This problem becomes formidable when the researcher attempts to deal effectively with triads of teachers, children and methods. Therefore, when one designs an experiment that includes children (who vary) and teachers and, possibly, some other adults (who vary) in classrooms, the notion of homogeneity of variance that assumes there is similarity in the way a treatment occurs in different classes with different teachers and different children is questionable. In attempting to deal with group comparability, some researchers have utilized random procedures (or substitute methods) to gain group comparability in the assignment of children, teachers and methods. Unfortunately, although this may solve certain theoretical problems if the randomization procedures are maintained—which they rarely are in field studies—other problems are hardly dealt with and certain new ones are created.[3]

---

[2] Presenting a compelling argument, Shulman (1970) encouraged educational researchers to leave the safe and sterile atmosphere of the conventional laboratory for the classroom setting. Because the current "gap between such studies ('conclusion-oriented') and needed educational applications is simply too great," what is needed is another form of investigation "to bridge that gap and create the basis for educational theory" (p. 377). Shulman concluded that, in view of its complexity, "it might be in the long range interest of both psychological theory and education to ignore those theories for the moment and proceed along a relatively atheoretical path in the study of education" (p. 383).

In a personal communication, Samuel A. Kirk, pursuing a line of reasoning similar to Shulman's, speculated that "one of the research approaches that could get at process and some of the things that you are talking about is through idiographic studies. I always think of the report by Itard which has become a classic . . . I think that in our field we need more intensive studies of cases: how they learn, what obstacles there are to their learning, etc. in order to understand their learning processes. When we have enough hypotheses from this kind of approach, we could do better controlled research. As you indicated, we tend to jump on comparison of methods, without making a real analysis of what ought to be done."

[3] Accompanying the randomization strategy is the assumption that factors which do not interest the researcher, or with which he cannot deal, will "randomize out," i.e., will equalize across groups. Although, as we stated above, this may provide a theoretical solution for the researcher—if the randomization procedure does not break down—it is entirely possible that those variables with which the researcher has attempted to deal through randomization may be the very factors upon which the research might have profitably focused.

Our review of recent literature relating to how and under what conditions the mentally retarded learn, reveals continued major emphasis on experimental studies that attempt to control various independent factors. This research has assessed differences among several independent methods of teaching the mentally retarded. Investigators have designed research utilizing randomization procedures in which groups of children learning to read under one method are equal to those assigned to another method. Further, the researcher randomly assigns teachers to each group, hopefully to ensure that one teacher would be more or less as well adjusted to his group and method as any other teacher would be to any other group and method; and, lastly, to give greater assurance to the assumption of group equality, other pertinent variables would be measured to check the randomization. Consequently, the researcher is in a position to claim that these two variables, children and teachers, were held constant for all of the groups studied.

The above research strategy is based on the belief that the method of teaching (or the curriculum or the curriculum organization) is the most significant independent variable. In such studies the kinds of children and the personalities of the teachers are considered to be intervening variables that have importance but are peripheral to the experimental comparison being made. Therefore, controls are employed to equalize the other potentially independent variables. One objective of this chapter is to present a rationale that is a reversal of the above example. By this, we intend to discuss the possibilities and values that may obtain by specifically assigning—for the purposes of field research on teaching—major independent variables which relate directly to teachers and children, and intervening variables which relate to method and curriculum content. Although this approach is suitable for the study of classroom situations per se, it appears to be especially appropriate for the study of the educational environment of mentally retarded or most other disabled children.[4] In those special programs, the "usual" curriculum goals are generally subordinate to ones pertaining to interpersonal relationships. Emphasis is not primarily on achievement, and methods of teaching are not generally considered to be of greatest importance and are, in fact, de-emphasized. This is another way of saying that the independent variables which *should be* given most attention in such settings—teachers, children, and their interactions—*have not been* subjected to careful measurement and control.

There are several technical reasons for experimenting with only one

---

[4] In a personal communication, James J. McCarthy echoed support of the above assumption: ". . . during the past months, the thought has been occurring to me that the real differences in treatments have often hinged on affective variables (e.g., motivation) and, therefore, we ought to put our research effort there. To your view that most research on teaching the retarded ignores 'processes,' I can only say, amen!"

or two fairly discrete variables at a time; on the other hand, there are as many reasons for analyzing the complex interactions of children in natural settings (Shulman, 1970, p. 383). In the latter case, classroom situations can be manipulated in order to provide the observer with limited structure in a natural setting. Data obtained could then be used to compare programs and curricula for children in order to enhance the possibility of favorable behavioral changes which will depend upon prior maximization of the principal sources of variance—teachers and children. Through such study we begin to confront the following questions: What anomalous behaviors are displayed by the children and how are they connected to the evolving class atmosphere? What are the specific effects of various procedures upon individual and group behaviors?

To continue this line of reasoning, much attention has been given to the proposition that the teacher-child relationship is critical to the teaching process, suggesting the importance of not only the "how" of teaching but the relationship that develops between the teacher, on the one hand, and both individual children and the total group on the other (Rosenthal & Jacobson, 1966). An example of this phenomenon is the "Hawthorn Effect," one that persistently appears in psychological and educational experiments and which seems to be more consistently related to improved performance than any particular method or curriculum. Stated another way, the excitement generated by a research project (e.g., the "Hawthorn Effect") is an experimental side effect that appears to have more research significance than so-called main effects. Therefore, one assumption the researcher might consider is that something like the "Hawthorn Effect" is necessary to the development of a significant interaction. Yet another way of stating this is to specifically design "Hawthorn Effects" as sources of independent variation in research on teaching.

Although we believe that something akin to the "Hawthorn" is necessary, we also believe that, in itself, such an effect is not sufficient. There are other questions to be answered. How do children spend their time in classrooms? Do they attend to what is going on? How is their attention monitored? How are they dealt with when they succeed and when they fail? What kinds of questions do they ask? What kinds of questions are asked of them? Questions such as these—and a good many others—must be studied and answered if we are to learn more about behavior and how it can be affected. Yet rarely do we pose such questions; rarely do we judge a teacher's effectiveness, for example, by other than an estimate of her acquisition of knowledge concerning her "subject" or her "teaching."

In spite of the neglect and ignorance we have mentioned, there is sufficient evidence to reconsider this particular pervasive focus on teaching. To begin, variables in the usual educational situation are of such a nature as to discourage the rigorous experimentalist from dealing with them. The classroom situation is antithetical to an experiment that demands rigid application of certain a priori determined conditions. Personalities of teachers and children, social interactions and creative processes are examples of difficult-to-measure factors that must be dealt with if we are to do more than produce sterile descriptions of curricula. As stated earlier, since these factors cannot be measured easily, or perhaps not at all with presently available techniques, they are not usually included in the design of an experimental study.[5] For purposes of clarification, we may discuss these factors in terms of the *process* and the *substance* of classroom life.

Process refers to the way in which relationships are initiated, develop and endure among individuals, and the extent to which they exist. *Substance* is concerned with that well-defined content of relationships which can be tested formally. In studies of children in school, substance has received considerably more attention than process. Thus, in terms of what is here called substance, an extensive body of literature provides hypothetical and empirical constructs that describe how children differ from one another and how individual children's test scores change. However, the literature is not at all clear on how to produce changes most efficiently, especially in dealing with children who have cognitive or other disorders. In terms of the present discussion, process has received less attention because it is less amenable to study. This is to say that the measurement of children's abilities (substance) is less difficult than the measurement of their social interactions and motivations. It is understandable that psychologists and educators have concentrated on variables that are relatively easy to measure, even though such variables may be of trivial importance to learning.

For example, an intelligence quotient is a good predictor of academic success. However, academic success is a function of both substance and process variables. The latter, being difficult to measure, are more or less ignored. Why, then, is IQ such a good predictor of academic success if it measures essentially the substance and not the process? It is probable that process variables affect IQ in the same way that they affect academic success, and the predictive efficiency of the IQ is, to a greater or lesser extent, due to indirect measurement of the process. Therefore, it is important for those engaged in research on teaching to explore not only the components of the IQ but those of academic success as well. Such ex-

---

[5] In recent years the works of Amidon, Bales, Flanders, and Medley and Mitzel, among others, have developed interesting and potentially illuminating observational systems. However, with very rare exceptions, these newer observational approaches have been noticeably excluded from the design of research dealing with teaching the handicapped. What such exclusion suggests is impossible for us to determine.

ploration calls for intensive investigation of the total field of child behavior with minimal attention to conventional aptitudinal criteria and maximal attention to processes. Although this is neither a new nor profound idea, it remains conspicuously absent from research and evaluation programs. Such a focus is clearly a reversal of what generally takes place in research on teaching.

In summary, the focus and rationale of this chapter suggest the development of research strategies that are in harmony with discovering and evaluating what actually occurs in classrooms. It is further concluded that such research should assign, as bases for comparison, the variability that exists among and between interactions rather than among and between either teachers or children. Possibly this orientation to research on teaching offers a solution to what Blackman (1969) described as the serious and ambivalent dichotomy between those so-called logical positivists who prefer experimentation as the method of proof and those who view education essentially as an art form, one which would lose its color and vitality if the movement to fractionate the teacher-pupil interaction achieves its apparent goal.

CHAPTER OVERVIEW

During the past decade, more textbooks, monographs, research studies, and journal articles concerning the mentally retarded have been published than in all the previous history of man's efforts to describe and understand this group of people. As in other fields, and in spite of valiant efforts by individuals and organizations to catalogue and retrieve information and to prepare bibliographies and reviews, it is impossible for even the most diligent scholar to keep up with all of the literature in this field. Fortunately, in recent years a number of superior substantive reviews have been published. In the past *The Review of Educational Research* regularly devoted one of its issues to "exceptional children," and the reader will want to examine the still timely analyses of Dunn and Capobianco (1959) and Blackman and Heintz (1966). In 1963 the Council for Exceptional Children published Kirk and Weiner's *Behavioral Research on Exceptional Children*. The chapters by Heber on the educable retarded child, and Charney on the trainable retarded child, present a valuable collection of abstracts that have recently been updated by the contribution of Spicker and Bartel in Johnson and Blank's (1968) *Exceptional Children Research Review*. Several other important reviews of research on teaching the mentally retarded should be noted for readers wishing to pursue the literature beyond this chapter's limits, dictated by the ever-present compromise between space allocations and chapter focus: Guskin and Spicker (1968), Kirk (1964), McCarthy and Sheerenberger (1966), and Quay

(1963). Lastly, among the many related books that have been published in recent years, the following are particularly noteworthy in that each presents comprehensive reviews of literature that, in direct and tangential ways, are relevant to our central concern: Ellis (1966a, 1966b, 1968), Jordan (1966), Phillips (1966), Robinson and Robinson (1965), Sarason and Doris (1968), and Schiefelbusch, Copeland, and Smith (1967).

The review of literature to be presented in this chapter will not attempt to duplicate, or even elaborate upon, the aforementioned reviews. Rather, we will deal briefly with only recent literature pertaining to teaching the mentally retarded and, beyond that, discuss the general research in this area in terms of our hypotheses relative to the study of teaching and our theoretical formulations that have obtained from both the evaluation of prior work and our own research experiences.

The remainder of this chapter will be concerned with, first, the continuance and elaboration of our earlier discussion of research on teaching. Second, a selected critical review of the most recent relevant research has been divided into three sections: studies concerning variations in home and community settings, studies concerning variations in educational atmosphere, and studies dealing with variations in children and teachers. Lastly, the chapter will conclude with a discussion of the nature of research on teaching, the importance of hypothesis-generating studies, and possibilities for the development of new scientific traditions that may enable field researchers to deal with heretofore insuperable problems in the study of teaching and its effects.

RESEARCH ON TEACHING

A Polemic

Nearly all research on teaching-learning is plagued by a paradox: on the one hand there is the need to support generalizations about teachers, children and methodologies, and on the other hand lies the problem of individualization, i.e., which children work best with which teachers and under what methodological conditions (Vale & Vale, 1969). The need for generalizations produces research which attempts to structure supposedly categorical uniformity over qualitatively different inputs. Independent variation is assumed to exist a priori, as is the case with comparative studies of methodologies, curricula or teacher styles. Such propositions set forth the premise that given discrete independent variation of particular teacher, methodological or curriculum variables, there will be measurable differences in output as inferred from either the later measurement of observed behavior or through the use of standardized or specially constructed tests which specifically measure independent variation that is a function of independent variables. This approach lends itself to the study of many different classes and teachers who may be assigned to points on a scale of independent variation. This assignment can be random or it can be ex post facto in terms of the given characteristics of a general environment, teacher, classroom, physical facility, curriculum or chosen pedagogy.

A second major approach implicitly assumes that class variation is secondary to individual variation and that the primary research unit should be either an individual child or an individual child with a specific teacher or class. Without doubt this leads to a far more tedious research procedure and does not lend itself to the random assignment of children to treatments. This molecular approach suggests that the search for what promotes difference must center on the longitudinal dynamic interaction between specific children, their teachers and their peers; further, it implies that between-class differences will not be as important as variations of children within particular classes.

This is not to say that there will never be uniform class (i.e., classrooms of children) differences but, rather, that such differences will be relatively rare since they would be dependent upon uniform application of specific kinds of subject matter and goals across groups of children of widely varying abilities, interests, values and motivations. The factor that is brought into bold relief when we study the education of mentally retarded children, as opposed to children in regular classes, is the impossibility of applying uniform academic goals. This reasoning, which follows from those factors, leads to the placement of mentally retarded children in special classes, the structure and continuity of those classes and the powerful variations—vis-à-vis the handicapped—that exist between different school systems, classes and teachers.[6] The extent to which within-class variation is trivial will depend upon the existence of powerful and uniform differences between classes, which is by way of saying that no matter what the differences are within classes they are not nearly as important as the commonality that exists over groups of children in their abilities, goals, and acceptance of basic educational assumptions regarding why they are in school, what they hope to achieve, what rules they have to attend to, and their sources of gratification.

---

[6] For example, an impressive literature fails to demonstrate the superiority of either special curricula, administrative organization or special methods in the educational treatment of the retarded (Blatt, 1958; Cain & Levine, 1963; Cassidy & Stanton, 1959; Goldstein, Moss, & Jordan, 1965; Hottel, 1958; Kirk, 1958; Mullen & Itkin, 1961; Wrightstone, Forlano, Lepkowski, Sontag, & Edelstein, 1959). We speculate that these rather consistent findings are due, in part, to the nature of "special child" identification and, in part, to the pervasive effects of such identification, which together provide both extraordinary variation between and within each class *as well as* an equally extraordinary variation between those classes and so-called regular classes.

Our argument is not that there is a categorical difference between regular and special education with regard to critical sources of variation; rather, the fact that special education consists largely of children who are rejects from the regular system suggests that greater within-variation and less uniformity of behaviors and attitudes than generally are encountered in typical academic situations will be found here. However, it should be added that gross models used to compare different teaching methods or curricula have failed as badly in studies of regular classes as they have in studies of special classes (Gage, 1963).

An illustration of this phenomenon (i.e., the effects and importance of within- and between-class differences) may be found in research related to home and community effects on learning. Where there is relatively little variation between homes and within a community with regard to academic progress, one can expect school inputs and processes to contribute strongly to output variance; and it may not be necessary to be specially concerned with out-of-school variables. (However, this assumes that variation in academic behavior of children includes success and failure. There are schools where there is no important variation—virtually everyone succeeds or everyone fails.) On the other hand, where there is significant effective variation—i.e., effective in the sense that what takes place in the home and in the community will alter school behavior significantly—it is necessary to consider out-of-school environmental factors seriously, to measure them carefully and, perhaps, to contribute to independent variation in them (i.e., to actively manipulate) in order to assess change more adequately.

It is our contention that special classes in general, and special classes for the mentally retarded in particular, are heavily loaded with effective sources of variation other than those pertaining to academic activities in the school. With regard to constitutional variation (including genetic factors) which is relatively constant within educationally relevant time periods, we must, at the present time, consider ourselves to be more or less ignorant and must, therefore, remain open-minded. The literature on stability and change in children from various social classes does not offer a solid foundation from which to theorize about educational programs. Consequently, our position about the potential and probability for change in children has to be derived from other than (or in addition to) a strictly experimentally designed empirical base. This has been incisively demonstrated in the debate that has taken place recently between Jensen (1969) and Deutsch (1969), Kagan (1969) and others.

If constitutional (physiological) variation is eliminated from a total input-process-output design for the study of teaching—and where the primary criteria for the appropriateness of input are based on the careful measurement and description of process rather than presumptions about capacity (IQ) or potential, and also where we can assume the importance of community, home and nonacademic school variables in the process of change—it becomes imperative to assess research on teaching the mentally retarded in terms of the aforementioned questions and assumptions.

Goodness of Fit

In numerous ways individuals function differently. Research attempts to record these ways and explain the whys. For some researchers description is an end in itself. However, the history of social science has at least one certainty about it: description always leads from and to something. There is no "unbiased description." For example, when several groups are given IQ tests, almost invariably they will have different means. Are these objectively derived differences? We believe not! A good deal went into the development of the IQ test, selection of items, and procedures for administering the test. The testing format is, itself, a very special structure for communication. Tests are validated in specific ways using specific criteria. They are developed to do *something*. The narrower that *something* is, the easier it is to validate the test; however, the test becomes more biased when used with other groups at other times.

We often talk about variability. What makes the greatest difference? Is it heredity or environment? Is it school or home? Latin or home economics? Discipline or therapy? If a child has a problem, what (or who) had most to do with it? What is the main, most significant, most pervasive cause? What is the best, very best, way of undoing the problem? Does the answer to the first question (cause) lead to the answer to the second (undoing)? Does what is wrong indicate what should be done?

Eventually the question is: What should we do? And, how do we obtain that answer? Does it depend on who does it, or where it is done, or how much time there is? It is wishful thinking to expect that there is a clear relationship between what exists, why it exists, and what to do about it. Useful reductions are impossible, at least in the usual sense. Prescriptive education is a reduction. Montessori, Frostig, Kephart, Cruickshank, Bereiter and A. S. Neill all offer reductions. They say *this* is what to do with children who present or behave in *this* manner. Whatever *this* is, there is the assumption that *this* can be identified, described and distinguished from something other than *this*.

What contributes to difference? Children are poor, come from families who have inadequate housing, food, medical services, space—are crowded into cities (or rurally separated)—and they do not do well in school!—or on tests!—or on the cello! Often, they are migrants, emigrants or immigrants. And they do not speak standard English. They are different. They do not fit well.

A lot of confusion exists about what people should do, how they should do it, and when it should be done. Who is to judge? Are the judges' values my values? Or yours? How can it all be put together: poverty, delinquency, migration, retardation, language, values, disability, learning? Or, can it be put together? Is it psychology, sociology, anthropology or epistemology? Some individuals in some groups do not fit. The first problem is to decide about fit: individuals who do not fit, groups that do not fit, and individuals who do not fit groups that do not fit.

There are several differences to being an individual who does not fit (I-no-fit) rather than being in a group that does not fit (G-no-fit). Special education "rides" the I-no-fit local. Black power "rides" the G-no-fit express. The new field of learning disabilities has epitomized the I-no-fit way (Blatt, 1969a). Find out what is wrong, then treat it. The patient subsequently will get better. Mental retardation has always been in the I-no-fit category, but it was a strategic error to assign the retarded to it. Either in special classes, institutions or at home, many do not have the skills to make it on their own.

A G-no-fit means there is something wrong with the society, or the culture, or with the G, or with everything. What do you want your child to become? Or yourself? Or Lee Harvey Oswald? But whatever it is, it has little to do with the child, with you, or Lee Harvey.

With any problem there are I-no-fit and G-no-fit alternatives. For example, we can examine juvenile delinquency. According to the I-no-fit strategy, the delinquent can be treated individually (or in groups) as a sick, ill-advised or alienated person requiring rehabilitation, therapy, education, counseling or, possibly, vocational training. A G-no-fit policy leads to a dilemma. Do we categorically change G? Or the rest of society? Are delinquents to be understood and treated as a collection of individuals who have something superficially in common with each other? They all have done something illegal. Therefore, should we impose or prescribe a common treatment? Enter, G-no-fit analysis. It is absurd to talk about a thousand or 10 thousand adolescents getting the same treatment. The G is at issue. But that either leads backwards—lock them all up, vengeance, punishment, retribution—or to an examination of who does not fit what, and when. Whoever and whatever does not fit has to apply to the total G. Whatever is to be done has to apply to the total G. How can we speak in these terms without descending to an absurd reductionism? In other words, if the G-justifying generality cannot apply to G, maybe there is a generality that can uniformly be applied to non-G. What is it that can be said about non-G that connects it to G—that forces G to be G-no-fit? What does non-G do, think, believe, feel, worship or deny that operates on G? This is not simply a question of prevention versus treatment. The kind of prevention or treatment will depend on which no-fit track is being used.

The learning disabilities movement has pushed for the identification of a particular kind of child—perceptually impaired—who is supposed to be different from mentally retarded or emotionally disturbed children. Each of these children is to receive individualized assessment and treatment. This appears to be a bastard G-no-fit strategy. But, in reality, it is not. It is I-no-fit all the way. The G is supposedly identified, but it is always quite clear that it is really I that does not fit and must be dealt with. Again, we ask what makes a difference. Are children with learning disabilities going to be any different if we view them as different from mentally retarded or emotionally disturbed children? Or is the real difference going to center around the goodness or badness of fit? To what extent do we change individuals, or at least try to change them, and to what extent do we change groups and structures? For example, programs that change the structure of services for mentally retarded children, that go beyond the requirements of any given individual child or adult who has been designated as being mentally retarded, are clearly G-no-fit programs. The greater the inclusiveness of the G—therefore, including diverse disability groupings—the more it leans in the direction of G-no-fit. The introduction of more refined diagnostic categories is a push in the I-no-fit direction. This is certainly justified, at times, by the special needs of some disabled individuals and some disability groups. For example, a special diet for a child who has been identified as being phenylketonuric is the appropriate I-no-fit strategy. However, in our view, this is a proper exception to, not regularity of, our philosophical and clinical orientation.

Curriculum and Learning

The preceding section leads to a primary concern: whether any particular educational strategy—be it related to methodology, teacher, peer group or curriculum—"takes" in more or less the same way as an inoculation does or does not take. It is easy to establish whether an inoculation was administered, but there is considerable uncertainty in knowing whether or not it accomplished its purpose, i.e., before its effects can be verified by long-term follow-up. Thus, in the case of our analogy, it is one thing to judge whether an inoculation has "taken" by examining the individual some time after it was given; it is another to analyze whether or not it "took" in terms of its effect. The latter circumstance involves questions about whether the inoculation influenced susceptibility or, on the other hand, whether the individual was susceptible but never in contact with the disease-producing germ.

Similar questions exist with regard to educational input, process and output. The input can be there for various groups of children and it might or might not "take" depending upon personnel, timing and method of application. If there is reasonable evidence that, in fact, it did "take," it still does not mean that it will affect output. For example, it might or might not generalize to other situations and materials. Or appropriate situations and materials may not present themselves and, therefore, although the process originally "took," follow-up will offer no evidence of this.

Most research on teaching the mentally retarded (and, for that matter, most research on teaching) tends to concern itself with input and output phases but to ignore process. At best this can seriously decrease the power of a study and, at worst, it can destroy entirely the meaning of such research because of the "noise" that exists in a system that results in an error-ridden process that often has an overwhelmingly negative effect on children for whom there is a misfit between their needs and the educational situation.

Teachers and Teaching

The model used here assumes that research on teaching covers a finite period of time where certain individuals and groups are exposed either naturally or through manipulation to ordinary or extraordinary interventions, with measurements taken at various points during this period. Criteria for effectiveness can consist of a sequence of measures, a final measure or a series of measures in the last phase of the period. Studies can concern themselves with any one or all of the following stages: input, process and output. These are not meant to be mutually exclusive but, rather, useful for raising provocative research questions.

Input includes teacher, child, facility, methodological and curriculum variables that are given sources of independent variation and that may or may not be affected by the interventional process. Input variables may or may not be measurable even though they can be conceptually described. They may or may not include nonschool variables such as those concerned with home, community or other external conditions and processes which are operating upon children, teachers and schools at the time of the intervention. They necessarily include the choice of the sampling unit to be studied, whether it be individual children, teacher-child dyads, classrooms, schools, or other units either defined externally or in terms of input characteristics.

Process variables are concerned with what takes place during the intervention and the ways in which input variables are modified as a result of the intervention. They include the quantity and quality of verbal and social interactions, the ways in which materials and activities are used by children, the ways children and teachers spend their time, and the interrelationships that exist between school and nonschool activities. Process variables can be conceived both in terms of teaching and learning, or in terms of what we might call the teacher-learning process. They can be the end product of a study—namely, to affect process by certain input—or they can be a means to producing stipulated goals.

Output is the effect(s) produced by a given intervention, with given inputs, and with either certain assumptions made or certain conditions ascertained about processes. Output can be measured with standardized or specially constructed tests, observational scales, or by measuring behaviors in subsequent extra-experimental situations. The strength of inferences about the relationship between input and output will depend upon the extent to which processes are identified, measured, and included in the data analysis.

Studies of the effects of educational interventions must be concerned with the extent to which observed behaviors are child-specific or situation-specific. Child-specific behaviors will be relatively unchanged by situational variation, whereas situationally specific behaviors will vary for any given child as he enters into different kinds of situations. Inputs that do not attend to situational variance will necessarily have marginal effects on children. But it is unlikely that the differential effects of situations will be identified unless considerable attention is paid to process measurement and input variation, which permit attention to specific and systematic situational variation.

This is not to say that child-specific behaviors are accepted as being immutable but, rather, the existence of situational variations suggests strategies of teaching which attempt to re-create elements of other situations in which desired behaviors are known to exist. If a child's behavior varies with different adults, and this information is critical for generating effective interventions, it is unwise to leave to chance the study of factors which are closely associated with, or cause, behavioral variation, particularly with children who have repeatedly demonstrated situational failures. To assume that all situational failures are also child failures is both dangerous and misleading. Similarly, an excessive preoccupation with child-specific behaviors without careful recognition of their implications for teaching can only reinforce the expectation that the total behavior is child-specific and that educational programs can be little more than holding operations which keep children occupied and, hopefully, happy.

REVIEW OF RESEARCH

As mentioned earlier in this chapter, this review has been arbitrarily divided into three sections. Further, it claims neither depth nor does it include all possible variables that deserve consideration. It is designed to augment more comprehensive reviews and, secondly, it is included to illustrate both the kinds of research programs currently receiving support and the status of the field with respect to the nature and correlates of teaching the mentally retarded. Lastly, because there have been several recent substantive reviews (e.g., Guskin & Spicker, 1968; Spicker & Bartel, 1968), this section will be brief and will focus on subsequently published literature—our purpose being to provide a basis for discussing research trends, interests and strategies.

Variations in Home and Community Settings

Review of recent literature indicates that little attention has been given to studying the effects of the home and community on learning ability and achievement. This is surprising in view of the enormous support to compensatory education and the documentation, during the last 10 years, of a strong, persistent and pervasive relationship between socioeconomic class and educational achievement. The authors' own research with so-called "high risk" children (Blatt & Garfunkel, 1969) found, on secondary analysis, a significant correlation (0.52) between family organization and family (sibs) school behavior. That finding is consistent with the Coleman et al. report (1966), Hurley (1969), and unpublished follow-up data from our aforementioned study. With such modest exceptions as the few studies describing the effects of family counseling or community recreation programs (e.g., Pumphrey, Goodman, Kidd, & Peters, 1970), there appears to have been little research activity in this area. Further, there is an equal paucity of studies that seek to illuminate or modify the attitudes of community groups or individuals toward the handicapped. Although several studies did report parents' attitudes toward their mentally retarded children, only one recent study was located which attempted to assess general community beliefs (Meyers, Sitkei, & Watts, 1966).

The dearth of research dealing specifically with variables of home and/or community—especially those studies that bear directly on social, emotional and cognitive aspects of school behavior—is particularly discouraging in view of what we had thought to have been deep interest in this area. Most related research, little as it has been, was concerned with intelligence as the critical, and usually as the only, independent variable. There has been a growing acceptance of the importance of home and social class factors, but these are not taken very seriously. Witness the design of Coleman et al.'s survey on *Equality of Educational Opportunity* (1966) and of evaluations of compensatory education, including Head Start. It is not that variables from home and community are not used. They are usually present in most current research studies but are visibly trivial. That is, they do not have particular meaning or importance and contribute very little to the researcher's understanding of the problems confronting him. Asking parents of Head Start children questions about how they feel toward their children, Head Start and their community does not deliver revealing data. It amounts to using a teaspoon to do the work of a steam shovel. Similarly, attention to socioeconomic status does not, in itself, attend to the relationship between poverty and the ways that poor families or families with mentally retarded children deal with schools.

Our review of literature indicates either the general belief that the home and community have little influence on school-related development or—as is more probably the case—the belief that current experimental research capacities and techniques do not lend themselves to the adequate examination of that multitude of interrelated variables connected with families and communities. To be sure, experimental methodologies have not been as useful or productive as the so-called "soft" approaches of Edgerton (1967), Glaser and Strauss (1967), or the general model of participant observation as described by Bruyn (1966). However, there are other reasons—perhaps more important—why scant research attention has been given to home and community variables:

1. It is easier to use well-established instruments, with known reliabilities, short administration times, and presumed conceptual clarity. As soon as one gets into other methodologies it usually requires months of observation.
2. Apparently there is a degree of satisfaction in doing relatively "clean" research, even if it may not have important meaning or relevancy.
3. Possibly a covert factor is related to whatever biases researchers have against the concept of "change." To discover that others can and have changed means that the researcher could have changed. He could be somebody other than what he is. Expectations for change are tied up with the lives of the expecters as much as with those for whom they have greater and lesser expectations. Designs, variables, procedures and analyses are certainly influenced by these expectations.
4. If retarded individuals (or any other group) are studied in environments that are maximally different from what they are used to (certainly not necessarily a special class), and criteria are selected that are tied up with that difference and, furthermore, if those criteria have not been operationalized to demonstrate reliability (short-term consistency) and stability (long-term consistency) as a major function, but rather have been intentionally constructed to get at change (even at the sacrifice of predictability), then we can expect to be able to document change (see Blatt & Garfunkel, 1969). Most special classes do not radically alter children's lives and most homes do not change very much. But there are variations between homes and between communities that are probably much more compelling than formal

educational variation—including school, teacher, methodology and materials.

Variations in Educational Atmosphere

Our review confirms the continued popularity of so-called efficacy studies, curriculum studies and evaluations of teaching methodologies. The abundance of research of this type is disconcerting in light of frequent expressions in the literature relegating such research to positions of minor value with little possibility for either shedding new light on tired questions, or generating new hypotheses for the study of heretofore puzzling problems. Kirk (1964) expressed the belief of many educational researchers with his comment that research on efficacy of special classes will yield little return in relation to the effort and resources required. Insofar as studies of special methodologies or curricula are concerned, the literature discloses the near universal failure to reject the null hypothesis, i.e., no difference between various experimental and control groups of children (Blatt, 1967).

What have we learned from these efficacy and methodology studies? Or how may we interpret their relatively uniform findings? We have concluded that the accumulation of evidence leads to a clear rejection of even the legitimacy of the form and content of these two questions asked rhetorically. The special versus regular class dichotomy is not a defensible independent variable. Although there may be powerful exceptions to this hypothesis, the regularity of data findings suggests strongly that children's experiences are not systematically different in a consistent way if they are in one or the other class. A child can have individual attention, warmth, support, friends and an exciting program in either class. Furthermore, his home can vary independently of the kind of class he is in. For many children, the home contributes so potently to variance that it may well drown out any differences connected with educational programming.

The most recent efficacy studies are in the familiar tradition. Welch (1965) compared the effects of segregated and partially integrated school programs on self-concept and achievement of educable retarded children. She found that those educable children who remain in a regular classroom one-half day were significantly less self-derogatory than those who were completely segregated, i.e., had no contact with typical youngsters while in school. Further, the partially integrated children improved significantly in reading in contrast with the academic achievement of the comparison group. Grounded along similar theoretical lines, Zito and Bardon (1969) investigated differences in achievement motivation between two groups of Negro educable adolescents, one group in a special education program and a second group in a regular school program. A third group, adolescent

Negroes of typical intelligence in regular classes, comprised the remainder of the study sample. The results indicated that retarded adolescents were more influenced by success than failure and, further, that their achievement motivation was comparable to that of typical subjects from similar socioeconomic backgrounds. Insofar as comparisons between special and regular class youngsters, the special class experience appears to have made these adolescents more cautious in setting goals and more likely to anticipate failure, while the regular class children anticipated success and, in fact, showed greater achievement. In a study similar to Johnson's (1950) now-classic sociometric research on friend selection, rejection and acceptance of mentally retarded children in public schools, Rucker, Howe, and Snider (1969) administered a sociometric instrument in 30 regular junior high-school classes. The results of their investigations, designed to measure the social acceptance of the educable mentally retarded participating in both academic and nonacademic regular classes, supported the conclusion that retarded children enrolled at least half time in regular junior high classes were less accepted than their nonretarded peers. Further, these children were equally rejected in nonacademic and academic classes.

Other recently reported "efficacy" research has dealt with such matters as the effectiveness of cooperative programs between special education and rehabilitation departments (Bloom, 1967), off-campus work placement for the educable retarded (Howe, 1968), the effectiveness of special education on perceptual-motor performance (Krop & Smith, 1969), and integration versus segregation as related to success expectation and achievement (Schwarz & Jens, 1969). Each of the above studies, although relatively well controlled, has added little more than new layers to the massive ambiguity surrounding such questions as they concern curriculum design, administrative organizations, and the efficacy of special interventions or treatments.

Preschool studies are being reported with increasing frequency, due—at least in part—to the favorable conditions vis-à-vis federal and state support of both service programs and research in this area. Guskin and Spicker (1968), Spicker and Bartel (1968), and Blatt and Garfunkel (1969) have all reviewed this rather impressive literature. Since the work of Skeels and his associates to the most recent studies, several theoretical threads reappear and, if for no other reason than their consistency and frequency, may be noteworthy. There continues to be marked interest in the study of so-called "cultural-familial" mentally retarded children and their families. More broadly, there is a significant escalation of interest in studies concerning the correlates of social class and intelligence. However, whereas during the first decades of this century cultural-familial cases were viewed as a specific etiological grouping of genetic origin, they tend now to be viewed as part of that much larger group labeled "culturally deprived" (Blatt & Garfunkel, 1969).[7] Insofar as genetic processes are concerned, the argument of Jensen (1969) and his adherents is by no means original. Even before Goddard's infamous "Kallikak" study, and through all of the decades to the present, there has been general agreement in the psychological and educational communities that genetic processes represent an important source of influence on the biological foundations of intelligence (see Blatt & Garfunkel, 1969, or Sarason & Doris, 1968, for discussions of this history). However, there has also been recognition, which is now increasing remarkably, that far too little is known about the nature of intelligence—except, perhaps, that it is vastly more complex than what is indicated by the IQ score—to justify anything more than the formulation of hypotheses and sheer speculations about the role played by multiple genetic factors (Blatt, 1970; Bodmer & Cavalli-Sforza, 1970). As we have stated elsewhere (Blatt & Garfunkel, 1969), the nature-nurture controversies of the past are being superseded by the realization that earlier positions (either nativist or environmental) were oversimplifications which served certain polemicists' personal opinions far better than they clarified the problem. This important shift in viewing the nature-nurture controversy as neither settled nor understood, together with the emergence of cultural deprivation as a major political, economic, social and educational problem in our society, seem to have set the stage for systematic research and social action on environmental changes that might prevent intellectual deficits.[8]

---

[7] Although the "technical" definition of cultural-familial mental retardation is stated somewhat differently (Heber, 1959, pp. 39–40), substantively it suggests at least five characteristics which have long been descriptive of these individuals: 1) by traditional methods of evaluation their intelligence is subnormal, 2) the intellectual level and social adequacy of at least one parent and one sibling appear also to be subnormal, 3) there is no discernible central nervous system pathology giving rise to the subnormality, 4) they were born into, and reared in, a cultural milieu which is "inferior" to other strata of our society, and 5) they represent a disproportionately large part of the case load of many social agencies.

[8] For a full discussion of classification and terminological problems in mental retardation, tied so intimately to each shifting nature-nurture "fashion," see Blatt and Garfunkel (1969) and Heber (1959). Traditionally, mental retardation was defined as a constitutional condition of the central nervous system existing from birth or early age, incurable, and irremediable, oftentimes resulting in the inability of the individual to profit from ordinary schooling. This traditional definition was joined to a classification system that utilized arbitrarily determined IQ scores to categorize levels of intellectual capacity; e.g., 25–50 IQ was in the "trainable" category; 50–75 IQ was in the "educable" category. More recently (Heber, 1959), a new and widely used definition and classification manual was developed by a committee of the American Association on Mental Deficiency. This new manual defined mental retardation as subaverage general intellectual functioning, originating during the developmental period and associated with impairment in adaptive behavior. This definition did not assume a constitutional condition as a necessary requirement for mental retardation (e.g., in "cultural-familial mental retardation," pp. 39–40). It referred to function rather than, as is traditional, to capacity, and it did not preclude possibilities for prevention, cure or amelioration of mental retardation and its associated consequences.

To date, relatively few well-controlled studies bear directly on the effects of planned intervention on the intellectual development of culturally deprived or cultural-familial mentally retarded children (see Sarason & Doris, 1968, for a perspective on this problem). The accumulated research in this area varies greatly in methodological sophistication and quantity of descriptive detail about sample selection, differences in contrasting environments, and control of bias in collection of data. Although findings generally tend to suggest that planned interventions have the predicted effect of increasing intelligence test scores, these studies have neither produced compelling data nor have they permitted us to draw other than the most cautious conclusions concerning the correlates of intelligence. The three most recent preschool studies, not previously discussed in the aforementioned reviews, have had little more success than their predecessors in contributing to either educational theory or practice. Using groups of disadvantaged children of average intelligence, Karnes, Hodgins, and Teska (1968) compared the effects of traditional and highly structured experimental preschools. Kodman (1970) observed the effects of a special enrichment program designed for Appalachian children, and the third study, conducted at the University of Washington's Experimental Education Unit, dealt with behavior modification procedures for Head Start children (Haring, Hayden, & Nolen, 1969). All three studies reported significant changes in the predicted directions. However, each employed very small samples and, with the exception of Karnes and her associates, there was little attempt to deal with the harassing problems of internal validity. Of the three, Haring et al. was most encouraging, first because the investigators were able to meaningfully depart from the tradition of IQ change as the major dependent variable and, secondly, because their design permitted the systematic study of teacher-child interactions and the modifiability of behavior.

In spite of the educational community's current interest in programmed materials, textbooks and, further, in elaborate new "hardware" systems to promote pupil learning, only a handful of studies relating to the education of mentally retarded children have been reported in recent years that dealt with assessing the potentialities of these newer educational technologies. Of those reviewed, Blackman and Capobianco's (1965)—the most sophisticated in terms of research design and conduct—reported disappointing results with a carefully developed teaching machine program in reading and arithmetic. Other studies by Bradley and Hundziak (1965), Miller and Miller (1968), and Rainey and Kelly (1967) reported greater possibilities with time-telling programs, programmed textbooks, and a unique method for teaching word recognition and discrimination, respectively. However, both Bradley and Hundziak's research and the Millers' study of "symbol accentuation" should be considered exploratory in view of both their small samples and limited research objectives.

Several other methodology studies are worth mentioning. Cawley and Goodman (1969) hypothesized that trained teachers, employing a well-planned program, could effect significant improvement in the arithmetic problem solving of mentally retarded children. Utilizing two control and two experimental groups—three of these classes for the retarded and one a regular class—it was demonstrated that, when teachers were trained during a two-week workshop, mentally retarded children improved significantly. Rouse (1965) found significant gain scores resulting from the involvement of educable mentally retarded children in a training program designed to enhance their productive thinking. However, Budoff, Meskin, and Kemler (1968) were unable to improve productive thinking scores in a general replication of Rouse's experiment. Working with 30 institutionalized retarded children, Bradley, Maurer, and Hundziak (1966) demonstrated the effectiveness of milieu therapy and language training in incrementing psycholinguistic functioning. In a study of the effects of group counseling on educable boys, Mann, Beaber, and Jacobson (1969) found that those who received counseling exhibited anxiety reduction and improved self-concept, deportment and school grades. Lastly, Vergason (1966) compared the effects of a traditional and an autoinstructional method on retention of sight vocabulary. Although there were no differences between groups after one day, superior retention for words learned by the automated self-instructional procedure was found during several follow-up periods.

Elsewhere we have reviewed and discussed an almost endless sea of studies relating to physical performance and capacity of the retarded child (Blatt, 1957, 1958, 1969b). For good and sufficient reasons, few of the traditional strength, motor ability and physical ability studies are currently being reported. Replacing the physical fitness comparison and survey research of three and four decades ago is a renewed interest in perceptual-motor training and performance. Certainly, this interest is a reflection of a major educational movement—learning disabilities—which is now literally sweeping the country and obviously has broad and important implications for the field of mental retardation (Blatt, 1969a). Kahn and Burdett (1967) found that, by utilizing practice and reward schedules, mentally retarded adolescents improved significantly in motor skills. Employing specially designed training programs, both Lillie (1968) and Ross (1969) reported similar results, i.e., with training, mentally retarded children improved in motor proficiency. Edgar, Ball, McIntyre, and Shotwell (1969) reported gains in adaptive behavior after a program

of sensory-motor training with a small group of organically impaired retarded children. However, Alley (1968) was unable to demonstrate significant effects resulting from a systematic perceptual-motor training program. Lastly, both Corder (1966) and Solomon and Pangle (1967) found
that physical education programs significantly influenced the development of retarded children. However, most of these studies suffer from
one or more serious design problems: samples that are too small or ambiguous, very short-term treatments, and dependent variables that seem
unrelated to the experimental treatment (e.g., Corder, 1966, with an experimental sample of eight boys, designed a 20-day program of physical
education using the Wechsler Intelligence Scale for Children as a dependent variable).

Since the theoretical work of B. F. Skinner in the fifties, the field of
behavior analysis and modification has gained increasing attention and
importance. A perusal of the literature in mental retardation generously
testifies to the prominence and influence the operant conditioning movement has had in this field. Although much of the work reported emanates
from the laboratory, a growing literature, anchored in the field, can now
be found regularly in journals dealing with the education and treatment
of the mentally retarded. Much of this literature is concerned with the
severely retarded and the modification of such self-help skills as toileting,
dressing and eating. A number of other studies have been successful in
extinguishing destructiveness, aggression and self-abuse. The following
reports are examples of behavioral studies that have succeeded in modifying the performance of mildly and severely retarded children—some
institutionalized and others in the community: Bensberg, Colwell, and
Cassel (1965); Broden, Hall, Dunlap, and Clark (1970); Doubros (1966);
Karen and Maxwell (1967); McKenzie, Clark, Wolf, Kothera, and Benson
(1968); and Siegel, Forman, and Williams (1967). Undoubtedly, a great
deal more can be said concerning the influence of this movement on the
development of theory and practice in the field. There appears to be
almost no possibility for other than escalated activity in this area and
prominence and support for its advocates, in spite of shortcomings and
limitations inherent in the concept of behavior modification as well as
increasing misuse of this potentially important area by its unsophisticated
advocates (Macmillan & Forness, 1970). For example, the senior author
served recently on an HEW panel reviewing proposals to improve conditions in state schools for the mentally retarded. With possibly one and
no more than two exceptions each of those 60 applications communicated
neither a glimmer of interest nor even an awareness of other than one or
another variation of behavior-modification programming. Again, we have
come full circle; as psychotherapy was the mental aspirin of the forties

and fifties, it seems certain that our current era will be noted for the influence of this rediscovered approach we term "behavior modification."

Variations in Children and Teachers

The preponderance of research dealing with the learning characteristics and behavior of mentally retarded children originates in the laboratory and emanates from the experimental tradition. Experimenters continue to be interested in the laboratory examination of: paired-associate learning (Baumeister, Hawkins, & Davis, 1966; Hawker & Keilman, 1969; Milgram & Riedel, 1969; Ring, 1965); short-term recall (Baumeister, Hawkins, & Holland, 1967; Gallagher, 1969); discrimination learning (Riese & Lobb, 1967); curiosity behavior (Morgan, 1969); learning transfer (Gerjuoy & Alvarez, 1969); and attention (Follini, Sitkowski, & Stayton, 1969).

The contrast between the great number of basic research studies and the scarcity of field or applied studies is remarkable. Except for the organizational, efficacy, and methodology studies, there is almost no recent research to report in the latter area. Lovell and Bradbury (1967) observed the learning of English morphology in educable retarded children. Huber (1965) studied the relationship of anxiety to the academic work of retarded institutionalized children. Jacobs and Pierce (1968), Laing and Chazan (1966), and Levine, Elzey, and Paulson (1966) reported on the social status of retarded children in various in-school or school-excluded settings. Lastly, a number of personality-type studies—reminiscent of the familiar comparison and status reports of the thirties and forties—have appeared from time to time during recent years, neither adding to our knowledge nor worthy of further discussion here.

We found but four studies dealing with teachers, their prestige, turnover and characteristics: Knox (1968); Meisgeier (1965); Sharples and Thomas (1969); and Sparks and Younie (1969). Finally, we found only two studies (Jones, Marcotte, & Markham, 1968; Strauch, 1970) that dealt with the attitudes typical children have toward the retarded.

We have said little here beyond noting for the reader's attention references to a sample of the more recent reports dealing with characteristics and variations of children and teachers. We have said little because little deserves saying, not because these are poorly designed or poorly executed studies; on the contrary, there is at least equal overall research precision here as contrasted with research more comprehensively discussed in other sections of this chapter. We choose to merely list the above reports because, first, laboratory research has yet to offer more than a promise for useful application to classrooms, teachers and children (a promise that we believe will be realized one day) and, secondly, because much of the remaining research mentioned in this section reveals little that was not reported as long ago as the forties and fifties, and whose value might have been questioned then.

DISCUSSION

During the 1969–70 academic year, the Council for Exceptional Children asked both of the authors of this chapter to participate in a unique experience involving the organization of what they termed an "invisible college." Due to limitations of time and resources, and because the Council needed some fairly reliable data concerning the kind of research that is currently being conducted and who is doing it, a core of key researchers in special education were interviewed by telephone to ascertain their opinions concerning current research efforts, issues and controversies. Eventually, the consensus on several topics will form the base for convening the "invisible colleges." A total of 55 telephone interviews were conducted, the interviewers asking each participant to:

1. Identify projects they found interesting and significant
2. Describe their own work
3. Identify the "hottest" controversy in the field
4. Identify technical or methodological problems delaying research efforts
5. Name the creative mavericks

In the general field called "special education," the categories of behavior modification, early childhood, strategies in special education, curriculum development in mental retardation and innovations in personnel training were the most frequently cited. Pupil characteristics, methods and materials, and speech, language, and communication disorders were mentioned with lesser, but impressive, frequency. Although the above survey assessed research interest in a much broader area than ours—mental retardation—these findings accurately reflect how we would respond to such questions as they might deal specifically with the field of mental retardation. Our brief critical literature survey revealed the great and increasingly influential position now enjoyed by those engaged in behavior modification research. When—for the purposes of categorization—reinforcement, applied behavior change and classical conditioning studies are grouped together, they probably constitute the greatest percentage of articles on mental retardation to be found in current major journals. Further, although the Council for Exceptional Children has a somewhat different constituency and mission than the American Association on Mental Deficiency or other organizations focused specifically on mental retardation, literature reviews in our field would, undoubtedly, disclose the majority of basic studies to be concerned with: verbal learning, discrimination, reinforcement and applied behavior change, and—to a lesser extent—generalization and motor learning. (See Gardner, Solomowitz, & Saposnek's paper, "Trends in Learning Research with the Mentally Retarded," unpublished but reproduced in the Council for Exceptional Children *Planning Report for Information Analysis Products*, 1969.)

Our literature survey and the results of the Council's telephone study have both indicated that the preponderance of published research in mental retardation is experimental. Most studies of teaching have used traditional designs, whether they were efficacy studies, follow-up studies of children in special and regular classes, studies of different reading approaches, or studies of different curriculum approaches. Although these kinds of studies are more amenable to design modifications which may account for dyadic variation, we believe that there are more appropriate ways to study teaching-learning in classrooms or tutorial situations. Guskin and Spicker (1968) commented upon what, to us, is the most important lesson we could learn about the effects of our current style of research with the handicapped (i.e., our research has contributed almost nothing of value for the educational practitioner and, may we add, for the educational theoretician). It is well known that researchers, especially doctoral students, engage not in what they want to do but what they are able to do, not in what is important but what is possible, not in what is risky but what is safe and gives assurance of completion. People do what can be supported and most of us engage ourselves in activities that are comfortable and appreciated by others. Possibly the most accurate judgment we can make about the research in mental retardation now being published is that this is what the people in the field want or, possibly, there is not anything else known that they can or wish to substitute for their current mode of activity.

We conclude that:

1. There is nothing intrinsic in mental retardation—or in any disability— to produce handicap. Further, it is not the primary responsibility of the behavioral sciences to determine the validity of the aforementioned statement, but to make it become valid. We have supported far too many studies purporting to demonstrate differences between groups or the disorders of one type of child in contrast with another. All these years we should have promoted and encouraged research that sought to make it true that a child would learn after participation in a special program or curriculum. To state this another way, we are less than enthusiastic about the possibility that "all or nothing"— i.e., either we find something (significant) or we find nothing—research has anything to offer, either to our understanding of the handicapped or to pragmatic solutions to their learning problems. As an aside—we believe an important aside—in such "all or nothing" stud-

ies, one can see important and, perhaps, insidious relationships between the needs of research design and programming. That is, it is certainly seductive to randomly assign groups of children to treatments in order to see whether those treatments are effective, disregarding questions concerning the desirable way to develop educational programs for children.

2. The above leads directly to our second recommendation, viz., the study of particular methods for the purpose of demonstrating their efficacy is rather fruitless and whatever is demonstrated will eventually be contradicted by subsequent research. Such "all or nothing" studies of methodologies prove little. By "all or nothing," we mean studies that compare the efficacy of one method with that of another or compare the superiority of one type of individual with that of another.[9] As methods do not exist outside of a psychoeducational setting, and as they are implemented by unique groups of human beings, only a naive researcher could conclude that the demonstrated superiority of his method has direct and specific transferability to other educational settings.[10] Our research preference is to study children and how they change in different educational environments. We believe it is more defensible, and will make a greater difference, to generalize about children interacting with each other and with adults in situations than it is to generalize about procedures. It is from evaluations of varieties of methods, with varieties of children in more or less formal and informal settings, utilizing teachers with heterogeneous backgrounds, that hypotheses will be generated that will lead to viable theories concerning human development and learning. It appears to us that, in this kind of strategy, theory construction shifts from methodological concerns to those involving human interactions.

3. Every researcher is confronted with a decision concerning the number of variables and sample size to be studied. Consequently, in light of limited resources, manpower, and time, to the degree that the researcher does not restrict variables of the study, he will have to restrict his sample, or vice versa. Our recommendation is to restrict—to the necessary degree—sample size rather then number of variables.

---

[9] Or, as Campbell and Stanley (1963) incisively concluded, "we must increase our time perspective, and recognize that continuous, multiple experimentation is more typical of science than once-and-for-all [what the present writers term "all or nothing"] definitive experiments. . . . we should not expect that 'crucial experiments' which pit opposing theories will be likely to have clear-cut outcomes" (p. 3).

[10] On the other hand, we are not ready to suggest that there is *nothing but* uniqueness in an educational setting. There must be possibilities for building generalizations, for, if "knowledge" is an objective, we must be concerned with the degrees of nonuniqueness. Unfortunately, as we stated above, the numerous dimensions of child-teacher interactions have been neglected and, consequently, hardly understood.

In studying the complex problems of the handicapped on the one hand, and teaching them on the other hand, the restriction of variables to be studied and accounted for may lead to a distorted impression of results that either mislead the researcher or tell him very little about that which he has so diligently attempted to investigate. Therefore, although it is desirable to use as large, unbiased and representative a sample as possible—especially if one is interested in the generalizability that a study may provide—in respect to the aforementioned realities and compromises that must be made, we cannot help but recommend that the research payoff will be greater if compromises are made with sample size rather than number of variables.

4. Leading from the above discussion is our recommendation that a great deal more work is needed before we truly comprehend the varieties and natures of educational settings for the mentally retarded. Education and psychology are now just beginning to appreciate the dictum that before the researcher attempts to manipulate variables he should describe the natural setting. What are so desperately needed today are studies describing how and under what conditions handicapped children are admitted to school programs, how and under what conditions they perform in such programs, their attitudes and the attitudes of their instructors, and the interactive effects of such programs on those children, their families and other involved children.

5. Finally, the enormous current interest in specialized education strategies—e.g., Montessori, Bereiter, Special Classes, Head Start, token reinforcement, compensatory education, operant conditioning, and various learning disabilities programs—is testimony to the wide acceptance of a view of learning that places high value on teachers and learners rather than on teaching and learning. All of those strategies are attractive, in part because they are self-contained and can be discussed, described and set up as independent variables. Similarly, single-dimensional teacher differences as a factor in differential learning places us in a comparable trap. Such distinctions as structured versus nonstructured, directive versus permissive, child-centered versus teacher-centered, do not appear to make much of a difference other than that which is specifically tied to the behaviors under consideration. It would appear that other factors in teaching and learning are more important, that they cannot be simply described by the aforementioned methodologies or style labels, and that they are best studied by looking at differential processes.

In this chapter we have presented the position that, before we can adequately measure and understand quantitative differences in children and their teachers, we will first have to deal with and understand qualitative differences and processes. Our goal as educational researchers is to examine the components of the teaching-learning interaction. We conclude that, to accomplish this goal, individual components cannot be amputated; that is, as we amputate, we both change the natural setting and destroy much of any understanding we might have gained from a more holistic view. To extend this analogy further, the surgeon might more easily examine and operate on the brain if it could be removed from the skull. However, notwithstanding modern medicine and its miracle workers, that trick is not yet possible. We in the behavioral areas seem not to believe that the variables we study and manipulate are more complex and less well understood than the surgeon's.

REFERENCES

Alley, G. R. Perceptual-motor performances of mentally retarded children after systematic visual perceptual training. *American Journal of Mental Deficiency,* 1968, 73, 247–250.

Baumeister, A. A., Hawkins, W. F., & Davis, P. A. Stimulus-response duration in paired-associates learning of normals and retardates. *American Journal of Mental Deficiency,* 1966, 70, 580–584.

Baumeister, A. A., Hawkins, W. F., & Holland, J. M. Retroactive inhibition in short-term recall in normals and retardates. *American Journal of Mental Deficiency,* 1967, 72, 253–256.

Bensberg, G. J., Colwell, C. N., & Cassel, R. H. Teaching the profoundly retarded self-help activities by behavior shaping techniques. *American Journal of Mental Deficiency,* 1965, 69, 674–679.

Blackman, L. S. *A scientific orientation for special education.* New York: Teachers College, Columbia University, 1969.

Blackman, L. S., & Capobianco, R. J. An evaluation of programmed instruction with the mentally retarded utilizing teaching machines. *American Journal of Mental Deficiency,* 1965, 70, 262–269.

Blackman, L. S., & Heintz, P. The mentally retarded. *Review of Educational Research,* 1966, 36, 5–36.

Blatt, B. The physical, personality, and academic status of children who are mentally retarded attending special classes as compared with children who are mentally retarded attending regular classes. (Doctoral dissertation, The Pennsylvania State University.) Ann Arbor, Mich.: University Microfilms, 1957, No. 57–425.

Blatt, B. The physical, personality, and academic status of children who are mentally retarded attending special classes as compared with children who are mentally retarded attending regular classes. *American Journal of Mental Deficiency,* 1958, 62, 810–818.

Blatt, B. A hypothesis of theories and methods in special education. In Jerome Hellmuth (Ed.), *Disadvantaged child.* Vol. 1. Seattle, Wash.: Special Child Publications, 1967. Pp. 65–76.

Blatt, B. (Ed.). Learning disabilities. *Seminars in Psychiatry,* 1969, 1, 237–361. (a)

Blatt, B. Time's passage—unchanging times. Keynote address in *Physical education and recreation for handicapped children.* Washington, D.C.: American Association of Health, Physical Education and Recreation, 1969. Pp. 50–56. (b)

Blatt, B. On the educability of intelligence. *Syracuse Scanner*, 1970, 15, 7–10.

Blatt, B., & Garfunkel, F. *The educability of intelligence.* Washington, D.C.: Council for Exceptional Children, 1969.

Bloom, W. Effectiveness of a cooperative special education vocational rehabilitation program. *American Journal of Mental Deficiency*, 1967, 72, 393–403.

Bodmer, W. F., & Cavalli-Sforza, L. L. Intelligence and race. *Scientific American*, 1970, 223(4), 19–29.

Bradley, B. H., & Hundziak, M. TMI-Grolier Time Telling Program for the mentally retarded. *Exceptional Children*, 1965, 32, 17–20.

Bradley, B. H., Maurer, R., & Hundziak, M. A study of the effectiveness of milieu therapy and language training for the mentally retarded. *Exceptional Children*, 1966, 33, 143–150.

Broden, M., Hall, R. V., Dunlap, A., & Clark, R. Effects of teacher attention and a token reinforcement system in a junior high school special education class. *Exceptional Children*, 1970, 36, 341–349.

Bruyn, S. T. *The human perspective in sociology: The methodology of participant observation.* Englewood Cliffs, N.J.: Prentice-Hall, 1966.

Budoff, M., Meskin, J. D., & Kemler, D. J. Training productive thinking of EMRs: A failure to replicate. *American Journal of Mental Deficiency.* 1968, 73, 195–199.

Cain, L. F., & Levine, S. *Effects of community and institutional school programs on trainable mentally retarded children.* Washington, D.C.: National Education Association, Council for Exceptional Children, 1963.

Campbell, D. T., & Stanley, J. C. *Experimental and quasi-experimental designs for research.* Chicago: Rand McNally, 1963.

Cassidy, V. M., & Stanton, J. E. *An investigation of factors involved in the educational placement of mentally retarded children.* Columbus, Ohio: Ohio State University Press, 1959.

Cawley, J. F., & Goodman, J. O. Arithmetical problem solving: A demonstration with the mentally handicapped. *Exceptional Children*, 1969, 36, 83–88.

Charney, L. The trainable mentally retarded. In S. A. Kirk & B. B. Weiner (Eds.), *Behavioral research on exceptional children.* Washington, D.C.: National Education Association, Council for Exceptional Children, 1963. Pp. 90–114.

Coleman, J. S., Campbell, E. Q., Hobson, C. J., McPartland, J., Mood, A. M., Weinfeld, F. B., & York, R. L. *Equality of educational opportunity.* Washington, D.C.: U.S. Government Printing Office, 1966.

Corder, W. O. Effects of physical education on the intellectual, physical, and social development of educable mentally retarded boys. *Exceptional Children*, 1966, 32, 357–364.

Deutsch, M. Happenings on the way back to the forum: Social science, IQ, and race differences revisited. *Harvard Educational Review*, 1969, 39, 523–557.

Doubros, S. G. Behavior therapy with high level, institutionalized, retarded adolescents. *Exceptional Children*, 1966, 33, 229–233.

Dunn, L. M., & Capobianco, R. J. Mental retardation. *Review of Educational Research.* 1959, 29, 451–470.

Edgar, C. L., Ball, T. S., McIntyre, R. B., & Shotwell, A. M. Effects of sensory motor training on adaptive behavior. *American Journal of Mental Deficiency*, 1969, 73, 713–720.

Edgerton, R. B. *The cloak of competence: Stigma in the lives of the mentally retarded.* Berkeley: University of California Press, 1967.

Ellis, N. R. (Ed.). *International review of research in mental retardation.* New York: Academic Press, Volume 1, 1966(a); Volume 2, 1966(b); Volume 3, 1968.

Follini, P., Sitkowski, C. A., & Stayton, S. E. The attention of retardates and normals in distraction and non-distraction conditions. *American Journal of Mental Deficiency*, 1969, 74, 200–205.

Gage, N. L. (Ed.). *Handbook of research on teaching.* Chicago: Rand McNally, 1963.

Gallagher, J. W. Short-term recall of sentences in normal and retarded children. *American Journal of Mental Deficiency*, 1969, 74, 57–61.

Gardner, J. M., Solomowitz, S., & Saposnek, D. T. *Trends in learning research with the mentally retarded.* Unpublished manuscript. Washington, D.C.: Council for Exceptional Children, 1969.

Gerjuoy, I. R., & Alvarez, J. M. Transfer of learning in associative clustering of retardates and normals. *American Journal of Mental Deficiency*, 1969, 73, 733–738.

Glaser, B. G., & Strauss, A. L. *The discovery of grounded theory: Strategies for qualitative research.* Chicago: Aldine, 1967.

Goffman, E. *Asylums: Essays on the social situation of mental patients and other inmates.* Garden City, N.Y.: Anchor Books, 1961.

Goldstein, H., Moss, J. W., & Jordan, L. J. *The efficacy of special class training on the development of mentally retarded children.* Cooperative Research Project No. 619. Urbana, Ill.: Institute for Research on Exceptional Children, University of Illinois, 1965.

Guskin, S. L., & Spicker, H. H. Educational research in mental retardation. In N. R. Ellis (Ed.), *International review of research in mental retardation.* Vol. 3. New York: Academic Press, 1968. Pp. 217–278.

Haring, N. G., Hayden, A. H., & Nolen, P. A. Accelerating appropriate behaviors of children in a Head Start program. *Exceptional Children*, 1969, 35, 773–784.

Hawker, J. R., & Keilman, P. A. Prompting and confirmation in paired-associate learning by retardates. *American Journal of Mental Deficiency*, 1969, 74, 75–79.

Heber, R. A manual on terminology and classification in mental retardation. Monograph supplement to the *American Journal of Mental Deficiency*, 1959, 64(2), 111.

Hottel, J. V. *An evaluation of Tennessee's day class program for severely mentally retarded children.* Nashville: George Peabody College for Teachers, 1958.

Howe, C. E. Is off campus work placement necessary for all educable mentally retarded? *Exceptional Children*, 1968, 35, 323–326.

Huber, W. G. The relationship of anxiety to the academic performance of institutionalized retardates. *American Journal of Mental Deficiency*, 1965, 69, 462–466.

Hurley, R. L. *Poverty and mental retardation: A causal relationship.* New York: Random House, 1969.

Jacobs, J. F., & Pierce, M. L. The social position of retardates with brain damage associated characteristics. *Exceptional Children*, 1968, 34, 677–681.

Jensen, A. R. How much can we boost IQ and scholastic achievement? *Harvard Educational Review*, 1969, 39, 1–123.

Johnson, G. O. A study of the social position of mentally-handicapped children in the regular grades. *American Journal of Mental Deficiency*, 1950, 55, 60–89.

Johnson, G. O., & Blank, H. (Eds.) *Exceptional children research review.* Washington D.C.: Council for Exceptional Children, 1968.

Jones, R. L., Marcotte, M., & Markham, K. Modifying perceptions of trainable mental retardates. *Exceptional Children*, 1968, 34, 309–315.

Jordan, T. E. *The mentally retarded.* (2nd ed.) Columbus, Ohio: Charles E. Merrill, 1966.

Kagan, J. S. Inadequate evidence and illogical conclusions. *Harvard Educational Review*, 1969, 39, 274–277.

Kahn, H., & Burdett, A. D. Interaction of practice and rewards on motor performance of adolescent mental retardates. *American Journal of Mental Deficiency*, 1967, 72, 422–427.

Karen, R. L., & Maxwell, S. J. Strengthening self-help behavior in the retardate. *American Journal of Mental Deficiency*, 1967, 71, 546–550.

Karnes, M. B., Hodgins, A., & Teska, J. A. An evaluation of two preschool programs for disadvantaged children: A traditional and a highly structured experimental preschool. *Exceptional Children*, 1968, 34, 667–676.

Kirk, S. A. *Early education of the mentally retarded.* Urbana, Ill.: University of Illinois Press, 1958.

Kirk, S. A. Research in education. In H. A. Stevens & R. A. Heber (Eds.), *Mental retardation: A review of research.* Chicago: University of Chicago Press, 1964. Pp. 57–99.

Kirk, S. A., & Weiner, B. B. (Eds.). *Behavioral research on exceptional children.* Washington, D.C.: Council for Exceptional Children, 1963.

Knox, S. C. Turnover among teachers of the mentally retarded. *Exceptional Children*, 1968, 35, 231–235.

Kodman, F., Jr. Effects of preschool enrichment on intellectual performance of Appalachian children. *Exceptional Children*, 1970, 36, 503–507.

Krop, H. D., & Smith, C. R. Effects of special education on Bender-Gestalt performance of the mentally retarded. *American Journal of Mental Deficiency*, 1969, 73, 693–699.

Laing, A. F., & Chazan, M. Sociometric groupings among educationally subnormal children. *American Journal of Mental Deficiency*, 1966, 71, 73–77.

Levine, S., Elzey, F. F., & Paulson, F. L. Social competence of school and nonschool trainable mentally retarded. *American Journal of Mental Deficiency*, 1966, 71, 112–115.

Lillie, D. L. The effects of motor development lessons on mentally retarded children. *American Journal of Mental Deficiency*, 1968, 72, 803–808.

Lovell, K., & Bradbury, B. The learning of English morphology in educationally subnormal special school children. *American Journal of Mental Deficiency*, 1967, 71, 609–615.

Macmillan, D. L., & Forness, S. R. Behavior modification: Limitations and liabilities. *Exceptional Children*, 1970, 37, 291–297.

Mann, P. H., Beaber, J. D., & Jacobson, M. D. The effect of group counseling on educable mentally retarded boys' self concepts. *Exceptional Children*, 1969, 35, 359–366.

McCarthy, J. J., & Sheerenberger, R. C. A decade of research on the education of the mentally retarded. *Mental Retardation Abstracts*, 1966, 3, 481–501.

McKenzie, H. S., Clark, M., Wolf, M. M., Kothera, R., & Benson, C. Behavior modification of children with learning disabilities using grades as tokens and allowances as back up reinforcers. *Exceptional Children*, 1968, 34, 745–752.

Meisgeier, C. The identification of successful teachers of mentally or physically handicapped children. *Exceptional Children*, 1965, 32, 229–235.

Meyers, C. E., Sitkei, E. G., & Watts, C. A. Attitudes toward special education and the handicapped in two community groups. *American Journal of Mental Deficiency*, 1966, 71, 78–84.

Milgram, N. A., & Riedel, W. Verbal contex and visual compound in paired-associate learning of mental retardates. *American Journal of Mental Deficiency*, 1969, 73, 755–761.

Miller, A., & Miller, E. E. Symbol accentuation: The perceptual transfer of meaning from spoken to printed words. *American Journal of Mental Deficiency*, 1968, 73, 200–208.

Morgan, S. B. Responsiveness to stimulus novelty and complexity in mild, moderate, and severe retardates. *American Journal of Mental Deficiency*, 1969, 74, 32–38.

Mullen, F. A., & Itkin, W. Achievement and adjustment of educable mentally handicapped children. Cooperative Research Project SAE 6529, 1961, Board of Education, City of Chicago, Chicago, Illinois.

Phillips, I. (Ed.). *Prevention and treatment of mental retardation*. New York: Basic Books, 1966.

Pumphrey, M. W., Goodman, M. B., Kidd, J. W., & Peters, E. N. Participation of retarded children in regular recreational activities at a community center. *Exceptional Children*, 1970, 36, 453–458.

Quay, H. C. Academic skills. In N. R. Ellis (Ed.), *Handbook of mental deficiency*. New York: McGraw-Hill, 1963, Pp. 664–690.

Rainey, D. S., & Kelly, F. J. An evaluation of a programed textbook with educable mentally retarded children. *Exceptional Children*, 1967, 34, 169–174.

Riese, R. R., & Lobb, H. Discrimination learning in retarded children: Non-reward vs. reward. *American Journal of Mental Deficiency*, 1967, 71, 536–541.

Ring, E. M. The effect of anticipation interval on paired-associate learning in retarded and normal children. *American Journal of Mental Deficiency*, 1965, 70, 466–470.

Robinson, H. B., & Robinson, N. M. *The mentally retarded child: A psychological approach*. New York: McGraw-Hill, 1965.

Rosenthal, R., & Jacobson, L. Teachers' expectancies: Determinants of pupils' IQ gains. *Psychological Reports*, 1966, 19, 115–118.

Ross, S. A. Effects of an intensive motor skills training program on young educable mentally retarded children. *American Journal of Mental Deficiency*, 1969, 73, 920–926.

Rouse, S. T. Effects of a training program on the productive thinking of educable mental retardates. *American Journal of Mental Deficiency*, 1965, 69, 666–673.

Rucker, C. N., Howe, C. E., & Snider, B. The participation of retarded children in junior high academic and nonacademic regular classes. *Exceptional Children*, 1969, 35, 617–623.

Sarason, S. B., & Doris, J. L. *Psychological problems in mental deficiency*. (4th ed.). New York: Harper & Row, 1968.

Schiefelbusch, R. L., Copeland, R. H., & Smith, J. O. *Language and mental retardation*. New York: Holt, Rinehart & Winston, 1967.

Schwarz, R. H., & Jens, K. G. The expectation of success as it modifies the achievement of mentally retarded adolescents. *American Journal of Mental Deficiency*, 1969, 73, 946–949.

Sharples, D., & Thomas, D. J. The perceived prestige of normal and special education teachers. *Exceptional Children*, 1969, 35, 473–479.

Shulman, L. S. Reconstruction of educational research. *Review of Educational Research*, 1970, 40, 371–396.

Siegel, P. S., Forman, G. E., & Williams, J. An exploratory study of incentive motivation in the retardate. *American Journal of Mental Deficiency*, 1967, 71, 977–983.

Solomon, A., & Pangle, R. Demonstrating physical fitness improvement in the EMR. *Exceptional Children*, 1967, 34, 177–181.

Sparks, H. L., & Younie, W. J. Adult adjustment of the mentally retarded: Implication for teacher education. *Exceptional Children*, 1969, 36, 13–17.

Spicker, H., & Bartel, N. The mentally retarded. In G. O. Johnson & H. Blank (Eds.), *Exceptional children research review*. Washington, D.C.: Council for Exceptional Children, 1968. Pp. 38–189.

Strauch, J. D. Social contact as a variable in the expressed attitudes of normal adolescents toward EMR pupils. *Exceptional Children*, 1970, 36, 495–500.

Vale, J. R., & Vale, C. A. Individual differences and general laws in psychology: A reconciliation. *American Psychologist*, 1969, 24, 1093–1108.

Vergason, G. A. Retention in educable retarded subjects for two methods of instruction. *American Journal of Mental Deficiency*, 1966, 70, 683–688.

Welch, E. A. *The effects of segregated and partially integrated school programs on self-concept and academic achievement of educable mental retardates.* Unpublished doctoral dissertation, University of Denver, 1965.

Wrightstone, J. W., Forlano, G., Lepkowski, J. R., Sontag, M., & Edelstein, J. D. *A comparison of educational outcomes under single-track and two-track plans for educable mentally retarded children.* Cooperative Research Project No. 144, 1959. Board of Education, Brooklyn, New York.

Zito, R. J., & Bardon, J. I. Achievement motivation among Negro adolescents in regular and special education programs. *American Journal of Mental Deficiency*, 1969, 74, 20–26.

CHAPTER 4

Poems and Aphorisms

VERSE

The most personal, the words that cut and sting,
are the words men call "poetry."
These words are little more than the accumulated
pain and reason of each man who denudes his mind and his
soul and his heart—for himself.
For to himself he will be true, as he knows there
is no truth
As he knows that truth eludes him and he is
incapable.
But less incapable than others who have tried,
and have failed.
As he has failed.

REFORMATION OF PANDEMONIUM

Pandemonium is the capital of Hell. It is the fantasy of Milton, yet, to
many, it is the reality of being. One does not describe Pandemonium but
reacts to it. Let us examine the mentally retarded in Pandemonium and
the reformation that is attempting to return them from the brutality of
institutional back wards to the realm of human awareness, compassion,
and interrelatedness.

In Pandemonium, there are many aliases: solitary
confinement is therapeutic isolation; restraint is protection; punishment is negative feedback; and
indifference to all of these is thoughtfulness.
In Pandemonium, a girl has seven healthy teeth
extracted to prevent her from eating threads of the
day-room rug.

During the years, I've published more than a little poetry, aphorisms, and fiction, such
work representing not only other sides of my life but also other sides of the *same* questions
dealt with in my scholarly publications. Here in this chapter are a few selections from
Exodus From Pandemonium: Human Abuse and a Reformation of Public Policy (1970) and
Souls in Extremis: An Anthology on Victims and Victimizers (1973), both published by Allyn
& Bacon, Boston.

In Pandemonium, the physically handicapped become
more disabled as each day passes each identical
day and as each old contracture is the cause of new
contractures, and as both old and new are the
effects of indifference and ineptitude.

In Pandemonium, we appropriate such progressive
terms as "comprehensive," "community," "regional,"
and "prevention," but nothing changes,
or we wouldn't be in Pandemonium.

In Pandemonium, there is little drug addiction, but there
is pervasive, more destructive, environmental
addiction with its accompanying withdrawal
syndrome and sickness.

In Pandemonium, the cry of the anguished is, "I am
here!"

In Pandemonium, children are locked and forgotten in
solitary confinement cells for such crimes as
breaking a window or speaking disrespectfully to
an attendant.

In Pandemonium, the tunnel is endless, the darkness
unendurable, the light extinguished.

In Pandemonium, weakness is strength and strength
is weakness.

In Pandemonium, causing nothing to change is Power.

In Pandemonium, trivial questions are answered
erroneously while meaningful one are
never asked.

In Pandemonium, Utopia is anywhere else.

In Pandemonium, humanists dislike people.

In Pandemonium, both labor and management are
represented by one collective negotiator,
the devil.

In Pandemonium, we find new ways to express horror
and debasement.

In Pandemonium, to embrace life is to kiss death.

In Pandemonium, the humanists are inhuman,
the theists are atheists, the lovers are
haters.

In Pandemonium, you die before you live; the end
precedes a beginning.

In Pandemonium, the luxury of life is death.
In Pandemonium, labeling someone or something
  makes it fact.
In Pandemonium you are in the eye of the eye
  of that mischief named hell.

> Pandemonium is the sophist's paradise.
> Pandemonium disguises inertia as reasonableness.
> Pandemonium demonstrates the tautology of the "evil
>   of massive institutions" and the non sequitur in
>   "excellent large institutions."
> Pandemonium is entranced with medical curiosities
>   rather than concerned with human necessities.
> Pandemonium is a phantasmagoria which is
>   real.
> Pandemonium proves the gnostics' thesis that man is
>   wicked and the world is an evil place.

Pandemonians hope for their nightmares to end while
  knowing their terror is permanent, for the
  floods to subside while expecting the deluge.
Pandemonians have learned that the meaninglessness
  of one's question is only exceeded by the
  valuelessness of its answer.
Pandemonians respect an equality that understands no
  difference between "he" and "it."
Pandemonians have learned that the next hour will
  be a greater catastrophe than the last.
Pandemonians who are deaf never speak, who
  are palsied never walk, who are retarded never
  think; in Pandemonium, the blind have
  no eyes and the lame no feet.
Pandemonians know that life is war.

> Good works are inherited from evil deeds in
>   Pandemonium.
> We are trapped because the priest *does* practice what
>   he preaches in Pandemonium.
> There is no need to talk through one's problem
>   as there is no shade of difference, just an omnipotent
>   MAN who proclaims what *is* in Pandemonium.

Artists distort reality to present reality; distortion is
  the reality in Pandemonium.
Naïveté and innocence cannot survive in Pandemonium.

Subterfuge is the shortest distance between two
    conspirators in Pandemonium.
One man lives in the future, another in the past, while
    no one has either in Pandemonium.
Nothing changes, yet there is an illusion of
    change, for things do not change differently, now,
    from the way they have not changed before in
    Pandemonium.
There are many liberals but few equalitarians
    in Pandemonium.
No one is dehumanized *because* he is a man, but many
    are dehumanized *because* they are residents
    in Pandemonium.
Sick people live in a healthy culture and healthy
    people live in a sick culture; the mix is Pandemonium.
Today is Doomsday in Pandemonium.

> The law of Pandemonium is to know right and do
>   wrong, think well and behave poorly.
> The law of Pandemonium is to believe that nothing can
>   be done so nothing need be attempted; the
>   system is wrong while we are right.
> The law of Pandemonium is to treat other humans as if
>   they *weren't*, then treat ourselves as if *we were*.
> The law of Pandemonium is to promote the
>   administrator's pseudo-giftedness while he promotes
>   the patients' pseudo-custodialness.
> The law of Pandemonium is not to believe in the
>   fulfillment of every human being.
> The law of Pandemonium relates more to *ahumantia*
>   than to *amentia*.
> The law of Pandemonium is to present a public image
>   that disguises closed systems as open systems.

The law of Pandemonium unfolds the animal
    ethos leading the human spirit.
The law of Pandemonium is to build ideational and
    physical tunnels to deny man the sensation
    of natural light and experience.
The law of Pandemonium is to learn geography while
    neglecting etiology.
The law of Pandemonium relies on the truth of its deceit,
    the courage of its cowardice, and the love of hate.

The law of Pandemonium is for the state to give the
  patient everything but he gets nothing.

Pandemoniacs destroy relationships.
Pandemoniacs respect chaos.
Pandemoniacs build evil.
Pandemoniacs exude unforgiveness.
Pandemoniacs induce pain.
Pandemoniacs cause mental retardation.
Pandemoniacs revolt against competence.

> What will the reformation of Pandemonium bring? We
> will agree that mere intention is meaningless; mere
> speech is noise; behavior is character. We are what
> we do! And, we will question not only truth but
> value!

In our relationship with humanity, we have learned that:
Love penetrates hate.
The heart moves mountains while the mind moves only
  the heart.
And the soul is man's ultimate triumph.

> The saga of humanity has its glory in the human value.
> The glory of humanity is its saga of humanhood.

In the cause for humanity, we must agree that:
All men are human beings.
All human beings are valuable.
And all the rest is commentary.

THE LONG WAIT

In the institution, everyone waits—patients, attendants, doctors, the superintendent. But, the patient's wait is longest: first, because it *is* longest and, second, because it usually is for no reason, toward no goal, no achievement. He waits for nothing. This is his destiny. And, if he is lucky, he is not surprised by its discovery.

One asks, "How long is endless?" It is an instant past the end, a shadow after meaning would have been comprehended, a shade of time later than too late.

In the institution, everyone waits. But, the patient's wait is longest. His wait is endless, having had a beginning long forgotten or never known, endless or senseless, dimensionless, a vacuum in time, a ghost in space— nothing, in nothing, for nothing.

Here, people are squeezed between the place and the system, less important than the former and subservient to the will of the latter.

It is a lucky and rare patient—and a sad one—who *knows* that The Long Wait leads to the next wait. I have found that *knowing* one is waiting for nothing, however long the wait, makes for a shorter wait than believing one is waiting for something to end so there may be, then, a new beginning. Being fully prepared to wait for nothing makes time pass quickly, much like a long, deep sleep. The lucky patient hardly ever realizes he's lived.

APHORISMS OF A BURNED-OUT PESSIMIST

I have confronted the foul,
and we are all people.
I have been to the bottom,
and it is part of the human continuum.
When appearances tell you that nothing remains,
you either die or become an optimist.

Optimism is not in believing that
things will turn out well, objectively,
But in believing that one can face things,
subjectively, however they turn out.
Optimism is not in feeling good,
But in feeling that good has a chance to survive.
Optimism flows not from defeats
and bitterness or victories and joys of the past,
But in being here now, knowing that
the past has strengthened you.

Optimism is in believing there is a grand design
that holds eventual Good—for each of us.
All optimists are lucky people.
As all lucky people are optimists.

The lucky man neither works to live,
nor does he live to work.
His work is a necessary one part of his life.
He has difficulty deciding what is work
and what is pleasure, not because he
cannot recognize joy in leisure but because
he does not encounter drudgery in work.

The lucky man knows that the language
of computers will not replace the language of
        humans,

The hardware of technocrats will not
decelerate the thinking of thoughtful people,
The technological process will not obscure
the humanitarian ethos.
And the Group will not overwhelm the
person.

The lucky man is rarely asked to
climb a mountain of Moriah,
He is rarely forced to choose between
love and duty,
Between compassion and justice,
Between humanity and integrity,
Or between friend and friend.
When he is required to choose, he makes his
own decision.

The lucky man is judged for those things he did,
not for those things others believe he should have done—
For his accomplishments as well as for his failures—
For that which he attempted as well as for that in
which he succeeded—
For his lovely defeats as well as for his glorious victories—
For his intentions as well as for his credits—
For his credits in spite of his intentions—
And for the style and process as well as for
the content and achievements of his life.

The lucky man walks with the belief
that his friends are steadfast, in spite of
his defects, not because of his virtues—
In spite of his thoughtlessness,
not because of his generosity—
Not because of what he may give to them,
but because of what they must do for him—
Because they need him as he needs them.

The lucky man has been taught to
love, because he has been loved.
He has learned to care, because he
has known those who care.

He can give something he values,
because he has been given all that is priceless,
He has learned that there is never shame

in true emotion, never embarrassment
in true feeling, and never fear in truth.

The lucky man has a wife who believes
he is a lucky man.
He has children who, in their maturity, continue to
believe he is a good man.
He has parents who respect as well
as love him.
And he has brothers and sisters,
and uncles and aunts who do not envy his luck.
He has everything,
and he has this time to reflect and to understand.

PRIMARY CONNECTIONS

Scientists turn eventually to philosophy,
As theologians turn to Man,
As men turn to God,
As those who seek faith bring it,
As each man returns to the beginning,
As he turns inward to cope with the universe,
As he seeks to discover his being,
As he learns how the self reveals and illuminates.

PARADOXES

The butcher washes blood from his hands and then fondles the lamb he leads to the slaughter.

The Crusaders have killed in the name of, and for their faith in, God's only son.

Men wage wars, destroy the guilty and the innocent without discrimination or rancor, annihilate all in their paths—for the glory of men and the sanctity of God.

Men behave as if means justify ends and have faith that their means cause them to be judged worthy of glorious ends.

Men pray that their unholy means are just in the face of holy ends, which would not only cause means to justify ends, but would cause ends to cleanse and beautify means.

A man hates the woman he loves, and a woman loves this man she hates—he behaving knowingly about that which he knows so pitifully little and she responding haltingly about that which she was born to experience and to understand.

The fool is sure he has the answer because he sees no alternatives, while the wise man becomes less sure in his wisdom, less decisive by his experience, less adroit in knowing black from white, and hardly ever daring to choose a shade of gray—yet wise enough to appreciate the talent some fools have for making the correct answer and for performing the heroic, the perfect, act.

Man has faith that he will be judged, not by his behavior, but by his justification of his behavior—as he is compellingly certain to judge all other people, not by their infinite desires, but by their finite acts.

A man may see himself as an unfolding, developing creation in the process of becoming. Who has not, at some grand time, viewed himself with pleasure and satisfaction? A wonderful feeling, yet one that few men have the strength and pride and love for all men to admit!

Living is a paradox, but life is a simple and self-revealing truth. Man follows his mortal leaders, but invents and destroys his immortal ones. He has conquered pain and hunger, but not torture and debasement. The wisest among him learn from living, while the proletariat learn from their wise men; and those who find learning most difficult are admonished to learn from living.

Paradoxes and puzzles obtain when outsiders stare at insiders and insiders gaze at outsiders. There will be fewer such conflicts when both outsiders and insiders disregard those conditions that cause relationships to occur and concentrate on whatever factors there are that contribute to the continuance of these interactions and involvements.

Men will struggle with fewer paradoxes when we better understand that, inevitably, each of us must—and should—do certain things, in spite of the knowledge that there is no excuse for such behavior; and we must not—and should not—do other things, in spite of clear justification to the contrary.

Perhaps the ultimate paradox may be that there are no Children of Light and no Children of Darkness. Men separate from each other in many ways and forms, but not by divisions of true belief or goodness and evil motives or falseness. All men have confronted the Way of Darkness and all men have attained truth. All men are neither Good nor Bad, all having been Good and Bad. And if judgments are made of these matters— including judgment of this judgment, a final paradox—they will not be made by mortal man.

ON INSTITUTIONS

In the special world of institutions,
One learns the rules only by breaking them,
And is happy if he's not depressed,
With full control when not unhinged,
For he's alive just because he's not dead,
But dead while he lives.

HUMANNESS

Secretiveness is the handmaiden of anxiety
Anxiety is the enforcer of repression
Repression is the progenitor of violence
Violence is the catharsis of madness
Madness is the escape from reason
Reason is the revolt from chaos
Chaos is the sperm of control
Control is the harbinger of abuse
Abuse is the device of totalization
Totalization is the process of evil
Evil is the flight from humanism
Humanism is the hope for mankind
Mankind is the center of the being
Being is the life of the physical
Physical is the shell of the soul
Soul is the essence of the humanness
Humanness is the universal truth.

POINT-COUNTERPOINT

There is virtue in sin and sin in virtue.
There is good in evil and evil in good.
There is right in wrong and wrong in right.
And black is white.

The just are unjust and the strong are weak.
The foolish are wise and the hateful are loving.
The honest man lies, the cheat fulfills.
And the cowardly braves.

Laws are good, and to obey them is virtuous,
And to obey some is sinful.
Laws that permit a man to:
      devalue another man
      hold him in contempt
      remove his liberties
      lay bare his defenses
Or to:
      destroy his humanness
Are sinful, and those who believe in them are sinful.

Traitors may be evil, and to follow them is folly,
And to follow some is wise.

Traitors who are traitorous to the ideals of:
    War
    Murder
    Genocide
    Enslavement
    And humiliation
Are virtuous, and those who support them have virtue,
And we, who turn from their deeds, are less virtuous.

Philanthropy is piety, and to give is loving,
And to give can be prideful and self-serving.
Those who give to:
    Degenerates
    Institutional cases
    the Slothful
    the Putrid
    and the Tainted
Give neither to humanity nor to man,
Give not to human beings but to piousness.

They give to save themselves, not to serve their brothers.
They give to live at the expense of others who perish.
They give to become better as others are made worse.
Their virtue is sinful as their goodness is greedy.
    Each point has a counterpoint,
    As the wisest man alone knows his infinite
foolishness,
    As the just man understands his capacity for
injustice,
    As the thief never loses conviction he will walk
somehow,
    With the righteous.

    Each point is its own counterpoint.

MOUNTAINS TO NOWHERE

    I have climbed mountains but
missed reaching lovely heights.
    I have scaled the precarious peaks while
stumbling on familiar ground.
    Man has accomplished much, but what
has he accomplished?
    We have done our job, but what
have we done?

Does it matter how high one climbs,
how hard he works,
how much he completes,
how difficult is his task?

For where does a man climb?
Why does he work?
What are his ends?
To what end are his means?
He who engages himself for the devil
finds something worthy in his slothfulness and
would accomplish proper deeds by his laziness—
and his industry further faults him,
While the good man can contribute only good.
He who believes that mountains are, themselves,
important and scaling them is, itself,
an accomplishment may know not the difference
between an object and its relevancy,
Nor the virtue in thought,
Nor the dependence of Man to his ideals.

STRANGE ALLIES

The man who suffers with his institutionalized
brothers and the man who hardly knows they exist
Both seek alternatives to commitment—
The former to save humanity,
The latter to conserve prosperity.

One educator finds little comfort in new school laws,
modern buildings, and fashionable slogans,
While another expects few improvements with increased
school support, greater attention to individual needs, and
community participation;
The former, who has learned that laws, and architecture,
and words do not guarantee progress,
And are not harbingers of greater wisdom and behavior;
The latter, who wishes only to return to the halcyon
days of memory so dimmed,
That he no longer sees the pinched faces, the pained
expressions, the empty school desks, and the totally controlled
environment,
In his mind's eye.

One citizen votes not to tear down the old and build
a new state institution,
As another votes not to build a new rehabilitation center.
The former, who is resolved to witness the destruction
of all institutions.
The latter, who is committed to a philosophy of individual
responsibility and governmental passivity in these matters.

A mental health professional seeks support for a
community-based program, while another for an institutional
program,
Both being against the construction of a new community
mental health center.
The former, because he visualizes those plans as the
portrait of a mental institution at conception.
The latter, because he visualizes those plans as the
enemy of his institutions' justified share of the public
treasure.

We ask ourselves if there is any profit for men to
ally themselves with one another when their destinies differ,
But they share common tactics and immediate goals.
We must ask if a cause is violated as allies are recruited
who are not allies,
And as enemies are identified who are not enemies.
Essentially we need to review our fateful journeys;
those who have joined us, and why they remain; and those
who have left us, and why they departed.

This is but another way of asking for an audit of means
and ends,
And of reminding each other that—in our struggles—
the means must be the ends.

BENCHMARKS OF CIVILIZATION

Mutism, nudity, and fetters are the enemies of the civilized.
And language, clothing, and freedom are the benchmarks of
civilization.
Language prompts a man to engage symbolically with other men.
Language prompts him to communicate that which he cannot
demonstrate,
To demonstrate that which he must communicate.
Clothing permits a man to walk among other men.

Clothing permits him to seek out the larger society,
To physically and spiritually go beyond his room and his pallet.
Freedom persuades a man that he is a man.
Freedom persuades him that there is dignity on earth, that man's
civilization is for all men.

What are the benchmarks of civilization?
Noise and talk, and laughter,
And crying, and sighing, and responding,
Giving answers, asking questions, prompting,
And seeking out to touch, to hold, to caress.
A cover, a dress, a robe,
A cover to hide the flesh, and free the body,
A cover to soothe the wounds, to conceal man's trembling
uncertainty,
Man's unshakable humility and unquenchable vanity.
And freedom!
Freedom to walk, to talk, to think.
Freedom to contemplate one's destiny and contrive one's future.
To leave, to stay,
To wait, to flee.
Freedom to disdain that which another man loves dearly.
And freedom to cherish that which all other men disdain.
Mankind, if you yet have one,
Return all the incarcerated to civilization.

ANTECEDENTS AND CONSEQUENCES OF EVIL*

The public has conquered, and the danger is gone.
The burden is lifted, and our souls have won.
In Boston, little old ladies will lay aside their
tennis shoes.
While in Syracuse, men will breathe easier,
And women will return to household chores with
stronger spines and softer smiles
The seals will live and long live the seals.

The baby, cuddly, snow-white seals will live until—
They live a month,
And until they turn brown,
And until they weigh eighty pounds,

---

* Written on October 25, 1969, a day when *Time* (p. 35) and the *Syracuse Herald-Journal* (p. 4) reported on the Canadian Government's change in policy regarding the killing of seal pups.

And until they leave their mothers,
And until they are no longer as cute as they were.
Then their time comes, the once-baby cuddly, snow-white seals
will not be—
Clubbed to death
or
Skinned alive
or
Garroted

When their time comes, these two- or three-month-old
brown animals will be
Shot:
With a modern clean rifle,
or
With sleek and swift arrows.
And when their time comes, heed
Prime Minister Trudeau's admonition:
"Those who protect won't be shown the same photograph of
baby seals with their big blue or brown eyes."

And when their time comes, protect your government,
Complained Minister of Fisheries Davis, for:
"A lot of young people in distant
Countries now think of Canada only in terms of
Seals."

A lot of young people in distant countries now
Think of the U.S.A. only in terms of
Vietnam, Chicago, and Selma.

And legions of people in all lands have thought:
Of Germany, only in terms of Nazis,
Of Rome, only in terms of lion pits,
Of U.S.S.R., only in terms of cancer wards,
Of Russia, only in terms of czars,
Of Chamberlain, only in terms of "Peace for Our Times,"
Of King John, only in terms of murder and deceit,
And of evil, only in terms of its ability to flood out
Goodness.

And the baby seals will lead mankind out of the wilderness.
And we will learn from them:
That evil thrives as the being is devalued,
That evil flourishes as it is rationalized,
That evil is Man's unique gift to the universe.

And that man will learn that he, and all men,
are judged and judge by that which makes us less than men,
By that which we hate, not that which we love,
By that which shames us, not that which gladdens us.
By that which is in our hands, not that which is in our
hearts.
By that which makes Man the animal, not that which makes
the animal Man.

The antecedents of evil require a disregard for life,
As he who is selected for debasement *must* be judged
A less equal being—
As consequently, he who so judges *must* be known
For that judgment.

WHEN YOU WALK WITH MOLOCH

When you walk with Moloch you pay,
More than you have,
You pay more than you know,
Less than he wants.

When you walk with Moloch you're with the devil,
Beelzebub!
Harpies,
And Yahoos.

Tread with care!
Step in slime, and you slip,
And you're trapped,
Engulfed.

Avoid state schools,
And state hospitals,
And state humanitarians,
And the state!

Each can make you wish for Moloch,
As each seeks to prove its goodness,
As each confirms the evil one,
And their gifts to his grand design.
And their murder of the kindest Brownie!

THE SMELLS OF HELL

Urine, trickling down naked flesh,
Running on smooth terrazzo,

Streams of hot piss inching toward the center,
As gravity pulls the wicked, sticky yellow,
From one hole to another,
Leaving its markers here and there,
Straight lines of dried piss,
Amid islands of old, old shit,
As attendants in gleaming white,
Step daintily to avoid the inmates,
While bravely they navigate through the oozing slime,
Gleaming white and untouched by human hands.

IN VACUO

Not real lives that move and mouth,
With skin so smooth and eyes near blue,
And hair that's thick and red or white,
Almost perfect, almost real.
Look through those eyes that look through you,
Those eyes that see through you to walls,
Through walls to walls through walls,
To you through you to finiteness.

And out of the mouth of a babe who spake,
Who saw those lives and knew their plight,
And saw that to see all is not to see,
And to love all is not to love.

Without guile or shame or layers of muck,
He taught us with trust and grace,
That there is terror to no end,
And nothing to infinity.

Together, inching to the puzzle,
We observed the shuffles, sought out the eyes,
Grasped some arms, embraced the flesh,
And found our answer.

They move and speak,
And look like Man,
So damned real,
Creatures, so man-damned.

VICTIMS AND VICTIMIZERS

In the back ward, who is the
victim, and who is the victimizer?
Each is; all are.

Who is dehumanized, who are the
cruel, and what is cruelty?
     Each is; all are; everything!

In any institution, if there is a
back ward, can there be anything but
back wards?
     In that institution, as the back
ward continues to exist, are all people
chronic victims and pervasive victimizers?
     In that institution, is not the
     term "back ward" a synonym for
     "institution"?

He who victimizes others is the victim
of his inevitable dehumanization,
     As he who is dehumanized must contribute
to the dehumanization of others.
     All men—willing or unwilling, knowing
     or unknowing—are victimized during the
     trials of living as their debasements and
     agonies victimize other men.
     Our way of living tests each man's
humanity, assaults it, and sometimes is its conqueror,
     As each man contributes
     to our way of living, to his
     own dehumanization, to the dehumanization
     of all others,
     As each man is his own victim and victimizer.

HUMAN ABUSE AND PERSONAL RESPONSIBILITY

The most beautiful words in our testament admonish us
not to wrong a stranger,
     For we were strangers in the Land of Egypt.
     These words are beautiful, not in the morphological sense—
for alone they are no more than ordinary words—
     But in their pristine elemental truth concerning man,
     His needs,
     And his anxieties.

Each man must live alone, must be consumed or learn to deal
with his being,
     And his mortality.
     Each man must find his way to:
          Fight the perils,

Ignore the demons,
Sustain a personal meaning of the Cosmos and his share
and place in it.

In the intimate sense, each man is a stranger to all
mankind.
In the social sense, too many men are total strangers,
Are globally estranged.
In the intimate sense, each man must face the omnipotent
alone and resourceless.
In the social sense, some men find their brothers and,
thus, find their strength and their contentment.

What responsibility do I have for you,
And you for me?
Am I my brother's keeper, and are all men my brothers?
If all men are my brothers, is there meaning to the word
"brother"?
What are the links between us, between your life and mine,
your past and my future?
What are our ties from:
The genetic pool,
The metaphysical relationship,
The human reality and mutuality?
Is each man a responsibility of all men, and is each man
responsible for all men?
Am I my brother's keeper, and are all men my brothers?

I am and they are.
We are intertwined as one.
And, as one, each man must pursue his individuality and unique
destiny.
And, as one, when my brother suffers, I suffer.
And, as one, until the world is righted for all people,
No one is safe,
Neither you, nor I, nor our progeny.
And, as one, each man is part of all men, as all mankind is
the sum and effects of each man.
My issue, my brothers and I are all mankind.

THE HUNGERS OF MAN

The creature cries first as the soul cries most persistently.
The needs of the flesh precede the yearnings of the heart.
When man's belly is satisfied, devotion
turns to the mind and the heart.

What man lusts for initially is not what he hungers for
    endlessly.
What man hungers for, each man must find in
    his own manner and in his own time.
And what each man finds does not satisfy
    the hungers, but deepens the pit.

What lies at the bottom of the pit,
    at the endless and formless need?
Is it triumphant and noble man,
    the vain and glorious seeker and taker?
Is it what man seems to appear as,
    or is it what man seems to avoid?
What manner of man stands there?
What manner of man is the Essential Man?

No man knows, yet each man must ponder
    that question.
No man dares know, yet all men dare not turn
    aside for such thoughts.
And, as each man seeks his answer,
    each man must offer his personal truths.

The truth that each man finds a relationship,
    as he seeks a oneness and uniqueness with self?
The truth that man is not an island,
    nor is he the sum of a maze of bridges?
The truth that man is not dust to return to dust,
    nor was he, nor is he eternal?
The truth that each man envisions his truth
    as he strives to deny the truths of others?

Man hungers to change,
    to plan for his future while he anchors his present.
Man hungers to grow,
    while he denies his need to change.
Man hungers to improve,
    while he behaves as if his reasoning is omnipotent.

Man hungers to be,
    to struggle, to find, to sense.
Man hungers to act,
    on his terms, or on the terms imposed upon him.
Man hungers to feel,
    with others and alone.
Man hungers to be alive.

ON MAN ALONE

While he's alone, and while we're together,
Most of a man's time is with but himself.
He is born alone,
And he'll go alone.
Amid the trumpets of life and the drums of death.
In joy and gloom, he is and he'll be but one,
Alone.

There's color and liveliness and zestful things,
To entice and seduce the mind and the heart.
But a man has pride,
As he resists his relatedness.
A man does engage himself in the swirl of life
With three billion others with him here,
And with each alone.

While each one comes,
And as each stays,
And goes,
Alone.

EZEKIEL'S PROPHECY

The Lord set Ezekiel in the midst of a valley,
        a valley full of bones.

And the Lord asked, "Son of man,
        can these bones live?"
And Ezekial answered, "O Lord God,
        Thou knowest."
And ever since, sons, and their sons,
        prophesied over dry bones.
For the Lord has caused men to reflect,
        on His work and on His omnipotence.
The Lord can cause breath to enter into you,
        can cause life.
The Lord can enter the valley of the dry bones,
        can lay sinews, bring up flesh and skin.
The Lord knows if the bones can live,
        when the bones should live.
But man has been commanded to have faith,
        and to have desire that these bones will breathe.

The bones that are the whole house of Israel,
    the whole house of the mad,
    the whole house of the feebleminded,
    the whole house of all the abused,
    and all of the houses of all of the dehumanized,
All of these bones will live in their own green lands,
    when man believes they could and should rejoin mankind.

FOR NOW, LAST WORDS

from the enemies of the *American Solid Waste Disposal Authority: Department of Subhuman Affairs*, and the enemies of those who romanticize the Therapeutic Illusion, and from the friends of all who try to remove the curtains surrounding crazy houses.

To hold a pen is to be at war.
        —Voltaire

Mark my words, young man, one day you will remember that it's a *human* universe we live in.
        —Martin Buber to Allen Ginsberg

    Living is plotless,
        As all lives are part of a Grand Design.

The first principle of living is to endure.
The last principle of endurance asks what was learned.

If you condemn one for things accomplished with the "left hand," you may miss the products of the "right."

    In the end,
        Artists should be judged by their best works,
        Individuals by their finest hours,
        And societies by their worst behavior.

    Bon chat, bon Rat—
    this book is good or bad.
    I, the writer, whose words
        flow from the blood and spittle of others,
        Disagree!

This book is good, in part,
*   and bad, in part,*
And, if I remove the bad (if I knew the bad),
*   I lose the good (if I knew the good).*
The whole is the book,
*   the parts nothing.*

Woe to the man who has eyes but will not see,
Ears and will not hear,
*   A brain, yet will not think.*
Woe to him and God bless us all.

If you ask me to explain this I won't,
I can't, and if I would try, you may be offended,
And if you would try, I may not understand.
Read as I wrote, for oneself.
In matters such as these, one must first explain,
and answer but to himself.

The jaundiced man might conclude that, for functional efficiency, good works should be observed microscopically and evil deeds with a telescope;
    But, for self-improvement, probably vice versa.

He who purposefully turns away from success,
*   and seriously dogs failure,*
*   has a passion.*

The ultimate creative act lies not in its freedom of expression, but in its discipline, not in the unfoldment of one's self, but in the control— and, as this process requires focus and thoughtfulness, it must exist in, its necessary dimension must contain, freedom and openness, self-expression, novelty, and rule-breaking.
    And, the parts do not contradict the whole.

Each man must first discover his magic to find his passion.

Since the beginning, I have been engaged in but one work, sections of which have been published as research monographs, papers, polemics, prose, verse, and books. The focus of my work is Man, his capability for changing, his perfectability.
    The mission of my work is to reform the human race.

There is no end to the horror,
This closing is nothing more than a technical break,
The chapter is completed but the madness will continue,
For, as all chapters must end, so too must life and death remain,
And so, too, will evil persist and cruelty endure.

CHAPTER 5

How to Destroy Lives by Telling Stories

Someone once told Rabbi Mendel that a certain person was greater than another whom he also mentioned by name. Rabbi Mendel replied: "If I am I because I am I, and you are you because you are you, then I am I and you are you. But if I am I because you are you, and you are you because I am I, then I am not I, and you are not you.

Author Unknown

GOD AND POPEYE

Perhaps there is no more human activity than the telling of stories. Perhaps nothing better characterizes the human being than his ability to tell stories. The rational person exhibits his humanity by telling rational stories, while the religious person explains and guides his life by stories from the Scriptures. And where our ancestors sought to understand the world by telling stories of giants on the backs of turtles, scientists today tell stories of a Big Bang and relentless entropy. People seem driven to capture or construct their reality through stories. Each of us has a memory filled with stories which explain the world and ourselves, stories of Santa Claus and storks delivering babies, stories of our origins and hopes, stories of misplaced ambitions and good and bad excuses. When a child is born, no developmental milestone is as eagerly awaited or as crucial to attain as the miracle of language. And what is so astonishing is that, soon after birth, almost every child is on the way to being a teller of stories. In a fashion and with a suddenness which even the experts don't fully understand, only the truly exceptional baby fails to develop an elaborate system for communicating. Hence, almost all people participate in the human drama of storytelling.

It is a drama, of course! It is the drama which binds people to a common cause, as it is the drama which separates others and leads to conflict. Our stories not only stir people to want to live together but also to want to live apart—to make war, to kill. While there are people who live by the word, and while there are still some who would die for it, too

---

This essay will be published in the *Journal of Psychiatric Treatment and Evaluation*.

many of us are eager to kill if the right words are spoken, if proper orders are given. Consequently, those few people who do not have stories have, instead, grave troubles. It's probable that, more than anything else, their inefficient language causes trouble for people who are mentally retarded. And it is certain that the language the rest of us employ so effortlessly deepens those troubles. We tell stories about people who can't tell stories, people who can't stop us from telling our stories about them. Our stories have been known to kill the mentally retarded.

Because language has such power and importance, and because not to have it is to be in such serious trouble, I want to spend some time thinking not so much about retarded people as about the stories we tell, what kinds of consequences stories have, and what guidelines there might be to steer us through the inescapable dilemmas of human language and life. Because their inability to use language defines and causes trouble for people who are mentally retarded, because we live in a world constructed of stories and the mentally retarded cannot tell their own stories, and they cannot stop us from telling destructive stories about them, I want to concentrate here on stories as both antecedent to abuse as well as reflection of concern. In this way, I intend to build a case for stories as the context in which to understand the harm we cause other people, even those whom we profess to regard as brothers.

When God says, "I am," and when Popeye says, "I am what I am," both are affirmations that everyone—that even God—has and tells stories which define us. When God says "I am," He warns us of course that there is nothing more to be said, that He is everything. But when the sailor says "I am what I am," he, too, announces that nothing more need be said—imperfections notwithstanding—that you could take him or leave him, but if you take him, you must take the total person, the coarseness as well as the good nature, the spinach with the muscles. You can't have one without the other. That's why, while "I am" is the most serious story, "I am what I am" is the most serious individual's story. A person is defined by the stories he tells about himself as well as the stories that are told about him. But sometimes, one's definition of oneself is challenged, and this signals the beginnings of abuse.

Language is such a miracle! It begins with the infant, who very soon after birth achieves a sophisticated system for communicating. Language stirs people to make love, to initiate wars, to lay their lives down for their country, or their God, or their youth, or their excesses. Language drives away boredom, enriches our lives, makes life worth living. Language also hurts, may make one's life unbearable. Language can kill! Nothing is more certain than that there are inescapable consequences of language. That is, one can rarely if ever say, "I'm sorry" and, thus, patch things up as if nothing had occurred after announcing to a lover that the relationship had ended. One can't simply say, "I didn't mean it" and get away with it after telling someone something for his "own good." One can't always say, "I made a mistake," after declaring that so and so is mentally ill or he or she is mentally retarded. Writers live to produce language, others have died to rid themselves of mischievous language. Is it any wonder that telling false stories about people can destroy their lives? Is it any wonder that the process of abuse is initiated at the invention of a disease assigned to a person? By merely telling a story, the scene is set for abuse.

Once upon a time, there was an old woman who lived alone in a very old house which had been her father's house, which had been his father's house. Everyone in the town said that she had a mattress full of money. One night while she slept, three young men stole into the house, killed the old woman, and tore open the mattress. They found old feathers.

Once upon a time, an old man and an old woman lived together in the same house for sixty years. When the old man died, the couple's children decided that the old woman couldn't take care of herself any longer. She needed "care." They placed her in a nursing home, although she didn't need "care" until after she was placed there.

In the first of these stories, the intention was to do harm. In the other, good. But *both* stories about these old people had evil consequences. Intentions aside, stories which are not true usually have evil consequences. Abuse is to be expected from stories about mattresses filled with money. The most benign consequence of such a story is that it is made false, that the thieves and murderers find out after invading her privacy that the old woman doesn't have any money hidden in a mattress. The most benign consequence of doing something for someone's "good," in spite of that person's objections, is that the "busybody" doesn't get away with it. When Socrates said that you can't have good ends from bad means, he must also have meant that you can't do people good if you lie to them or about them, if you invent stories about their lives.

Centuries ago in this country, there were stories about women who were witches, women who cast spells or who gave birth to calves. Such women were hanged, not because they broke any laws, not because they weren't church-going or honest, and not because they didn't watch over their families. The women were hanged because they were witches, and witches were hanged. That was surely not history's first example, but murdering witches illustrates what can occur when abuses are invented to deal with invented diseases. In many quarters, a "67" means "educable mentally retarded," and stories are told about the "educable mentally retarded." And a "44" means "trainable mentally retarded," and stories are told about those people. In 1969, 200,000 people lived in state institutions for the mentally retarded, and one of the stories about virtually all of those people was that they were not able to take care of themselves out of the institution. And while there are fewer people in such institutions today, that same story persists for those who remain there. Indeed, by definition, most people in institutions are there today because they are presumably unable to manage their affairs competently, if at all, in the larger society. *We* wrote that story, presumably on their behalf.

When God says, "I am," He tells us to hear in our hearts what He says, and see with our souls what He does. He informs us that He is everywhere, that He is everything, and that we should know Him from the stories which are told about Him, all the stories, even those which mortal man *can't yet fathom*. And Popeye? Popeye isn't merely the spinach-eating strong man. He's also what he thinks about Olive, and what she thinks about him. And not only is he defined by his friends, but by Bluto, too, and by Popeye's other enemies. The stories about us, true and untrue, those we tell and those which are told about us, represent the substance of the human dictionary. That's why it has been said that to know all is to understand all and, thus, to forgive all. That's why it can be said that no one ever has the complete story. Hence, we had better be careful about what incomplete stories we tell.

INVENTED ABUSES FOR INVENTED DISEASES

Stories based on false premises are almost *necessarily* abusive. Of course, not every abuse is of this kind. Old women are murdered in their beds by people who neither know them nor the stories about them. My point is that invented stories often cause a lot of harm, and rarely if ever do any good. And the other point is that invented stories—i.e., invented diseases—lead to invented treatments, which never do anyone good and often do them a great deal of harm. Virtually any treatment designed to deal with an invented disease is abusive because it is based on a story which isn't true. Even when we invent a story that compliments a man, that announces his wisdom or courage, it will cause him to suffer eventually. If we try to convince our child that he plays the fiddle like Heifetz or the piano like Rubenstein, it's all very nice until reality inescapably reveals itself. Sometimes in our eagerness to be "nice" to people, we impose burdens upon them which are as hurtful as if we wanted to hurt. *We must be true to people.* And, consequently, our stories about them must be true. Of course, there are dilemmas, which I will get to but not deal with well.

Mental retardation is an invented disease, an untrue and unnecessary story about a large group of people. In some families, old age is an invented disease, while in other families it is an honored state of being.

In some families, manual work is an invented disease, while in other families it is an honored occupation. But *always*, mental retardation is an invented disease. That is, to understand the disease of "mental retardation," one needn't be a neurologist, a psychologist, a social worker, or a teacher. Of course, to do something about neurological impairment, it's good to have a neurologist handy, as it's good to have a teacher available if a child is waiting to be taught. But mental retardation, itself, can't be appreciated by a study of marbles and holes or neurons and dendrites. Mental retardation, *itself*, requires the study of our prejudiced inventions about certain people who have wires loose or who read poorly. Illiteracy is real. Blindness is real. However nonrevealing and misinforming it may be, the 50 IQ is real. The chronological age of 80 is the truth about the octogenarian. But mental retardation is an invention, an untrue story. And as nothing good obtains from such untrue stories, the treatments for mental retardation are necessary inventions and, consequently, are always abuses.

WHAT PRACTITIONERS SHOULD KNOW

I cling to the conception of practitioners who are determined to benefit society, who are less interested in finding out whether a person can or can't be helped. The role of the school psychologist should be more to find a way for the child to profit from the regular class than to find the law or the reason to place the child in a special class. The role of the teacher is to find a way to help teach the child rather than to find a reason for excluding the child, physically or psychologically. I cling to the belief that practitioners should develop optimistic stories concerning their clients. But I say that every person is entitled to have only true stories told about him! Yes, but I also admit that there are dilemmas here. For example, parents should never tell trivial stories about their own children. Indeed, their stories about their children should be more on the grand side, if not so grand as to mislead or burden the child. Parents should tell stories for their children to live up to and not stories to shame them and to live down. And that's what professionals should do, tell stories that their clients will want to live up to. Quite literally, the intention of therapy is to get people to change their stories, to rescript their lives, *to learn*, which is merely another way of saying *to change*. But what does a therapist do when the man in the bughouse proclaims, "I'm Napoleon"? Is the only goal of therapy to correct a false story? And if so, how is it accomplished? Do we shock it out of him? Or condition it out of him? Or drug it out of him? Or beat it out of him? Possibly, the man is entitled to his fantasies. Maybe he is Napoleon, even if not the same Napoleon who fought the battle of Waterloo. Maybe the therapist deals with Napoleon well only when he remembers the Golden Rule: "You should believe and tell stories which, if you were in that person's shoes, you would be willing to have told about you." That is, telling someone's story is also believing your story. And so the question is, "Could there be an institutional story, a Willowbrook or Pennhurst story, that someone—client, staff, someone who knows—would want to live up to, or own up to?"

Many of our books and discussions in the field of mental retardation seem to concentrate on what can be done to our subjects. But ironically, the most important research question we have is what can be done to help those who aren't retarded to live more compatibly with those who are retarded. The obsessive commitment of professionals to remain outsiders is a logical and absolute barrier to our ever becoming important in the lives of our clients. For example, what can we tell the couple whose marriage is troubled by the presence of a severely retarded child? Is there a curriculum for marital happiness? Not really, yet we think it is important to have our students learn about the "Impact of Mental Retardation on the Home." Retarded people have problems of mobility, perception, articulation, reading, and arithmetic. But these are not the problems that students of mental retardation need to address. Mobility problems of the mentally retarded will be solved by the architects and by the application of the sort of technology that makes travel on the moon possible. In a sense, that is a trivial problem, not that a child or "anyone" can solve such a problem, but that we have sound methodologies for tackling such problems in the same way that the cure of some cancers is trivial. The serious problems we have in the field of mental retardation are the ones related to the cultivation of moral attitudes and to securing respect for the rights of others, and not merely in complying with the laws guaranteeing such rights. Our scholarship in the field of mental retardation hardly touches upon these serious problems, except to the extent that it "proves" what *doesn't* help, how administrative strategies *break down*, and what *not* to try. Of course, there are "intuitive" understandings we have of what it is to be intelligent and what it is to be retarded. Not only professionals but *all* people think of *something* when they hear the word "retarded." That's the point! While ranging widely in quality and frequency of such thoughts, there are common understandings which transcend occupational level and even personal involvement. And although these thoughts can dominate and blind us unless we attend to them very carefully, they also help to keep us honest, because they give us a sense of what we actually think in contrast to the modish words we usually employ. At times, science and scholarship curiously muddle our comprehension. That is, science and scholarship make it easy for us to compose and tell nonrevealing, unrelated, or erroneous stories ostensibly connected with mental retardation. Of course, science deepens understanding and increases knowledge, but there is also a sense in which science may have nothing to do with ordinary experience, such as what it means to be a person labeled mentally retarded. We must be careful lest science leads us away to its own lofty but irrelevant domains. For example, science tells us that black is not a color, but the absence of color. What are we to make of this? Sensible people entirely disregard such information. The thing to realize is that neither science nor sensible people are wrong. Science has discovered something important about the portion of the electromagnetic spectrum which is detectable by human eyes. However, science makes no contribution to the ordinary person's deliberations in choosing new clothes or cars because those are deliberations which, by their nature, can't be facilitated by increased knowledge of the properties of light. A harmonious wardrobe is not based on a knowledge of optics. But this is not to say that we would want the lenses for our eyeglasses to be designed by fashion experts based on their knowledge of colors. The scientist teaches that matter is "mostly empty space." Then, if I go to the refrigerator after stocking it with groceries, what should I expect to find? "Mostly empty space" in refrigerators means "no food," even though that's not what the scientist means. While saying something true, the scientist obviously isn't speaking about refrigerators. Science can illuminate the universe as well as muddle our tiny portion of it. Consequently, we have to remind ourselves of our subject, *mental retardation*, and make sure that it is being illuminated rather than distorted or obscured. In mental retardation, the problems to be addressed must be problems which arise in *life*, not in the laboratory. Neurologists have much to learn from studying mental retardation, but mental retardation must not be confused with neurology. Certainly, there are inquiries which can be most satisfactorily addressed in the laboratory. If not exclusively, we may profitably study intelligence and learning in the laboratory. But such research questions are no more about retarded people than they are about any other people. Consequently, when we call upon the laboratory sciences, we must understand that the questions we ask, however important they may be, are removed from the direct study of mental retardation. Scientists curing mental retardation is the quintessential science fiction story in our field.

PREVENTING ABUSES

There may be some truth to a story which nevertheless leads to abuse; the old woman indeed had a mattress, never mind the lies about what was in it. Then the question is, "How can we make sure that we tell "true" true stories about people? Any intervention based on the premise that a person can't learn anything is a story almost certain to destroy that person. The story that a person's condition is hopeless, or that mental retardation is incurable, or that mental retardation is genetic (i.e., in the same way that Tay-Sachs disease is genetic) are either not at all or not sufficiently true and, thus, can destroy people. Practitioners, administrators, and policymakers need to be guided by the conviction that human capability is educable, that there are procedures and conditions and stimulations which can bring out an individual's capabilities for changing. And abuses are prevented when individuals are given opportunities to contribute to and not merely to cope with society. Abuses are prevented when more of us behave as if people can learn, but even more so when we vigorously support each person's right to his fullest development possible, irrespective of the course of his life or his actual contributions to society. It is with that belief in human educability as well as in our common relatedness and natural rights as human beings that people find ways to prevent abuses. Such stories truly prevent abuse.

REDISCOVERING THE 19TH CENTURY

The story I heard was that Indonesia has but one inconsequential residential facility for a few mentally retarded children, located near Jakarta, its largest city. The story I heard was that the institution, as the country itself, was very poor and scientifically backward, and that I should not expect to see much there. There was truth to that story but, as I learned, even more that was untrue. Here again was a story which was not only descriptive but diagnostic; while the facts about this Indonesian institution were true, what I was led to believe was untrue. Constructed from my notes from that visit several months ago, this is the "true" story, or as much of a true story as somebody could give who hardly knows the country, its history, or what it thinks about itself.

Indonesia is the fifth largest country in the world. Then how could it be that this place we were about to visit was the only institution for multiply handicapped children in the entire country? How could it be that an ordinary looking house for 16 children is *the* country's institution for multiply handicapped children? They also told us that this was our lucky day: the Rupiah is devalued approximately a third and we're sitting on a hotel bill which, therefore, will be reduced a third. But if we're so lucky, why don't we feel lucky sitting in the back seat of a car that is propelling us back in time to an institution, the likes of which were more commonly seen in rural America 100 years ago. And as we ride on that bumpy and dust-generating road, with windows closed in order to keep out the choking pollution which hangs heavy everywhere and remains until the car is far out of the city, we sit frozen, hoping that our faces do not betray the anxieties which we're trying to keep in check. We don't want to insult Julie, our volunteer guide. So, with eyes darting here, then there, we fill ourselves with exotic scenes of lush vegetation pushing against homes made of paper and sticks. And everywhere there are milling people; everywhere there are teeming mobs. And the amazing thing is that everyone seems to be doing something; everyone seems busy. The car moves too quickly to figure out what is going on, so we hardly have time to notice that it's midday; yet, the children too are on the streets. We hardly have time to think about why the children don't appear to go to school and why the adults aren't working someplace. But don't misunderstand, this is not like a scene in New York's or Detroit's ghetto. In America's ghettos, no one seems to be moving, everyone stands still, seems frozen except when something bad is happening, then chaos is boss. We've been driving approximately 40 minutes. There are more open spaces here. We see people who must be farmers working what must be their fields. The air smells cleaner. Some of our anxiousness is submerged, possibly because the fresh air and real countryside cause us to forget for the moment how many people are needed to support one of us in the style to which Americans have become accustomed. We've forgotten for the moment how many people here seem to live by the narrowest of margins, without any support from industry, government, or even the elements. And as we're thinking about these matters, the car slows down, makes a sharp right, and stops. We're here. We had to travel 13,000 miles to learn again what our forefathers knew, what the Amish know, and what we know in our souls. But while everyone knows what we're about to say, it seems that only those whose religions require them to believe it actually believe it. That's why the Amish don't need to read this, and that's why we don't expect many of you to buy this story.

The institution was built about eight years ago. Before that, nothing of a group residential nature was provided for such children. What happens to the thousands of others in this country who are born very delicate and very handicapped is anybody's guess. You don't rule out the possibility that some of those children do survive and are cared for by family or others, and I won't rule out the possibility that thousands of children die needlessly because there is no one to care for them or to fix their broken spines or misfunctioning enzymes.

We're met at the door by the nurse in charge. She's an old woman, recently retired from a position in a general hospital. She's assisted by eight or ten young women who are also called nurses, but who probably don't have any formal nursing training. There's also an old man who serves as some sort of caretaker for the facility.

The main floor consists of a couple of small dormitories, a staff dining room, some sort of a reception room, possibly another small room or two. The cribs are lined up side by side. And that's it.

In some respects, this institution is exactly like Willowbrook, Belchertown, Fernald, and the others. Of course, it's much smaller; there's hardly anything to this place. Of course, there's also nothing here for the residents to do. It's a typical institution. But to conclude that is to miss the point, to construct an erroneous story.

We go from crib to crib. One blind child is trying to get about. He's the only child who seems to have the freedom of the dormitory. We ask if he is being taught anything. No, there's no itinerant teacher of the blind to come to teach him. There's no Anne Sullivan for this child. We move on. In the next crib is a child with hydrocephalus. His enormous head tells us that there may be little hope here. Through Julie, our interpreter, we ask the head nurse whether a shunt operation was attempted. We are told that it was not only not attempted but is unknown. We move on to a child with beautiful eyes who lies in his crib staring. He seems to want to say something to us, but we don't understand Indonesian. We move on to the next crib, and the next, and then to the next room, and on to the next crib, and the next. We ask about the rest of the institution. But this is it. There is a second floor, which is a dormitory for the nurses. We chat for a few more minutes, thanking each other for the same reason: our visit. We are grateful, but they too seem grateful.

The ride back to Jakarta is quicker, quieter. Each of us is thinking about what we've just seen. We have been to an institution whose entire operating budget is 10,000 American dollars a year, less than $700.00 a resident. And we're soon going back to a land where yearly institutional budgets for 3,000 residents often run higher than 75 million dollars, $30,000 a resident, sometimes higher than $90,000 a resident. Of course, we know that the average Indonesian doesn't earn $700.00 a year, and if he did, so what; one cannot compare Indonesia to the United States in this regard. And we know that, in America, children with hydrocephalus are afforded shunt operations to sometimes prevent the devastating effects of this malady. And while we know that even 75 years ago in America, there was an Anne Sullivan for a Helen Keller, we know some other things too. We know that in our multi-billion dollar mental retardation system, children lie in beds unattended. We know that what happened between Helen Keller and Anne Sullivan was an official miracle. We know that institutions which spend $50,000 a year per resident still send their clients to bed without proper food, still can't find ways to provide their clients with clothes which they would own, still have dormitories which stink. We know that everything is supposed to be better in the United States, and lots of things are better in the United States, but not so many things are better in the United States for severely and multiply handicapped children.

How could it be that this country, which hasn't yet discovered shunt operations, a country that spends only $700.00 per year per child in an institution, a country whose capital city has open sewers, could have created an institution whose dormitories smelled sweet? How could it be that a country whose money was devalued a third during the few days we were there, whose average citizen doesn't read, whose institutional superintendent doesn't have a college degree, who doesn't know about Braille, who doesn't know about perinatology, who doesn't know about all the things which make life beautiful in the United States, can run a cleaner and more decent institution than we in New York State run? There might be a howl about the assertions here—a howl not only from commissioners of mental retardation but even from some of my friends who will point out all of the flaws in this argument. But I wonder if there would have been a howl from Jean Marc Gaspard Itard, Edward Seguin, Maria Montessori, Samuel Gridley Howe, or Albert Schweitzer. Was it really as bad as we'd like to say it was before the dawn of science? Are we as good as we like to think we are, as we marvel at the wonders created during this modern era? Or is it that while science does a lot of good, it does good in such a narrow way that only a very few or only a small part of each of us profit from it? Is the magic bullet of science miraculous for only the few with PKU, Rh, and the handful of others with specific and controllable conditions, while it ignores the throngs?

OTHER STORIES AND OTHER DILEMMAS

Stories about our people today are more important than ever before. In the 19th century, the diagnosis that someone was an incurable idiot would be known to the few who treated him, to his family, to possibly a handful of others. Today, in western society that information is stored by computers, can be transmitted anywhere, is retrieved instantaneously, and need never be destroyed or discarded. What happens in an Indonesian institution is learned by few of that nation's millions, which is a useful definition of the nontechnological culture. What happens at Willowbrook or Partlow is known by anyone who owns a television set and wants to listen to Geraldo Rivera. Stories are increasing at an exponential rate. Computers, telecommunications systems, direct dialing across the world, airplanes, the other modern wonders quickly spread untrue stories. Worse, whoever notices, much less believes, retractions? And it is the handicapped and other fragile people who are the likeliest and easiest victims of untrue stories in this age when everybody has "the right to know" and demands to know everything about anything. Of course, anyone—you or I—can be hurt. A teacher's notation about a clumsy first grader is filed to haunt an adult decades later. A computer fouls up, then refuses to desist spewing forth its erroneous information, thus causing one's credit to be impaired. How many untrue stories has the FBI filed? How many have been filed by the elementary school you attended?

Stories are told about women with big breasts, others about women with small breasts. Stories are told about male nurses, others about people whose parents were immigrants, or Jews, or alcoholics, or Anglo-Saxons. One man's story is his poison but, to another man, that same story is the antidote. One doctor's treatment is to cut the leg off, while another doctor tries to talk that same patient out of his neurosis. In King Farouk's mind, each of his issue was born with a birth defect, the female gender. He didn't want to hear about chromosomes, only male heirs to succeed him. Kings and pawns, every one of us has a story. Or better, each of us has many stories which comprise "the story." Here are a few from among the countless stories about how the mentally retarded are treated. But these together, even these and many more, do not tell "the story" about any one person, much less about the mentally retarded.

Recently, in a northeastern state, the Deputy Commissioner of Mental Retardation and Developmental Disabilities visited with a group of home owners in an affluent community. His purpose was to explain to those "good and substantial citizens" why the State had intentions to invite other citizens—mentally retarded people—to live in that home. The Deputy Commissioner felt the meeting had gone well, that the discussion was reasonable and the local citizens understood the State's point of view in the matter. He certainly never expected what happened only a few hours after he left the community. A torch was put to the home. What horrible stories had these "good and substantial citizens" contrived to drive them to arson?

This letter sent by a state official responsible for "quality of care" to another official responsible for "employee relations" tells another story:

Dear _____,

I am writing to call to your attention a significant problem in the current contract between the State and the _____ Employees Association which adversely effects the ability of a facility director to take actions which he deems essential for assuring quality patient care.

Recently, an employee at _____ Children's Psychiatric Center was charged with patient abuse as a result of an assault upon a fourteen-year-old child which necessitated several stitches in the child's face. The employee was found guilty and a penalty of two months suspension was imposed. When the employee returned to work, the Director of the facility, Dr. _____, decided to reassign him, at the same salary, to a function that did not involve direct patient contact.

The employee has challenged the director's decision and litigation has ensued, since the contract does not recognize the director's right to make such a reassignment without the employee's consent. In the judgment of the employee relations and legal staff of the Office of Mental Health, it appears that the employee will very likely succeed in his lawsuit and that the director will have no choice but to assign such an employee to his old job which involved direct patient contact.

At _____ Psychiatric Center, an employee was disciplined for ripping a patient's face with a can opener. The arbitrator permitted a *temporary* reassignment of unspecified duration of this employee as part of the penalty awarded. The director of _____ Psychiatric Center will confront the same dilemma that the Director of _____ Children's Psychiatric Center has already confronted.

While denying a director the right to keep employees with patient abuse convictions from direct patient contact may be protective of the employee's interests, it is a measure that seriously erodes the director's ability to be responsible for quality care within the mental hygiene facility.

The Commission on Quality of Care strongly recommends that a better balance be struck between the employee's right to continued employment and the patient's right to be saved from forseeable harm. Where an employee has been found guilty of patient abuse after all the due process safeguards provided by the disciplinary procedure, it appears to us that the facility director ought to have reasonable latitude in ressigning such an employee, at no loss of pay or other benefits, to functions that do not involve direct patient contact.

Sincerely,

_____

Chairman

Recently, in a large state institution for the mentally retarded in a northeastern state, a nonambulatory client was fastened to a hoist in order to transport him from a swimming pool to his wheelchair. In the process, the hoist snapped. The client crashed to the tile floor, breaking his neck and dying instantly. The next day, the State Department of Mental Retardation issued orders to have every such hoist inspected in every institution under its jurisdiction. What stories are created in attempts to humanize systems that must function in a manner similar to how the airlines function when a motor falls off a plane? Is there a story to normalize the "DC-10 syndrome"?

A teacher whom I work with has a child in her class with many problems, a fragile, handicapped, and neglected child. Because we live in a small community, and people who run things in the human services tend to know each other rather well, we were able to piece this story together about that child's family. This little girl and her brothers and sisters are on foster placement in the care of their maternal grandparents. Meanwhile, the children's actual parents are caring for five unrelated foster children. At the time of this account, those parents are enlarging their home in order to expand their foster care business. Everything is legal, or at least allowable. Of course, there are uplifting stories written and told about foster children and foster parents, but there are indecent stories, too, for situations such as the aforementioned to be enacted. Much of the interest in "child abuse" these days centers around what I call "unintentional abuse," the abuse which a parent usually inflicts upon a child, sometimes deliberately so, but even then without intent to abuse. However, every now and then, especially when the State or the County gets involved, parents behave like workers for the State, and then the abuse is indeed intentional. The difference between institutional abuse and parental abuse is usually the difference between intentional and accidental abuse. And while related, these are very different problems. They are similar, on the one hand, when the parent acts as a disinterested party might act, either for profit or to do harm. They are similar, on the other hand, when officials act as parents would, out of love or frustration, worry and concern, stupidity or madness. In either case, parents rarely act like state officials and state officials rarely act like parents. Rarely do parents and state officials abuse children for the same reasons. But in both types of situations, wrong stories about the children are the underlying culprits.

Quite recently, I was asked by the Attorney General of a New England state to serve as an expert witness on behalf of that state, which was defendant in one of the now-common deinstitutionalization cases. Not a week later, I was asked by the United States Justice Department, representing the plaintiffs, to be their expert on the same matter. I proceeded to point out to attorneys for both defendant and plaintiff that, as both had independently agreed that I was indeed an expert, wouldn't it be simpler, least expensive, and most logical for me to serve as a "true" friend of the court, an expert for *both* parties. No! Apparently, a person can be an expert only if he curses one house while blessing the other. I don't like such stories. A pox on both their houses. And besides, all of this litigation is becoming tiresome and doesn't seem to lead to much in the way of improved programs for plaintiffs. And also besides, the story is getting around that every decent gesture and act must be witnessed in court. If that's what we've become, nothing can save us. Then we're doomed.

I serve as President of the Board of Visitors of our region's developmental center. As part of their orientation and inservice training, employees there are required to enroll in a course on "the gentle art of self defense." And from the looks of my mail, such courses are now the rage. For example, one such 30-hour program advertised as "nonabusive physical intervention," is designed "to teach control of aggressive outbursts of behavior." It was created primarily for "direct care mental health and retardation workers, as well as psychiatric nurses, with quick and non-violent solutions to such client behavior as biting, punching, kicking, choking, and the resistance of transport." The reader is informed that the course "will be thoroughly grounded in the principles of crisis inter-vention and team leadership." How ingenious! Who could have envi-sioned during one's innocence that combat training could be couched in such professionally appealing language? And for those who don't want or need the full dose offered by the 30-hour course, there is a 16-hour option, "designed to give the direct care force the ability to intervene effectively in an occasional problem situation." The last words of the program's originator insisted that, upon completion of the full program, each graduate will be able to protect himself and others from the following aggressive behaviors: punching, kicking, biting, choking, hair-pulling, being pinned on the floor, being choked on the floor, ankle and clothing grabs, flailing, and resisting transport. I'm not new to this work, and I don't get my kicks taking cheap shots at people who, for the most part, are as dedicated and decent as I aspire to be. Work with severely and multiply handicapped people is arduous. Work with aggressive and acting out clients is very difficult. But why do we have so many aggressive and acting out clients? And whatever the reasons for the inappropriate behaviors of severely handicapped people, what kinds of stories must we teach ourselves in order to prepare in such fiendish ways to deal with not only psychologically but, *by state definition*, physically defenseless human beings? And does a state teach its employees about mental retar-dation when it inflicts such a course, such a story, on its hundreds or thousands of employees? Even when such courses "work," they tell untrue stories about the people connected with them.

From the period between July, 1978 and June, 1979 at that institution which I serve, there were a total of 2,391 reported incidents involving the approximately 500 residents. An incident ranges in seriousness from a death to a scratch, a resident argument to the abuse of a client. By far, the most prevalent incidents were "accidental injury" (647) and "assault" (423). When, during the course of a year, there is one reported accidental injury per client, and when during the course of a year, the average client is assaulted, would you say that clients at this facility are abused? Not according to the state's recordkeepers. During 1978–79 only 13 abuse incidents were reported at our facility. The story at our developmental center, which in my view is a good facility compared to most others, is that residents fight a lot with one another or with staff, that they fall down and hurt themselves, and that they are fragile and need lots of drugs, lots of protection from each other and the outside world, and lots of doctors around to mend their wounds and their spirits. So far, that story is more or less true. It becomes a lie when we say, "Yes, there are too many accidents, too many assaults, too many medication errors, too many other errors, but there is hardly any abuse here."

Is this abuse, as reported by my colleague, Wolf Wolfensberger, in a manuscript-in-progress:

> During the 1960's, Dr. _____, a pediatrician, distinguished hepatitis researcher, and chairman of the Vaccine Board of the U.S. Food and Drug Administration's Bureau of Biologics, had operated a research program at the _____ State School for the Retarded. In this project, retarded children between the ages of three and ten were experimentally infected with live hepatitis B. Despite all of the exposés of the atrocities committed at _____, Dr. _____ proposed as late as 1979 that retarded children should continue to be used as subjects in experiments designed to test out vaccines made from the diseased blood of hepatitis victims. A major rationale he advanced in support of this proposal was that because of crowding, unsanitary conditions, and poor personal hygiene, retarded institution residents would get hepatitis anyway.
>
> On top of the fact that German physicians were pronounced guilty at the WW II medical war crime trials for experiments of this nature, the ideology of rejection and destruction embodied in such a stance were further underlined by 1979 actions of the _____ Board of Education. In _____ state, governmental structures at various levels have waged systematic warfare against retarded people for decades, and tried virtually every ruse to exclude them from services other than institutions, and especially from education. The latest strategy, after all previous strategies had been ruled illegal, was to exclude those retarded pupils from the schools who had been ascertained as being carriers of hepatitis B—the very same condition with which Dr. _____ had infected the children at _____. The school board declared that these pupils posed a significant health risk to other children in the schools. After efforts to exclude these pupils from the schools were blocked by the courts, the board fell back on the next typical line of defense: segregation in separate programs. As far as the facts of the school board claims go, hepatitis B is generally thought to be communicated only through blood-to-blood contact, and the judge ruled that there was no documentation of even one actual transmission from a retarded pupil to another child. The profound irony in all this is that most of the pupils in question had contracted the disease as guinea pigs in Dr. _____'s researches. This kind of event illustrated the "blaming the victim" strategy: victimize someone, then use the inflicted affliction as an excuse for inflicting even further affliction.

There are more stories which I could tell. But a book would not be big enough to contain them all. Neither would a lifetime. I've written books, possibly too many, and papers, certainly too many, and I haven't been able to tell all of the stories I know which treat the problem of intentional and unintentional abuse, of sanctioned institutional abuse as well as unsanctioned child abuse. Those I told here are "merely" some which I recently learned about and which I haven't told before.

HOW TO REDUCE HUMAN ABUSE

Mental retardation is an invented disease. The only treatments possible for invented diseases are those which are themselves invented. And in that sense, all treatments for mental retardation are abusive. To be sure, lots of people have problems which can be treated, which a caring society will want to treat. And probably people who don't read well, specifically, or don't think well, generally, would benefit from treatments to ameliorate their disabilities. But in each such instance, the "disease" is not mental retardation, but something else. One way to reduce abuse is to better control our cravings for inventing diseases and, then, treatments to cure them. The best way to cure an invented disease is to forget it. The best way to reduce abuses of those people unlucky enough to have "caught" invented diseases is to offer no treatment, because abuse is the only treatment for an invented disease.

Another way we can reduce human abuse is to be *very* careful about the stories we tell about people. Invented stories are like plays. In very good plays, believable characters and situations are invented so brilliantly that even the actors believe the truth of the fiction they portray. In very good plays, not only for the audience but for the cast as well, invention replaces fact and, thus, becomes truth. So, too, with ingeniously invented stories concerning mentally retarded or fat people. Being fat today is an invented disease. Of course, Hitler's inventions became "true." So convincing was he that the Jews were monsters, that they became monsters to the citizens of the Third Reich. Hitler's response to the "Jewish Problem" was the correct response if he told a true story. Obviously, a sufficient number of people believed the story. And there are people today in our own country who yet believe that very story. And just as surely as Hitler tried, they would eradicate the Jews.

I assume that, since the first woman, there has always been a menopause. But today, the story is surely different from that first story. What was once a natural expected consequence in life is now treated medically as a disease. The illiterate's story has changed from a person not being able to read to one not being able to think, from being a common man to being mentally retarded. Before we became so affluent, what we didn't know wouldn't kill us. Today, we worry to death about what we don't know, even though we often don't know what to do now that we know what we didn't know. Thirty years ago, there had to be a fairly serious reason for a patient to be subjected to an electroencephalogram. There are so many people given such tests today that it is estimated that 15 percent of the total population have abnormal electroencephalograms. But our doctors don't know what to make of the enormous number of people with abnormal EEG's who are in every respect perfectly normal. Consequently, through the widespread usage of electroencephalograms, electrocardiograms, x-rays, and blood tests of almost infinite variety, we have uncovered more and more abnormal, *but irrelevant*, characteristics in people. Maybe we ought to go back to the idea that what we don't know won't hurt us. But if you won't buy that radical suggestion, maybe you will consider the possibility that what we do know can hurt us, especially if it encourages us to invent stories about ourselves. Maybe overall, Alfred Binet's test was good for civilization. But maybe also, it did and does mischief.

While we are attempting to reduce human abuse, we may keep our spirits up by remembering that people change very slowly. Of course, that's both good news and bad news. The bad news is of the kind which led Chrysler to announce that it was going under. That is, people change so slowly—even big-boss industry people—that with all the evidence and expertise available to them, Chrysler refused to believe that we didn't any longer want their big cars, that not only were the people worried that a big car would cost us 30 or 40 cents more a day to run but that, for any amount of money, we might not continue to get gas for our cars without a lot of waiting and struggle. Further bad news is that the principles of normalization, least restrictive environment, zero project, and mainstreaming will not easily be implemented because other competing principles must first die. The good news is that people inevitably change!

In this chapter, I have attempted to uncover the rules of story-telling.

A. Those about whom stories are told have:

1. The right to tell their *own* story. A man has the right to claim he is Napoleon. Children have the right to "explain" themselves with whatever fantasies they find useful. Even "madmen" have that right.
2. The right to have *true* stories told. Every human being is entitled to the story that he is educable.
3. The right to *good* stories. I am valuable. You are entitled to stories which confirm your value. Even criminals are entitled to stories which do not deny their value as human beings.
4. The right to withhold participation in another's story about them and, thus, the right to stick to their own story. **I am what I am!**
5. The obligation to live up to good stories. Parents try to live up to their stature as parents as children attempt to live up to parents' expectations.

B. Those who would tell stories about others must respect these rights. They have the obligation to:

1. Listen to the stories of those about whom they tell stories. Profes-

sionals must be especially vigilant, because they *always* have their own versions to "sell."

2. Tell good and helpful stories. Of course, there is always the question, "Help whom? And how?"
3. Tell true stories. We must be vigilant because professional truths tend to be irrelevant and are usually sterile. More often than not, the injuries we inflict are by neglect and not by design.
4. Take responsibility for the stories they tell. Professionals don't enjoy such responsibility. We blame "syndromes" or our victims.

C. Those who hear stories by or about others must:
1. Distrust bad or destructive stories.
2. Seek to *know* the *truth* of stories, and to *understand* the *good* of stories. Knowing and understanding can be entirely different matters.
3. Remember that they become (we become) the sum total of stories they (we) believe. It becomes their (our) story.
4. Dismiss *any* story presented as finished. Even dead peoples' stories are not ended. There are stories that need to be told about Hitler, about Sacco and Vanzetti, about Moses, and about the billions of all the "ordinary" people who left legacies and lessons to be learned.

Of course, most of the above rules are at odds with each other. Sometimes, we must fabricate a good story and *make* it true. That's why I said earlier that there are dilemmas which I cannot adequately deal with. That's why stories about a Hitler or an Idi Amin must be told, but must also be regarded as "over" if not "finished." Consequently, these are rules which are safe to have *only* accompanied by judgment, concern, friendship, and respect for all life and our common mortality.

There are other dilemmas. Not everything that is true about people belongs in the stories we should tell. It was true that Sacco and Vanzetti were Italian, but it did not belong in the story of what happened at Braintree that day. Of course, there shouldn't be harm in gratuitously throwing into a story a few extra facts, but the reality of human nature is that it can and does cause confusion and mischief. Consequently, good stories have to stick to the story; the "red herring" is never part of a good mystery. There should be enough complications in such a story to sustain interest without it, as in real life there always are enough complications to sustain interest without "red herrings." And that's why there are many things true about mentally retarded people which do not belong in the stories we tell about them, things such as IQs, head circumferences, distance between eyes, shoe sizes, national origin, and educational prognosis. As scientists and professionals we can only be helpful by putting our clients in a position to have stories in which head circumference is only relevant in a hat store, shoe size is only relevant in a shoe store, and national origin is perhaps relevant in choosing a church or bowling club. And we will only be helpful when IQ is hardly ever relevant. As for educational prognosis, our job is not to predict such futures but to start enacting a story in which they unfold naturally and compellingly, as in a *good story*. And of course, it is no crime when a good story ends happily.

The good news is that in between catastrophies, ideological wars, real wars, true stories and invented stories, ordinary life goes on. There is hope, even in the most fragile human being. And there is sustenance and stability because there is hope, but also because everyone knows that state management is horribly inefficient and, consequently, not much changes unless the masses want things to change. That is, when 100 years ago the "menace of the mentally retarded" was once proclaimed as the state's story, the people didn't believe that invention. The people don't easily believe lies any more than they believe true stories. Yes, the bad news is that things change slowly, but that's also the good news. The bad news is that ordinary life proceeds while people suffer horribly. But the good news is that ordinary life proceeds in spite of wars, lies, and other catastrophes.

In this chapter, I have attempted to indicate how words and language are important. I have attempted to show why stories must be true, why false stories—for bad *or* good—cause harm, how false premises lead to false conclusions, false treatments. I also tried to speak to the dilemmas which will not go away, but which can be understood better. That is, while what we say should be true, the laws of life are not like the laws of physics. The laws of life are rules of thumb, not rules of science; stories about people must be true but also deeper than the merely factual. To be decent, all human truths—truths about one's children, one's country, one's friends—require judgment and magnanimity.

Somewhere I once wrote that while illnesses are man's curse, handicaps (stigmas attached to illnesses) are his invention. I wondered then when we will learn the difference between what we must endure and what we bring upon ourselves. I complained that while we still have lots to learn about illnesses, we seem to have everything to learn about handicaps, that while not all illnesses have effective treatments, all handicaps are preventable and curable. Handicaps are conditions of the soul. Therefore abuse won't be "cured" by scientists, for the same reason that mental retardation won't be conquered by science; abuse is a disease of the spirit. When, earlier in this century, people looked to invent a war, they murdered an archduke. We've invented this disease, mental retardation, then we needed to invent treatments for the disease, now we strive to invent treatments for the treatments. We are all foolish people.

REFERENCES

Wolfensberger, W. Personal communication from manuscript in progress, Syracuse University, 1979.

PART II
DISABILITY

CHAPTER 6

Purgatory

All hope abandon, ye who enter here.

Dante

With a good deal of anxiety, I waited for the white-uniformed attendant to respond to my knocking and unlock the door to hell. And, in America, we have our own special inferno. I was a visitor there during the Christmas season, 1965, while studying five state institutions for the mentally retarded, located in four Eastern states.

As I awaited entrance to the building, which was a residential dormitory, my anxiety belied the ostensible situation. In the 18 years that I had been professionally active in the field of mental retardation, I had been to scores of institutions. I had served on numerous commissions to evaluate or advise such institutions. In fact, the building I was about to enter—and which terrified me now—was no stranger to me. Over the years, and for one reason or another, I had found it necessary to visit this building, never giving it any particular thought; one might say I had visited it thoughtlessly.

However, my fears were not the neurotic outcroppings of an unhinged mind. I had a great deal to be worried about, and my thoughts flashed back to the circumstances that brought me here.

In the early Fall of 1965, Senator Robert Kennedy visited several of his state's institutions for the mentally retarded. His reactions were widely published in our various news media, shocking millions of Americans as well as infuriating scores of public office holders and professional persons responsible for the care and treatment of the mentally retarded. Most of the laymen with whom I discussed his visits reacted to the Senator's disclosures with incredulity. For it is difficult for "uninvolved" people to believe that, in our country, and at this time, human beings are being treated less humanly and under more deplorable conditions than are an-

---

This essay was originally published in the author's *Exodus from pandemonium: Human abuse and a reformation of public policy.* Boston: Allyn & Bacon, 1970. A summarized portion appeared in *Look*, October 31, 1967. Parts were also published in R. B. Kugel & W. Wolfensberger (Eds.), *Changing patterns in residential services for the mentally retarded.* Washington, D.C.: President's Committee on Mental Retardation, January 10, 1969, and in G. Clark, M. Kivitz & M. Rosen (Eds.), *A history of mental retardation: Collected papers* (Vol. 2). Baltimore: University Park Press, 1976.

imals. A number of the "involved" citizenry—i.e., those who legislate and budget for institutions for the mentally retarded and those who administer them—were infuriated because the Senator reported only the worst of what he had seen, not mentioning the worthwhile programs that he undoubtedly was shown. Further, this latter group was severely critical of the Senator for taking "whirlwind" tours and, in the light of just a few hours of observation, damning entire institutions and philosophies.

During the time of these visits, I was a participant in a research project at The Seaside, a state of Connecticut regional center for the mentally retarded. The superintendent of The Seaside, Fred Finn, and I spent a considerable amount of time discussing, in particular, the debate between Senator Kennedy and New York Governor Nelson Rockefeller. We concluded the following: it does not require a scientific background or a great deal of observation to determine that one has entered the "land of the living dead"; it does not require too imaginative a mind or too sensitive a nose to realize that one has stumbled onto a dung hill, whether or not, as Cervantes wrote, it is covered with a piece of tapestry when a procession (of distinguished visitors) goes by; it is quite irrelevant how well the rest of an institution's program is being fulfilled if one is concerned with that part of it which is terrifying. No amount of rationalization can mitigate that which, to many of us, is cruel and inhuman treatment.

It is true that a short visit to the back wards (the hidden, publicly unvisited living quarters) of an institution for the mentally retarded will not provide, even for the most astute observer, any clear notion of the causes of the problems observed, the complexities of dealing with them, or ways to correct them. It is not difficult to believe that Senator Kennedy could not fully comprehend the subtleties, the tenuous relationships, the grossness of budgetary inequities, the long history of political machinations, the extraordinary difficulty in providing care for severely mentally retarded patients, the unavailability of highly trained professional leaders, and the near-impossibility in recruiting dedicated attendants and ward personnel. Further, I do not believe the conditions Senator Kennedy claimed to have observed were due to evil people. As Seymour Sarason, Professor of Psychology at Yale University, wrote in the preface to our book (*Christmas in Purgatory: A Photographic Essay on Mental Retardation*), these conditions are ". . .not due to evil or incompetent or cruel people but rather to a conception of human potential and an attitude toward innovation which when applied to the mentally defective, result in a self-fulfilling prophecy. That is, if one thinks that defective children are almost beyond help, one acts toward them in ways which then confirm one's assumptions."

However, regardless of their antecedents, I believe, as well as do thousands of others who have been associated with institutions for the mentally retarded, that what Senator Kennedy reported to have seen he very likely did see. In fact, I know personally of few institutions for the mentally retarded in the United States that are completely free of dirt and filth, odors, naked patients groveling in their own feces, children in restraints and in locked cells, horribly crowded dormitories, and understaffed and wrongly staffed facilities.

After a good deal of thought, I decided to follow through on what then seemed, and what eventually became, a bizarre venture. One of my friends, Fred Kaplan, is a professional photographer. On Thanksgiving Day, 1965, I presented the following plan to him. We were to arrange to meet with each of several key administrative persons in a variety of public institutions for the mentally retarded. If we gained an individual's cooperation, we would be taken on a "tour" of the back wards and those parts of the institution that he was *most* ashamed of. On the "tour" Fred Kaplan would take pictures of what we observed, utilizing a hidden camera attached to his belt.

Through the efforts of courageous and humanitarian colleagues, including two superintendents who put their reputations and professional positions in jeopardy, we were able to visit the darkest corridors and vestibules that humanity provides for its journey to purgatory and, without being detected by ward personnel and professional staff, Fred Kaplan was able to take hundreds of photographs.

Our photographs were not always the clearest. On the other hand, in these conditions of secrecy it required a truly creative photographer to be able to take any pictures at all. Although these pictures cannot even begin to capture the total and overwhelming horror we saw, smelled, and felt, they represent a side of America that has rarely, if ever, been shown to the general public and is little understood by most of the rest of us.

I did not believe it was necessary to disclose the names of the institutions we visited. First, to reveal those names was, assuredly, an invitation to the dismissal of those who arranged for us to photograph their deepest and most embarrassing "secrets." However, involved was not only a matter of promises made to altruistic people but also an avoidance of the impression that the problems exposed were and are local rather than national ones. I was completely convinced that in numerous other institutions across America I could and would observe similar conditions—some, I am sure, even more frightening.

Had I known what I would actually be getting myself into and had I known what abnormal pressures would subsequently be exerted upon me as a result of this story and my efforts to bring it before the American people, I might have turned away from that first dormitory entrance as I was, finally, being admitted; and I might have fled to the shelter and protection of my academic "ivory tower" to ruminate on the injustices prevailing in society. As it was, I was in no way prepared for the degradation and despair I encountered.

As I entered this dormitory, housing severely mentally retarded adolescents and adults, I was still reminiscing about Senator Kennedy, Governor Rockefeller, and our fateful Thanksgiving dinner, when an overwhelming stench enveloped me. It was the sickening, suffocating smell of feces and urine, decay, dirt and filth, of such strength as to hang in the air and, I thought then and am still not dissuaded, solid enough to be cut or shoveled away. But, as things turned out, the odors were among the gentlest assaults on our sensibilities. I was soon to learn about the decaying humanity that caused them. This story—my purgatory in black and white—which, ironically, was conceived of and written on the 700th anniversary of the birth of Dante, represents my composite impressions of what I consider to be the prevailing conditions of certain sectors of most institutions for the mentally retarded in this country. It is in the hope of calling attention to the desperate needs of these institutions and, thereby, paving the way for upgrading all institutions for the mentally retarded in all dimensions of their responsibilities that this study was undertaken and this story written.

Several things strike a visitor to most institutions for the mentally retarded upon his arrival on the institution grounds. Sometimes there are fences, once in a while with barbed wire. Very frequently, the buildings impress him with their sheer massiveness and impenetrability. I have observed bars on windows and locks—many locks—on inside as well as outside doors. As I entered the dormitories and other buildings, I was impressed with the functional superiority of the new buildings but, on the other hand, the gross neglect in many of the older ones. I have observed gaping holes in ceilings of such vital areas as the main kitchen. In toilets, I frequently saw urinals ripped out, sinks broken, and the toilet bowls backed up. In every institution I visited—with the exception of The Seaside, which will be discussed later—I found incredible overcrowding. Beds are so arranged—side by side and head to head—that it is impossible, in some dormitories, to cross parts of the rooms without actually walking over beds. Oftentimes the beds are without pillows. I have seen mattresses so sagged by the weight of bodies that they were scraping the floor.

Before I go further, it would be well to point out a crucial factor giving rise to the overcrowdedness, the disrepair of older buildings, the excessive need for locks and heavy doors, and the enormity of buildings and the numbers of patients assigned to dormitories. In 1962, the President's Panel on Mental Retardation estimated that approximately 200,000 adults and children were cared for in residential institutions for the mentally retarded. States and localities spent, at that time, $300,000,000 a year in capital *and* operating expenses for their care. At first glance, this appears to be a great deal of money and a cause for comfort, i.e., the mentally retarded have finally received their due. However, simple arithmetic tells us that $300,000,000 divided by 200,000 amounts to $1500 a year per person, or less than $30 a week, part of which is for capital development, *not only clothing, food, care, and treatment.* Nationally, the average per capita cost in institutions for the retarded was, in 1962, less than $5.00 per day, less than one-sixth the amount spent for general hospital care. Six states spent less than $2.50 a day per patient, while only seven states spent over $5.50 per day. In some checking that I have done recently, I learned that in our better zoos the larger animals require a much higher per capita expenditure. The average per capita daily cost for maintaining a retarded resident in each of the four institutions I first describe was at that time less than $7.00 and, in one state school, less than $5.00. In contrast, The Seaside, a regional center for the retarded sponsored by the Connecticut Department of Health, spent $12.00 daily for care and treatment of each resident. Although it may be true that money corrupts, it may be equally true that its absence is similarly corrupting.

> Inasmuch as ye have done it unto one of the least of these my brethren, ye have done it unto me.
>
> Matthew 25:40

All of the doors in institutional buildings visited that are used as living quarters for young children, and moderately and severely retarded residents of any age, have locks. These locks are on all outside doors as well as all inside doors. Many of the doors are made of heavy gauge metal or thick wood. It is routine, second nature, for attendants to pass from room to room with a key chain in hand unlocking and locking doors as they pass.

Many dormitories for the severely and moderately retarded ambulatory residents have solitary confinement cells or what is officially referred to, and is jokingly called by many attendants, "therapeutic isolation." "Therapeutic isolation" means solitary confinement—in its most punitive and inhumane form. These cells are usually located on an upper floor, off to the side and away from the casual or official visitor's scrutiny. (Coincidentally, a United States senator had visited a dormitory at a state institution three days prior to one of my visits there. In discussing this with him weeks later, I showed him pictures taken of solitary confinement cells in that dormitory. As one might expect, he had not been shown these cells during his tour and I believe he was not absolutely sure that I had not concocted this coincidence to impress upon him the urgency of my mission.) Isolation cells are generally tiny rooms, approximately

7' × 7'. Some cells have mattresses, others blankets, still others bare floors. None that I had seen (and I found these cells in each institution visited) had either a bed, a wash stand, or a toilet. What I did find in one cell was a 13- or 14-year-old boy, nude, in a corner of a starkly bare room, lying on his own urine and feces. The boy had been in solitary confinement for several days for committing an institutional infraction (as I recall, it was directing abusive language to an attendant). Another child, in another institution, had been in solitary confinement for approximately five days for breaking windows. Another had been in isolation, through a long holiday weekend, because he had struck an attendant. Ironically, in the dormitory where this boy was being incarcerated, I saw another young man who had been "sent to bed early" because he had *bitten off* the ear of a patient several hours previously. Apparently, it is infinitely more serious to strike an attendant (and it should not be misunderstood that I condone this) than to bite off the ear of another resident.

In one institution I saw a young man who was glaring at me through the screen of the door in the solitary cell, feces splattered around this opening. He, too was being punished for breaking an institutional regulation. In this particular dormitory, I had a good opportunity to interview the attendant in charge. I asked him what he needed most in order to better supervise the residents and provide them with a more adequate program. The attendant's major request was for the addition of two more solitary confinement cells, to be built adjacent to the existing two cells that, I was told, were always occupied, around the clock, day in and day out. Unfortunately, I have recent confirmation of the constant use of the solitary cells. Seven months after the above incident I revisited this dormitory. Both solitary confinement cells were occupied and there was a waiting list for other youngsters who were to receive this punishment.

I often saw restraints used with children. I observed many children whose hands were tied, legs bound, or waists secured. After discussion with a number of attendants and supervisors in the four institutions, I was convinced that one of the major reasons for the frequent use of solitary confinement and physical restraints was the extraordinary shortage of staff in practically all of these dormitories. The attendant who requested the construction of two additional solitary confinement cells was, with one assistant, responsible for the supervision of an old multi-level dormitory, housing over 100 severely retarded ambulatory residents. Almost in desperation he asked me, "What can one do with those patients who do not conform? We must lock them up, or restrain them, or sedate them, or put fear into them." At that point, I did not feel I had a response that would satisfy either him or me. I suffered in silence in much the same way, I imagine, men of conscience suffered upon reading Reil's description in 1803 of institutional problems that were astonishingly similar to those I encountered. He said then, "We lock these unfortunate creatures in lunatic cells, as if they were criminals. We keep them in chains in forlorn jails . . . where no sympathetic human being can ever bestow them a friendly glance, and we let them rot in their own filth. Their fetters scrape the flesh from their bones, and their wan, hollow faces search for the grave that their wailing and our ignominy conceals from them." My thoughts also went back to that anonymous writer who, in 1795, said, "A humanitarian is bound to shudder when he discovers the plight of the unfortunate victims of this dreadful affliction; many of them grovel in their own filth on unclean straw that is seldom changed, often stark naked and in chains, in dark, damp dungeons where no breath of fresh air can enter. Under such terrifying conditions, it would be easier for the most rational person to become insane than for a mad man to regain his sanity."

I sometimes hold it half a sin to put in words the grief I feel.
Alfred, Lord Tennyson

In each of the dormitories for severely retarded residents, there is what is called, euphemistically, the day room or recreation room. The odor in each of these rooms is overpowering, to the degree that after a visit to a day room I had to send my clothes to the dry cleaners in order to have the stench removed. The physical facilities often contributed to the visual horror as well as to the odor. Floors are sometimes made of wood and, as a result, excretions are rubbed into the cracks, thus providing a permanent aroma. Most day rooms have a series of bleacher-like benches on which sit denuded residents, jammed together, without purposeful activity or communication or any kind of interaction. In each day room is an attendant or two, whose main function seems to be to "stand around" and, on occasion, hose down the floor, "driving" excretions into a sewer conveniently located in the center of the room.

I was invited into female as well as male day rooms, in spite of the supervisor's knowledge that I, a male visitor, would be observing denuded females. In one such dormitory, with an overwhelming odor, I noticed feces on the wooden ceilings, and on the patients as well as the floors.

Early in the evening, sometimes at 5:00 p.m., patients are put to bed. This is to equalize the work load among the different shifts. During the day, I saw many patients lying on their beds, apparently for long periods of time. This was their activity. During these observations, I thought a good deal about the perennial cry for attendants and volunteer workers who are more sympathetic and understanding of institutionalized retarded residents. One of the things I realized was that attendants might be sympathetic, might interact more with patients, if institutional administrators made deliberate attempts to make patients cosmetically more appealing.

For example, adult male residents should shave—or be shaven—more than once or twice a week. Dentures should be provided for any patient who needs them. It seems plausible to believe that it is much more possible to make residents more attractive, and therefore more interesting, to attendants than it is to attempt to convince attendants that they should enjoy the spectacle of unwashed, unkempt, odoriferous, toothless old men and women.

My friends forsake me like a memory lost.

John Clare

The living quarters for older men and women were, for the most part, gloomy and sterile. There were rows and rows of benches on which sat countless human beings, in silent rooms, waiting for dinner call or bedtime. I saw resident after resident in "institutional garb." Sometimes, the women wore "shrouds"—inside out. I heard a good deal of laughter but saw little cheer. Even the television sets, in several of the day rooms, appeared to be co-conspirators in a crusade for gloom. These sets were not in working order, although, ironically, the residents continued to sit on their benches, in neat rows, looking at the blank tubes. I observed adult residents during recreation, playing "ring-around-the-rosy." Others, in the *vocational training center*, were playing "jacks." These were not always severely retarded patients. However, one very quickly got the feeling that this is the way they were being forced to behave. Or, as Hungerford said, ". . . in an institution there is always tomorrow so that he who starts out a student ends up, by default, an inmate." Lastly, I viewed old women and very young girls in the same dormitories and old men and young boys as comrades in the day room. In the "normal" world, there is something appealing—even touching—about such friendships. In the institution there is something opportunistic, sinister, and ludicrous.

Suffer the little children . . .

The children's dormitories depressed me the most. Here, cribs were placed—as in the other dormitories—side by side and head to head. Very young children, one and two years of age, were lying in cribs without contact with any adult, without playthings, without apparent stimulation. In one dormitory that had over 100 infants and was connected to nine other dormitories that totalled 1,000 infants, I experienced my deepest sadness. As I entered, I heard a muffled sound emanating from the "blind" side of a doorway. A young child was calling, "Come, come play with me. Touch me." I walked to the door. On the other side were 40 or more unkempt infants crawling around a bare floor in a bare room. One of the children had managed to squeeze his hand under the doorway and push his face through the side of the latched door, crying for attention. His moan begged me for some kind of human interaction.

In other day rooms, I saw groups of 20 or 30 very young children lying, rocking, sleeping, sitting—alone. Each of these rooms was without doors or adult human contact, although each had desperate looking adult attendants "standing by."

During my visit to the above institution, I was told about the development of a new research center on the institutional grounds. The assistant superintendent mentioned to me that the "material" for the research center would come from the institution and this center would require the addition of approximately 30 or 40 "items." I was quite confused by this statement and, as a result of some verbal fumbling and embarrassment, I finally did understand what was being said to me. At that institution, and apparently at others in that state, patients are called "material" and personnel are called "items." It was so difficult to believe that this assistant superintendent was not either "pulling my leg" or using some idiosyncratic jargon that, during my subsequent visits to dormitories in that institution, I asked the attending physicians, "How many 'items' do you have in this building? How much 'material' do you have?" To my amazement, they knew exactly what I was asking for and gave me the numbers immediately.

In another dormitory, I was taken on a tour by the chief physician, who was anxious to show me a child who had a very rare medical condition. The doctor explained to me that, aside from the child's dwarfism and misshapen body, one of the primary methods for diagnosing this condition is the deep guttural voice. In order to demonstrate this, he pinched the child. The child did not make any sound. He pinched her again, and again—harder, and still harder. Finally, he ensured her response with a pinch that turned into a gouge and caused the child to scream in obvious pain.

In some of the children's dormitories I observed "nursery programs." What surprised me most was their scarcity and also the primitiveness of those in operation. Therefore, I was not unprepared to see several children with severe head lacerations. I was told these were the "head bangers." Head banging is another condition that some people think is inevitable when confronted with young severely mentally retarded children. I challenge this. I have reason to believe that head banging can be drastically reduced in an environment where children have other things to do. Alice Metzner once said, "There are only two things wrong with most special education for the mentally handicapped: it isn't special, and it isn't education." From my observations of the "nursery programs" conducted at the state schools visited, I would have to agree only with the second part of Miss Metzner's complaint. The special education I observed at the state schools bore no resemblance to what I would consider to be "education." But, it was special. It was a collection of the most especially depressing "learning" environments I have ever had the misfortune to witness.

One may find his religion in the clinical setting.

Albert T. Murphy

I have learned a great deal during my visits to these institutions about the treatment of the severely mentally retarded and of young children who are institutionalized. But, essentially, and possibly most importantly, I have learned something about the dominating factor that influences Man in his treatment of other human beings. And this is a concept that is worth striving to understand. No doubt, the reader of this piece has asked himself several times, "Why do attendants and supervisors treat mentally retarded patients in the way this author describes?" It is probably almost impossible for you to believe that such conditions are allowed to exist. Because of my years in observing these affairs, I may have been a little further along the way in rationalizing and, to my shame, accepting them. That is to say, I knew with certainty that these conditions existed. However, I was about as puzzled as anyone else in explaining why we permit them to continue. Now, I may have a glimmer of enlightenment that I want to share with you.

It has always intrigued me to think about why anti-vivisectionists are so passionate in their beliefs concerning the use of animals for scientific experimentation. To me, animals have always been creatures to enjoy, to act kindly toward, and not to inflict any unnecessary punishment on. I believe this is the way most thoughtful human beings view the animal kingdom. I think of myself as a reasonable man. I have no interest—in fact I have revulsion—in inflicting unnecessary pain on any creature. However, I would be less than candid if I did not admit that stories about carefully controlled, and apparently necessary, animal experimentation never offend me. Further, I have never really lost any sleep or had any sustained grief in hearing about or observing cruelty to animals. I do not enjoy such spectacles; on the other hand, I have never been motivated enough to intervene directly to prevent them. However, there are people, some of our closest friends, who cry real tears and display deep emotions when confronted with cruelty to animals. During this study, I began to understand, finally, why antivivisectionists are the way they are and why I am so different. Further, I began to understand how human beings can be treated so dispassionately and cruelly in institutions. Anti-vivisectionists must conceive of animals in ways other people conceive of human beings. If you look at the anti-vivisectionists in this light, it is not difficult

to understand their anguish in observing inhuman behavior to animals.
On the other hand, certain human beings have been taught or trained—
or this is part of their nature—to conceive of other human beings in ways
that most of us think of animals. If this is so, it is not difficult to understand
why, and how, institutional attendants and their supervisors can treat the
mentally retarded in the ways they do. It isn't that these attendants are
cruel or incompetent people—although, all too often, they are—but they
have come to believe, for various reasons, that those in their charge are
not really human. The words that are used in institutions describing certain mentally retarded residents give substance to my notion. When one
views a group of human beings in an official kind of way as "material,"
an increased per capita expenditure for resident care and additional staff
are not sufficient alone to bring about the massive changes in institutional
treatment that are necessary. The use of such terms as "basket case,"
"vegetable," and others too offensive to record here indicate that the
basic problem to be surmounted before state institutions for the mentally
retarded will change substantially lies in the realm of our conception
about human behavior and its amenability to change or, as Sarason has
said, ". . . When one looks over the history of Man the most distinguish-
ing characteristic of his development is the degree to which Man has
underestimated the potentialities of men." Whatever ways we implement
a program to reconstruct the philosophy and practices of institutions for
the mentally retarded, our most forceful thrust must be in our attempts
to reconceptualize our understanding of the nature and prerogatives of
Man. More important than the desperately needed increased per capita
expenditure for institutional care, more important than the obvious necessity of reducing the size of institutions, more important than the al-
leviation of their crowdedness, is the necessity for infusing a fundamental
belief among all who work with the mentally retarded that each of these
individuals is equally human—not equally intellectually able, not equally
physically appealing, but equally a human being. Carl Sandburg stated
this much more eloquently than I could: "There is only one man in the
world; And his name is ALL MEN."

The Promised Land always lies on the other side of a wilderness.

Havelock Ellis

I have just returned from a four day visit to The Seaside Regional
Center, a small state institution of approximately 250 residents and somewhat over 100 staff, located in Waterford, Connecticut. This was one of
many trips I had made to The Seaside during the past four years. However,
this visit was somewhat different. I had returned for a specific purpose.
I wanted to understand, for myself, why this residential center for the
mentally retarded is so different from others described in this chapter and

others I have seen throughout the country. On each of my visits to The Seadside, I could always anticipate something new and exciting. On this occasion I was not disappointed. However, I wanted something more— much more. I wanted some reason for the uniqueness of The Seaside, a reason other than the obvious. I knew that The Seaside expends approximately two times the per capita costs for its residents as compared with other institutions discussed in this chapter. Further, I knew a great deal about the sincerity, the zeal and hard work, of its staff and administration. All of those factors contribute to an institution that does not deal with "material" and "items," that does not deal in "human warehouses." All of those conditions contribute to the development of an extraordinarily dedicated and involved staff, in a setting small enough to allow every child care worker—as well as every teacher, nurse, and administrator—to know every child in the institution, and vice versa. But, at The Seaside, there is something more and I believe I now know a little of what that is.

A recent book by Kurt Vonnegut, Jr., developed what I believe is a profound insight, "We are what we pretend to be, so we must be careful about what we pretend to be." Reality is what we do, not how we wish things to be. Whether or not the staff at The Seaside feel deep compassion and tenderness toward residents—although I want to believe they do— is quite immaterial, for they behave in ways that can only lead to good for the children and others there. Whether the staff at The Seaside are better people—as people—or are wiser or more sensitive than other institutional staffs is not particularly important, for they behave as if they are. I am fatigued, exasperated, with professional and attendant staff who offer multitudes of excuses, rationalizations, and explanations for their behavior in institutions for the mentally retarded. Although I am not entirely unsympathetic to their plight (insofar as inadequate budgets, undermanned staffs and overcrowded dormitories may lead to the concessions they make and the kinds of programs they conduct), their behavior speaks volumes more about their character than does the "good will" which supposedly lies behind their compromises. For myself, I now prefer the man with the "black heart" who behaves decently for reasons neither he nor others know than the man of sterling mien who, because of "unavoidable circumstances," behaves in ways which depress and compromise him.

I imagine I am saying that mental retardation can bring out the best in some people—as well as the worst. At The Seaside, I have found that it brings out the best in a lot of different adults who are involved professionally, interpersonally, and tangentially with the residents. The Seaside has more people who demonstrate interest, show kindness, have feelings toward the residents and other staff, than do other places for the mentally retarded—notwithstanding the fact that every institution, large as well as small and those discussed earlier in this chapter as well as at The Seaside, has superb and dedicated attendants and professional staff as well as its quota of mediocre and poor staff. In my opinion, The Seaside has more superior personnel and fewer of the inefficient and uninterested. In the above, I believe, is the major difference between The Seaside and other institutions for the mentally retarded. But these warm-feeling and acting human beings are not indigenous to one small state institution. They are found everywhere and there would be many more if a higher value were placed on uncovering them, encouraging them, and nurturing their natural talents for helping other people.

About ten years ago, I made several trips to a large state institution for the mentally retarded, one not visited during this study. I became interested in and, for several days, visited a dormitory housing severely retarded ambulatory adults—one that was very similar in population to those living quarters discussed earlier in this chapter. However, this dormitory was, in a very important way, different. What made this dormitory different can best be illustrated with the following story.

On the occasion of one such visit, I was hailed by one of the attendants and asked to come into the day room. Upon entrance, the attendant called over a 35- or 40-year-old, partly denuded, incontinent male and said, "Dr. Blatt, you remember Charlie. Charles has learned how to say 'hello' since your last visit. Charlie, say 'hello' to Dr. Blatt." Charlie grunted and the attendant, literally, went into a kind of ecstasy that is rarely shown by adults, and when it is, radiates warmth enough for anyone lucky enough to be touched by it. It should not be misunderstood that Charlie's grunt resembled anything like a "hello," or any other human utterance. In a way, this attendant's reaction to Charlie might have been considered as a kind of psychopathology of its own. However, I have a different understanding of it.

What type of man was this attendant? In 1938 he walked, literally off the streets, into that institution—an alcoholic, without a home of his own, purposeless and without a future—and asked for a job. He wasn't then, and isn't particularly now, an educated man. For 28 years he has served as an attendant in a dormitory for severely retarded patients. He knows every "boy" there and actually thinks of them as his children and they of him as their father.

Sometimes, in despair and helplessness, I ask myself why were these severely retarded human beings born. When one observes an attendant of the kind just described, it is possible to find at least a semblance of an answer. If not for the mentally retarded, this attendant might have been a drifter, an alcoholic, much less of a person than what he actually is. Would it be unfair to say that this attendant *needed* mental retardation in order to fulfill his own destiny and realize the greatest good he could render to society?

Maybe the mentally retarded will enjoy the care and education they deserve when institutions cause those who minister to their needs to become better people, rather than more insensitive ones. During my last trip to The Seaside, I had the opportunity to see their magnificent day camp, which enrolled 100 community children in addition to the residents. I also took the time to visit all the living quarters, the workshop, and the vocational activity areas. Lastly, I reviewed case folders of children who particularly interested me. The following are excerpts of letters sent, unsolicited, to The Seaside from parents of children in residence there.

Mr. and Mrs. Richard LaCourse, of Groton, Connecticut, wrote:

> We are the parents of a seven year old retarded daughter who is at Seaside Regional Center. When she first went there she was not toilet trained, couldn't dress or undress herself. Her temper tantrums were quite often and severe. We certainly had no idea she'd be able to learn so much in such a short time, as she is a microcephalic. Today she goes to school, is toilet trained, can dress and undress herself, and she can talk a little more clearly than before. She has very few temper tantrums and gets along well with the other children and staff at Seaside.
>
> The way Seaside is conducted, we are able to have Debbie home quite often. We appreciate this very much. Since it is our wish, as well as Seaside's, to have her remain a part of the family.

Mr. and Mrs. Charles R. Watson, also of Groton, Connecticut, reported:

> As our son was fortunate enough to be one of the first to go to Seaside Regional Center, we can honestly say that a year has done him a world of good and it almost seems like his rebirth. Formerly at_____he was unable to walk or speak, having suffered from a paralysis, coupled with a brain injury and epilepsy. Today he is the picture of health and walking and running with the other children. He is also attempting to regain some speech.

From Mrs. Evelyn Mirable, of Manchester, Connecticut, Superintendent Fred Finn of Seaside received the following letter:

> I am afraid that if I had not visited your Center I would have been forever devoid of hope for all residential retardates, inasmuch as my visit to _____was such a shock. I am still going to endeavor in my efforts to get David admitted to your Center, or to a comparable setting, and I have made a firm vow that when and if he is so situated, I will turn as much concentrated effort as I can to helping those poor lost children that I saw at_____. I still can't get them out of my thoughts.

Mrs. Viola Hance, of Uncasville, Connecticut, wrote the following to Mr. Bert W. Schmickel, Deputy Commissioner of Health, in charge of the Connecticut Office of Mental Retardation:

> At the time Gloria (her daughter) was admitted to_____she was five years old and could walk as well as any child of that age. In the past three

years, however, she had stopped walking almost altogether. She didn't know me and looked so bad that I expected a call any time that she had left us. In the eleven months that she has been at Seaside, she has gained weight, is walking better again, and always knows me when I visit her.

I could easily reproduce a dozen or two case histories of children and adults who have changed dramatically since reassignment to Seaside from other state institutions. However, the following, excerpted from a statement by Mrs. Sally Hughes Carr, who has a daughter at The Seaside, tells a great deal more about The Seaside environment:

We knew that by the time Betsy was one year old she would require institutional care, as her retardation was not mild. In spite of most of the medical advice we received which was in favor of placing her as soon as possible since it was obvious she would have to go eventually, we decided to keep her at home until she was about five if possible. It has proved to be a rewarding experience for all of us. Her father, her brothers and sister and I have all had the job and satisfaction of seeing her slow but steady development and have the opportunity to get to know the quiet, withdrawn but sweet and loving soul within her. Once one accepts the fact and degree of retardation of the child then every new accomplishment, however small, is exciting. This last year she has been attending a local day school for retarded children and the progress she has shown since she started is remarkable. Two months ago, just shortly after her fifth birthday, we had the fun and joy of seeing her start walking all on her own. She is soon to enter Seaside, a marvelous state training school for retarded children in Waterford, Connecticut.

I can truthfully say that, while we are all going to miss her dreadfully when she starts up there, we are much better prepared for the change now than we would have been even a year ago and I would hate to think of having missed the last five years with our sweet silent little Peter Pan. We now know her, and have had a chance to give her something of our love and receive hers in return. There are heartaches and frustrating moments with a retarded child at home, but the benefits just in term of the increased patience, understanding, and tolerance of the other members of the family far outweigh the problems. At least that has been the case for us.

A year has passed since I wrote the above, and I would now like to add a postscript.

Betsy entered Seaside Regional Center for Retarded Children in Waterford, Connecticut, a year ago last August. There has been much newspaper publicity lately about the terrible conditions in some state institutions for the mentally retarded. Seaside is the living proof that it doesn't *have* to be this way.

My husband and I drove up to look the school over for the first time with a considerable amount of apprehension. I must confess that my mental picture of a state school for the mentally retarded was very close to my picture of a penal institution. I was afraid that once Betsy entered the doors we would have lost her forever. I knew she'd get three meals a day but I wasn't at all sure she'd get the love I felt she needed. Would she get any exercise, or only sit tied to a chair to keep her out of trouble?

It was a very different couple who drove back after our day's tour of the school. We had expected to be shocked by the many children we would see who would be more severely and grotesquely retarded than our Betsy. Oddly enough, we saw these children, many of them, and yet we found to our amazement that instead of shock and sadness, the strongest emotion in our hearts on our drive back was a feeling of joy. We had been shown everything from the kitchen to the nursery. While the cleanliness and order were immediately apparent, what impressed us most was the overwhelming feeling of love and happiness, a wonderful cheerful warmth greeted us at every turn, from the children who ran out of their classroom to give us a hug and a kiss to the patient smile of an attendant crooning a nursery rhyme to an infant as she changed her diapers. This was no prison, but a big loving home. And so it has proved to be.

There are no restrictions on visiting or taking Betsy home. She comes home about once a month for a weekend, and, of course, for all the holidays, and it's always a pleasure to go up to get her or bring her back. She is no number at her school but a very special person. The director insists that the children each have their own lockers with their own clothes in them, for although this necessitates infinitely more sorting and separating of laundry, he feels very strongly that the children must keep their own individual identities and not become "institutionalized." The playground is literally teeming with fascinating swings in the shape of animals, merry-go-rounds, and what not. Many of them have been constructed by neighbors who not only have not resented the fact that they have a school for mentally retarded in their midst, but have given of their time and money to make the lives of the children as happy and full as possible.

I guess if I were able to talk to parents who have just learned that they have a retarded child I would tell them two things. First, don't be afraid to love and to get to know your child no matter who advises you to the contrary. And second, don't be afraid to investigate your state institutions. You may be pleasantly surprised as we were, and if you aren't, join those who are trying to do something about it. It can be done.

Life is a struggle, but not a warfare.

John Burroughs

The Seaside is people! It is small! It is expensive to operate! But it isn't as expensive as one might imagine. The Seaside appropriates approximately twice the amount, per patient, that other institutions for the retarded appropriate. However, in contrast with per capita costs in penal institutions, The Seaside has a very modest expenditure. In terms of human suffering—and the potential for human growth—places like The Seaside are among the few really economical government-sponsored facilities that I know of.

At The Seaside there is time, time for teaching a young child to use a spoon or fork, time for helping a child learn to use a zipper, time to heal a wound—either of the body or the soul. But, at The Seaside, there is no time for tomorrow. There is a fight against inertia. Children must be helped today, for in too few tomorrows children become adults and residents become inmates.

At The Seaside, there is schooling. Some children attend school at the institution. The older and more capable youngsters attend school in the community—public school—with other children who are living at home. At The Seaside, it is not difficult to tell that this is an environment designed for children. The lawns are filled with swings and jungle gyms and bicycle paths. During Christmas time, each room is decorated welcoming Santa Claus and the spirit of Christmas. Rooms are clean and orderly. Furniture that children use is designed for children. Furniture that adults use is designed for adults.

There are adult residents at The Seaside. However, they are not in the same dormitories, or programs, with the children. Adults have other needs and the following may illustrate how some of these are met.

One of our difficulties in photographing activities at The Seaside was in our inability to take very many pictures of adult residents. There is a very good explanation for this. Most of the adults at The Seaside are working during the day—they are on institutional jobs or out in the community. Some, who could not be returned to their own homes, live in a work training unit. Here, they are together with friends and co-workers, under the careful supervision of cottage counselors. During the day they are on placement—working in the community—and in the evening they return to their "home" where they can receive special help and guidance in their successful attempts to integrate into normal communities and become contributing and useful members of society.

At The Seaside there is love, and love is believing in the fulfillment of another human being.

AFTERTHOUGHTS AND RECOMMENDATIONS

It is many months since I have visited the institutions described here. During that time, I have shown and discussed this story with a formidable, very heterogeneous, but selected number of individuals. Their backgrounds range from those in very high public office to undergraduate college students preparing as special class teachers. The sentiments of the aforementioned individuals, and others too numerous to mention, convinced me that this story must be brought to the American people as speedily as possible. In discussing this work with my colleagues, I have been able to resolve some of my anxieties insofar as the possible adverse consequences of publication. Further, I have been able to conceptualize a plan that might correct those antecedent conditions that led to the horror I observed.

The major questions that dictated caution and painful deliberation concerned themselves with whether or not this work represented an invasion of privacy of certain individuals, on the one hand, and whether the general public has a right to be protected from the knowledge of degradation, on the other. Insofar as invasion of privacy is concerned, I must question some types of privacy on moral grounds. I believe that the so-called privacy of the back wards of these institutions contributes to suffering, for outsiders do not know the conditions within these buildings and, therefore, do little or nothing to promote improvements. When privacy contributes to suffering, it loses its significance as a cherished privilege. For those who could so reason, I do not believe that there would be many in the institutions who would object to my exposure of these frightening conditions if such exposure offered some possibility for a better life and chance for the residents. Lastly, as I discussed this issue with a number of people, I began to wonder whose privacies were being protected, institutionalized residents' or ours?

This leads to the second consideration. Do people have a right to know, whether they request this knowledge or not, the unvarnished nature of human activity? In order to avoid hysterical reactions to this study, I have deliberately shied away from comparisons of what I have seen with what took place in another country, with other kinds of human beings, toward the solution of other problems. I do not want to, in any way, leave the impression that what goes on in American state institutions for the mentally retarded is, by administrative design, barbaric, inhuman, or callous. However, I see certain obvious major problems, not the least being the general public's unawareness of conditions in our back wards.

The American people have the *right to know*. In spite of what we wish to know, in spite of the pain that knowing may bring to us, we have the right to be informed about any serious conditions that affect the human condition. There is a maturity that comes to a people when it no longer needs the protection of ignorance and, thus, of ignoring what needs to be attended to. Only very young children, with their fantasies, or sick adults, with theirs, believe that ignoring a problem can make it go away.

My recommendations derive from many sources: my experiences prior to this story, what I observed during the study, the reactions of many astute individuals to this study, and the advice of students and colleagues. In addition to the emergency need for at least doubling per capita expenditures in state institutions and for reducing the sizes of institutional populations wherever and however possible, my study of this problem leads to an additional set of recommendations that may contribute to an improvement of institutional programs and facilities:

1. In each state, a board of institutional visitors should be appointed by the governor or other constituted authority. This board would be responsible for reporting directly to the highest state officials. Appointments to this board should be made irrespective of political party affiliation, and these appointments should be contingent on both

knowledge of the broad field of human welfare and demonstrated public service. Members of this board of visitors would not be, concurrently, members of any particular institution's staff or board of trustees.

2. Within each state institution for the mentally retarded, each department (e.g., medical, psychological, educational, nursing, cottage life) should have a board of advisors. This board of advisors, through periodic visits and consultations, would know the institution and its problems intimately and thus be in positions to advise and assist in the resolution of difficulties. In essence, the advisory board would be organized for direct consultation and assistance to the institutional staff. As this board would not be responsible for rating institutional personnel or recommending their salary increments or promotions, it is possible that members of this board would become involved with the most pressing and severe problems of the institution—without "endangering" the positions of the staff that trusts them. In this way, it would be possible for problems currently secreted from the outside world to be given the exposure and ventilation needed for satisfactory solutions to them.

3. Can one any longer ignore the needed relationship between the state institution for the mentally retarded and the state university? In each state, a state university should be given responsibility and resources to provide comprehensive in-service training and consultation for all institutional employees, from the chief administrative officer to the rawest attendant recruit.

4. In each state, at least one state institution for the mentally retarded should be designated as a center for the in-service training of *all* personnel to be employed for state service in institutions and clinics for the mentally retarded. As a condition for employment as institutional superintendent, psychologist, teacher, nurse, or attendant the candidate would have to spend a specified period of time at the training center. His preparation program would range from a few weeks to one calendar year, depending upon his background and experiences and the nature of the position he intends to assume. During this training program, the candidate would be involved in clinical experiences that relate directly to this future employment, would participate in seminars, colloquia, and other instructional experiences designed to prepare him for the sensitive and demanding activities of work with the mentally retarded. At the end of the candidate's training program, the director of this facility and his staff would rate the candidate and recommend him, or not recommend him, for employment. To the degree that this program is workable with currently employed staff, every inducement and encouragement should be provided to permit them to complete this preparation.

There is a shame in America. Countless human beings are suffering—needlessly. Countless more families of these unfortunate victims of society's irresponsibility are in anguish for they know, or suspect, the truth. Unwittingly, or unwillingly, they have been forced to institutionalize their loved ones into a life of degradation and horror.

I challenge every institution in America to look at itself, now! I challenge each institution to examine its program, its standards, its admission policies, its personnel, its budget, its philosophy, its objectives. I challenge every institution—and every governor and every legislator—to justify its personnel and their practices, its size and development, and its budget.

My experiences during Christmas 1965 require me to call for a national examination of every institution for the mentally retarded in America—an examination that will inspect the deepest recesses of the most obscure back ward in the least progressive state. I call for a national examination of state budgets for the care and treatment of the retarded. I hold responsible each superintendent, each commissioner of mental health, each governor, each thoughtful citizen for the care and treatment of individuals committed for institutionalization in their state.

To some degree, all of us talk and behave as if we will not change. Yet, it is absolutely certain that we will change; what we profess now, in one way or another, we regret later. By the above I mean that the most difficult truth each of us has to learn and live with is the knowledge that we aren't perfect. It was my intent in this article to point out some of the more serious imperfections of state institutional programs for the mentally retarded in this country. It is my belief that, now that our most indefensible practices have been laid bare for public scrutiny, men of good will from all walks of life and all professions will sit down at the planning table and seek solutions to the plight of our brethren.

POSTSCRIPT

It is not necessary here to discuss the flood of extraordinarily encouraging mail and calls I have received in response to the first edition of *Christmas in Purgatory*. It may be instructive to mention some of the negative, or otherwise puzzling, comments and hectoring that came to me.

One well-intentioned clergyman believes that I exhibited bad taste in reproducing photographs of nude men and women. An acquaintance in our field thinks our use of a concealed camera immoral and he believes our work to be a fake, comparing the atypical worst I had seen with "posed pictures" theatrically staged at The Seaside. A wise and beloved Commissioner of Mental Health asked me if these conditions exist in his state's institutions. (How can I tell him about something he, as the principal responsible officer, should be aware of—and doing something about?)

In another state that I have deep feeling for, a legislator who has championed mental health legislation circulated copies of *Christmas in Purgatory* in the vain hope that it would help in the passage of social welfare legislation. He received scant support from his own party, who did not want the "opposition governor" to gain stature through such legislation in, this, an election year. The bill appeared doomed for many weeks, but subsequently passed, due, I have been informed, in some part to the influence of our book.

Albert Camus wrote, "Again and again there comes a time in history when the man who dares to say that two and two make four is punished with death." I have written the truth, as plainly and as simply as I see it—not for power or fame, for there has been precious little of either connected with this assignment and there has been a good deal of grief. I would be surprised if this work changes radically the nature of institutions. My current depression will not permit such grand thoughts. On the other hand, Camus wrote further, "Perhaps we can't stop the world from being one in which children are tortured, but we can reduce the number of tortured children."

In spite of those who protest this presentation, there will be no turning back; the truth can no longer be concealed. Some good must come from all this pain and anguish to so many institutionalized residents and their families. Once seeds are sown, one only has to wait for the crop to harvest. It has also been said that, when the bellman is dead, the wind will toll the bell.

So hurry wind! Or revive yourselves noble bellringers.

CHAPTER 7
Exodus from Pandemonium

ANTECEDENTS

By 1956 I had completed approximately seven years of what I considered to be a deep involvement in the field of mental retardation—and had visited a total of two state institutions for the mentally retarded.

My first visit was made during an early graduate year, sometime in 1949 or 1950. It was to a very large state school in New York and was arranged by the professor in mental retardation with whom I was studying. My recollections of that visit are not completely clear. However, I do remember that I was impressed with the beautiful grounds. On the other hand, I also remember that, upon our return home, I complained to my professor about what I thought to be a disgraceful and very distressing etiological conference that we attended there. Patients were presented to our group of about 100; they were seated in a row at the front of an auditorium and, one by one, were asked to stand and to exhibit themselves to this audience. As each patient was moved and turned and poked, the presenting physician would recount the history, family background, current status, and activities of the patient. I'm certain that now any reader who has had even a minimum experience in state schools knows about these kinds of case presentations. I was forced to sit through all too many of them until—some years ago—I vowed never to subject myself again to a presentation of this kind and, I am proud to report, this is one vow that I have kept.

I do not recollect visiting any institutions for the mentally retarded during the years between the completion of my master's degree and my return to The Pennsylvania State University for the final year of doctoral study. During those five years, I taught a special class for the mentally retarded in a Brooklyn public school and, although I was continuing some graduate work in mental retardation and was very deeply involved in this field, not once did I visit a state school nor, even more surprising to me now, do I remember ever thinking seriously (or, for that matter, casually) about a state school. In retrospect, it is perfectly clear to me that I had,

Comprising several portions of the author's book, *Exodus from Pandemonium: Human Abuse and a Reformation of Public Policy*, Boston: Allyn & Bacon, 1970, this chapter reflects his concerns during the period immediately after the writing of *Christmas in Purgatory*.

for many years, neither an understanding nor an interest in institutions, their residents, and their problems. Further, and not in any defense of that thoughtlessness, I do not believe that any of my colleagues (i.e., those who taught special classes and were part of "our crowd") and few of my professors were any more knowledgeable or interested in this problem than I. Still further, I do not believe that the situation is very much, if any, different today. Public school special class teachers, principals, and university professors appear to understand little and care less about the institutionalized mentally retarded and the problems confronting those attempting to change the institutions.

During my last year at Penn State (1955), I made several visits to Laurelton State School, an institution for the mentally retarded located twenty or thirty miles from the university campus. Again, I was struck by the beautiful grounds and bucolic setting of the school. As in the earlier visit, I did have negative reactions. These were concerned mainly with the unavailability of schooling opportunities for the residents, many of whom were mildly retarded and, so it seemed to me then, some of whom appeared to be of normal intelligence.

It was not until I completed doctoral studies and began my college teaching career that I became a regular visitor to state institutions for the mentally retarded. After my appointment to New Haven State Teachers' College (now Southern Connecticut State College), I was responsible for the supervision of student teachers in special education, several of whom were assigned to the Southbury Training School and the Mansfield Training School, at the time the two state schools for the mentally retarded in Connecticut. Further, with Fred Finn, then the Director of Training at Southbury, I organized a workshop each summer for teachers of the trainable mentally retarded. These involvements caused me to become a very frequent visitor to the state schools. I attended staff conferences, child study committee meetings, and numerous other activities in these facilities. I visited all of the dormitories on innumerable occasions and, quite literally, became a kind of quasi-staff member, especially at the Southbury Training School.

In 1959, Governor Ribicoff appointed me to the first Connecticut Advisory Council on Mental Retardation. For the first time, I was now required to observe the institutions and to consider their needs from the viewpoint of someone who had responsibility for them and who pledged his commitment to serve them. However, during my years in Connecticut, including those on the Advisory Council, I had a general feeling about institutions that, although not completely positive, permitted me to sleep soundly and not worry about them or about their residents. Obviously, I had visited numerous back wards (although Connecticut did seem to have fewer of these than did other states and did seem to be doing more for its institutionalized retarded than other states) and attended innumerable etiological conferences. Even then, in my naïve, less jaundiced stage of development, I was able to observe all of the obvious and many of the subtle barbarisms that seemed to be perpetrated daily in state institutions. I explained those observations to myself by using stock reasonings: "nature of things in institutions," "the invariant characteristics of the severely retarded," and "we are doing the best we can."

A glimmer of a more mature understanding of the things that are, and the things that need be, began to take hold during the last year of my service on the Advisory Council, just prior to my move to Boston University. Ernest Roselle, the first superintendent at Southbury Training School, articulated during the early 1950's a view of regionalization and community participation in programming that was brought to fruition a decade later by such individuals as Bert Schmickel and Fred Finn. Bert Schmickel, Deputy Commissioner for Mental Retardation, Connecticut Department of Health, and Fred Finn, Superintendent of the Seaside Center, with the approval and encouragement of the first Advisory Council, established a center that began to demonstrate the obsolescence of back wards, certainly, and the inappropriateness of large institutions, probably. We began to understand that the condition we termed "back ward life" is an invention of the nonretarded and a reflection of their character rather than a necessary concomitant to severe mental retardation. As we grew to appreciate the certainty that back wards could be eradicated, some of us learned with ever increasing anxiety and torment how truly evil these monuments to inhumanity were. While we could convince ourselves that back wards were necessary—were, in a way, providing the best care possible under intolerable circumstances—we were able to abide them. With the advent of clear alternatives, our defensive moat—"the nature of things"—crumbled. What was being demonstrated was that the architects of back wards, the progenitors of the feces-smearers, the culprits of this holocaust are normal men with good intentions. This realization did not come to me overnight and, in fact, I am still struggling with it.

In the Fall of 1961 I assumed the chairmanship of the Special Education Department at Boston University. Among my responsibilities was the inauguration of a research program sponsored by the United States Office of Education and involving three- and four-year-old children from disadvantaged homes. For any readers interested in our activities during those years, an account of that study and other involvements may be found in my book *The Intellectually Disfranchised*, published in 1966 by the Massachusetts Department of Mental Health. I mention that preschool study for two reasons. First, it embarked us on a series of studies and programs designed to test the hypothesis that intelligence is educable, that it is plastic, that it is a function of practice and training. Essentially, I view the hypothesis undergirding that project as synonymous with the hypothesis that back wards may be eradicated or, as you will read in the section on *Jimmy*, every human being is capable of changing and learning (in fact, when I view in retrospect my research and clinical activities during the past twenty years, it is not very difficult to conclude that practically all of these activities were concerned with the hypothesis that man underestimates his potential and man—all men—are capable of changing.) Secondly, I mention this preschool study because the intervention phase of the program was conducted at a state school for the mentally retarded. Thus, I had an opportunity to visit the Walter E. Fernald State School almost every day for two years.

In the fall of 1965, United States Senator Robert Kennedy visited several institutions for the mentally retarded in New York State. His shocked reaction to those visits brought a storm of protest from many sources. An account of my own reaction to these protests and the eventual decision to produce *Christmas in Purgatory* (a presentation in words and photographs of the horrifying conditions in back wards) are found in the previous chapter.

But it is not necessarily easy, once you know the facts, to get them put before the public. Fred Kaplan, the photographer, and I prepared the manuscript and photographs for presentation to publishers. One publisher, William Morrow, turned us down because they felt much more text was needed and, secondly, some of the pictures might be considered offensive. Two publishers, those I have had affiliations with in the past, turned us down without asking to see the manuscript. Both believed this type of book would be unsalable and difficult to produce. Neither the Kennedy Foundation nor the non-profit *Special Child Publications* felt able to sponsor the book. Allyn and Bacon, the publisher who eventually brought out the second edition, turned it down, originally, saying it was an important book but one that presented too many problems to consider sponsoring. We went to the magazines. *Life* was very interested. I'm certain that their editor, Mr. Billings, will not forget me. After viewing our pictures, he remarked that he would not be able to have lunch that day. *Life* wanted to publish a two-part series on *Christmas in Purgatory*. However, they insisted that their editorial policy required the naming of names, the designation of institutions, and the identification of states. For reasons that are brought out in the next section, we were unable to agree to those conditions.

Eventually, we decided to publish *Christmas in Purgatory* ourselves and, if necessary, pay for all of the publication costs. Happily, as things turned out, a parent association for retarded children in Connecticut agreed to advance us the money to print the first edition. After publication of the commercial edition, all royalties have been assigned by both Fred Kaplan and myself to that parent association. (Contrary to any possible misbeliefs, neither Fred Kaplan nor I received any royalities from the publication of either the first edition or the second edition of *Christmas in Purgatory*.)

In 1966, at the time we were arranging for the publication of the book, I received a call from Charlie Mangel, senior editor of *Look*. He had heard, through an unnamed source in "high governmental office," that we had completed a study of institutions for the mentally retarded and were having great difficulty in arranging for the publication of our report. After several meetings with him, I prepared an article and it was scheduled for publication in an issue planned for the coming fall. Actually, it was not published in *Look* until October 31, 1967, one year later. Several factors delayed its appearance, including a last minute objection from a very high-ranking official of Cowles Communications, Incorporated, publishers of *Look*. He did not believe that a "family magazine," catering to the tastes of the broad mainstream of America, should publish this type of article, but in the end the article was printed. It drew a phenomenal reaction, powering the beginnings of a national movement to eradicate the conditions we exposed.

We distributed the first edition of *Christmas in Purgatory* in the early fall of 1966. One thousand copies were sent to a list of those individuals whom we believed would be in the most advantageous positions to support a reform of institutions. The response to this publication was absolutely overwhelming. We received letters from the President of the United States, Mrs. Hubert Humphrey (several letters, requests for additional copies of the publication, and an eventual meeting), practically every United States Senator and practically every governor, and many, many commissioners of mental health and mental retardation, superintendents of state schools, professors of special education or fields allied to mental retardation, presidents of parent associations, and many hundreds of other people from all walks of life who had read the book.

With the publication of the second edition, which was held up so that it could be brought out simultaneously with the *Look* article, reviews began to appear in professional journals and in newspapers. The mail continued to flood in to us and, for about six to ten weeks after the *Look* article, we received request upon request for appearance on radio programs or television discussion shows.

When the opportunity presented itself for us to spend the summer of 1967 in Europe, teaching for Boston University in its overseas program, we accepted this respite from the almost daily pressures and activities that had, by now, become a "normal part" of our lives since the first publication of *Christmas in Purgatory*.

Upon our return to the United States, I found several messages to call Dr. Milton Greenblatt, newly appointed Commissioner of Mental Health. Dr. Greenblatt succeeded Dr. Harry Solomon, who had retired the previous spring after a long and distinguished career as Harvard professor of psychiatry and, later, Commissioner of Mental Health. An appointment was made and Dr. Greenblatt quickly came around to his purpose in asking for the meeting. In March of 1967, the Commonwealth of Massachusetts passed legislation reorganizing the Massachusetts Department of Mental Health. For those in the fields allied to mental health and mental retardation, it will be enough to mention that this reorganization was in compliance both with the dissatisfactions voiced in our Commonwealth concerning the care, treatment, and services offered the mentally ill and the mentally retarded, and with the federal guidelines requiring the establishment of mental health–mental retardation regions and areas for states wishing to be eligible to receive federal support for construction and staffing of mental health–mental retardation programs. The Massachusetts legislation was, in my opinion, a landmark, a pioneering achievement. It provided for the utilization of nonmedical personnel in high administrative positions. Further, it required the participation of citizens on area and regional boards. It mandated the development of community programs and the provision for alternatives to institutionalization for the mentally ill and mentally retarded. Commissioner Greenblatt asked me to become the first nonmedical director of the newly organized Division of Mental Retardation. I explained to him that I was not prepared to leave Boston University or university life. He explained to me that it was his understanding that I was scheduled for a sabbatical leave of absence for the coming spring semester. Why, he asked, couldn't I request a leave of absence, instead of a sabbatical? My first reaction was to refuse the directorship. Probably, the prime arguments for my later change of decision were the remarks made by several people in state government— remarks that I knew to be perfectly valid and to which I had no ready response. Essentially, I was reminded that men of good conscience cannot turn away in the face of their responsibilities to attempt to remediate those problems. I had articulated those problems and aroused a public storm. Here was my opportunity to do more than talk about them. How could I refuse it?

I began this new assignment with the Department of Mental Health on January 2, 1968, expecting to return to Boston University on September 1. Sometime during the late spring and early summer of 1968, after appropriate telephone calls from Governor Volpe and visits from Commissioner Greenblatt and myself to university officials, my leave was extended through the fall semester. In the late fall, a similar "attack" was mounted by various state officials and citizen groups, including Governor Volpe, but without Commissioner Greenblatt's or my participation (we had promised the University that I would return for the spring semester). I returned to the University in January, with a great many mixed feelings—excited and happy to be "back home," and, at the same time, regretting the friendships that must now be neglected, the "action" of the past, and the mission that must now be continued indirectly and without—to use a favorite term of Dr. Greenblatt's—governmental "clout." These were the antecedents.

In May I was invited to address a joint meeting of the Massachusetts House and Senate on the problems confronting our state schools for the mentally retarded. As matters were presented to me, it was one of the most important and delicate assignments I had ever been challenged with. If we could arouse their interest and support in ways that we had never been able to before, there was a chance that the legislature would take extraordinary measures to relieve the plight of back ward patients and other state school residents. I was acquainted with some of these legislators, a few of whom I admired very much. I was aware that most of the legislators knew of me and knew of *Christmas in Purgatory*. Senator Beryl Cohen, of Brookline, one of the spearheads most responsible for the passage of the Commonwealth mental health–mental retardation bill mentioned earlier, stated publicly that his distribution of our book, *Christmas in Purgatory*, in the final hours of Senate debate of that bill caused sufficient numbers of senators to reverse their earlier stands and tipped the balance to ensure favorable passage of the legislation.

I consider that address to the legislature, "The Dark Side of the Mirror," the most important public address I have ever given. It can be found in *Exodus from Pandemonium*. The chapters there by Dorothea Dix and George Albee, written more than a hundred years apart and concerning different times and places, indicate that time passes but times change grudgingly. All three addresses are so strikingly similar in purpose, so plainly clear about a problem that should interest every one of us, and reveal conditions so outrageous, that one wonders what is actually required before things change as time passes. I am optimistic that times will change and things will be better. However, I realize now that we must present with unremitting regularity the raw data of institutions, descriptions upon descriptions upon descriptions of what transpires in those dungeons of hell. The purpose of the following is to present those raw data, most from my own observations and reactions, with a perspective from Dix and Albee—and hope from Jimmy. Jimmy's story shows both the horror that we permit to exist and the beauty that can be nurtured anywhere.

SPOILED HUMANITY

On January 4, 1968, I had a nightmare. I awoke terrified, not being able to forget the ghoulish textures and sounds of that experience. We were in the jungle, fighting—whom?

One of our men was hit very hard. His head was almost gone and parts of his body were torn away. He wouldn't die. He continued to talk, to ask for water, to hope he wasn't causing us too much trouble. And my reaction? During the nightmare, or after I had returned to the real illusion—wakefulness—I kept saying, over and over again, "Die, die you louse!" The nightmare was not in his dying but in his living. I would tolerate death but not life that does not resemble life, that is disguised as death but is too obstinate to die. I was embittered with this man who was beginning to smell, with this offensive spoiled piece of humanity, who had not the decency, character, and good judgment to die without the agonizing fuss he perpetrated on us.

Which parts of the above were in the nightmare and which were the aftermath meanderings of a disturbing experience is impossible to judge. However, as I drove that morning to the _____ state school for a meeting with its superintendant, Dr. _____, I could not erase from my thoughts the inhuman wish I had for the death of another human being.

Say it is fate, coincidence, retribution, or immanent justice for moral transgressions of the night before. For whatever the reason, the nightmare continued at _____. That afternoon, I learned or reconfirmed several things I now believe:

1. The realities of life can be as terrifying as our subconscious ghosts swirling through the blackness of those pits we construct in our brains between midnight and dawn.
2. Over a period of time, being forced to contend with "spoiled humanity" dehumanizes us.
3. We cannot tell people to act as human beings and expect that they will heed our advice or command. Under certain conditions, people will behave as we suppose humans should behave; under other conditions, they will not.

On that afternoon at _____, I asked to see _____ building, their domicile for male severely retarded ambulatory adults. Accompanied by the institutional steward and John Callahan and Phil Dick of our central office, I revisited purgatory for the first time since those eventful days of late 1965 and early 1966. Goading John and Phil to enter that foul-smelling, evil-sounding den of disaster—they preferring to go directly to lunch, not wanting to risk Herculean tests of their appetites—I pushed the three of us into the rancid kitchen as we entered from the sweet smelling outdoors, surrounded by towering pines, picturesque snow-covered glades, meadows, and country walks.

Stumbling amidst those buried lives, the indelicate care, the blatant—and subtle—pandemonium, were shapeless forms who milled about mumbling incoherently, incognitant, incognizant, inert. One hundred and forty-eight grinning, frowning, shrieking, silent, wasted, and forsaken brothers greeted us. Their welcome made me suck in my breath, clench my teeth, resolute in my purpose to expiate for some debt or abnormal obligation, to once again tremble through this bitter experience, see every room, every cell, every defiled body, and ask the same warped questions:

How many patients do you have?
How many attendants are on duty here?
Where are the solitary cells?
Why does it stink here?
God! How can you work here? YOU appear to be human.

We were taken first to the dormitory, where beds were lined—row upon row, sides and heads abutting—beds without pillows, without a sign that this one's yours or that one's mine, beds arranged and covered "by the numbers" assigned to men who long ago ceased to exist as men, who were now on the cruelest of journeys nearing road's-end in _____ Building.

On several of these beds we saw huge mounds of tattered, colorless clothing, waiting to be sorted and stored. In attendants' areas, closets, and even in one solitary confinement cell, we noticed piles and piles of garments—unrecognizable, faded and shapeless (clothes for unrecognizable, misshapen people)—assigned randomly to building residents and collected periodically on washday for eventual countless reassignments. I have read descriptions of the beauty and loftiness of communal life. Possibly, devotees of such systems have some valid argument. However, I am irrevocably persuaded that there is nothing implicitly uplifting or ennobling in communal underwear, and I feel certain that no political or welfare manifesto can convince me otherwise.

From the dormitory, we proceeded to the day room. A day room is that place in the residential facility intended to resemble most the family or living room. This is the area for group interaction and fellowship or, possibly, for television, quiet games or parties. The _____ Building day room is quite large, I should guess 40' × 50', contained by peeling walls and ceiling, and a cement floor—the center of which has a circular sewer of about one foot diameter.

Entering the day room, we observed 50 to 60 adults in varying degrees of nakedness—most of them completely bare, others with a shirt, underwear, a sock. Some were standing, others lying on the cement floor, and a group were sitting or sprawling along benches that circled much of the room. In the center stood the matron. (I always believed this term was reserved for women attendants in institutions; in our state institutions, all charge attendants are officially matrons.) Mr. _____, the matron, is a young athletic-looking man. He was wielding a slop broom seemingly trying to push the recently accumulated debris, feces, and urine into the floor sewer—conveniently installed for such purposes by our efficient engineering service. He was facing away from the entrance and, as the moans and other noises of the room were quite vigorous, we now accidentally became undetected observers.

I am not certain how many minutes we remained unnoticed. I do know that I walked to the left of the day room, having been told that an isolation room was located off that section. Further, I remember peering into that confinement window and observing a teenage boy wrapped in a blanket, lying on the bare floor of the cubicle—no bed, no toilet, just the hopeless, unremitting and inevitable program toward the destruction of a man. I further remember that, as I turned to rejoin our group, I stumbled over one young man lying on the floor adjacent to the isolation room and that that clumsiness, in turn, caused me to trip onto another one, lying nearby. Possibly, all of the aforementioned lasted no more than 60 or 80 seconds for, as I returned to the day room entrance, Mr. _____ was still engaged in his sweeping chores. Why didn't I call out to him to announce our presence? I prefer to think—yes, I truly believe—our failure to make our visit known, to either shout out or stride out across the room, resulted from our hesitation to interrupt him while he was performing his work and our unwillingness to negotiate a walk through that horrible, surrealistic, irrational arrangement of life. It may be that John Callahan and I huddled together, unwilling to retreat from the reassurance of our togetherness, and the comfort of swift escape, if need be, through the exit an arm's length away. Of this I am certain, there was no mendacity to our behavior, if for no other reason than the fact—consciously obvious even to us—that we were overwhelmed by the situation and incapable of then planning anything so cunning as a secret observation.

We stared, gazing rigidly in fear and wonderment, for possibly a minute, no more. In an instant or two the setting changed totally. Mr. _____ shouted some command at one of the denuded men who was seated on a bench. I didn't hear his words but it seemed that he was issuing some instructions or orders. Apparently unsatisfied with the man's reaction to his message, before our horror-struck eyes he lifted that filthy slop broom and, over and over and over again, beat it down upon the naked cowering body, a steady stream of curses spewing from his enraged tongue.

As with all nightmares—at least those I have—this one lasted no more than two or three minutes. As with all nightmares, it is the preoccupation with the morbidity of our reactions that has lasting and telling effects on our personality and behavior. One may ponder why these fleeting seconds so profoundly disturb me and, on the other hand, why those responsible for the System and who perpetrated and were participant to the specific misdeed toss off with incredulous disdain my indictment that evil inhumanity permeates that environment. I believe that any discomfort the Superintendent and Mr. _____ derived from the incident obtained not from the fact that a staff member acted cruelly, but from the embarrassment and threat of my accusation which was made forcefully and officially.

The question I ask is: What was so offensive to me but not to them? Rhetorical and essentially unresolvable questions usually expect no answer. However, I have an answer, albeit metaphysical and introspective. I cannot tolerate spoiled organic matter, expecially spoiled humanity. I gag at the sight and smell of piled garbage and decay, with its swarming maggots and oozing slime that pulsates in its primitive living cellular and animal parasitic kingdom. Neither, I suspect, can Superintendent _____ tolerate spoiled garbage, for didn't he include in his newest building a specially built walk-in refrigerator for *Garbage*—so it wouldn't spoil between the time of its storage and removal to the institutional dump?

I cannot tolerate human garbage and that is what these patients have been turned into, and that is how I believe they are now viewed at _____ Building.

It is always fruitless—more, a denial of rational life—to attempt to convince someone that supercrescence, filth, slime, all things scatalogical, and all things uretic are natural and, consequently, completely acceptable facets of our human eminence. Yet, there are those among us who, rather than conceive of and develop programs for people that are ideational counterparts to refrigeration and sanitary engineering, delude themselves and others into accepting and perpetrating environments nurturing human garbage. Their ministry is not education or social welfare. Their mission is not rehabilitation and a return to human dignity and participation. Their ministry is delusion and deception and hypocrisy—to accept for their brothers that which they would not tolerate in a barrel of garbage. They have traded their brothers' birthright for a stainless steel walk-in cooler and have been able to accept and justify the coexistence of fresh unspoiled garbage and humanity turned sour and rotten. In so doing, they have traded their own birthright and humanism. Words cannot describe how deeply all of this offends me.

RESTRAINT, SECLUSION, AND PUNISHMENT

Woe to the misbegotten, the senile, and the legally incarcerated! Woe to anyone we think subhuman, for the becoming is in the thinking and the being is not what is but the apprehension of what will be. Pity those who believe that God is dead or that death is God. Beware of the gods who live, who deign to judge the humanity of a man as well as his spirit, worth, and utilitarian competency. Beware of he who will forsake a human for the cause of humanity. Look carefully at philosophies and institutions that explain and justify to human beings, and at systems that brutalize both the offender and the offended.

For some time, I have been studying first-hand the various forms in which brutality is permitted to be expressed in our state schools for the mentally retarded. Some of man's inhumanity is legal; some is quasi-legal; some, if detected, would result in dismissal or, possibly, criminal proceedings. It is hoped that studies of these types of behaviors may lead to some notions concerning the foundations of human abuse, notions that may give rise, eventually, to universal practices divested of the cruelty, brutality, and human divisiveness that we, in our generations, are noted for and accept as natural conditions of civilization.

At one state school, in the dormitory housing the most severely retarded ambulatory women, four solitary confinement cells are continuously filled, and a waiting list exists for their use. During a recent visit, I found two young women in one cell, lying nude in the corner, their feces smeared on the walls, ceiling, and floor—two bodies huddled in the darkness, on a bare terrazzo floor, without competency or understanding of the wrongs they have committed and with no hope that those on the other side of the cell will ever comprehend this unholy incarceration. On the next floor was a girl who has been in a solitary cell for five years, never leaving—not for food or toileting or sleep. This cell—this concrete and tile cubicle—without furniture or mattress or blanket or washstand, is one human being's total universe. Across the hall, on the other side of the day room, is another cell where paces a sixteen- or seventeen-year-old girl, nude and assaultive, incontinent and non-verbal. One day each month her parents call for her. She is washed and dressed and they take her home or for a ride in the country or, possibly, to a restaurant. One day each month her clothes remain on her, she communicates, she is a human being.

At the above institution, an attendant in another dormitory was found kicking a patient who was in the throes of an epileptic seizure. The attendant was dismissed by the superintendent. Many employees became angered by this and a "work slowdown" erupted, with a genuine strike imminent. During one tense moment, while negotiations and recriminations were exchanged between labor and management, an employee told the superintendent that management had committed the one unpardonable sin, placing the welfare of patients above that of employees.

Recently, a retarded boy was accepted to a state school for the mentally retarded. During the admission interview with a school physician, the child's mother was told that her son would be placed in the "worst building" with 140 residents, most substantially older than he, with no more than three attendants on duty during any one shift. She was told that she could not see her son until three months after his admission. The physician added that after six months, if the family should want to take their son home for a visit, a state school social worker would conduct an investigation to determine if the family was suitable for such an arrangement. The mother said that as she had adequately cared for the child since birth such an investigation seemed somewhat out of place. The mother was also told that most of the residents in the dormitory were nude and many were abusive in their behavior. She learned that there were no chairs in the dormitory because the "State" did not provide them. In answer to the question, "Do the residents have anything to do?", the admitting physician replied, "No." This parent decided, on admission day, to withdraw her application for placement, despite the family doctor's warning that she was in poor health and physically unable to care for the child any longer.

Recently, a patient at a state school hospital become critically ill with high fever, shock, and coma. The staff physician diagnosed a "severe virus infection" and prescribed penicillin. At postmortem, the patient was diagnosed as having had acute purulent meningitis, due to pneumococcus infection. The case was presented at a clinical-pathological conference, attended by an outside consultant, resident physicians, and three of the twelve school staff doctors, one of whom was the physician attending the case. The consultant, in presenting the postmortem finding, concentrated on the birth injury which had caused the patient's retardation and, undoubtedly to avoid embarrassment for the staff, only briefly mentioned, without further comment, the existence of the acute and fatal meningitis. It is general medical practice that in a case such as this, the diagnosis of an acute viral illness is made only after all treatable bacterial infections have been ruled out; lumbar puncture, to exclude meningitis, is mandatory under such circumstances. Penicillin was given for this presumed "viral infection," yet it should be general knowledge that penicillin is ineffective against viral infections. Penicillin, improperly prescribed, happened to be the correct treatment, but to have been successful it would have required a larger dosage administered intravenously. Since neither the superintendent nor assistant superintendent attends the clinical-pathological conferences, they probably do not know of this medical error. Neither do the nine staff doctors who failed to attend this conference nor, most disturbingly, do those who did—including the physician involved—since in an attempt to spare feelings, the error was not discussed.

Recently, in a state school, a senior physician recommended that a resident have seven healthy teeth extracted in order to prevent her from eating the threads of the day-room rug.

At another institution, a child was found to be in severe diabetic ketoacidosis on a Friday, after a Thursday holiday (a "skeleton duty" day). The emergency request for blood sugar measurement was begun by the laboratory technician more than five hours after the initial request. Other key laboratory tests were unavailable. This medical emergency requires expert nursing, frequent and immediate monitoring of blood and urine tests, and even then has a significant mortality. The physician recommended immediate transfer to a community hospital, where these facilities were available. The assistant superintendent flatly refused this transfer because of a shortage of funds for this purpose, and considered the matter closed. The staff physician, through personal contacts, was able to arrange transfer to a research ward at a large city hospital at no charge to the state. That research unit is not supposed to provide this type of emergency service. The physician in charge of the research unit, however, admitted the patient since he recognized that without this subterfuge, the patient would have died.

Recently, in a state school, a severely retarded child choked to death when an attendant fed her a whole hard-boiled egg. There was no subsequent postmortem, inquiry or investigation, or even a staff conference to determine the possibility of any negligence or other unusual circumstances surrounding this unfortunate incident.

Within twenty-four hours, during a hepatitis epidemic at a state school, twenty-seven of seventy-one patients in one building were diagnosed as having this dread disease. A request was made by the physician in charge of the building to the director of nursing for extra personnel, since only three staff members were on duty at that time. The director promised to send help several times, but left suddenly for a three day vacation without assigning additional help or someone to succeed him in his absence.

At one state school, a seven-year-old was tied—hands and feet—to the four corners of her dormitory crib. The physician explained that this restraint was necessary because the child had tied an elastic band around her finger until it became gangrenous, and subsequently attempted to eat the finger. When mittens were put on, she began eating a toe. Now she is restrained in bed to prevent her from biting herself.

At another state school, George is described by the dormitory physician as a "monster." He is in seclusion twenty-four hours a day because, the physician explains, when permitted freedom he bites and kicks the other children. The physician, describing George as one who "Frankenstein's monster would be afraid of," pointed out a victim of George's behavior who now has only half an ear lobe.

I was once visited by a member of the Parent's Association of one of our state schools. She wanted me to know, just as she knew, of certain conditions existing in a particular building at the school. She was especially concerned with that building since she was its representative to the Parent's Association and her own son is a resident there. The building she described is very old and was meant to house approximately 75 people. Now it must serve 117. About 20 of these soil frequently and cannot feed themselves. Twelve of the residents are aggressive and violent. On the other hand, 70 of the residents can dress and care for themselves and 17 have attained the status of "worker boys." These are residents who are able to help the attendant with chores around their dormitory, primarily with feeding others.

All of these residents, with the exception of the "worker boys," are crowded each morning into the incredibly drab day room, many of them naked and all without shoes. Under these conditions, even the more capable ones regress when placed with the profoundly retarded and the violent. This visitor also described extraordinarily inadequate bathing and showering facilities. The residents aren't even soaped and, with so many being untidy, permanent odors remain on their bodies. At 4:30 p.m., everyone is brought into the dining room for supper, the majority of them naked. She has never seen pajamas or nightgowns on any residents, yet she claims parents often supply these. She said that each person has only one threadbare blanket to use for cover, this being inadequate on cold winter nights. When new blankets come to the building, they "disappear fast." Sleeping arrangements are so crowded that beds are touching, end to end and side to side. The doors of the sleeping wards are locked. When my visitor inquired about the fire hazard, she was told it was necessary to lock the wards so that attendants may take turns having their evening meal. During the night (11:00 p.m. to 7:00 a.m.) there is only one attendant on duty for the entire building. Should there be a fire, it would result in a catastrophe, especially during the winter when piles of snow block the fire escape doors. This visitor, whom I regard as an intelligent and sensitive person, feels insulted, degraded, and humiliated by a state which forces her son to live under such circumstances. These conditions are unfit to be called humane or decent and, ironically, the family is charged $7.70 each day for such care.

In 1911, Dr. L. Vernon Briggs framed for Massachusetts the first state law on the use of restraint. Our pioneering illustrious history does not exclude us from the perpetration of abuses, couched in the legal terminology of "restraint" and "seclusion." During a recent month, at one of our state schools, there were 11 seclusion orders and 103 restraint orders issued. At another school, during the same month, there were no seclusion or restraint orders issued.

How is it possible for one state school to conduct its affairs without the necessity to restrain or seclude its residents while another state school—with ostensibly the same kinds of patients with the same kinds of problems—must resort frequently to the restraining jacket and the solitary cell? Where is the influence of our illustrious predecessors, those great humanists who conceived of and built residential centers for the care and humane treatment of those afflicted with amentia? What are the causes of brutality, callousness, insensitivity toward another human being, professional malpractice and incompetence, unreasonable or excessive or unnecessary restraint or seclusion? Is it only the budget that is deficient? Or the overcrowded conditions of the state schools? Is it the understaffed and overworked employees? Surely, the aforementioned are very much related to the unforgivable conditions described in this chapter and elsewhere in this book. Surely, more funds, more appropriate staff, and less crowded conditions would have obviated a multitude of sins, some more horrible than even those reported here. However, funds and staff and physical conditions are only part of that total fabric, human abuse, which we must better understand some day.

I have developed two hypotheses concerning the conditions leading to human abuse and the consequences of such practices. Hopefully, these hypotheses will provide us with a way of studying an aspect of human behavior that, although unpleasant and frightening, may well be the cornerstone of an eventual theory of group behavior leading to an eventual society of civilized men.

It is hypothesized that human beings conceived of as animals, or not as human beings, are treated as animals, or not as human beings. Secondly, animals conceived of as other than animals are not treated as animals. The following is, with the exception of two word changes, a direct quote from the *Boston Globe*, June 5, 1968:

> Each year the U.S. Food and Drug Administration condemns millions of children to death by poisoning. The FDA does this, it says, to test the safety of drugs.

The test children suffer horribly. Their bodies shake with spasms, they stagger, they arch and roll in agony, their eyes bulge from their heads and discharge tears, and they go into convulsions. The more fortunate die in hours, but many suffer for weeks—or even months. The luckless survivors are re-used.

The above is unbelievable, horrifying, excruciatingly painful to the reader. Our civilization has not degenerated to the degree where such practices occur. I have substituted the word "children" for the word "animals" which appeared in the original advertisement sponsored by United Action for Animals. Why did I deliberately mislead you? As long as one believed that this report concerned with children was a news story, in a reputable newspaper, the horror of it all became an overwhelming burden. However, how often have we read such advertisements or newspaper stories concerning animals? This we can contend with and, in fact, most of us aren't even slightly affected or moved by such cruelties. The hypothesis, stated above, and discussed elsewhere in this book, is that it is almost impossible to deliberately torture another human being (unless the torturer has a rare pathology of his own) without agreeing and believing that the victim is not "really" human. Once that belief is inculcated, man can—and does—perpetrate the ultimate abuse and inhumane treatment. The problem before us is that of developing better ways of ensuring that those dealing with people are given every opportunity and encouragement to develop conceptions that continuously confirm and reconfirm the basic worth of these human beings.

It is hypothesized that a society is judged most harshly by that of which it should be most ashamed, and that judgment is the most accurate reflection of the society's sickness. Further, from the multitude of conditions and situations which can bring shame to a society (that which demonstrates inhumane treatment of humans is the most shameful) that sickness has the power to flood out whatever good the society is accomplishing.

What are the consequences of the above hypotheses if, as you can agree for purposes of discussion, their repeated testing would not cause us to disown them? We may come to understand that our most difficult task ahead in a national program to reform residential and community settings for the mentally retarded will not be how to raise sufficient funds, or build better facilities, or pass more appropriate legislation. Our most formidable hurdle will be to engage the support and involvement of people whose conceptions of human potential are optimistic and whose views of humanity do not exclude any one segment from membership in the human family. Our task will be not only to enjoin those with such conceptions to enlist in the movement, but to find ways of helping people without such convictions to deal more effectively with their prejudices and biases concerning the possibilities that all human beings are valuable and changeable. Society's judgment of the progress that has been made on behalf of the mentally retarded will continue to be harsh and, in its own way, prejudiced, until such time as the most severely retarded and the most severely neglected receive the treatment due them as human beings.

Earlier this year, I received a telephone call from the assistant superintendent of one of our state schools who, during the superintendent's vacation, was acting as chief officer. This assistant superintendent has been at the school for many years, the same institution described earlier in reference to a budding insurrection resulting from the dismissal of an employee for kicking a child. He has had the reputation of being a kindly man, although one not noted for relishing "head-on" encounters with employees, a mild person with distaste for controversy or disagreement. He called for advice or, rather, reaction. A chief nurse reported to him that an attendant kicked a child and, although only grazing her, severe disciplinary action was indicated. The assistant superintendent told me that after a lengthy hearing, and in consideration of the 10-year employment record of the attendant, he placed her on three-week suspension without pay. Yesterday, I received a carbon of a letter he sent to this attendant, informing her of his action and his displeasure with her behavior. Although I find it difficult to be happy receiving news of anyone's suspension or discharge, I felt a sense of progress and timeliness and hope when I received that suspension notice. Maybe, at least at that state school, the corner has been turned and the reformation has begun. Maybe, it is a portent of things to come when a conservative administrator has the conviction and courage to suspend a permanent employee for what, heretofore, has been a common and unnoted occurrence. I will keep that carbon, and, someday long after my tenure as commissioner is completed, I may well frame it. It is truly a symbol of what we have been and what lies ahead for all of us.

LIMBUS: MAN'S SUBTLE CATASTROPHE

A child, Debbie, who is in treatment at our University Psycho-Educational Clinic, wrote a poem:

> *Snow is very white,*
> *Snow is oh so very white,*
> *But it will get dirty.*
>
> *Ants are so small,*
> *Ants are interesting,*
> *But they will die off.*

Winter is a season,
It is very pretty,
But it will leave us.
Bees buzz all the time,
It seems that they never stop,
But they do.

Debbie has expressed for me, better than I ever could, the feeling of hopelessness and helplessness that permeates the minds and souls of those in our institutions and those others of us who visit there. For the ordinary condition in our institutions is not one involving violence or brutality or illegal treatment—although these are much more ordinary in institutions than they are in the community. The ordinary condition is boredom more than brutality, legal abuse more than illegal assault, and a subtle degradation rather than a blatant holocaust. However, this genteel catastrophe is deadening, it's overwhelming, for it floods out whatever opportunities residents and staff have to rise together in some common attempt for personal dignity and mutual human concern. This subtle catastrophe is the mortar filling in the cracks and anchoring the devastation and permanence manufactured by the heavy hand of the System. The subtle catastrophe is the belief most have that everything—anything—will either get dirty, die off, or leave us. Nothing can escape the plague, everyone and everything is doomed eventually to ignoble demise or perpetual anonymity, dying as we all must but never having lived. The subtle catastrophe is knowing that all is forsaken, that not only is God dead but He never was and neither are we. One cries, not because he is in pain but because he does not know what pain is or what love is. To be in pain, one must be alive. The previous section illustrates examples of restraint, seclusion, and punishment. This section will deal with legal abuse, sanctioned mendacity, and chaos as a reflection not of a deliberate program but of the consequence of a hopeless System.

About a month ago, I visited one of the state schools, having been invited to meet with and address a group of attendants who were working on a project designed to habilitate our so-called "back ward" residents. By prearrangement, I went directly to the Administration Building for a brief meeting and informal discussion with one of the institutional administrators, concerning a couple of then current problems. He was in a highly agitated state. During the previous night, in the building housing the most severely retarded ambulatory male patients, a forty-year-old resident was stabbed in the testicles by an unknown assailant. The attendant on duty bandaged the wound as best she could and wrapped it in a diaper. She noted on her building chart that the man should be seen by the building physician in the morning. The patient was returned to bed and remained there, alone, throughout the night, without any medical attention, other than the treatment of a night attendant. By morning, the physician's examination disclosed that the man required immediate surgery and hospitalization.

Until recently, in many of our institutions, a major responsibility of the institutional dentist was to extract teeth of those who bit themselves or other people or ate "inedible" matter. I have seen and spoken with innumerable girls and boys—ten, fifteen, twenty years old—with hardly any teeth in their mouths, because teeth have been removed in years past for committing such "offenses." Today, in one institution, the dentist may not extract teeth without the authorization of a staff physician who will rule on the medical need for such treatment. In another institution, finally, appliances are used for those who bite themselves or others. These appliances—although not very comfortable-appearing to the observer—discourage enthusiasm for extracting healthy teeth.

In another institution, as one enters the main Administration Building, he reads a prominently displayed sign, stating: NO VISITORS ARE PERMITTED ON LEGAL HOLIDAYS. As institutions attempt to get along with skeleton staffs on legal holidays, thus permitting personnel to enjoy these days with their own families, the decision had been made that it would be inconvenient to permit visitors on such days. At times, I found it difficult to convince—really convince, so that programmatic changes were implemented—colleagues and certain institutional staff that it is morally wrong to base administrative policy on whether it is or isn't convenient for the staff. This is not to say that staff needs and conveniences should receive no consideration. The staff are entitled to as much consideration as possible, *as long as the needs of residents are the first priority*, rather than the last. To this day, I am not able to convince the institutional superintendent who made the ruling about no holiday visiting that it is an insensitive disregard of the needs of his residents and their families.

In one state school, children in a particular dormitory go to bed each night wearing dungarees instead of pajamas, on mattresses without sheets or pillows. In that dormitory each child is given a pair of socks, a shirt, and dungarees (usually not underwear) each day. There is no "ownership" to these garments, only temporary usage until the next batch of laundry comes in and the child receives another pair of socks, another shirt, another pair of dungarees. At this same institution, in another dormitory for children of approximately the same age and level of ability, each child has pajamas. Each bed has a clean sheet. There is order to the building and sufficient supplies and equipment to maintain basic health and care. The matron in the first building is new at the job, doesn't know her "way around" too well, and doesn't know how to get all the things she needs for the children in her building. The second matron has been at the institution many years, is friendly with the steward and the treasurer, has a good deal of personal prestige and power. Her children are well cared for. In one of the infirm buildings of this institution, inhabited by sixty children—most of whom are in cribs much of the day—two attendants are on duty during feeding time. In one hour, these two attendants are required to spoon feed sixty children. Averaging two minutes per child, they complete this arduous task with an incredible degree of good humor, warmth, and good will—this, in spite of the inescapable conclusion that some of those children require at least one half hour for feeding. When one understands that "feeding time" may well be the only human contact of any durable length (two minutes!) that some of these children have, the viciousness of this practice becomes excruciatingly clear. As a minimum essential, and incredible as this may sound to a State Bureau of Personnel, the proper feeding of such children requires twenty to thirty matrons, attendants, and volunteers, if it is to be accomplished in a one hour period. Problems such as this, incidentally, require us to consider and reconsider the feasibility of unitizing a residential school along geographic lines rather than along etiological or competency lines. Such unitization—e.g., placing all children from a particular geographic home area in residence together, regardless of etiology or level of functioning—distributed through many residential facilities of the institution would include difficult management problems as well as residents who facilitate care and treatment programs. There are many problems to be found with such unitization, problems that we have not begun to understand—much less solve. However, the spectre of sixty young unable children being fed by two attendants in an hour's time makes it clear that some change—some radical change—in the System is required. Lastly, it should not be necessary to give any further evidence to support the need for change. We must begin with this need as a "given." If we cannot agree on this, we are in desperately unimaginable difficulty.

Several months ago, I was presented with a critical problem concerning a twelve-year-old boy and the need for his placement in a residential facility for disturbed children. The child was evaluated by the one children's unit the Commonwealth maintains for the disturbed as "disturbed with primary mental retardation." Our state school Community Evaluation and Rehabilitation Center evaluated the child as "retarded with primary emotional disturbance." The children's facility for the disturbed did not feel competent to accept this youngster; nor did the state school for the mentally retarded. All the while, during this period of diagnosing and rediagnosing and classifying and reclassifying, the child was excluded from any community treatment or care facility. He was not in school, he was not in treatment, he was not in day care. He was creating incredible disorder and tension in the home. In order to ease the unbearable strain at home, he was placed, eventually, in a state hospital for the mentally ill. As the state hospital had no facilities for children and no patients younger than sixteen years, it was thought best to place him in a living unit with the youngest adult male patients. However, it was soon learned that this child could not possibly remain in this dormitory. He was physically and sexually abused by several aggressive patients and, literally, his well-being was imperiled as long as he remained in that situation. Consequently, he was transferred to a unit housing older and, oftentimes, senile patients. In this setting, the child became the aggressor and physically assaulted several of the older men. At the present time, this boy is in solitary seclusion at this institution, and has been in seclusion for several months. We have not succeeded in placing him in a more appropriate children's unit for the disturbed. We have not succeeded in interesting the state school for the retarded in accepting responsibility for him. Nor have we developed or planned to develop new special facilities for the disturbed retarded child. This child may well continue to remain in solitary seclusion until such time as he is old enough to fend for himself in an adult dormitory in the state hospital. I am pessimistic that facilities and programs will be made available quickly enough ever to benefit this child. Lastly, there are more than a few children with problems of a similar nature, children who "fall between the cracks," children who are neither eligible for one program or another, children who are excluded from school and exempted from the state facility, children who are called "retarded" by the adolescent unit of the state hospital and "disturbed" by the state school for the mentally retarded, children who are "encouraged" to leave school at the earliest possible age (sixteen) yet are declared "not feasible" for vocational rehabilitation, children who are—as a colleague once remarked to me—CLINICALLY HOMELESS.

Such a child is "David." David was born at full term, with a normal delivery, but mother reported delay in reaching infantile milestones. Further, she reported the onset of continuous rocking behavior commencing at ten months and David's failure, ever, to cry. Reputedly, the boy acquired a vocabulary of approximately twenty words by age two, but subsequently discarded verbal communications and became increasingly egocentric and hyperactive. Mother, nevertheless, thought of David as bright, fully comprehending of her speech, and remarkable for his ability to demonstrate perfect musical pitch and rhythm, the latter skill acquired some time beyond the age of two. Father, now divorced from mother, was described by her as ineffectual, frustrated, and abusive. The marriage was dissolved in David's third year. Mother is described by clinic as alert, vivacious, and attractive, somewhat aggressive, and currently combating a mild overweight problem. At the present time, she is remarried and describes the situation as quite satisfactory. David has been evaluated at numerous hospitals, clinics, residential centers, and state schools. There has been more or less general agreement vis-à-vis the diagnosis, with most evaluations concluding with "Infantile Autism," "Schizoid Reaction, Childhood Type,"or "Kanner's Syndrome." Under the provisions of our Commonwealth legislation for the emotionally disturbed, Chapter 750, David's parents succeeded in entering him in a first-rate residential center for disturbed children. However, because of his hyperactive and assaultive behavior, as well as the minimal progress he was making there, the school returned him to Massachusetts in February, 1968. Since that time, David has been evaluated at one state school and rejected as not eligible for admission due to the presence of "Kanner's Syndrome." At another state school, he was rejected because that facility's "present staffing pattern, groupings of children, open visiting and parent participation policies preclude a residential admission, at least at the present time." The children's unit of the state mental hospital will not accept the child as they evaluate him as "severe mental defective with behavioral reaction." After repeated case conferences, one could conclude that the Commonwealth had little to offer David or his family and that "diagnoses" are very valuable insofar as controlling who is admitted and who is excluded from a treatment facility. It appears ironic that, in spite of the vigorous build-up today of facilities and programs for disturbed and retarded children and adults, there continues to be greater and greater numbers of *clinically homeless people*—those neither wanted by any agency nor the clear-cut responsibility of any agency and, more often than not, those who present the most serious and urgent problems and needs.

We have a System whereby, if a clinical home is found for a child, we may deprive him of rights, privileges, and resources guaranteed to those "on the outside." "Sonny" was admitted to the state school at the age of one month. Now twelve years later, recent evaluations of Sonny indicate that his long-range outlook was reasonable enough to warrant efforts at rehabilitation. Sonny suffers from a rare disorder which limits severely the movement of his tongue, lips, and lower face. This causes people to undervalue his intelligence; for example, having a somewhat blank expression, he is thought to be less alert than he actually is. Even more damaging to his general development and his unfolding self-concept is the fact that he is increasingly unwilling to attempt to use speech or voice as a means of communication. An eminent reconstructive surgeon associated with a nearby large general hospital outlined a specific treatment program designed to increase the strength and usefulness of the chest musculature, to improve the pharyngeal and palatal musculature that he does possess and, eventually, to involve Sonny in an intensive speech therapy program. Further, certain operative procedures dealing with the restoration of speech components would be considered. Lastly, Sonny would be afforded a complete dental therapy program designed to bring the teeth in proper alignment so as to allow lip closure and formation of fricatives. The surgeon had agreed to arrange for the medical expenses for Sonny's treatment. However, the hospital expenses, which would be considerable, were an obligation that faced the state school if the child was to receive this chance for rehabilitation. The total budgeted allocation available to this institution for the hospital care of its residents is $4,000 a year. Sonny's hospitalization, alone, would exceed that amount. Essentially, the Commonwealth does not allocate funds for anything more than the most emergency and necessary outside hospital treatment. Because of these budgetary restrictions, so-called "elective surgery" is rarely viewed by the Commonwealth as its responsibility. Very intensive and dedicated investigation and follow-up by the institutional assistant superintendent revealed that an institutionalized child is not eligible for Medicaid even though the child's family meets the eligibility requirements for this program, which was the case in this situation. That is to say, had Sonny lived at home he would have been eligible for the surgery, therapy, and hospitalization under the provisions of Medicaid which his family was eligible for. However, because he is in the Commonwealth's custody, the Commonwealth is responsible for his health and welfare. However, the Commonwealth did not then—and does not now—allocate sufficient funds to discharge such responsibilities. Consequently, children such as Sonny do not receive the care and treatment that would have been guaranteed to them had they not been placed in a state facility that, one would suppose, should guarantee each such resident adequate care and treatment. Fortunately, in this particular case, the devotion of the aforementioned assistant superintendent to this child and his needs led him to a satisfactory solution to the problem and Sonny, eventually, received the treatment he needed through sponsorship of another Commonwealth agency.

Such cases as David's and Sonny's lead, almost inevitably, to angry confrontations, denials and denunciations, irreparable breaks in relationships, and lasting enmities—not only between and among families and professionals, but between one professional worker and another and between one "good" person and another "good" person. Too many times, our battles are virtuous but, unfortunately, so are our opponents' battles. Unfortunately, our opponents might well have been our friends and our causes often are forgotten before they are realized and long, long before we forgive our enemies their transgressions. We have not learned well enough that Institutions and Systems, much more than individuals, are responsible for the earth's good and evil. When we attempt to comprehend and cope with good or evil, we persist in studying individuals and individual actions. We hardly recognize Institutional and Group and System influence. We do not understand that the true and pervasive mendacity is the mendacity of the System. While I was in office, I had a rather thick file on the activities and correspondence concerning a Mrs. Baker. Mrs. Baker is a member of a church group, committed to provide volunteer service to one of our state schools. In the course of her involvement there she became very frustrated—enraged—at the conditions she observed at the school. An articulate and forceful, as well as humanitarian, woman, she goaded herself to, eventually, petition the governor for his support in changing the conditions she was forced to observe at the state school. After repeated attempts to communicate and receive support from the Administration, the Commissioner of Mental Health, my office, parent groups, newspapers, and numerous other individuals and organizations, she succeeded eventually in having the Board of Trustees of the state school hold a special meeting to consider her specific charges. I attended that meeting as did other members of our central office staff and the superintendent and key staff of the state school. Essentially, she called for a replacement of the superintendent, a reorganization of the state school administration, an increase in budgetary allocations to the school, more active involvement, inspection, and supervision of the facility by the central office, and legislation enabling the modification of certain practices and the development and enlargement of Commonwealth-supported care and treatment programs. She disclosed that there is ample documentation supporting the following conditions of neglect and mistreatment. I quote from her report:

1. We found the children not only nude, filthy, and bruised, but also sitting, sleeping and eating with moist and dried feces covering them and their surroundings.
2. We found children heavily medicated and lying on filthy sheetless beds, uncovered and with flies crawling up and down, and in and out of their noses and mouths.
3. We found children playing in and eating garbage.
4. We found cockroaches and other bugs infesting exposed foods and greasy dishes, and having the run of the building.
5. We found unlocked medicine cabinets, and observed unsupervised and poor dispensing of medicines.
6. We found poor plumbing, locked bathroom doors, exposed electrical cords, poor ventilation, poor lighting, broken windows and screening, knobless and broken doors, drainless floors, filthy and chaotic laundry room conditions, broken and inadequate furnishings.
7. We found hopeless, apathetic, and frustrated patients and employees with no supervision, no evident instruction in procedures, and no schedule or program to follow; their plea to us was that there was continual lack of cooperation from the nursing office.

She reported that the minimum medical care and the minimum standards of fitness for human habitation were not available to children or employees, and that conditions that existed at this state school were due directly to a lack of leadership, supervision, inspection, and training which should have been provided by both the central office and the superintendent of the state school and his administrative staff. Her petitions included reference to inefficient health, sanitation, and safety maintenance control and inefficient methods for recording pertinent data on resident and personnel status. She attempted to document a lack of qualitative purchasing, resulting in false economy. She alluded to misappropriation of funds and unjust distribution of funds as well as inefficient inventory control leading to a tolerated frequent pilferage. Mrs. Baker wrote letters of protest to the governor who sent them to us to prepare responses for his signature. She charged and accused and we justified and defended. Finally, at the Board of Trustees meeting, I found myself almost—but not quite—defending our policies and programs at the state school and denying the charges Mrs. Baker had been making. Obviously, there was a good deal more truth in her charges than falsification. Obviously, I—as well as many other individuals around that Trustees' table—was as anxious as Mrs. Baker to change the conditions she described. However, I—and perhaps others there too—realized that she (and all of us at one time or another) was attacking "evil people" rather than "an evil System." Certainly, some superintendents are more creative than others and some have more good will than others and some are more optimistic than others. However, to get at the root cause of the problems she so eloquently delineated and discussed, what is needed is a great deal more than just changing superintendents and certain staff. The subtleness of man's subtle catastrophe lies not only in what is around us but who— and, more likely what—caused what is around us.

> Snow is very white,
> Snow is oh so very white,
> But it will get dirty.

I hope that, some day, Debbie can write that there is always time for a new snowfall, for a second chance, for one more opportunity. There is always tomorrow.

LEAVES FROM A EUROPEAN DIARY[1]

August 27, 1968: 2:00 A.M. Natick, Mass.

One year ago today, Edward (then age 13), Steven (10), Michael (7), my wife Ethel and I, boarded a plane for return home to Natick, Massachu-

---

[1] Some readers, mostly younger ones, may be puzzled about the inclusion of a section concerning a summer trip to Germany in a book of this kind. Although they have read about Nazi Germany, the Holocaust is about as removed from their lives as the American Revolution is from ours. The author asks those readers to accept—on faith—the logic supporting such inclusion.

setts. Our trip had begun on June 11, and during the ensuing eleven weeks we visited the Scandinavian countries, the British Isles, Luxemburg, France, Austria and, for seven weeks, West Germany. Of all the places on Earth, why should we set foot in that dread land that inspired Dachau, Auschwitz, Treblinka, and ONE HUNDRED OTHERS?

Several years ago, Boston University developed overseas graduate programs in a few selected fields, primarily for servicemen and teachers assigned to American dependent schools in the European theater. One such program is in the field of education and I had been asked to teach my course "Nature and Needs of the Mentally Retarded" during one of the summer sessions sponsored in Germany. After considerable family discussion, over a period of several months, we agreed to participate in this program. The plan was for all of us to travel to Munich for a briefing period early in June, drive to Heidelberg for participation in the graduation ceremonies for the preceding year's students, teach a three week intensive course in Stuttgart, and return to Munich for a repeat of the Stuttgart course. At the conclusion of that assignment, we would have one full month remaining for travel through Scandinavia and the British Isles.

What were the advantages, as we envisioned them then, and what were the liabilities of such a plan? The opportunity presented would permit our family to spend three months together, much of this time free to explore, to visit the museums, to enjoy the scenery and countryside. This opportunity would permit a retreat, albeit temporary, from what had been a very rigorous year and what was expected to be a continuation of work pressure and personal demands once the new academic calendar and schedule dominated the fall season.

Why did we hold back, have reservations about this trip, refuse an identical invitation of the previous year? It was Germany! Why couldn't we be asked to teach in France, or England, or—better yet—Israel? That which at first had made us hesitant about going to Germany later made me resolute, determined to live for a period of time in that land. I must admit that my determination to go to Germany, once I had made up my mind, was a minority position in our household, as well as a selfish one. Further, my reasons for this determination did not fully crystallize until we were firmly ensconced in that country. From the time when the possibility of a summer in Germany first presented itself until our plane landed in Munich, I had been slowly—but increasingly—developing the notion that it would be important for me to observe and study the German people, in light of the holocaust of the 30s and 40s, a period in history to which I had become morbidly attached. It was not until several weeks after our arrival that I began to think seriously, in fact regularly, about the striking correlates of Nazi Germany and its concentration camps and American mental health and its institutions for the retarded. That summer in Europe gave me a perspective of things that increases in importance as I review them.

It is hoped that this presentation of selected passages from that summer's diary—impressions recorded not with any thought for eventual publication but in keeping with the roles we were assuming as travelers and tourists—will contribute something toward comprehending mankind's capabilities for destruction, and the conditions that appear to be present during these periodic barbarisms in which human beings participate. I had already spent considerable time observing attendants in some of our most wretched back wards. I had spoken to these men and women, calmly and rationally, eye to eye. Now, I wanted to observe the German citizen, speak to him calmly and rationally, eye to eye. I wanted to visit Dachau and try to understand what was then—and now—an incomprehensible and fiendish period of inhuman history. Certainly, these excerpts can make no pretension insofar as unraveling the puzzle of The Third Reich or understanding the German culture as it is known today. Far more sophisticated and erudite attempts toward these kinds of understandings are available to the reader. However, these impressions may be useful within the context of a book on human abuse. There is no doubt in my mind, after reading too many histories and personal accounts of the German death camps, that the Germany of our generations will be recorded as the most savage, inhuman, ungodlike tribe ever to inhabit this Earth, the likes of which we pray will never be seen again. For one interested in the foundations of human abuse, in retrospect, it seems clear that the German people should be studied from every angle possible, with even an *ex post facto* analysis likely to prove valuable.

June 17, 1967: 6:15 P.M. Bayrischer Hauf, Heidelberg

Most aspiring Germans carry briefcases. I am told these are used to store lunch and other necessities. Usually, middle class workers—both male and female—carry these briefcases, although some blue collar workers also find them valuable accessories. Those blue collar workers that do not carry briefcases, oftentimes an "old time factory hand" or "laborer," generally wear what we in America call "laboratory coats." Some workers wear boots and knickerbockers. All bellhops wear green aprons and bus and street car conductors have uniforms indentical to my sterotyped conception of a German military officer. It must be an overreaction, but my impressions lead to the conclusion that there is some design to all of this.

June 20, 1967: 3:45 P.M. Robinson Kaserne, Stuttgart

From a few discussions and observations, it is clear that the Germans build private homes to last at least a hundred years. It isn't unusual for a family to buy a modest home, which is terribly expensive, after many years of saving. Unfortunately, the family cannot possibly keep up the mortgage payments with their family income. So they buy the house to rent it, using income from the rental to meet mortgage payments. During these many years of mortgage obligations, the family that owns the home lives in a small apartment elsewhere or in a small section of the house, oftentimes the basement. The plan is to complete the mortgage payments sometime before the retirement of the head of the household when, at that time, the family moves into their "new home."

One may ask why this is necessary in order, eventually, to own a home. And why is housing so expensive? One would think that the Germans—especially the Germans—would have the affluence to be able to afford to purchase, and live in, homes in the same way that Americans do. I don't have the depth to understand the so-called German mentality, if there is such a special mentality. However, I do know that their homes are built to last many generations. The walls are very thick, the doors appear to be designed for banks, the window sashes and other woodwork are hand cut on the building site. It seems that, in order to sell a home in Deutschland, the builder must: make it strong, thick, aplastic, sensible, dark, and functional. Don't make it fragile, elegant, or graceful. What that country might need is a Levitt and a Levittown. It seems to me that, especially in Germany, fewer permanent-type homes would be an appealing economy. There doesn't seem to be much point in building a home to last a hundred years while, at the same time, preparing for or waging wars that destroy the homes every thirty years.

June 23, 1967: 1:15 A.M. 77 Lembach Strasse, Stuttgart

We spent the best part of a beautiful day in Killesberg Park, a short walk from our house. This park is dedicated to the millions of Jews killed in German concentration camps and, ironically, it must be the most beautiful park we had ever been in. The Germans enjoy and take care of their parks, which are very safe and comforting. Everywhere around us is kindness, consideration, dignity, and contentment. The Germans are not arrogant about their language. Unlike the French (so we've been told) they will try to understand you and help you if you make an attempt to speak their language. They have no false pride, so it seems, when confronted with a fumbling tourist who is trying to communicate while relying on long forgotten high school German and faint remembrances of a grandmother's Yiddish. How could these kind, thrifty, and bright people have participated in such horror? Killesberg Park, and the people we encountered there, do not make sense in the light of history.

July 8, 1967: 7:00 P.M. The Grand Hotel, Nuremberg

In this city where the Trials were held, I compared my daily observations of black GI's with the riots and troubles in the States that are reported here daily. I have noticed—possibly wrongly—that the black GI in Germany is less alienated, less alone, more integrated in the Army than in Boston, Massachusetts, or anywhere else in civilian life with which I am acquainted. I have noticed no special groups of black GI's, but rather, blacks and whites together. I don't want this reaction to appear to be something it shouldn't. However, compared to what I have seen in the United States, black GI's in Germany seem to have a better deal than black civilians in New Jersey.

Why do we have prejudice? This diary, now to the point of embarrassment, continues to disclaim any special insights or depth concerning the questions raised. However, I have noticed that most of the poverty, misery, and suffering in the world is in the Southern Hemisphere. So-called "civilization" is in the Northern Hemisphere. Color seems to be less important as a determiner of either income or racial bias than is place or residence. Men of color populate the Northern Hemisphere and are not viewed—because of their color—in pejorative ways, e.g., the Chinese and Japanese. It almost seems as if color isn't inferior; the South is or the heat is. White isn't superior; the cold is. What might be needed is not more civil rights legislation but a good cold wave in the Southern Hemisphere or continent-to-continent air-conditioning.

What are the trappings of the favored? Geographically, living in the temperate zone is tremendously important, probably necessary. We must also include such items as: a religion, preferably Christianity; whiteness; cleanliness; the written word; monogamy; and taking the past seriously (e.g., museums, antiques, catalogues, tours). Symptoms of the favored are ties, briefcases, symbolic expressions of wealth, Culture. Most of the favored can be located in Western Europe, the British Isles, North America (with the possible exception of Mexico), and Japan, which is becoming White in attitude. The USSR will soon be as favored as any nation and is now, practically "White." China is "Red." Soon they will be colored "White." Find a little "Blue" and you have Old Glory, McCarran Act and all.

July 11, 1967: 5:15 P.M. McGraw Kaserne, Munich

We went to Dachau today. It's a short, pleasant drive on the autobahn from Munich to Dachau, really just a few kilometers before reaching the autobahn exit sign "Dachau." After a drive of about four kilometers through level farmland, you arrive in the middle of the town. We stopped a passing pedestrian, asking, "Pardon, wo ist der koncentrazion Kamp?" in our best school German and pidgin Yiddish-English-gesture. No response! Possibly, the pedestrian was a stranger in Dachau or didn't understand you. So, you ask again, and again, and again. You don't give up. You ask, in a German dialect that had been very well understood until now, "Where is the concentration camp where 200,000 Jews, French, and clergymen from many nations were tortured during the years 1933–1945?" You ask, "Where in your town are the crematorium and mass graves?" Finally there is an answer from a man you were able to intimidate sufficiently to respond to your, by now, enraged questions. "Ah! Sie gehen zu dem Americana Kamp!" You don't understand the answer but you get the directions and, within a kilometer or two, you are standing at the entrance to the infamous Dachau KZ.

Certain things must be cleared up. Is this Kamp so unknown to the local population or is our German so poor that our inability to locate the camp was the result of unintentional roadblocks—nonfeasance rather than malfeasance? What did my informer mean by "the Americana Kamp"? I'll try to answer those questions, and hopefully unravel a number of puzzles that confronted us this morning in Dachau. First, anyone who lives in Dachau must know exactly where the concentration camp is and how to get there. Literally, one can see the camp from parts of the town. Secondly, to date, more than 300,000 people from 30 different countries have visited the camp. Since the camp had been developed as a memorial and museum, it appeared impossible that any citizen of this small town had not been asked directions to the camp on innumerable occasions. The most frequent answer I received to my question for directions to the Kamp was, "Es gibt kein koncentrazion Kamp hier in Dachau." ("There is no camp . . . ") Lastly, the Kamp is called the "Americana Kamp" by the townspeople because, after World War II, our army occupied Germany and, to this date, we have not returned this camp to the German Republic. That is, in a legal and technical sense, the Dachau Concentration Camp is an American camp. This is one instance where changing the label cannot remove the history or the stench of the product.

July 12, 1967: 10:35 A.M. 17 Badelschwingh Strasse, Munich

More on Dachau. The first German concentration camp was opened here on March 22, 1933. During the ensuing 12 years, 13 million defenseless human beings were slaughtered by the flower of Germany. There is little I can say that hasn't already been much more eloquently said. What struck us, really hit us hard, was the list in the museum of all the concentration camps and the destruction each had wrought. Imagine, over 100 such hells strategically placed both in Germany and conquered nations! As you visit the crematorium, the grave sites, and the memorials—as you examine the documents on display in the museum—over and over is the reminder, "Remember us. Do not forget." You see a warning to the living, for all time to come or until there are no longer any people, "Help us to testify of the past. Help us to protect the future." And as you see pictures that, two generations later, can torture, you ask "How can anyone have participated in such barbarism?'' And when you look out across the bucolic splendor of Bavaria, passing idle moments in pleasant conversation with a good man, a decent and honest German, answers don't come easily.

How can these good Germans continue to live in the town of Dachau, with a constant reminder of their inhuman past? How can a young family move into a new garden apartment, a couple of hundred yards from the entrance to the concentration camp? How can the townspeople claim ignorance of what transpired in a camp located on Route 471 that existed for a dozen years, almost in the middle of the town? How can they plead ignorance and why do we believe them? It's too frightening to remember the terror they participated in and it's too frightening for us to disclaim their innocence. Human beings can understand—even tolerate—pathology or sickness among some of our less fortunate. However, it is probably too terrible to contemplate an evil such as Germany perpetrated. A conspiracy of the sick and degenerate and psychopathic is unpleasant but manageable. We must remove these sick ones from the mass, the healthy, the group that can be called human beings. A conspiracy of this kind led by the cream of the nation, the harvest of its years of toil and drudgery, is an affront to all mankind. It is an assault on our personal eminence as human beings and it demonstrates what man is capable of, given certain conditions and opportunities.

To understand Nazi Germany—to comprehend what drove them to their terrible misdeeds—will lead to our understanding the treatment of blacks in the United States, our past treatment of the American Indians, and the care we provide for the mentally retarded in the back wards of our state institutions. To understand Nazi Germany, or to understand the background to any of the evils mentioned, is to help unravel what I consider the most important and basic problem known to man. What are the conditions required before a man can abuse another man? I cannot believe that the abuse of individuals or, for that matter, the abuse of groups proceeds in a random or haphazard manner. I believe that the proper study of human abuse will reveal a theory leading to understanding the factors that give rise to it. The results of this study may, some day, provide us with ways to prevent human abuse or—at the very least— sublimate or mitigate mankind's apparent need to inflict pain and cruelty.

July 17, 1967: 9:20 A.M. Bachelor Officer's Quarters, Garmish

We were invited to the Casa Carioca International Ice Review last night by two friends we had met in the States. After what really was a most enjoyable ice show, all of us went to a local restaurant for coffee. We talked about many things, including responsibility, even had a mild argument. The husband is an unusual man who has remained a classroom teacher for many years despite strong pressures from government school authorities to promote him to one or another administrative post. I understand completely his decision in this matter, and both congratulate him and agree with his logic. However, the point I made to him was that if part of his decision were dictated by an absence of any personal ambition, then I should understand with reluctance and regret. People who have little personal ambition may be as dangerous to society, possibly more so, as those who have driving personal ambition. People without ambition, but with talent, abrogate the positions they should have taken (or sought) to those with the ambition (but not always with the talent). One shouldn't overstate the line of this logic but, in these troubled times, one must at least raise the question as to how much individual freedom a man has in accepting or rejecting responsibility. There may be a kind of collective concern that each individual must respect with whatever insight he has to bring to bear on the decision.

We discussed Dachau with them; the husband had visited there, and his German wife had lived in Munich during the war. His wife, who is a wonderful woman, doesn't appear to feel any more personal guilt about such places as Dachau than most Americans would feel about institutions in the States where atrocities have been known to occur. I believe she feels a kind of responsibility as a citizen of the Third Reich. However, I don't believe she feels any individual responsibility for Hitler, the KZ, or 13 million humans slaughtered. Who can fault her? The ambivalence and vacillation between the horror I saw at Dachau and the horrors I am acquainted with in the United States trouble me and, at the same time, permit me to understand something about how abusive situations are allowed to arise and to continue unchecked by "civilized" people. Don't most of us in the United States deny any individual responsibility for the "black problem," the "migrant worker problem," and the problem of back wards in state institutions?

July 20, 1967: 11:30 A.M. 17 Badelschwingh Strasse, Munich

We had a marvelous day yesterday visiting the great Munich art museum, Alte Pinakothek, with George and Julie Tsiramokes. George is a major in the Air Force, stationed with the American consulate in Munich. Some random thoughts: 1) Why are we surprised with reports of brutality, murder, and terror coming from the emerging African countries? After spending a day at the incredible Alte Pinakothek, one must become convinced that the relationship between Culture and Decency is a very obscure one, if it exists at all. It is probably true that the Germans weren't cannibals. Their industrial inventiveness led them to manufacture lamp shades. 2) Toilets in public places are sometimes free to the user, but more often there is a charge of ten to twenty pfennigs. At such public toilets where there is a charge, the attendant on duty is usually an old lady. This woman, anywhere from seventy to eighty years old, lurches about the foul smelling men's room, placing the fees collected in nondescript, grubby looking folds of clothing. It seems to be an affront to the dignity of old age to permit someone (anyone) to work at this occupation. First, the smell is horrid (which questions the tradition of German cleanliness). Second, it desexualizes this woman who, by the very nature of her work, is either a disinterested observer of male genitalia or a female voyeur (a neat trick at eighty). On the other hand, after occasional visits to nursing homes in the United States, it is difficult to decide which of the two would be the more appealing existence. 3) Every day, I have been reading reports of riots in Newark and Detroit and New York. Today, suburbia is good; the city is not good. It hasn't always been that way. Most of us can remember when the "poor" countryman left the farm for the luxury and richness of the city. When he came in sufficient numbers to the city, the wealthy cityman (whom the countryman came to emulate) moved to the country. Now certain urbanologists are suggesting that we take undeveloped suburban areas and plan housing for the poor. If this succeeds too well, it will only drive the middle and upper classes back to the city. The favored land is where the favored are, not necessarily where the birds are.

July 25, 1967: 3:00 P.M. 17 Badelschwingh Strasse, Munich

We will be leaving Germany in less than forty-eight hours for Scandinavia and, then, on to the British Isles. What has it been like to spend seven weeks in Germany? Our daily existence forgives the Germans for what they have done. Our hearts and our minds—even our so-called logic—can't forgive. We play the part as they, in another way, play theirs. We are civilized to them, engage them in pleasant conversation, feel—for the moment—very warmly towards them. They have been the most polite of all the Europeans during our limited experience here. Surprisingly, we have been most comfortable with them. They are not arrogant about their language and customs, easily forgive the frequent mistakes that tourists are wont to make, and are honest and reliable people.

But, we must never forget what they did. We may forgive individuals but we must never forgive the Third Reich. We must be remorseless and relentless. No one can give us a "testament" to ensure remembrance, as others have been given testaments to ensure other thoughts and deeds for all the ages. Our individual zeal to remember and to pass on what transpired here must be in our "mortal to mortal" and, thus, "immortal" insurance.

August 30, 1968: Natick, Mass.

I have just completed the preparation of this section taken from my diary of last summer in Europe. One particular thought keeps returning to my mind, a thought I heard chanted continuously two nights ago. "The whole world is watching, the whole world is watching." Those brave words, chanted by the demonstrators on the Chicago streets as the television cameras recorded it all, did not stop the policemen's clubs, the gas, and the strong-armed forces of Mayor Daley's order, if not law. Now that the whole world has observed, what will we do? History has taught me that the chances are excellent we will do nothing. Good German citizens did nothing. The Northern White liberal did nothing. The humanitarian Chicagoan will do nothing. I am fearful that the administrator of the back ward will do nothing.

The more I study the problem of human abuse, the more convinced I become that the ancient Chinese proverb, "Virtue is not knowing, but doing," is as profound as any words put together by man. Further, I am persuaded that unless we find better ways to convince the man-who-knows that knowing isn't enough, our children's children will pay homage to memorials yet to be conceived, protesting horrors yet to be imagined. For too long, the good people have sought solace from human outrage in their religions or have told their troubles to the wall. Possibly, this is the time we might convince ourselves that our protection and salvation on Earth is with each other. We must tell each other and must act on behalf of each other.

JIMMY[2]

In early December of 1965, a professional matter required my presence at a state school. For reasons that are not germane to this report, my specific purpose was to observe in the "back wards." I met Jimmy during that visit. He was a resident of the dormitory housing the most severely retarded male adult ambulatory residents. It was a visit that I do not expect to ever forget. However, unlike so many other visits I made, it had a very happy ending.

An attendant was our guide during that tour of K Building. I noticed that few residents were on the ground floor or the dormitory floor above. I asked the attendant where all of the other people were and she said, "Have patience. We're going to see them now." We descended a flight of stairs, walked along a dark passageway and came to a heavy metal

---

[2] The author is grateful to Sumner Rotman, who, during much of Jimmy's recent development, was principal psychologist at the state school, and Dr. Edward Meshorer, superintendent there. Both encouraged me to learn more about their Hospital Improvement Program and provided the case material necessary to prepare this section.

locked door. In an instant, out came the inevitable key chain and ring of keys, a wrist turned, we bolted forward, the door closed behind us, and— in an instant—I observed the transmogrification of the sane and stable world I knew to the Day Room of K Building. I had been to many back wards and many Day Rooms but never before, or never since, had I ever seen or felt or smelled the clamor, the grotesqueness, the animal-like environment of this Day Room.

It is a large room, possibly 50' × 50', maybe larger, maybe smaller. The walls are made of a grayish white tile, the kind you see in hospitals or other Day Rooms. The windows are glass bricks, not really opaque but, on the other hand, permitting only light to pass through. The floor is constructed of a terrazzo-like substance. I remember that there is a metal pole rising from the floor to the ceiling, somewhere near the center of the Day Room. In recent days, during the preparation of this chapter, I have been haunted by my complete inability to remember anything more about this pole—except, to think now, how ludicrous it seems to construct a metal pole in the center of a Day Room for severely retarded residents. Along the walls of the Day Room are several wooden benches, very sturdily constructed and each capable of seating five to six adults.

Sitting on benches, standing around, sitting on the floor, pacing back and forth, lying on the floor, huddled in corners, standing by the door, mumbling, shrieking, laughing, crying, stony silent, fifty to sixty residents were crowded into that Day Room. About half of these men were com- pletely nude; about half wore some garment or another. Of the latter group, one man had a baggy pair of pants, a double-breasted sport coat, no shirt, no underwear, no socks or shoes. Another man wore pajama pants and a Harris Tweed sport jacket, 1930 vintage. A third man had another double-breasted sport coat, nothing else. Another man wore dun- garee pants and, instead of a shirt, another pair of pants wrapped around his shoulders. Those that used belts had pieces of rope or neckties for this purpose. Some had shoes—or one shoe—without socks; some had socks and no shoes. One or two men wore hats, nothing else.

Standing to the side, taking distance and observing this scene whose scenario might have been written by Lewis Carroll or Maxim Gorky or Dante, were two attendants—one male and one female. Yes, reader, I too was startled to find a female attendant in this dormitory, although it is not surprising that this institution will employ women in such positions since staff are desperately hard to get.

Each in a spotless white uniform, the two attendants stood off to the side, staring imperiously at the residents and, after we had entered, at us too. They did not come forward to introduce themselves to us, their manner suggesting to me that there was no point to any gesture we might make in this vein. The two attendants stood rigid, indomitable, spotless, and unsullied by the chaos surrounding them or by our intrusion into their special world. After several minutes of wandering amid the debris of the Day Room, my eye caught a closed solid door. I turned the knob, trying to open it. It was locked. I walked the thirty or forty feet to the male attendant (some kind of embarrassment prevented me from meeting the eye of the female attendant, much less speaking with her). My first words, ever, to this attendant—we had not, in any way, been introduced to each other nor had our presence been acknowledged by either attendant— were, "What's on the other side of this door?" The attendant replied that the door led to a toilet facility. I asked him if he would open it. He told me that the door had to remain locked because, during the day, it served as a seclusion room for a very destructive and dangerous twenty-year-old resident. I asked the attendant to please open the door so that I might see this resident. He explained, with some exasperation, that Jimmy was an unmanageable, quite strong resident and it would be best not to unlock and open the door. In a mild, but stubborn, way I persisted and, reluctantly, the attendant unlocked and opened the door. Before the door could be opened fully, out streaked a completely nude man. He ran here, then there, then back here again, then to some other place. There did not appear to be any thought to his movement or any language to the sounds he was making. He was tall, well built, without any apparent organicity or physical stigmata—with one exception. He had an enormous tongue, which kept darting out and in much like a snake's. I never did learn the clinical syndrome associated with this anomaly, if there is such a syndrome. It is enough to say here that Jimmy's tongue was (and still is) the largest tongue I have ever seen and it would flabbergast me to ever see another one like it again.

Jimmy did not remain very long out of the toilet room. Unfortunately, soon after his release to the Day Room, he ran to a nude man who was sitting on one of the benches. I had singled out this resident before because he had a very large ulcerated lesion on his shoulder. It was uncovered and without any apparent medication on it. The lesion was about four or five inches in diameter, quite bloody, and pus oozed from it. While the man sat, rocking back and forth on the bench, Jimmy snatched at his shoulder and began to suck on this festering ulcer, his tongue swilling up the cankerous rot. My companion and I viewed this in stark horror, he blanching and looking as if he was about to faint. I, not in very much better condition, turned away with a horrified look at the attendant. The attendant, immediately, walked to Jimmy and firmly, in a way gently, disengaged him from the rocking resident and guided him back to the toilet room, locking the door as he closed it.

After things had settled down, both attendants began to explain to us why they had to keep Jimmy locked up in the toilet room. The tones of their explanations made it very clear that, had we heeded their advice and minded our own business, this incident would never have happened—which is, obviously, quite true. We learned that Jimmy, now twenty years of age, was admitted to the state school at the age of three. On presentation to the state school, he was evaluated as "grossly retarded." The etiology was never clarified and he was classified as "undifferentiated etiology, functional diagnosis of idiot." We learned that, prior to his placement at the state school, Jimmy's early history was quite uneventful until his eighth month. At that time, he became quite hyperactive, chewed anything he could get his hands on, threw things out of the window, turned on gas jets, attacked other children and, literally, required twenty-four hour supervision and care. His bizarre behavior attracted so much adverse attention and notoriety that his mother was forced to move a number of times, being evicted from one apartment after another. By the age of three, his mother's health was at the breaking point and Jimmy was finally admitted to the state school. We learned, during this discussion with the dormitory attendants, that Jimmy's mother rarely visited him. In fact, in recent years he received no visitors at all.

I did not see Jimmy again until the spring of 1968. However, I had learned that shortly after my visit, the state school received a grant under the provisions of the federal Hospital Improvement Program. The purpose of the grant was to develop a program to maximize the functioning of 250 profoundly retarded residents, Jimmy included. Specifically, through the use of operant conditioning principles and techniques—including a graduated reward system from food reinforcement to token and vending machine reinforcement—individual resident programs were designed which emphasized the acquisition of eating, dressing, and toilet skills.

This program in behavior modification was spearheaded by two individuals at the state school—one the superintendent and, the other, the principal psychologist—who, to paraphrase Sarason, have a concept of human potential and an attitude toward innovation with the mentally retarded which is optimistic (not pessimistic) and who believe that all human beings have the potential to change and that all human beings—including people such as Jimmy—are capable of learning and improving their functional behavior. This superintendent, fairly recently appointed, and the principal psychologist rallied around them a group of dedicated and zealous workers, including one senior physician, the director of nurses, a nursing supervisor, and a teacher. For sixteen hours each day, the trainees (as these former back ward outcasts were now called) were given a great deal more attention than ever before, much more staff time and thoughtfulness, and a very special environment created for *their* needs. The barren Day Room of K Building was transformed into an activity room, where people spoke to one another and were clothed, where there was genuine human interaction, where gymnastic and other learning equipment was available and used, where there were books and records and things to do—and places to go and music to hear and something to learn. In the spring of 1968, I visited the state school to observe and discuss the progress these most severely retarded residents were making in the Hospital Improvement Program. I was especially interested in Jimmy, hoping that the reports I received periodically concerning him were not overly exaggerated, and not daring to remember the circumstances surrounding my last observation of him. Before discussing that visit and a summary of Jimmy's activities in the Hospital Improvement Program, it may be helpful to review, in some modest detail, Jimmy's history at the state school, the years of his admission, and his entrance into the Hospital Improvement Program in December of 1965.

Jimmy's History: 1948–1965

As mentioned previously, Jimmy was admitted to the state school in 1948, when he was three years and three months old, and diagnosed as having a mental age of one year and seven months and an IQ of 38. Initially, he was placed in a dormitory of so-called "crib cases," where he was regarded as a constant menace to the other children. One attendant recalled that Jimmy's crib was often turned upside down by an attendant, so as to protect the other residents from him. Probably, this was Jimmy's first acquaintance with seclusion although, undoubtedly, in subsequent years he experienced every form of seclusion, restraint, and punishment. Two years after admission to the state school, in 1950, he was re-tested, with a mental age now of seven months and an IQ of 11. Between that testing and 1966 (sixteen years later) he had not been evaluated, staffed, or programmed in any way that could be discerned from a review of his records or interview with staff members who had known Jimmy during those years.

The following comments were abstracted by the principal psychologist from reports and notations recorded, during the years, by physicians for inclusion in Jimmy's medical file. These vignettes provide an extraordinarily illuminating picture of Jimmy during that sixteen-year period, which he endured, and which others suffered through:

1948 . . . . A three-year-old colored boy brought to the school today by mother. Mother stated that child puts everything into his mouth, has no sense of danger and will deliberately run in front of automobiles.

1949 . . . . James requires supervision at all times, very untidy, no improvement.

1950 . . . . James likes to bother other children, does not go to school.

1951 . . . . Patient is a very active child, runs and yells most of the time, requires constant supervision, does not go to any entertainment.

1952 . . . . Jimmy is untidy and runs away from the building if not watched.

1953 . . . . Hard to manage, requires constant supervision.

1954 . . . . Will not keep clothes on. Requires care of an infant. Cannot talk, is noisy and cries a great deal. Cannot find his place at table or bed, runs and jumps all the time, licks walls, floors, or any furniture with tongue.

1955 . . . . Jumping and screaming, grabs for other boys.

1956 . . . . Very active, will not stay in bed or at the table while eating, will not keep clothes on.

1957 . . . . Hard to control him long enough to eat.

1958 . . . . Destroys everything in building. Getting more active and destructive.

1959 . . . . Jimmy continues to be a major problem in the building. Most staff members are afraid of him.

1960 . . . . Very active and destructive. "Colored boy idiot."

1961 . . . . Most destructive, no schooling, no change or improvement.

1962 . . . . Noisy, runs over and under beds, destroys blankets, hits his arms against his body and spanks his feet as he runs. He seems to be getting worse as he gets older and stronger.

1963 . . . . Pulls pillows, sweaters, anything made of wool, every chance he gets. Climbs out of shower unit window and jumps over the fence and runs around the grounds in the nude.

1964 . . . . Patient is kept secluded most of the day. Picks scabs from the children and eats them. Runs wild and escapes over the fence if let out and goes to rubbish barrel. Pulls his tongue out of his mouth and likes to lick people.

1965 . . . . Jimmy bites other boys and sucks the blood from the wounds. He mostly has to be kept separated from the other patients. He is very hyperactive, has no speech and pays no attention to commands. Is not toilet trained.

1966 . . . . Numerous mannerisms, rituals, stamping of feet, licking of objects, pulling tongue twice as long as a normal tongue. For the first time has had a grand mal seizure; may have been due to medication. EEG report is not compatible with a seizure pattern.

I was made acutely aware of the variety and frequency of injuries that befall a resident in a back ward after reviewing a compilation of

Jimmy's misfortunes, prepared by the aforementioned principal psychologist. On the other hand, knowing something about Jimmy and his behavior and something else again about the nature and quality of the supervision and attention given him during his years in K Building, the following documentation of Jimmy's "accidents and injuries" does not really surpise me, nor should it surprise any reader who has had even a limited experience observing in our so-called back wards:

July, 1955 . . . . Patient threw a hammer at Jimmy's right foot; deep laceration inner left ankle.

April, 1958 . . . . Contused right second toe, banged foot against a door.

October 1958 . . . . Patient threw Jimmy against wall in shower area. Left upper central tooth missing.

December, 1958 . . . . Patient has two ecchymotic eyes (black and blue) that he did not have on November 29.

April, 1961 . . . . Patient under treatment. Infection inner aspect left thigh.

May, 1962 . . . . Patient admitted to hospital; fractured hip.

August, 1964 . . . . Edema of nose.

August, 1964 . . . . While playing in the ward, James fell on the floor and cut upper lip. Received a small cut inside of his upper lip.

October, 1964 . . . . James reported missing from building. A short time later found in locker room. Broke several bottles of creolin.

Febuary, 1965 . . . . While jumping about, fell forward, knocking out upper right central and lateral incisors.

The above physicians' notations all were recorded between the year 1948, when he entered the state school, and his entrance into the Hospital Improvement Program in January of 1966. At the time of his placement in the H.I.P. program, Jimmy had been for many years a resident in K Building, where I had first observed him. Traditionally, this building housed adult male profoundly retarded residents and, in January of 1966, it had a complement of 135 residents cared for by twelve attendants. For those readers who are not acquainted with institutional shifts, days off, absences due to sicknesses, etc., a total complement of twelve attendants never permits any more than two or three attendants on duty in a building at any one time.

1966–1968

In January of 1966, Jimmy was one of the four most severely retarded adult residents at the state school selected to enter the Hospital Improvement Program. At the time, the staff of K Building evaluated him as unmanageable, destructive, denudative, and aggressive. He was unable to demonstrate any self-help skills involving eating, dressing, and toileting. He would defecate and urinate in the activity room and its surroundings, he would steal food in the dining room, he was completely and totally uncontrollable. The following are abstracted notations, prepared by the principal psychologist, covering the period from January, 1966 to February, 1968. It should be noted here—and will be revealed to the reader in a moment or two—that residents such as Jimmy, individuals who have started with so little and have suffered through so much, do not change very easily or quickly. However, change they do—at least, Jimmy did. (The parentheses in the following chronicle are this writer's, intended to either clarify the recorder's comment or explain why the staff member did or said a particular thing.)

January, 1966 . . . . Hyperactive, assaultive to trainees and employees, exploring with tongue.

February, 1966 . . . . Stealing food, banging with elbow and foot, assaultive during evening.

March, 1966 . . . . Stole food at breakfast, misbehaved all morning, settled down and became more cooperative, active but not hyperactive. Assaultive on afternoon shift. No supper, due to lack of tokens. (Tokens are used as rewards for desirable behaviors; trainees must earn sufficient number of tokens to "buy" meals; this writer does not wish to make any moral judgments or comments here about this procedure.)

April, 1966 . . . . Banging mirrors, stamping on furniture. Sodium amytal given, $7\frac{1}{2}$ grains, 10:30 a.m. without effect.

May, 1966 . . . . Wanting to go to the store on various occasions. Stamping feet and crying if not allowed to go.

June, 1966 . . . When I give Jimmy a token, I try to get him to put it in his pocket without licking or sticking it in his ear, or banging it on the wall. I think this will be very helpful in the long run because it will tend to civilize him a little bit more. It is crucial, however, that everybody else (other staff) do the same thing.

July, 1966 . . . . Active, stamping feet. Charged one token each time. Was rewarded too when he refrained from it any length of time. (Rewards are given for approximating desired behavior.)

August, 1966 . . . . He feels more at ease when he is around me and I am not quite as afraid to discipline him because I know just what limits he has. This brings up another point that I am discovering; each child has certain limits within which he will obey a person. In other words, if the screaming or stamping continues, you can be firm with him and get him to stop but you can only be so firm. If you are too strict with him, then he will simply become a lot worse than before.

September, 1966 . . . . I feel that in order to keep Jimmy's interest, it's necessary to take him to the store twice during activity period. I make sure, though, that Jimmy still has enough tokens for lunch.

October, 1966 . . . . To my amazement, James began crying real tears. Apparently he felt I had changed my opinion of him. He was pathetic. I tried to calm him down and he then became all right.

November, 1966 . . . . We started with the lacing boot. This was laced twice but he still refused to tie a bow. He put all the pieces back into the boot. He had some difficulty with the round piece. I let him experiment and he finally found it. He then worked with the nuts and bolts. He will always choose red before any of the colors. Second color appears to be yellow. He will not screw nuts and bolts on but will screw them off.

December, 1966 . . . . There are outbursts of temper when he is pushed too hard. This may be displayed by slaps and licking other patients.

January, 1967 . . . . Onset of afternoon, beginning with lunch, James became increasingly temperamental and peevish. He stole food and slapped Sophie. I still feel that it is his teeth which are bothering him.

February, 1967 . . . . Was wide awake at 6:45 a.m. Seemed to sense I was the only one in the room and began jumping from bed to bed on bureaus and radiators. Laughed when I couldn't catch him. I feel that to chase him was the wrong thing as he likes being chased. (Staff person ignores undesirable behavior, a common operant technique.)

March, 1967 . . . . Loud and lovable, that was James. What a character! He laughed and laughed for a solid 15 minutes. Enjoyed the mat (gym mat). It really looked as if he wanted to laugh because he forced himself. He's a "kook" but I love him.

April, 1967 . . . . James, being likable guy that he is, I have not heard one employee working with the children saying that they dislike him.

May, 1967 . . . . Jimmy is in the hospital having his teeth removed.

June, 1967 . . . . Wonderful day for Jimmy. He returned from the hospital and his joy knew no bounds. Laughed, smiled, and sang. No one ever saw a happier kid. He ate a good dinner consisting of mashed carrots, potatoes, gravy, pudding and tea.

July, 1967 . . . . On this day Jimmy and the group were taken to a nearby lake for a swimming outing. He conducted himself extremely well and was even able to get into a row boat. Several times throughout the afternoon Jimmy ran into the water, ducked himself and, in fact, splashed others. He undressed and dressed himself in the bedroom of a private home.

August, 1967 . . . . Out for a walk, went to E Building playground. Enjoyed himself. Seemed to single out the other Negro boys and stayed with them.

September, 1967 . . . . Jimmy has been very noisy and active the last few days. I think this is due to being stuck in one room. He needs to be outside or someplace where he can be more active. Was markedly noisy this afternoon because he wanted to go out. This couldn't be done because of lack of help.

October, 1967 . . . . After supper he was taken to the barn. He enjoyed the animals and also he "took to" a little kitten that was up in the barn. Laughing as he always does.

November, 1967 . . . . An experiment was conducted today with Jimmy. Aside from the usual walk in the afternoon, I opened the door and told Jimmy to go outside and take a walk by himself. After repeated requests to Jimmy, he soon left the dormitory and for two hours walked around the entire school. He slowly found his way to the school building. He went directly to the gym. Jimmy understands the importance of the gym because it is here where he uses the trampoline and other equipment so often.

December, 1967 . . . . At the Christmas party, Jimmy showed a momentary interest in toys; then he became a typical small child and played with ribbons and took a big interest in candy.

January, 1968 . . . . Jimmy dressed well this a.m. Ate both meals well. Went to the bathroom perfectly. Went to the gym and used the trampoline. Had refreshments at the Canteen. Excellent at both places.

On April 8, 1968, the principal psychologist evaluated Jimmy. Paraphrasing that report: Jimmy was observed in the dining room having lunch with a companion. He ate quietly, waiting for the various courses to be served to him, and using a spoon and fork correctly. Occasionally, he spilled very small quantities of food from his plate to the table. When he did this, he would glance furtively about, picking up the food with his fingers. Once, he picked up his plate and ate directly from it. However, he immediately stopped this activity when told to do so by the attendant. There was no food stealing observed, no ravenous eating, little use of his fingers in eating, no impatience between courses, and no improper use of food such as smearing or throwing. In quantitative terms, results of the Vineland Social Maturity Scale revealed a social age equivalent of three years and ten months, this in contrast to Jimmy's last evaluation (1950) where he received a mental age equivalent of seven months.

A Final Comment

On the day I visited the state school in the spring of 1968, I observed Jimmy in the Activity Room, sitting at a table with an instructor, listening to a story, and responding as appropriately as he could to the instructor's questions and comments. He was fully dressed, patient, well-mannered, and considerate of both the instructor and other trainees in the room. At that time, I commented to the principal psychologist and the superintendent that Jimmy represented, in my opinion, a remarkable demonstration of man's unquenchable human spirit and desire to live among men. I commented that, for me, Jimmy's progress is as important to understand and is as important for mankind to take seriously as other great documentations of the past: Victor, The Wild Boy of Aveyron; the lives of Helen Keller and Anne Sullivan; Rousseau's Emile; and May Seagoe's Paul. I mentioned that Jimmy's development is important for all human beings to rejoice in, as all human beings do when they learn that a man, once thought to be an irretrievable derelict, now walks among us, reborn a man again. Lastly, I mentioned that we—scholars and scientists and clinicians—could learn from such cases as we can learn from very few others. The concept of educability, the hypothesis that intelligence is plastic, the philosophy of optimism and faith and love, all of these concepts and ideas can be studied and better understood because some people had the motivation and faith to believe that Jimmy was capable of changing.

However, it was an offhand remark, made by an attendant to me that day, that washed away so many bitter memories and frustrations, and made so much seem worthwhile that seemed so foolish only the day before. As we were chatting, she mentioned to me that Jimmy's mother visits him regularly since he began to wear clothes and eat at the dining room table and "look" like a human being. The mother told this attendant, "After all of these years, I now have a son. I lost my child many years ago and you have helped me find him."

CHAPTER 8

This Crazy Business

The contents of this chapter derive from activities during my years as an administrator in government and academe. Essentially, the plan is to present a personal analysis of this crazy business we call "mental retardation." It may strike some readers that this chapter's organization is the reflection more of idiosyncratic conceptualizations than of logical processes. I must admit that I believe that, in this crazy business, one fights general craziness with any resources at one's command, even those which are paradoxical or illogical. In this regard, my long suit has always been independence. Some people may define such resistance as hostility, a transference mechanism, or whatever; I choose to interpret their definitions as other examples of this crazy business. In a world of continuous war on peace, where people incarcerate, and even kill each other, because of labels ascribed to or withdrawn from human beings, should anyone be surprised to read here that I call this business crazy, that there may be some who will think me crazy for it, and that I would find such reactions to be but additional illustrations of the craziness in our field?

DREAMS AND MEANS

One should start at the beginning, and the beginning for me must include the language of theory, laws, beliefs, and prejudice—statements of principles-goals and their pragmatic translations. So, first the principles and goals and, secondly, with a degree of diffidence, how I have interpreted them.

IDEAS

It seems entirely reasonable to suggest that goals represent important ideas to be achieved during some future period. Stated another way, I envision the term "goal" as including to some degree, and embodying

This essay is abstracted from one originally published in R. B. Kugel and A. Shearer (Eds.), *Changing patterns in residential services for the mentally retarded* (2nd ed.), Washington, D.C.: President's Committee on Mental Retardation, 1976, under the title "The Executive." I believe this, the original title, better identifies the substance here.

but not encapsulating, such other terms as "objectives," "hypotheses," "dreams," and—most of all—"ideas." At least while I write this chapter, I have persuaded myself that there are compelling ideas that seek expression, that there are people in this field who agree and disagree with these ideas, that one way of gaining a perspective on the "mental retardation" business is to evaluate those ideas.

The ideas are everywhere—in the literature, at the conventions, in the academy, in the field. Typically, we express them as researchable hypotheses or as pragmatic goals. Typically, we find them substantively discussed: 1) as the educability hypothesis, or the nature-nurture controversy, or the human potential movement; 2) in agreement that human beings are entitled to fundamental services and opportunities, or that there should be options available to all people; 3) in the belief that the state has certain responsibilities to the people, and the people have certain rights; 4) or as more specific goals, such as the recently publicized White House hope to reduce the incidence of mental retardation by one-half by the year 2000; 5) or as very general goals, such as to guarantee each person the right to be born healthy, the right to habilitation, the right to the least restrictive placement, the right to an appropriate education, or the right to equal protection and due process under the law.

There are goals, objectives, dreams, and hypotheses; but, at the beginning, there must be ideas. Unfortunately, one reason why many ideas are timeless and persistent, yet feeble, is that they haven't fully existed in reality; we don't feel compelled to implement them. And, one reason why we aren't so compelled is that ideas, like people, are themselves mixtures of weakness and strength—which itself may be an important idea. Possibly, such mixtures are inevitable, the products of dissonance between intent and practice, noble hope and dismal realization, and shared bitterness. The lesson is plain. Be humble or one has very little to rely upon.

The following are some ideas that I feel are now in the air, not always because they are loud or striking but, rather, because they are fundamental and each possesses the sound of truth:

The idea that each human being has unique value. Not only is each person educable, not only is capability a function of practice and training, motivation, and expectations, not only must all developmental programs be individualized, but so must one's life objectives. This is by way of saying that, although we believe that people can change, an individual's value as a human being isn't bound to his educability but to the intrinsic and inalienable right to be respected—because he is a human being, if for no other reason.

The idea that children represent our great hope to improve society. An individual is born and he dies, and during the interim, he struggles to realize his gifts, while the group—the government, the bureaucracy, what we call society—seeks to trap him, tame him, certainly standardize him. But, sometimes for good and sometimes for bad, there have always been people who would not be molded. They cause us problems; yet, they are our major investment for the future. The dilemma has always been to know who should be molded and controlled and who should be as free as the wind, who is dangerous and who is our prophet. And, so, we encourage freedom and individuality, while we weed out those who appear to be dangerous and maladaptive, while we pray that serious blunders have not been perpetrated in the name of society. And children must always exemplify humanity's universal continuing enthusiasm for a better future; therefore, if we fail with them we fail with everything.

The idea of the creative person. Each human being has a will to live, but also a dream to express himself, to realize his individuality in unique ways. Someone once said that living well is the best revenge. And, I truly believe, if we can agree that "living well" means living in one's unique manner, that living well is the only way. It's not enough to live, to exist, to be; all people seek to unfold, work to create something, and struggle for a principle or some different future.

The idea of freedom. A jaundiced assessment of our culture is that we revere life but disdain freedom. In our zeal to protect the weak, the aged, the so-called handicapped, and the ugly, we segregate and separate and stigmatize and make pariahs out of legions of people. We build industries to incarcerate—out of sight and out of mind—the blind and the retarded and so not only do we accomplish little to help them "see" and understand us but we preclude any possibility that we—the sighted, the brilliant, even the humanitarian—will "see" and understand them. Where is the liberty that our fathers wrote of in our declarations and constitutions? Where is the liberty that children every school morning across America claim their country guarantees for all of its citizens? Where can we find total implementation of the principle that a human being is entitled to freedom under the law?

ALL IDEAS HAVE HISTORIES

Each of these ideas has a history, long and bloodied. Wars were fought and lives were lost because of them; the idea that all people are entitled to freedom under a just law is one that has turned red the soil of most lands. So, today, these ideas struggle against other powerful ideologies, moving ahead, then falling back, in favor during one generation and out of favor in another. Today, at this very moment, it is no different, except for the difference in time and perspective. However, ideas dealing with freedom, individuality, human values and human resources continue to intrude into public consciousness, crying for legitimacy and support.

I have learned that one way to at least partly understand what our values are is to read the papers and listen to the public communicators. As the saying goes, look it up in the newspaper; everything begins with the birth announcement and ends with the obituary. Unfortunately, people may draw wrong conclusions from discrete facts; hence, this attempt to relate "word" facts with "deed" facts. It's necessary; for as all ideas have histories, so do all people. But some leaders tend to think they don't, that each day is a clean slate in a new world.

The following items have appeared in our New York State newspapers in recent months:

> A bill passed last month by the state legislature and sent to the governor for signature changes the names of all department facilities for the mentally retarded from 'State School' to 'Developmental Center' . . . . (1)

No longer will we have to contend with the Syracuse State School, the Willowbrook State School, the Letchworth State School, the Wassaic State School, or the Newark State School. Rather, there is a new model; new progressives and humanitarians appear to be in control. We now have the Willowbrook Developmental Center and the Letchworth Developmental Center. We change the names and, as if by magic alone, things are expected to get better.

> The playground of the Syracuse Developmental Center is going to be remodeled stressing safety and more creature comforts. Protruding bricks removed from all play areas and smooth epoxy applied to the sides of the slide to prevent abrasions are just two of the improvements to be made according to Al Clinton, assistant business officer of the Center. Improvements are being made to provide more safety to the retarded children that the Center serves. (2)

Some who read this announcement in our local paper remember that the Syracuse Developmental Center (formerly Syracuse State School) was once the oldest unremodeled and unchanged state school for the mentally retarded in North America and, just a year or two ago, it was torn down and rebuilt at an expenditure of approximately $25 million. The aforementioned playground, constructed at a cost of several hundred thousand dollars, received more than one national award for its innovativeness. Unfortunately, children couldn't play in this playground without submitting themselves to unusual physical dangers. Essentially, this award-winning playground built by the New York State Department of Mental Hygiene was, and probably still is, "unplayable."

> A State Comptroller's investigation of Matteawan State Hospital in Beacon, N.Y. has uncovered a pattern of fraudulent transactions and irreg-

ularities, including the bilking of inmates through doctored commissary records.

A still-confidential audit report obtained by the *New York Times* showed that, in one recent six-month period, inmates were overcharged $12,235 in commissary purchases.

In some of these cases, the report said, inmates "appear to have been charged for nonexistent items". (3)

Mental health and mental retardation are big business. In each state, not only is the state itself the "biggest" purchaser of new construction, but the state is in the position to offer millions of dollars in food, linen, garbage, you name it, contracts. Further, state employees handle transactions involving millions upon millions of dollars, oftentimes "on behalf" of incompetent, or presumably incompetent, inmates. So, the *New York Times* reports that "A Matteawan audit shows inmates were defrauded." What else is new?

It was a scientific experiment. For 30 years Federal health offices allowed 400 poor Black men known to have syphilis to go untreated despite the discovery that penicillin could cure their devastating disease . . .

Eight years ago, as part of a study of immunity to cancer, a leading New York cancer specialist injected live tumor cells into elderly clinically ill patients without ever telling them in plain English what they were being given and why . . .

Nearly 400 poor women—most of them Mexican-Americans who had already borne many children and had come to a San Antonio Family Planning Clinic for contraception—were enrolled in a study a few years ago to determine whether oral contraceptives did in fact cause psychological changes. All of the women were given identical-looking drugs, most of them active contraceptive agents. But 76 women received a 'dummy' or placebo drug. Seven pregnancies occurred before this study was ended, six of them in the placebo group.

In 1967, coercion was charged in conjunction with a study in which live hepatitis virus was injected into mentally retarded children at Willowbrook State Hospital on Staten Island . . . . (4)

Probably also reflecting its revulsion from the above kinds of human treatment, all of it despicable, probably some of it criminal, the *New York Times* headlined the above article by Jane Brody, "All in the Name of Science." Yet, let's now read a portion of a recent editorial in that same newspaper, reputed to be, and deservedly, the paper of record. Let's read the view of a newspaper that is not too modest to claim that it publishes "All the News That's Fit to Print."

A wasteful dispute has long been seething between civil libertarians and elements of the psychiatric profession. The issue, in effect, is whether the mentally ill should ever be hospitalized against their will or must at all times be left to their own resources as a recognition of their rights as free citizens . . .

What are needed are open halfway communities, preferably located in rural areas, where the less afflicted can work at farming or crafts . . . . (5)

Why did the *New York Times* print this lead editorial, titled "Civil Liberties for What?" With the world at war, Watergates, impeachments, runaway inflation, pollution, crime, Henry Aaron and the new baseball season, with a whole world of problems and happy and sad events to choose from, why did the *New York Times* feel compelled to report to the world that mental patients really need communities away from typical society, preferably located in the country? Apparently, even the *New York Times* can be misled, possibly by a few influential colleagues or, just as possibly, by a great many Mr. and Mrs. Citizens who plunk down their twenty cents on weekdays and one dollar bills on Sundays for the privilege of not only reading the paper of record but giving it advice.

Apparently, the people of New York City have "had it." So too, apparently, has the New York State Department of Mental Hygiene. For, in an April 28, 1974, front page article, also in the *New York Times*, it was reported that the ". . . Department of Mental Hygiene, in a private memorandum and directive, has made a major change in its policy by telling its hospitals that 'we should not take the initiative in discharging the patient to the community.'" Why, after the scandals of Willowbrook and Letchworth, the reports of joint commissions, with a new morality and in a supposed era of concern, does the *New York Times* ask us to slow down, if not apply the brakes? Why does it appear that the State Department of Mental Hygiene is doing one of its familiar herky-jerky about-face dances, tiptoeing in a 180 degree turn, skimming over the issues and principles that honest people would not ignore? Well, the Department of Mental Hygiene not only has "had it," but was "had"— by the "anarchists," the too-liberal psychiatrists, the reformists.

When they were persuaded to evacuate some of their more embarassing units, they were not told that many people would be unimpressed with the idea that mental patients should live in ordinary neighborhoods, especially unimpressed if the designated neighborhoods were theirs. The Department of Mental Hygiene apparently never did develop a contingency plan that would permit them to deal with community resistance. Further, the Department of Mental Hygiene doesn't quite understand that, when mental patients or state school patients are released, it would be best to diversify their placements, not consolidate them in one or a few locations. And when the residents of Long Beach, New York complained to the State Department of Mental Hygiene that, in fact, the Department was creating new quasi-institutions in the community with the purchase of converted motels or hotels for subsequent assignments of large numbers of mental patients to these facilities, the State Department of Mental Hygiene responded with lectures to the citizens on their moral responsibilities and the need for increased community acceptance and good will.

The irony of it all is that the community lay people had a much more insightful analysis of the situation, the problems, and possible solutions, than the State Department professionals. The community group said, "O.K., send your mental patients into our neighborhoods. However, if you want them to live in a normalized fashion, in ordinary neighborhoods, don't congregate them together. Permit us to continue to have normal communities—not places where there are large numbers of peculiar or different people, herded together in abandoned, dilipidated, or second-rate hotels."

The State Department of Mental Hygiene did not heed the community's advice, then pleas, then threats. They merely lectured at the community: to be good citizens, to accept differences, to have forebearance, to understand, to possess all of those virtues that the professionals in the State Department seemed to lack themselves. So we had the backlash, and a new and strange coalition of conservative average citizens—people such as our own mothers and fathers, our friends—and the *New York Times*. One wonders—and those who answer the question negatively are probably correct—will they ever cease? And so, we have a new state policy to slow mental patients' releases. Don't suggest discharge to them lest they request release. Cool it, boys; the natives back in the boonies are getting restless. Even the New York City sophisticates have "had it."

> The State Department of Mental Hygiene, defying city officials, plans to transfer 240 mostly helpless mentally retarded patients from Willowbrook to a four-story nursing home on Staten Island that has never been used because the city twice refused it a permit to operate . . .
> The (community) residents stress that they were not opposed to the plan because it would bring retarded people into the community, but because the nursing home in question would be a 'prison' and a 'zoo'. (6)
> The city's top health officials and the heads of psychiatry at leading hospitals here have clashed with the State Department of Mental Hygiene over state plans to reduce drastically the number of beds planned for the new Bellevue psychiatric center . . .
> 'Everybody who is a top professional in the city is absolutely agreed that the number of beds must not be cut' said one of those at the meeting . . . . (7)

Rebuff after rebuff; yet the dauntless State Department continues to seek solutions to the problems of this crazy business. Like Don Quixote jousting with windmills, our mental health leaders, ever sensitive to both the community and current professional metaphors and slogans, would evacuate institutions by creating new ones in the community, would evacuate them altogether. So they claim, but they don't have an analysis of what must follow. They are dedicated to "integration" and "humanization," as they integrate inmates by segregating them in nursing homes, and humanize the large institution by dehumanizing the community. Unfair? Probably! Is there another way of analyzing this news? Certainly! Yet, does the Department deserve the censure? No, if nobody deserves censure for what we have perpetrated; yes, if anybody deserves censure.

> The Elmira School Board was told Wednesday afternoon that the district may receive nearly $1 million more in state operating aid next year than was received this year . . .
> Weeks (the district business manager) said that he had nothing in writing and cautioned that $700,000 of the aid increase might have to be used in programs for the handicapped and students with special needs.
> However, School Superintendent Dr. Paul R. Zaccarine said that his impression is the district already offers the programs for which the $700,000 would be earmarked. (8)

Find a way, boys. Bring in the resources but, unless there is no other choice, don't use your precious scarce funds for the handicapped. You have more important priorities, even if those funds were earmarked for the handicapped.

> Manly Fleischmann, the Buffalo lawyer who was chairman of the Commission (on the Quality Cost and Financing of Elementary and Secondary Education in New York State), was asked last week what had happened to his recommendations (made two years earlier). His first reaction was to laugh . . .
> Cost of the Commission: $2 million. (9)

So, again, what else is new? Problems occur, statements are made, tempers rise, newspapers report, commissions are appointed, funds are allocated, and the more things change the more they remain the same; except, things remain the same differently from the ways they remained the same before. And, so it seems, that's all the people want. Things can remain the same so long as the color and rhythm of the sameness change hues and tempos from time to time. The major task is not to change but to satisfy everyone: first, the conservatives, but, also, the radicals; the conservatives, because they are in control and pay the bills and the radicals, because—if they are not under control—they will try to upset the delicate balance between no-change that appears as change and no-change that's discovered for what it is. Satisfy everyone, those who pay the bills because they pay the bills, and those who are potentially, or really, irritating to the true power groups.

The ultimate aim is to not only "freeze" the present but establish some type of "warrant," a hold on the future. It appears that one of the goals of a large segment of our society is to guarantee to their progeny what was guaranteed, and later delivered, to them—places of relative prominence and affluence in their society. And who could question that ideal? Who doesn't want to prepare for his coming generations? Who doesn't want a world for his loved ones that is at least as safe, and cozy, and comfortable as it was for him? The answer is obvious: those who never had anything, those who want something different for their children, if not for themselves. So, there is a conflict between variance and invariance, between the haves and the have-nots, between those who are more and those who are less selfish, between those who have more to protect and those who have more to gain, between the power block and the powerless, between the *New York Times* for the underdog and the *New York Times* for the overlord.

All ideas have histories, and the proper study of the histories may illuminate for us not only what occurs in the "name" of certain ideas but what the ideas actually mean. That's the first lesson; a goal or an idea is nothing without its history, and then it's only something in a special context and perspective. Therefore, let's continue examination of a few of the more provocative ideas that we seem to be romancing at this time. And, if these love affairs weren't made in heaven, there may be a more appropriate place to bear witness to such unions—and if not to the marriages themselves, to what they have become.

MAINSTREAMING, THE COMMUNITY, AND THE TEACHERS' UNION

As enunciated again and again, during informal discussions and in official or scholarly documents, our nation's educational leaders have now decided that handicapped children are best served in integrated settings. "Mainstreaming" will be, if it isn't now, the law, if not the practice, in this land. The Regents of the University of the State of New York urge a greater commitment by society to the education of handicapped children, with the primary responsibility for programs placed with local school districts and as integral facets of public education (1973). The litigation in our field exemplifies the centrality of the "integration-mainstreaming" issue (10, 11).

An analysis of the official reports of the various public committees and commissions responsible for formulating national policy on behalf of the handicapped indicates the marked escalation of concern about the integration issue. From the first annual report of the National Advisory Committee on Handicapped Children to then United States Commissioner of Education Harold Howe II in 1968 (12) to its subsequent reports to later Commissioners James E. Allen, Jr. (13) and Sidney P. Marland, Jr. (14), mainstreaming does not appear to be an important issue, at least an issue that deserves identification in annual reports. Contrast its virtual total absence during the late sixties and early seventies with the most recent report of the Committee (15). Now, priority recommendations reaffirm the Constitutional right of all handicapped children to a tax-supported appropriate education, regardless of their physical or mental capabilities. Further, the Committee now urges that regular education environments should be made available and, when there are differences between, for example, parents and school authorities, due process procedures should be operational to ensure an equal educational opportunity for each child.

A comparable analysis of *MR '67* (16), the first major policy statement of the President's Committee on Mental Retardation, and all of the subsequent reports, including its most recent one in 1974, *Silent Minority* (17), illustrates a major shift in policy discussions from an earlier deficit-oriented and categorical segregation model, based on the assumption that handicapped people need special and separate services to be delivered by professionals, to an avowal of principles of: advocacy, normalization, least restrictive alternatives, due process, and rights rather than privileges. Witness that, in 1967, the President's Committee appeared to be very proud of the fact that there were nearly 700,000 children in special classes for the educable and trainable mentally retarded. Note that, in 1967, there was little distinction made between special class and special education; special education was special class. Note, again, how "needs" were discussed in 1967, in terms of more services, not "open" or integrated services. And, although in 1974 the realities for people with special needs may not be very much different, the rhetoric surely is—with the language today expressing concern for an individual's rights, his freedom, his entitlements, his need to be a part of a world that includes rather than excludes him.

I don't know of a professional organization, or a municipal, state, or federal system or agency, that is plainly antagonistic to the mainstreaming principle. Certainly, there are individuals within those organizations and programs who take a dim view of the mainstreaming movement. However, mainstreamers seem to have the segregators on the run, at least for now. Or do they really?

Item 1: A debate is currently smoldering in Syracuse, and it will probably rage again as it did a year or two ago. It's a complicated matter, as all of these things are; suffice to say, I think there is one group who want a special school for the trainable retarded and another group who believe that a special school is neither desirable educationally nor responsible fiscally.

Although they have difficulty in believing they've won, the special schoolers have won; the Syracuse City Council, the Board of Education, and the school administration have all agreed that a special segregated school for trainable children is necessary, desirable, and defensible. Those of us who have raised questions concerning the need for a separate school, during a period of significant pupil enrollment decreases (e.g., a 600 drop for 1974–75 alone) and in a supposedly new egalitarian era, have been accused of insults against children. It seems ironic, at least to me, that in an age when unusual efforts are being exerted by local communities to integrate, for example, Black children, more unusual efforts are being exerted to segregate retarded children. While the courts in Boston and Detroit insist that minority youngsters be integrated—irrespective of long bus rides and significant program modifications and costly expenditures—the Syracuse City Fathers continue their plans to segregate handicapped children, whatever the costs.

Item 2: Syracuse is in Onondaga County and, reflecting the same "disease" of that city, the County Board of Cooperative Education (BOCES) has been seeking citizen approval for an additional new segregated school for the handicapped and for those youngsters enrolled in what was once called vocational education but now is referred to as career education. Probably, more out of anger in again having their "pockets picked" than for any reasons concerning principles or morality, the voters recently turned BOCES down—for the first time in New York State history denying a BOCES program the opportunity to expand its segregated mission.

Why does BOCES want a new school? Again, the polemics run rampant during these kinds of discussions and, trying to be fair but probably not succeeding very well, I should point out to anyone who hasn't noticed that I am singularly unimpressed with any efforts to expand or strengthen segregated settings for people. Having said that, I can now claim that the special education officials in the county want a new school because, since the beginning of organized society, bureaucrats want larger budgets, more staff, bigger and newer facilities, and control. Certainly, the current segregated school for the trainable mentally retarded in Onondaga County is inadequate. It is old, crowded, inaccessible to many families, and inappropriate. On the other hand, the only virtues I can see in constructing a new school is its newness and, possibly, its greater square footage per child. Yet, irrespective of its newness, size, or even beauty, a segregated school is still a segregated school; it will be centrally located and, therefore, inaccessible to many families; it will not permit the integration of the handicapped with the nonhandicapped and, as importantly, vice versa. However, exactly as with the Syracuse group, time is on the side of the county segregationists. Someday they will have their new school, if not after the new referendum, then the referendum after that, or the next one, or the next one.

Item 3: Ideological banners fly from the public relations staffs of the New York State Department of Mental Hygiene, proclaiming: deinstitutionalization, community programming, advocacy, priority reassessments, normalization. Yet, in the city of Syracuse alone, during the past three years, more than $50 million (plus millions more in interest) has been expended by the State Department of Mental Hygiene for the creation of new segregated institutions.

The Syracuse State School, created in 1854, the oldest state school for the mentally retarded in North America in continuous operation on its original site, has now been torn down and rebuilt, almost brick by brick, on that site. Where, formerly, it had a resident population of 250, the new state school is built to serve 750 residents. Permit me to remind you that not only is the facility larger but it is no longer a state school; we now have in our community a brand new concept as well as facility, the Syracuse Developmental Center, that has replaced the old state school. Similarly, what was once the small, essentially outpatient, Syracuse Psychiatric Hospital is now the brand new $25 million Hutchings Psychiatric Center, capable of "bedding down" 750 inmates.

Item 4: "Everybody" in Syracuse had agreed that we should return state school residents to the community as quickly as possible. Therefore, the school's director acquired a small residential facility to develop as a group home. Neighbors-to-be learned of this plan and, very quickly, drew up a petition which they presented to Mayor Lee Alexander; said petition denying any hostility to the concept of community integration but, on the other hand, providing a number of compelling reasons why this community residence would be inappropriately placed in that particular neighborhood. Mayor Alexander agreed with the petitioners. End of group home plan. And, when I was interviewed on television soon after the Mayor's decision, I received a number of rather hostile calls and letters, the following among them:

Dear Dr. Blatt:

You should live next door to mentally retarded like I do. On the weekend they go all over surrounding streets, scavenging big pieces of metal trash and wooden trash (they have superior physical strength to make up for lack of mentality), and so on Sunday the peace of the Sabbath is broken by their hammering on it (trash is picked up Monday a.m. in our neighborhood).

One looks about 30 and plays like a little kid. The other looks about 7 or 8. He thinks he is a method of transportation all the time. And goes down the street making like a motorcycle, an airplane, a racing car, etc. Sometimes he just stands and yells as loud as he can yell. They both do this.

They have not one but two dogs that bark 24 hours a day.

I say these people have no business living in a normal community— whoever sold them the house should get a medal!

I say these people should be provided with a community of their own; live with their own kind.

I understand there is one at Liberty, New York. I sure would like to be able to send these people there.

(Signed)
Has had it.

Item 5: Now, the most puzzling for last, the quintessential hypocrisy for the finale. My friends in the Syracuse City Schools, many of whom have been students in my classes, others of whom have served with me on committees, a few of whom are—truly—my friends, collectively agree that handicapped children deserve to be integrated in regular programs. Yet, circumstances and promises made by their predecessors force them to support the construction of the aforementioned new segregated school for the trainable in Syracuse. Yet, precedents, teacher prejudices, and practicality require them to continue their elaborate segregated special education program. However, if they had their way in the best of all possible worlds, they would integrate more children with special needs, especially the mildly handicapped. Similarly, members of the Board of Education agree fully with the concepts of mainstreaming and normalization.

And, as if to add insult to injury, in spite of public pronouncements in support of the principle of integration, the Syracuse Board of Education, with the concurrence of school officials, has entered into a negotiated agreement with my friends in the Teachers' Union which discourages school authorities from requiring regular class teachers to accept handicapped or disruptive youngsters in their programs.

It is the ultimate nonsequitur to claim to foster integration in a system where those same claimants support segregation. Not only is this crazy business, but it is also funny business.

THE YEAR OF THE CHILD AND OTHER INDECENCIES

Surely, there are reasons, related chains, that make indecencies almost inevitable. The reader has a right to ask why these indecencies occurred. I have some notions to "explain" them and you probably will develop yours. But I don't have truths, and you might not find those either. Someday, maybe, but for now, I only claim to collect and publicize indecencies, not adequately to understand them.

Item 1: Sometime during the spring of 1970, an administrator in the Massachusetts Department of Mental Health was in San Francisco. Upon his return, he remarked to colleagues that the California Chinese seem to always have a Year of something or another, and he suggested that this would be a good time for Massachusetts to have the "Year of the Child" (18). The idea caught fire. The Commissioner of Mental Health announced that 1971–72 would be the "Year of the Child" in the Commonwealth. Finally, attention would be given to the needs of children, priorities would be reordered, and an increased proportion of the Department's resources and programs would be allocated for children.

Unfortunately, this commitment to children was made *after* the Department of Mental Health had submitted its budget requests to the legislature. No resource shifts would be possible. Additional state assistance was equally impossible. Additional federal funds to meet the commitment didn't materialize. The "Year of the Child" was never more than a gigantic hoax, a public relations ploy created out of innocence, "implemented" by the cynical, and finally exposed publicly amid embarassment and frustrated disclaimers from the insiders and righteous anger from the muckrakers. The grand objective, the beautiful logo on thousands of wall posters, the fervent promises made, were all garbage, like confetti after the parade, like a kewpie doll the morning after in the noon day sun. All this from the chance notice of a wall poster in a Chinese restaurant. How easy it is to do something, and how difficult to accomplish anything.

Item 2: I can hardly wait to complete this next section on advocacy. In my study, I am surrounded with piles of books, monographs, chapters and papers—all dealing with the definition, theory, implementation and practice of various forms of human help we now term "advocacy." Who really knows but that, when I finish this section, I will find a paper I wanted to use earlier but is now hopelessly irretrievable in a morass of advocacy papers. But, to paraphrase what a colleague once said in an entirely other context, "Do we have a knowledge explosion on advocacy or merely a paper explosion?" One wonders, and here's why.

Wolfensberger described the various advocacy roles for children, including those that are primarily instrumental, some instrumental and expressive, and even one that is primarily expressive, the advocate-friend (19). As he and others noted, there are advocates who assume roles as guardians, friends, adoptive or foster parents, legal advisors, and "helpers." However, the one characteristic advocates must have in common is a partisanship, a primary interest to serve the client. Literally, the advocate is one who pleads the cause of another person, not conflicted by self-interests or loyalty to an organization or to one's profession. This partisanship, as a matter of fact, is one of the significant factors in the case Wolfensberger makes for the utilization of citizen-nonprofessional advocates on behalf of people who are mentally retarded.

The idea of advocacy has so captured the thinking in our field that, as happens to all good ideas, there are now groups attempting to appropriate—capture for themselves—the idea. Why must the advocate be professionally disinterested and nonpartisan, preferably a lay person? Why indeed? Wouldn't it be best for an advocate to be a spokesman for the deliverers of services so the program as well as the advocate can be held accountable for the work of the system? Would it? Some people think so.

As a matter of fact, the Regents of the University of the State of New York not only believe this but have developed a sure-fire method to implement an advocacy system that, in my opinion, will only lead to the destruction of the concept of advocacy in the public schools of New York State. The Regents have designed an ingenious method to co-opt an idea intended to serve clients but which now would serve the providers (20). They recommend the creation of a new advocacy system for children with handicapping conditions. They claim that a good advocacy system requires strengthened cooperation among agencies in the public and non-public sectors. Therefore, to be effective, any system of advocacy and service delivery must provide for cooperative arrangements agreeable to the Commissioner of Education and to those people responsible for the supervision of institutional programs at the state level. Consequently, the Commissioner of Education should be given the responsibility for the overall supervision of programs for handicapped children. Further, the state-wide system of advocacy should be vested by statute with the Commissioner of Education, and ". . . local school districts, BOCES, and other state agencies (should) have a proper role to play and that, wherever possible, parents represent the starting point."

Imagine a state-wide advocacy system, where the advocate is employed by the state yet uses his expertise or services only to serve his client, with the chief advocate being the Commissioner of Education, and with other state and local agencies and individuals having proper roles in that system—including last, but including wherever possible, parents. Just imagine!

Item 3: During the past several months, the R. J. Reynolds Tobacco Company, manufacturer of Camels, has been conducting a vigorous advertising campaign to attract the "honest and independent" smoker. Each of the advertisements in this series began with the question, "Can you spot the Camel Filters smoker?" The scene is in an airplane, at a party, or on the beach. Various people are pictured, saying something or doing something or appearing in some distinctive manner. The reader is to deduce who smokes Camels and, presumably, why. Surely, you have seen these ads. I have but, as with most advertisements, my obvervations were mindless; for so much of today's reading, advertisments or otherwise, mindlessness is a fairly safe and respectable condition to be in. If not for Liz Smith, an attorney who is a member of our Center on Human Policy staff, I never would have noticed that a particular Camel ad was vicious, bigoted, and unfair—but as typical of our culture as apple pie and baseball games. Among five other people on the beach, ranging in "beautifulness" from zero to everything, is Tyrone Shulace, "beach pest." We are told in the ad that the "58" on his shirt stands for his IQ. Further, Tyrone thinks that "off shore drilling is something Marines do." He smokes "Huff'n Puff" super filtered cigarettes. Obviously, that makes him retarded, unappealing, and deserving of whatever ridicule is heaped upon him.

Liz Smith wrote to the president of the R. J. Reynolds Tobacco Company, Mr. Collin Stoker of Winston-Salem, North Carolina. Within a week, she received a reply from C. A. Tucker, Vice President and Director of marketing for the company. He was apologetic. He said that:

> We do our best to create advertising that will appeal to large numbers of people. We have found one of the best methods to be humor. The 'Can You Spot' ads are intended to be much like a cartoonist's caricatures with the larger-than-life portrayal of the subjects not meant for literal interpretation . . .
> We have a great deal of empathy for the kind of public spirited work you are doing (our company supports local organizations involved with mental health). (21)

And, I think Mr. C. A. Tucker is right. This ad will appeal to large numbers of people. It will be thought very humorous. And besides, R. J. Reynolds does have a lot of empathy for the kind of public spirited work we are doing. And, I am sure, the company supports local organizations involved with mental health. They're as clean as a hound's tooth.

Item 4: Behavior modification, operant conditioning, behavior shaping, there are those and other names for a relatively new technique that has fast replaced psychotherapy as America's mental aspirin. The following bizarre story (22) is not intended to repudiate the importance or effectiveness of behavior modification techniques. There is no intention, at least on my part, to dissuade the reader concerning the great promise this method holds if used judiciously and appropriately. Rather, the Miami Sunland Training Center scandal is another indication of good ideas gone awry, good intentions misanthropically realized, potentially good people turned sour.

Sunland Training Center, in Dade County is a state institution in Florida, domiciling 900 people, each labeled mentally retarded. Like most state institutions, some of the residents are very retarded, some mildly retarded, some "retarded" only because they had once been labeled retarded. Like most large institutions, the age range represents a very wide spectrum indeed, young children to adults; and the range of behaviors represented at this institution is uncommonly broad and multidimensional. In essence, Sunland has a very heterogeneous group of residents, some of whom are at least adequately identified by the label "mentally retarded." Enter into this scene a new superintendent, one with a good reputation for "getting things done," for doing the right things, for being truly concerned about the mentally retarded. Enter also a psychologist who is given a free hand, who believes he has answers to the developmental problems these residents present, who is strongly devoted to behavior modification techniques as the foundation, the beginning direction, for behavioral improvements.

The consequences: homosexuals compelled to wear women's underwear; "thieves" who steal Cracker Jacks required to eat bars of soap and wear special signs noting each as a "thief"; those found masturbating, forced to masturbate in public; one inmate, who defecated in his pants while in seclusion, required to hold his soiled underwear under his nose before washing the pants out in the toilet; another "thief," caught stealing Sugar Pops, placed in restraints except to go to the "potty"; another boy who didn't want to go to bed locked up in a seclusion room; and on, and on, and on—children cleaning up their own vomit, rinsing their mouths with soap, denied meals, denied "privileges," tortured. Surely, this is not what Skinner planned for a new Walden. Surely, this is not what Barrett, Lindsley or Sidman envisioned. But, in this business, good ideas are often spoiled and altruistic motivations are corrupted.

Item 5: A letter to the author.

> In reviewing your book, *Souls in Extremis*, I am informed that the pictures in "Central" State School are in reality . . . State School. I would suggest that the material is quite out of date . . . the conditions you mention have definitely changed.
>
> One of my main criticisms would be the picture of the Community Store. I cannot identify the page as it does not have a page number, but the entire paragraph there is incorrect. The interest for residents is strictly regulated by law. There is a small amount left over because of bookkeeping difficulties. This amount is never used for the Community Store, never used for a retirement banquet, employees' gift fund, etc. The purposes for which this money is used must be itemized and presented to the Department of Mental Hygiene for approval. I take strong objection to this . . . . (23)

But here is an entirely different letter, from the above superintendent's immediate supervisor:

> By chance, I must confess, I was going through the Department library and found your book, *Souls in Extremis*. I have not been able to start reading it yet but was caught by the picture in the chapter, 'A Photographic Essay, 1971,' by Mark Blazey. What struck me was your straightforward description of Community Stores and the use of money for the benefit of employees. This came to my attention last Christmas when I found that these funds were used to pay for employee Christmas parties. I am enclosing a memorandum which was sent out concerning this problem and I think procedures are such that this misuse of money should be a thing of the past.

STATE OF
DEPARTMENT OF MENTAL HYGIENE

February 15, 1974

DIVISION OF MENTAL RETARDATION AND CHILDREN'S SERVICES

Memorandum No. 74-5

TO: State School Director, Deputy Directors for Administration
           Central Office Distribution Schedule 2

SUBJECT: Review of Community Stores, Donations and Patient Accounts by an Institution Ad-Hoc Committee

No proposed budget for community stores, donations, or patient interest accounts for fiscal 1974–75 will be accepted unless reviewed by a Committee whose size shall not be more than seven (7) members and whose membership shall consist of one-third parents, one-third residents, one-third employes, and one member of the Board of Visitors.

The Division policy will be that all funds from these sources shall be used primarily for residents' benefit. Recommendations will be made to the Director who will make final decisions.

Each institution will notify Dr. . . . .'s office in writing upon the selection of their review committee.

This memorandum will be in effect until superseded by future directives.

The supervisor adds:

I am also enclosing our memorandum on burials and maintenance of cemeteries (also discussed in book, with our treatment similarly criticized by aforementioned superintendent) which hopefully will start solving this problem.

August 12, 1974

DIVISION OF MENTAL RETARDATION AND CHILDREN'S SERVICES

Memorandum No. 74–30

TO: Directors, Deputy Directors, Clinical and Deputy Directors for Administration of all Division of Mental Retardation and Children's Services Facilities

Regional Directors

Central Office Distribution #2

SUBJECT: Burials and Maintenance of Cemeteries

It has come to the Division of Mental Retardation and Children's Services' attention that many graves in our institutional cemeteries are unmarked or marked only by a number. To correct this situation, the Division of Mental Retardation and Children's Services enunciates the following policy:

1. All graves in Mental Retardation and Children's Services' facility cemeteries will be distinguished by a marker with the person's name, date of birth and death, and appropriate religious symbol. No numbers will be used.

2. All burials will have a religious ceremony, unless such a ceremony is waived in writing by parents or guardians.

3. All state cemeteries will be maintained, and whenever possible, no new plots will be opened and community cemeteries should be used.

4. All graves, whether in state or community cemeteries, will be distinguished by a named marker.

The correspondent continues:

The other things that are photographically highlighted are obviously more difficult given the inertia of the system. However, we have a number of projects which I hope will make some dent in the problem (24).

The institutional superintendent claims that I am unfair, that the problems we portrayed have either been corrected previously or were never present. Her supervisor informs me that he has observed the same institutional abuses we described. He also tells me that, given the inertia of the system, other aspects of this photographic essay will not be corrected very easily. Yet, I am threatened in a subsequent letter by the superintendent who warns me that, because she is an advocate for the residents, she intends to "pursue this (our) transgression further." We have been waiting and, although I have heard several rumors that I will be sued, our last communication from this superintendent was January 23, 1974. Who is deceitful? Who are the advocates? And if, as claimed, the superintendent is an advocate, what does advocacy mean?

INNOVATION IS THE NAME OF THE GAME

Innovation is the name of the game, but it's not the stuff in the game. We may convince ourselves that we are truly in an innovative era in mental retardation. There is a plethora of monographs, books, and full journals devoted to innovative approaches to evaluating, placing, treating, dealing with, serving, and counting the mentally retarded; there are even claims that innovative approaches to paying for it all are now available. We read about innovation in special education (25) and innovation in other mental retardation settings (26) and we are tempted to believe. However, notwithstanding instructional materials centers, engineered classrooms, "hot" new dyslexia treatments, the effects of early educational intervention programs, new directions, and exciting frontiers emerging, notwithstanding the wish to believe, the jaundices and disappointments of the past remain, and therefore one tends to doubt. It isn't that we don't want to believe; we do or, I should say more correctly, I do. It's not that the evidence isn't piling up; we now have a Mental Retardation Source Book (27) and, believe it or not, I am currently serving on a committee that is optimistic enough to think it can develop a Mental Retardation Fact Book. Who would have thought that?

Nevertheless, I don't think that there is very much innovation in our field: first, because innovation requires new ideas (that's always a rare commodity) and, secondly, because we seem to be deliberately planning to achieve the antithesis of innovation and diversity.

Essentially, ours is a monolithic system, a single block of ideological stone; ours is a massive and solid, uniform, no-option, no-alternative, slot machine type of strategy that would seek the single best method, the single best procedure, the single best something or anything (28). The Monolith is not the special class, or even the segregated institution, or any other special setting or procedure or model. Rather, the Monolith is the one way, the unavailability of alternatives for clients, families, therapists and others concerned with the education and treatment of people with special needs. The Monolith supports "innovative" programs that evolve into either carbon copies of what is currently available or distortions of something that was once good, bad, or indifferent but will, surely, become tomorrow's new fad or the "magic" of the next modern-day alchemist. One thing that I've learned from all of this is the value we must assign to truly creative thinking and planning; it's an infrequent occurrence, often unrecognized, usually feared, and commonly disdained.

DEFINITIONS, LABELS, INCIDENCE AND PREVALENCE

Wedged by Executive and Squeezed by Academic Views

Years ago, when I first began seriously to study institutional life, I learned that, in New York State, residents of state schools were labeled "material" and their attendants and supervisors were labeled "items." More recently, while attending a meeting on the so-called geriatric problem in mental retardation, I learned that human beings are called "inventory" by some state department employees who have been designated responsible for their care and humane treatment. During the years, I have learned that labels are important, because they picture the feelings we have for people and things, and because they serve to peel away the concealment of our prejudices.

Labels may not be of consequence in a clinical setting; in fact, their usage with individuals should be restricted, if not discouraged. However, there are people who need service and the administrative assignment of resources to programs and groups requires the utilization of identifiers, labels. We can't even discuss policy priorities, much less programs, without naming people and things. For better or for worse, we have and will continue to have, and suffer with, labels. Hence, we will need to contend with an "epidemiology" of mental retardation—notwithstanding the knowledge that mental retardation is neither a disease nor a condition with "lawful" characteristics.

The labels we use are critical in understanding that epidemiology, because incidence and prevalence estimates have little meaning when separated from a definitional context. Therefore, notwithstanding the President's Committee on Mental Retardation, which has reported that there are 6 million mentally retarded individuals in the United States (a convenient application of the three percent estimate) and other approximations, I believe it remains essential for us to review what else may be known about these complex matters. I begin here with where I began the chapter itself, discussing metaphors, language, and the relationship between our words and our values. We should begin by noting again that incidence and prevalence data are not grounded only in objectively derived disease entities.

The American Association on Mental Deficiency has recently revised its definition of mental retardation. Before 1959, there was more or less general agreement that the incidence of mental retardation is approximately three percent. That is, mental retardation was assumed to be normally distributed in the population and it was further agreed that the psychometric "cutoff" would be seventy-five IQ or one and one-half standard deviations away from the mean. In 1959, the Association's terminology and Classification Committee, chaired by Rick Heber, redefined mental retardation and, included in the revised definition, there was the statement that subaverage intellectual performance refers to a psychometric score which is greater than one standard deviation below the population mean on tests of general intelligence (29). With that change in definition, 16 percent of a typical population would be, psychometrically at least, eligible to be designated as "mentally retarded."

In 1973, a subsequent committee of the Association, now chaired by Herbert Grossman, again revised the definition to include as mentally retarded only those who are "significantly" subaverage in intellectual functioning, where "significantly" means performance which is two or more standard deviations from the mean or average of the tests (30). With the figurative, and possibly literal, stroke of Herbert Grossman's pen, a committee sitting around a conference table reduced enormously the potential incidence of mental retardation, never having to see or dose or deal with a client, only having to say that, hereinafter, mental retardation is such and such rather than this or that. We cannot redefine measles, or cancer, or pregnancy with such external procedures. It's obvious; mental retardation and emotional disturbance, and even such seemingly objective conditions as blindness and deafness, are less objective disease entities than they are administrative terms; they are metaphors more than anything else.

It is important to understand that merely having a low IQ neither legally nor functionally jeopardizes how society views a person or deals with him. Sixteen percent of the population have IQs below 85; three percent of the population have IQs below 75; but probably no more than one percent of the population are ever in their lifetimes administratively adjudicated as "mentally retarded." This is by way of saying that the incidence, prevalence, and characteristics of mental retardation depend upon such influences as definition and criteria, program supports, cultural value, social class, and other factors that have more to do with political and administrative rather than biological or psychological matters. This situation exists across all so-called disability areas, and consequently, estimates of various categorical handicaps vary from study to study, from culture to culture, and from time to time. Disability means no more or less than being placed in a special class, a special program, or a special category or setting, as a consequence of that disability. The most relevant definition of a disability must refer to the fact that it is essentially administratively determined.

Incidence and prevalence estimates, predictions of program needs, and cost-benefit analyses are extraordinarily hazardous when dealing with these diverse administratively defined populations. For example, in one state, attempts are made to integrate so-called educable mentally retarded children in regular grades; in another area (e.g., Prince Edward Island, Canada) such youngsters are in regular grades and are not even thought of as "mentally retarded." In yet another state, every effort is made to place as many children as possible with IQs less than 75 in special classes for the mentally retarded. Then, we might ask, what is the prevalence of mental retardation in the public schools when, on the one hand, there are school systems that deliberately attempt to identify such children as retarded and others, equally interested in their well being, that deliberately attempt to integrate such children fully into the mainstream of educational life?

Table 1 summarizes prevalence estimates of handicapping conditions obtained from several recent studies. Some cautions should be emphasized: with the exception of our yet unpublished preschool data, summarized in Column One, the prevalence estimates are for age groups 5 through 19. Therefore, I am presenting prevalence of handicap among preschool children with prevalence estimates for school age children, while entirely neglecting adult prevalence rates. Secondly, none of these estimates account for what is now called minimal brain dysfunction, learning disabilities, or Strauss syndrome. Intentionally, I have not included prevalence estimates for this condition if, indeed, it is a separate condition; those that have made attempts to estimate the prevalence of learning disabilities indicate data ranging from a 5 or 6 percent estimate to 20, 30, and 40 percent. Next, it should also be noted that some of these prevalence estimates did not include multiple handicaps as a separate category; rather, they chose to indicate only the primary handicapping condition. Further, Table 1 hardly illustrates the enormous range of estimates available. For example, a recent Rand study on services for handicapped youth summarizes prevalence rates reported by 11 different groups (31). They range: in total prevalence of handicapping conditions, from 4.08 percent to 24.50 percent; in mental retardation, from 1.54 percent to 7.00 percent; in speech impairment, from 1.30 percent to 5.00 percent; in emotional disturbance, from .05 percent to 5.00 percent; and in learning disability, from .03 percent to 7.00 percent. Lastly, one should mention that, for most people in our field, prevalence and incidence estimates are either

Table 1. Prevalence estimates of various types of handicapped children

Handicap	Prevalence estimates by percent				
	1[a]	2[b]	3[c]	4[d]	5[e]
Educable mentally retarded	0.5	2.0	2.3	1.30	1.30
Trainable mentally retarded				.24	.24
Hearing-impaired	1.1	1.5	.575	.10	.575
Visually handicapped	.6	.2	.1	.05	.1
Speech impaired	3.4	2.0	3.5	3.60	3.5
Physically handicapped	1.0	1.5	.5	.21	.5
Brain injury and learning disabilities	1.7	(f)	1.0	1.12	1.0
Emotionally handicapped	1.0	2.0	2.0	2.00	2.0
Multiple handicaps	(f)	(f)	(f)	.07	.07
Total	9.3	9.2	9.975	8.69	9.285

[a] Estimates based on a Syracuse University-Systems Research Inc. Head Start questionnaire; T.M.R. and E.M.R. combined; no estimate on "Multiple Handicaps."

[b] Estimates by Romaine P. Mackie and Lloyd M. Dunn, College University programs for the preparation of teachers of exceptional children, USOE bull. No. 13, Washington: GPO, 1954.

[c] Estimates prepared for Bureau of Education for the Handicapped, USOE, in "Estimates of Current Manpower Needs in Education for the Handicapped, 1968–69," Washington, December 1968.

[d] Estimates used by Rossmiller, Richard A., Hale, James A., and Lloyd E. Frohreich, "Educational Programs for Exceptional Children: Resource Configurations and Costs." Madison, Wisc.: Department of Educational Administration, University of Wisconsin, 1970, p. 129.

[e] Conservative estimates used by "The Fleischmann Report on the Quality, Cost, and Financing of Elementary and Secondary Education in New York State," Viking Compass, vol. II, p. 260.

[f] No estimate.

meaningless or valueless, or both. Many such colleagues would claim that institutions, or schools, or clinics have what they have. What possible differences could these data offer?

While you may legitimately inquire, therefore, what value can prevalence studies provide, you might also ask what other comparable data are available to permit us to plan better, however crudely. And, while you ponder that unsatisfactory question, we should return to Table 1, and our data, and—eventually—some recommendations. The reader will find a rather striking similarity between data derived from our Head Start questionnaire and other estimates—with the exception of the prevalence of mental retardation. Ours is low (0.5 percent) in contrast with estimates of 2 percent and 2½ percent in the other studies. We believe this discrepancy is accounted for in our earlier discussion on factors influencing prevalence rates. Further, our reported low prevalence of mental retardation is entirely consistent with the numerous so-called educability studies concerned with the preschool deprived (32, 33). Specifically, we account for the low prevalence of preschool mentally retarded children in communities that traditionally include high prevalences of school age mentally retarded children to be a function of the nature of this thing we term "mental retardation." Mental retardation is essentially unidentified in the preschool years except when it is accompanied with central nervous system pathology or clinical stigmata and, therefore, usually with moderate or severe disability. So-called cultural familial mental retardation, quite common in later years, is essentially nonexistent among infants and preschoolers. What was probably reported to us as "mental retardation" by Head Start Centers were observable stigmata and moderate or severe cognitive disabilities. However, for this condition of "mental retardation" as well as others, it is not possible accurately to assess the influence of such factors as coercion, political motivations, and naivete, in the determination of our, and these other, prevalence estimates.

The ostensible purpose for defining groups, labeling individuals, and developing incidence and prevalence estimates is to serve better those individuals defined and labeled. If labeling does not lead to services, and it often doesn't, it reduces what might have been a helpful procedure to a pejorative and detrimental act.

Therefore, I too should at least present some estimates of needs and types of programs that may serve these special populations. I include in these estimates (Table 2) not only those whom we label "mentally retarded" but people who have other handicaps. The overlapping nature of these disabilities and the frequent occurrence of multiple handicaps among the moderately and severely disabled dictate a more global assessment of needs than what a single categorical approach could provide. Given all of the aforementioned caveats, and the additional one that I think I know a good deal more about the prevalance and incidence of mental retardation than about other disabilities, I nevertheless believe that these estimates may be helpful to those who have been forced to design programs without even the grossest notions of how many people they should plan for and what those people may need during their developmental and adult years.

In a perverse and ironic manner, we may be fortunate that needs seem always to be bottomless, endless and never met. That is, we haven't suffered from an overabundance of services for so-called handicapped people. On the other hand, especially with limited resources—which we will probably always have to confront—it may be useful strategically to place those resources where they can do the greatest good for the greatest number.

While many experts in the field of mental retardation have argued that, for example, 16 percent or 3 percent or 5 percent or 2 percent (AAMD) of the population are mentally retarded, or "psychometrically mentally retarded," our own study (34) indicates that a 1 percent estimate

Table 2. Estimated needs for special community and residential services for children and adults in a modal region of 500,000 population

Category	Percent of total population in categories	Estimated number in categories
I. Major Categories		
a. Percent of total population needing special services due to their mental retardation.	1% of total population: .75% EMR; .20% TMR; .05% SMR.	5,000
b. Percent of total population needing special services due to their behavioral disturbances.	1% of total population: .50% Severely ED or SM; .50% moderately or mildly ED or SM.	5,000
c. Percent of total population needing special services due to moderate and severe sensory and/or physical disorders.	1% of total population: including .03% blind, .08% deaf; .14% severely sensory and/or PH; remainder partially disabled.	5,000
II. Sub-Categories		
a. Mental Retardation		
1. Individuals in need of special programs in public school at any one time.	1% of total school population (125,000)	1,250[a]
2. Individuals in need of only minimum services other than special programs during school years.	50% of entire mentally retarded population	2,500
3. Individuals in need of residential placement, at any one time, with alternative programs available.	.1% of total population	500
4. Individuals requiring other services		
(a) Nursery and preschool programs	5% of known mentally retarded population	250
(b) Day Care Programs	5% of known mentally retarded population	250
(c) Sheltered Workshop Activities, Vocational Training, and Adult Day Activities	10% of known mentally retarded population	500
b. Behavioral Disturbances		
1. Individuals in need of special programs in public school at any one time.	1% of total school population (125,000)	1,250

[a] Estimates will slightly exceed those in major categories because individuals may require multiple primary services.

continued

Table 2. *Continued*

Category	Percent of total population in categories	Estimated number in categories
2. Individuals in need of only minimum services other than special programs during school years.	50% of entire emotionally disturbed population	2,500
3. Individuals in need of residential placement, at any one time, with alternative programs available.	.1% of total population	500
4. Individuals requiring other services		
(a) Nursery and preschool programs	5% of known emotionally disturbed population	250
(b) Day Care Programs	5% of known emotionally disturbed population	250
(c) Sheltered Workshop Activities, Vocational Training, and Adult Activities	10% of known emotionally disturbed population	500
c. Sensory and/or Physical Disorders		
1. Individuals in need of special programs in public school at any one time.	1% of total school population (125,000)	1,250
2. Individuals in need of only minimum services other than special programs during school years.	50% of entire sensory and physically handicapped	2,550
3. Individuals in need of residential placement, at any one time, with alternative programs available.	.1% of total population	500
4. Individuals requiring other services		
(a) Nursery and preschool programs	5% of known sensory and physically handicapped population	250
(b) Day Care Programs	5% of known sensory and physically handicapped population	250
(c) Sheltered Workshop Activities, Vocational Training, and Adult Day Activities	10% of known sensory and physically handicapped population	500

is more valuable for program planning and development. Similarly, estimates as high as 20, 30, or 40 percent in the relatively new category, "Specific Learning Disabilities," are provocative, certainly, but do not appear to be helpful in program planning. Further, prevalence estimates of various types of handicapped children (not including the new general category, "Learning Disabilities") conclude that approximately 10 percent of all school age children are "handicapped." Unfortunately, there are problems with this estimate for the same reasons that epidemiological data on mental retardation have never provided satisfactory guidance for program planning.

The studies that have been completed indicate that there are important differences between what we might call "administrative disability" and "objective disability." As mentioned, a clear example of this dichotomy is the discrepancy between psychometric mental retardation (at least two percent of the total population) and administratively designated (or known) mental retardation (approximately one percent of the total population). Therefore, taking these factors and their resultant problems into consideration, I believe it is reasonable to consider using population estimates that are based on available studies of known cases in the various disability categories.

From our own demographic studies of mental retardation, our evaluation of the epidemiologic literature in the field, and from a careful analysis of the data obtained from both our Head Start questionnaire survey and our observational studies of selected Head Start programs, we estimate that one percent of the total population (incidence) need special services because of their mental retardation, another one percent require it because of behavioral disturbances, and another one percent because of moderate and severe sensory and/or physical disorders (see Table 2). We would not include the so-called speech-impaired in such designations; nor would we include the so-called learning disabled.

We believe it is not in the best interests of either the children or the programs to label children with mild disabilities, who could otherwise be adequately dealt with in ordinary classes, as "handicapped," "retarded," "speech-impaired," etc. We believe it is in the interest of both the children who have been so labeled until now and those others who are now denied a normal interaction with them, to reserve the categories of handicap only for those who have such severe and moderate needs that they will not be able to be served adequately in ordinary classes under ordinary conditions.

For that group with such special needs, we estimate that there is no more than a three percent incidence across populations and age categories, and possibly, a four percent and no more than five percent prevalence during the preschool and school years. Therefore, mild speech impairment, as mild retardation or disturbance, could not be considered a handicap requiring special attention in the traditional sense. Those children with mild disabilities should be served within the context of regular school settings. Those with severe or moderate speech impairments will be found to have general language disabilities and, more probably than not, learning, behavioral, sensory, or physical disorders.

Obviously, the above recommendations will not solve all of the difficulties inherent in estimating the incidence and prevalence of conditions that are grounded more in political-metaphorical issues than in scientific ones. However, at least in some modest manner, we may be able to reduce the harmful effects of unnecessary labeling and the resultant stigma to many children and their families. We may also move from a disease-oriented planning model to a developmental model, one that seriously considers the benefits of integration and decategorization of both children and programs, one that is committed to the concept that people are educable, that development is a function of not only endowment but training and opportunity and encouragement.

BUSINESS AND FINANCE

The newly emerging literature on the economics of mental retardation is important and was long awaited by the professional leadership, the political community, and the consumers. I wish to address myself in this section to aspects of "business" that are rarely, if ever, discussed in professional publications or, for that matter, in polite society. And I believe what I am about to discuss is somewhat important for those struggling to understand why we make the decisions we make and why past experiences and data are incidental to such decision-making.

For one year, during a leave of absence from my university, I was the Commonwealth of Massachusetts Commissioner for mental retardation programs for the Department of Mental Health. At least theoretically, if not always pragmatically, I was responsible for the conduct of all of the Commonwealth's state institutions for the mentally retarded, and all of the Department's community educational and clinical programs for those people designated as mentally retarded who, for one reason or another, "escaped" institutionalization (35).

I will begin with the conclusion. Mental retardation is big business. It is very big business. One research group reported recently that there are 2,800,000 mentally retarded youth in the United States and that government agencies expend $2.8 billion annually to serve them (36). Its dollar volume does not approach expenditures for mental health. But how many businesses do? Let's look at some of the "evidence."

I have observed in several states that the largest purchaser of buildings in a state is the state itself. Further, within state governments, departments of mental health are oftentimes most consistently the largest purchasers of buildings. Even in the wake of a national clamor to invest our resources in programs, not real estate or buildings, giant steam shovels are ripping large chunks of land across this country, harbingers for institutional monstrosities that must always disillusion some and totally defeat others.

New York State, in the wake of public scandals and anguished outcries, after promises to do better and differently, continues to built large—although not as large as Willowbrook and Letchworth—ugly institutions at costs of $40,000 to $60,000, and more, per bed. Within the past few years, the state has been engaged in a half-billion dollar institutional building program in mental retardation. Why? Answers aren't easy and those that are readily available may be potentially libelous. However, even a school boy can deduce that 6 percent of a half-billion dollars—architects' fees—is a great deal of money. Even the most unsophisticated citizen will appreciate the importance major construction programs have for contractors, suppliers, land developers, the unions and, especially, the banks who together will "earn" a half billion dollars on this mental retardation construction. Even the most naive and apolitical citizen will remember that, when an official in a high federal government position was forced to resign for kickbacks taken while he was once governor, those who provided the "kick" and the "vigorish" were all either contractors, land developers, or architects. How can we terminate institutional building programs when, in many states, they are literally the source for political party, and even private, payoffs and patronage?

Let's look at operating expenditures. In New York State during the 1974 fiscal year, the mental retardation division in the State Department of Mental Hygiene was allocated a budget of $235 million. Of that amount, only $2 million was earmarked for community programs. Why? Well, one answer is that buildings, the staffs, and the inmates are there; so, the resources must go to the institutions. To a degree, this is a reasonable explanation. But why do we continue to use outmoded, sometimes disgraceful, always less than desirable or logical institutional settings?

First, there are unions, who find it convenient to have their members together in one facility; dispersal to many community programs may impair a union's strength and effectiveness. Secondly, there are administrators and supervisors who, similarly, find it compatible to have their staffs working in centralized facilities; dispersal of inmates leads to the dispersal of staff and the realization that neither all of the administrators nor all of the direct care personnel are necessary. Certainly, it would be difficult for an institutional superintendent to speak any longer about "his institution" if the institutional population were evacuated and re-settled in integrated communities. Thirdly, if there were no institutions there would be no million dollar laundry contracts, multimillion dollar food contracts, milk contracts, ice cream contracts, automobile contracts, service contracts, utilities contracts, even funeral contracts. Certainly, as matter is neither created nor destroyed, people must eat and soiled clothes must be washed. However, it's not the same, especially for larger influential businesses, to contemplate one contract for a million dollars as it is to contemplate competing for a thousand contracts for a thousand dollars each, or thousands of purchases by free citizens.

There are analogies in public education, contrasting segregated schools with integrated programs. There are analogies in comparing specialized clinics with generic clinics. As the Blacks learned, as the Jews learned, as the Indians are now learning, segregation, bigotry, and prejudice can be big business. In our field, considering our modest number of clients and our relative low priority in the scheme of things, mental retardation is big business, and it's big essentially because it's segregated and monolithic and, therefore, controllable. Either we must find a way to remove the overly attractive rewards that some people seek and find in this business or we must desegregate our programs and clients; otherwise little will change. Rhetoric, promises, or even good intentions will not alone discourage half-billion dollar state building programs or $50 million operating budgets for places like the Willowbrook Developmental Center. Either we demand a total moratorium on all construction, and quickly and efficiently remove other fiscal incentives, or we deal with this problem from the other end, reorder priorities (but, remember the "Year of the Child") and evacuate institutions and special segregated schools; otherwise mental retardation will continue to be big business— and great despair for those who truly want to serve others, and for those who must be served.

CONCEPTS OF MENTAL RETARDATION

Mental retardation is not something that can be simply and scientifically defined, discussed, dissected, applied or studied. Mental retardation is related to our very understanding of humanity, of human potential, of educability, of equality, of rights and privileges, of everything we are and everything that relates to us. Asking someone to comprehend a concept of mental retardation is akin to asking him to comprehend a concept of spirituality or decadence, beauty or ugliness, strength or weakness, good people or bad people. Mental retardation can't be encapsulated and "pictured" by I.Q. parameters, or even etiological descriptions, or behavioral assessments. It must always be anchored to other people, a community, values, expectations, and hopes. Therefore, the epidemiology of mental retardation can only be discussed in a psychological-social-political-economic context. Further, the economic factor, or any other factor or problem, can be appreciated only in this same context. Unfortunately, we have neither a manual on terminology and classification nor a curriculum that will permit us to shortcut this conceptual process.

Also unfortunately, one's concept of mental retardation may impair seriously otherwise good judgment. Prejudices concerning those whom society calls "mentally retarded" may cause even the most distinguished and wise among us to do thoughtless things and issue silly pronouncements.

REFORM OR REVOLUTION

I've asked the question many times, yet there is no answer for me. Possibly, there is no answer because I'm not pleased with the answers I see. I cannot tolerate the invidious comparison between the promises made and the institutions created. And, what were the promises that our field was to keep? What did the institution, the special education program, the community mental health-mental retardation movement contribute? We have been faithful, some have worked unselfishly, some have raised large sums of money, many have supported humanistic precepts and philosophies on behalf of people with special needs. What good was to come of all of this? The hope then, and remaining today, was that people would gain strength, would deepen their optimism and faith in the human ethos, would develop more genuine concern for our brethren, would eventually have the wisdom to believe that all human beings are equally valuable, and that our work is not to judge who can or can't change but to fulfill the promise that all people can change, that each person can learn. The promises made were to coalesce around the demonstration, especially to those of us most intimately involved, that society is each person, not multiplied but singular, each person unique and valuable.

Yet, what have we created? We find that, in institutions and in many special schools, both the caretakers and the clients victimize and are victims. In the institution, and in many special school programs, there are not sufficient options for children, for families and, equally important, for staffs. In plain fact, the research available confirms the shambles that too many special programs and facilities are.

Yet, in spite of powerful critical reports on institutional life (37), and the scientifically questionable but numerous reports on special class life (38), we continue to build more and more institutions and pass more and more mandatory rather than permissive special education laws—regardless of the well known fact that we have yet to demonstrate either the efficacy or moral rectitude in continuing, much less encouraging, those segregated programs. To turn to an earlier theme, such proliferation on the basis of trivial evidence is but another illustration of the monolithic influence.

We have made too many concessions, we have so bent the data to suit our ignorances and confusions, we are so anxious to please the people, that we lie to spare them the anxiety we feel because of what we have created. I'm expecting that, at any time now, somebody will propose a new concept, a remodeling of the old French triage system for sorting out and treating battlefield casualties. However, the neo-triage model will deal not with the militarily wounded but with those whom bad luck, accident, and society inflict their insults upon. I'm expecting to read someday an "erudite" paper advising us to set aside the hopeless, for their very designations demand we should not waste time with them; and, we might best benignly neglect those who will probably do as well without us, those who puzzle us, or those whose problems—although real—do not fully incapacitate them; and, consequently, we should reserve our resources and energies for those who most need our help. Possibly, in war, triage is a valid concept; where some will live and some will die, and resources are particularly scarce, the whole thing—ghoulish as it may be—makes at least a little sense. However, when the new triage is trotted out, will there be anyone to say, "But we are not at war"? And will there be anyone else to say, "No, we are not at war. Yet, we should have been. It was always a war, but most of us thought of it as merely a debate."?

REFERENCES

1. Mental Hygiene News, New York State Department of Mental Hygiene, 24.5.74, p. 1.
2. Syracuse Herald-American, New York, 7.7.74, p. 28.
3. New York Times, 7.7.74, p. 1.
4. Ibid, 30.7.72, Section 4, p. 2.
5. Ibid, 8.4.74, p. 34.
6. Ibid, 4.5.74, p. 7.
7. Ibid, 11.8.74, Section 1, p. 1.
8. Elmira Star-Gazette, New York, 9.5.74, p. 14.
9. New York Times, May 5, 1974, p. 45.
10. Collings, G. D. and Singletary, E: Case Law and Education of the Handicapped. Florida Educational Research and Development Council, Summer 1973.
11. Syracuse University Law Review: Symposium on the Legal Rights of the Mentally Retarded. Syracuse, New York, 23: pp. 991–1165, 1972.
12. National Advisory Committee on Handicapped Children: Special Education for Handicapped Children. Dept. of Health, Education and Welfare, Washington, D.C., January 31, 1968.

13. National Advisory Committee on Handicapped Children: Better Education for Handicapped Children. Department of Health, Education, and Welfare. Washington, D.C., June 30, 1969.

14. National Advisory Committee on Handicapped Children: Third Annual Report. Dept. of Health, Education, and Welfare, Washington, D.C., June 30, 1970.

15. National Advisory Committee on Handicapped Children: Basic Education Rights for the Handicapped. Dept. of Health, Education, and Welfare, Washington, D.C., June 30, 1973.

16. President's Committee on Mental Retardation: MR '67: A First Report to the President on the Nation's Progress and Remaining Great Needs in the Campaign to Combat Mental Retardation. U.S. Government Printing Office, Washington, D.C., June, 1967.

17. President's Committee on Mental Retardation: Silent Minority. U.S. Government Printing Office, Washington, D.C., 1974.

18. Task Force on Children Out of School: Suffer the Children: The Politics of Mental Health in Massachusetts. Task Force on Children Out of School, Boston, Mass., 1972.

19. Wolfensberger, W.: Citizen Advocacy for the Handicapped, Impaired, and Disadvantaged: An Overview. President's Committee on Mental Retardation, Washington, D.C., 1972.

20. Regents of the University of the State of New York: The Education of Children with Handicapping Conditions. The State Education Department, Albany, N.Y., November, 1973.

21. June 7, 1974.

22. Miami Herald, Florida, 5.4.72.

23. Personal correspondence, January 3, 1974.

24. Personal correspondence, August 16, 1974.

25. Aaronson, W. J.: Innovation in Special Education: Title III ESEA. Dept. of Health, Education, and Welfare, Washington, D.C., 1972.

26. Stedman, D. J.: Current Issues in Mental Retardation and Human Development. President's Committee on Mental Retardation, Washington, D.C., 1971.

27. Dept. of Health, Education, and Welfare: Mental Retardation Source Book. Publication No. (OSOS) 73–81, Washington, D.C., 1973.

28. Blatt, B.: The Monolith and the Promise. Therapeutic Recreation Journal, Vol. III, No. 4, Fourth Quarter, 1973, pp. 4–32.

29. Heber, R. (ed): A Manual on Terminology and Classification in Mental Retardation. Monograph supplement to the American Journal of Mental Deficiency, 64, 1959.

30. Grossman, H. J. (ed): Manual on Terminology and Classification in Mental Retardation. American Association on Mental Deficiency, Washington, D.C., 1973.

31. Kakalik, J. S., et al.: Services for Handicapped Youth: A Program Overview. Rand Corporation, Santa Monica, Cal., 1973, p. 276.

32. Blatt, B. and Garfunkel, F.: The Educability of Intelligence. Council for Exceptional Children, Washington, D.C., 1969.

33. Blatt, B. and Garfunkel, F.: Teaching the Mentally Retarded: in Travers, R. M. W. (ed): Second Handbook of Research on Teaching. Rand McNally & Co., Chicago, 1973, pp. 632–656.

34. Blatt, B.: Souls in Extremis: An Anthology on Victims and Victimizers. Allyn and Bacon, Boston, Mass., 1973.

35. Blatt, B.: Exodus from Pandemonium: Human Abuse and a Reformation of Public Policy. Allyn and Bacon, Boston, 1970.
36. Kakalik, et al., 1973, op. cit., pp. 2 and 13.
37. Blatt, 1973, op. cit.
38. Blatt and Garfunkel, 1973, op. cit.

CHAPTER 9

From Institution to Community: A Conversion Model

For too long, teachers have viewed their roles in society in terms of what takes place in the schoolhouse. Although we do not believe that such a model works very well for any child or, for that matter, any teacher, it works especially poorly and leads to serious problems when the children are the so-called handicapped and the teachers have been charged with the development of responsible programs to serve these children. All education is part of a larger social context, and seldom is it more important to recognize this than in dealing with children who are at high risk for placements in institutional environments. This chapter addresses itself to that larger social context and its relevance for teachers and other professionals associated with the schools.

This chapter begins with a brief discussion and definition of our Conversion Model, with the expectation that the reader will be receptive to the conclusion that deinstitutionalization is only one facet of any bona fide system of community options for individuals with special needs. We next describe the elements of a community model, followed by a discussion of the processes involved in conversion. The chapter continues with plan of action and, based on our analysis of relevant literature and our own investigations, an assessment of the magnitude of the problem. We conclude with a summary which sets forth the relevance of these issues for teachers and others connected with the schools. Finally, because we believe that a serious barrier to achieving a workable conversion model stems from imprecision in definitions of the population and in estimates of incidence and prevalence, the reader is referred to the previous chapter (pp. 226–234) for a discussion of the magnitude of this problem.

This abridged essay, co-authored with Robert Bogdan, Douglas Biklen, and Steven Taylor, originally appeared in E. Sontag (Ed.), *Educational programming for the severely and profoundly handicapped*. Reston, Va.: Council for Exceptional Children, Division of Mental Retardation, 1977.

CONVERSION DEFINED

If we do not reconceptualize deinstitutionalization, it will fail, either by inertia or by backlash. Deinstitutionalization is a federal policy mandated as a priority by Tile XX Social Security legislation, and by the Developmental Disabilities Act of 1975. Both as a policy and a philosophy, it has received general acceptance by state human service agencies, and by the public. Nevertheless, the practice of deinstitutionalization is occurring at a snail's pace (Conroy, 1976). The reasons are myriad, but the common denominator is our definition of deinstitutionalization.

Too often, deinstitutionalization has simply meant releasing people from state facilities by moving traditionally institutionalized people into community institutions. These have usually been nursing homes of two or three hundred people, or group homes, foster homes, and boarding homes that sometimes provide little more than bed and board. However, the goal of deinstitutionalization should not be simply to move people from one building to another, from one location to another, from a total-care institution to a partial-care one, or from a custodial-care facility to a non-care facility. The goal should be to transform a dehumanizing, segregated institutional model of services into a humanizing, integrated community model.

The task of achieving this goal has proven more difficult than first thought, mainly because it involves so much more than simply releasing people from institutions. There are several reasons for the difficulty. First, we have lacked a clearly articulated plan for community-based human services. Such a plan should address itself to these questions: Which children should enter public schools? Who will require special instruction? Who will need only resource assistance? Who will need more intense and individualized programming? What kinds of residential options will be necessary? Second, the states have vested interests in maintaining institutions whose construction has been financed by state and municipal bonds and loans. Institutional residents' Social Security, Medicaid, and insurance payments will be needed to repay lenders in the future. This mandates a continued full house in state-supported institutions. Third, deinstitutionalization will require changes in attitude throughout our culture. If the community is to offer experiences different from those offered by institutions, it must rid itself of prejudice and sterotyping and of the segregating, discriminatory policies that result from those attitudes. Fourth, the conduct of service providers must conform to principles of normalization (Wolfensberger, 1972), and of human dignity.

The roadblocks to deinstitutionalization will not be overcome by either moral or legal commitments to release institutional residents. What is demanded is a systematic approach to transforming institutions—a

Conversion Plan. By conversion, we mean an orderly transition from an institutional to a community-based system of services with concomitant plans to transform existing physical facilities, staff resources, institutional ideologies, community attitudes, and agency policies to alternative, more humanizing uses and postures.

When industries shift their direction and begin new production, they almost always attempt to convert existing facilities and staff to the new or alternative effort. It is time for institutions and communities to proceed in similar fashion in moving toward deinstitutionalization. Without conversion, deinstitutionalization will fail to yield its expected positive results and may possibly produce a powerful backlash.

Conversion to What?

We must conceptualize the problem of institutions and community programs as the *conversion* of a system, rather than as the deinstitutionalization of individuals. But what kind of system do we want? Are we advocating a transition from large institutions to smaller ones? Do we speak only for the mildly or moderately retarded? Are we asking for a new generation of enlightened professionals to decide how the retarded are to live? No. We have a vision of a world with dramatically different assumptions about the rights of people, and their potential for growth, individuality, and dignity. And we have a vision of a system of services that reflects the following principles:

1. Services must be provided as a right of citizens, rather than as a privilege (Biklen, 1974). Traditionally, services for those with disabilities have been considered a matter of charity and good will. As such, they have been denied on the basis of insufficient funds and other considerations. In the system we foresee, services will be offered to all who need them. This implies that all disabled individuals can benefit from community residential, educational, and vocational services and that they are capable of unlimited growth and development (Blatt & Garfunkel, 1969). It also means that no person will be deprived of services without due process procedures, whereby the burden of proof as to the inappropriateness of any service shall be upon the service agency. All persons, regardless of nature or degree of disability, shall be entitled to a full range of appropriate programs and services.

2. Services must be provided on a *non-categorical* basis. That is, a person's needs, and not his category or label, will determine the services he receives. No agency will categorize people as "mentally retarded," "emotionally disturbed," "learning disabled," or as any other disability type.

3. Services must constitute a *continuum* to ensure that each individual's needs are met in the most appropriate manner. Programs shall be designed to fit individual needs, rather than vice versa. Rather than group homes, there will be a range of community residences—short and long term group facilities—offering foster care, respite care, and a chance for independent and semi-independent living. Rather than special schools, there will be a range of educational programs. Individuals will be able to move from one program to another as their needs require.

4. Services must be provided under the *least restrictive, most normalized* circumstances possible (Wolfensberger, 1972). Every individual must have the maximum opportunity to be integrated into the community and to be among typical peers. This implies a preference for independent, rather than supervised, living; for integrated, rather than segregated, schooling; for regular, rather than sheltered, employment.

5. The agencies providing services must be *accountable* to consumers. There must be active and significant consumer involvement in the planning, implementation, monitoring, and operation of services at agency, local, regional, state, and federal levels.

There are some who will dismiss our vision as idealistic or impractical. And they may be correct. From our viewpoint, however, there has been far too much realism and far too little idealism in the past. We have written plans without goals, provided services without a purpose, and constructed a world without a vision. If nothing else, a vision offers hope and direction.

BARRIERS TO COMMUNITY CONVERSION

We have presented one way of conceptualizing the problem of institutions and deinstitutionalization, and some of the components of the system into which we are attempting to convert. It is also important to consider the barriers that interfere with our efforts at conversion, for it is possible that one reason for their persistence is our seeming reluctance to identify them.

Handicapism

Handicapism has many parallels with racism. It is a set of assumptions and practices that promotes the differential and unjust treatment of people because of apparent or assumed physical, mental, or behavioral differences. Handicapism pervades our society and, overall, presents the most important barrier to the development of community programs. Prejudice, stereotyping, and discrimination are its major components. (See Yinker, 1965, and Allport, 1954, for a discussion of the use of these terms in the study of ethnic relations.)

Prejudice toward the handicapped is indicated by assumptions that they are innately incapable and naturally inferior. It is revealed in the belief that the handicapped have personalities and characteristics so extraordinary that they have little in common with non-handicapped persons, and should therefore be kept "with their own kind" (Goffman, 1963; Wright, 1960).

Prejudice is a general disposition, while stereotyping refers to the content of the prejudice that is directed toward specific groups. Thus, the mentally retarded are believed to be forever childlike, to enjoy boring, routine activities, and to be oversexed (Wolfensberger, 1975). The blind are supposed to be melancholy (Scott, 1969). Stereotypes are frequently used to justify particular modes of treatment. Thus, the retarded are often treated like children, given boring work, and isolated from others.

Despite their inaccuracies, stereotypes are maintained by many processes. They are transmitted and constantly reinforced by the culture and by peers. Since the handicapped are isolated and have few opportunities for close or sustained relations with normal people, they have little chance of disproving the stereotypes about themselves. Since handicapped people are treated in ways that correspond to their stereotypes and are rewarded for stereotypic behavior, they learn to act out the role of the handicapped and fall victim to self-fulfilling prophesies (Merton, 1957).

Prejudice and stereotyping point to the cognitive and ideological substance of handicapism and lead to discrimination. At one time, slaves and women were considered to be not unfairly treated. Laboring in the field for the economic benefit of others or serving their husbands was viewed as their natural condition. Similarly, handicapped people are thought to have relative equality in our society, especially since the advent of categorical social service programs. Nevertheless, their differential treatment is evidence of deep discrimination.

Recognizing handicapism in a general way is important, but we must be more specific if we are to bring down this barrier. We must recognize that prejudiced assumptions are transmitted by the mass media—television, films, books, and newspapers. For example, in horror movies we see a clear association of physical and mental handicaps with acts of violence and hatred. In children's stories, there are the inevitable hunchbacks, trolls, and other deformed monsters who frighten pretty, normal children.

Cartoons, too, are important carriers of handicapist images. "Stupid idiot," "moron," "dumb," and "crazy" dot the landscape of such comic strips as *Beetle Baily* and *Archie*. These comics not only confirm prejudicial and stereotypic attitudes, but also prove that disability labels have become general terms of derogation.

In hundreds of ways, the mass media transmit and reinforce negative concepts of the handicapped that create barriers to their placement and acceptance in the community. (For a full discussion of the concept of handicapism, see Biklen and Bogdan, 1976. Authors who have described various categories of the handicapped as minority groups include Dexter, 1964; Wright, 1960; Yuker, 1965; and Gellman, 1959.)

Economics

Special education is big business. The Rand Corporation recently reported that government agencies expend $2.8 billion annually to serve mentally retarded youth (Kakalik, 1973). Mental health is also big business. Governor Carey of New York has recommended a $924 million Department of Mental Hygiene budget for the 1977 fiscal year, "part of the Governor's $10.7 billion austerity budget . . ." (*Mental Hygiene News*, January 30, 1976, p. 1). Contrast this with the $640.2 million appropriated for fiscal year 1973 in New York State.

Institutionalization is big business in New York, and in a fundamental sense, New York, our case example, reflects the national situation. The 1975 appropriation for the Willowbrook Developmental Center was approximately $62 million, more than a $20,000 expenditure per resident. In 1965, the per capita expenditure at Willowbrook, and at virtually every other state institution for the mentally retarded, was less than $4,000 a year.

Even deinstitutionalization is big business, for those engaged in trust-busting and monolith-wrecking and for others who create and manage community alternatives to institutions. There is no way to avoid the fact that special education-mental health-mental retardation is big business. We can, in fact, talk of a handicap industry (Blatt, 1976).

And it is sacred business too! How many people noticed recently that a presidential candidate's ill-fated $90 billion federal budget cut proposal avoided assault on allocations for the handicapped? Our pariahs have become holy untouchables, for the most part segregated and lacking normal opportunities, but surrounded by government and philanthropic agents who are committed to protect to the end their right to be different, and to back that right with big dollars. In this modern era, we seem to insist on creating problems, and then on spending heavily to support them.

The handicapped are big business, although the business resembles more closely the game of Monopoly than the work of people who buy, or sell, or grow. Like Monopoly, the handicap business appears unreal, the money expended seems like paper, the promises not really meant or taken seriously. Handicap monopolies are easily created and almost as easily destroyed; this moment's idea is the next moment's joke; today's victory is tomorrow's embarrassment.

When Rockefeller, Carnegie, Mellon, and others invented the philanthropy business, their efforts led to significant changes in the extent and manner in which the federal government aids those in need. Big business has taught us how to organize our philanthropies to serve the people and, further, how to organize the people—the state—to serve both business and philanthropy.

This is America. There is enough for everyone, for the rich and the poor, the healthy and the sick, the sound and the unsound, the philanthropist and the businessman. Some data:

Item: In 1965, New York State embarked upon a five-year $500 to $600 million mental hygiene construction program as part of a master plan for the mentally disabled (Construction of Mental Hygiene Facilities, 1973). Forty major projects were approved, at a construction cost of $320.3 million. Furthermore, the program included an additional $188 million for modernization of existing facilities, plus $100 million to help construct community mental health facilities. By 1972, 23 of the original 40 major projects had been completed or were under construction; these exceeded cost estimates by 50% ($94 million), a discrepancy that inflation in construction costs cannot fully explain. When the revised total plan is implemented, 28 projects will have been completed at a cost of $343.5 million, $23 million over the original estimates. If there are no further delays, inflationary increase, union demands, or bright new ideas, the 7,500 beds that will be the basic product of New York's master plan will cost the state's taxpayers approximately $45,000 each for construction, and an additional one and one-half to two times that amount ($65,000 to $90,000) to meet fund obligations, to the banks, foundations, and other bondholders who underwrote the cost.

Item: A recently completed study by the New York State Department of Mental Hygiene disclosed that residents in group homes for the mentally retarded required expenditures of $6,700 yearly, while institutionalized residents required $34,000.

Item: A recent report issued by the New York State Assembly (Swift & Melby, 1976) revealed that family care for the mentally ill and retarded requires approximately $7 a day, while residential services cost from $50 to almost $90 a day. While family care and other community placement admittedly may require additional educational and treatment services, such services are frequently available through resources provided by insurance, city, county, or state programs.

There are fixed costs, some of gigantic proportions, which are not accounted for above: pension costs, government and other grants, various kinds of interest rates, and hidden costs that even the most penetrating search has yet to uncover. The question that crops up again and again is: Why do New York State (and other states) continue to construct and support segregated facilities? Perhaps because there are currently 64,000 union employees in the New York State Department of Mental Hygiene, an increase of 10,000 in little more than three years. Perhaps because there are also contractors, builders, architects, real estate entrepreneurs, and many other people anxious to provide the best construction to any state for any purpose. Perhaps because there are merchants and manufacturers who would rather sell carloads of merchandise to institutions than run corner five-and-dime stores.

In 1963, at the behest of Governor Rockefeller, the New York Legislature created the Health and Mental Hygiene Facilities and Improvement Fund (HMHFIC), an organization that has had several name changes since, but has remained steadfast in its mission to execute the construction program of the Department of Mental Hygiene (Construction of Mental Hygiene Facilities, 1973). Its original responsibilities included completing work on a $350,000,000 mental hygiene bond issue. However, since its January 1964 takeover date, HMHFIC (or you may use its new name, the Facilities Development Corporation), has spent over one billion dollars on mental hygiene construction. Financing is arranged through the State Housing Finance Agency, which issues bonds to institutional and individual investors, who purchase them because they are tax-free and offer the lender a virtually fail-safe guarantee of earning from $3\frac{1}{2}$ to 7% interest on his money. You must remember that these bonds are tax-free (an important benefit to those in high tax brackets) and are rated as very safe by Standard and Poor and by Moody, even in the face of New York City's and New York State's various fiscal crises. One reason for the safety of these bonds and their high ratings is that income to mental hygiene facilities (income directly from patients or their families, or from federal or third-party sources, such as income from Title 19 of the Social Security Act) *is pledged first to the mental hygiene facilities improvement fund*. The bondholders must be paid first, as in any good business.

How do we convert segregated facilities for the handicapped and the elderly to useful purposes? How can these thousands of people return to normal community life, without the state's bankrupting itself in attempts to meet bond obligations and other commitments to the business community? First, we must recognize the depth and extent of commercial involvement in supposedly non-profit, philanthropic, and service agencies. Second, we must seek to interest other clientele in the segregated facilities and programs we have set up for the handicapped and the aged. A modest beginning might be to explore with business and state officials the possibilities for converting segregated facilities to new uses. To carry out the conversion, institutional operating budgets would be transferred to the community as each segregated facility is evacuated by so-called mental patients, state school residents, and the aged. This may require public support, special tax measures, and other inducements. The farmers have these advantages and so do others. Why not the handicapped?

The Schools

In its first five years (1971-1976), the Center on Human Policy (a Syracuse University facility devoted to the promotion of community-based environments for people with special needs) received over 4,000 requests for assistance from parents of children with disabilities and from teachers and other professionals in education. The vast majority of these requests concerned school placement and the right to education. The requests and complaints fell into several groupings. Some involved children who were excluded from school for behavioral reasons or because of severe disabilities. Others came from parents and guardians who sought to improve the quality of school instruction, or desired more specialized instruction. There were complaints about absence of auxiliary services, such as transportation and speech therapy. There was a recurring pattern of non-service; institution and social service agency professionals often found local school districts reluctant or unwilling to accept "state" children.

This last category is particularly significant. We found that, while parents were often willing to advocate tirelessly and for months on end to secure adequate services for their children, professionals were often as concerned with interagency harmony as with the fate of an individual child. Consequently, agency professionals often gave up trying to place institutional children in local schools, for fear of jeopardizing interagency harmony. These findings have been reiterated in several local and national reports (Task Force, 1971; Children's Defense Fund, 1974), as well as in our own research (Biklen, 1973; Blatt & Blank, 1971).

Numerous parent and professional cases brought the Center on Human Policy staff into frequent contact with school officials. Here we learned the language of exclusion, and its familiar ring from school district to school district, from professional to professional. We began to catalogue the many phrases that signalled exclusion. In some instances, they were typical bureaucratic doubletalk; in others cases, they reflected not so much the bureaucratic ethos as the social context in which prejudice toward the disabled is commonplace. *Taken as a whole, these phrases and the attitudes they reveal constitute a formidable barrier to successful deinstitutionalization.*

In the bureaucratic tradition, we frequently heard:

> "We do not have the funds to create a program for your child."
> "We agree with your philosophy, but we must be practical."

"The child is not in our jurisdiction. It is beyond our sphere of influence."

"Sorry, we do not make the rules."

"The unions will never buy it. They will not take on any extra work."

"We cannot change all at once. It will take time. We do not want to rush into things and possibly make it worse for everyone."

"We need evidence before we can act."

"We will need more time. You must learn to be patient."

There were other built-in biases against disability, expressed in exclusionary language:

"This child is an exceptional child among exceptional children. She just doesn't fit any category of student in our schools."

"Your child is too severely disabled."

"The schools cannot solve every need. We are not a babysitting service."

"If we included your child, we would have to cancel an art teacher for the typical children."

"We have always sent such children to the institutions or to private schools."

"We need at least ten of them with the same disability before we can set up a specialized program."

"We do not have a program for children at that level."

"We would like to help, but we need teachers first."

The effect of such phrases is immense (Task Force, 1971). Schools provide the core of every child's developmental experience, apart from home life. School exclusion, perhaps more than any other agency policy, threatens the whole deinstitutionalization process. Without schooling, community placement becomes a kind of custodial placement. So we must again turn to conversion, this time with an eye to overcoming prejudices, stereotyping, and bureaucratic red tape.

In part, that has already occurred in the form of court rulings, such as the PARC vs. Commonwealth of Pennsylvania litigation and the Mills vs. Board of Education case; national legislation, such as PL93-380 and PL94-142 (Abeson, 1974; Abeson et al., 1975; Gilhool, 1973); and consumer advocacy (Biklen, 1974, 1976; DesJardins, 1971; Ruskin, 1975). Court decisions like these and laws established on their basis insist on the right of children with disabilities to public education in the least restrictive (most integrated) setting possible. Children and their parents have also won due process rights by which they may question and challenge placement and exclusion decisions. Thus, there is an emerging new language replacing the language of exclusion. We are beginning to hear more about "rights": "every child can benefit from an education," "least restrictive services," "zero reject," "mainstreaming," and "individualized planning." These new words and phrases can be regarded as part of the conversion process.

Professionalism

Ironically, those who have been given the responsibility to provide services to the handicapped often erect additional barriers to changing our categorical service-segregated system to an integrated non-categorical one. Many professionals working with the handicapped think in terms of categories and segregated services. This is the way they have been taught to diagnose and prescribe. Thus, they may not have the philosophy or the skills needed to meet the requirements of conversion. Retraining can provide only a partial remedy; professionals do not change easily. Furthermore, not only is retraining a technical problem, but professional resistance to it can lead to a major undermining of conversion efforts.

Next, there is the brick-and-mortar, formal organization of the professions—physical and organizational elements that stand as defenses against the onslaught of change. For example, our buildings have been constructed to foster segregation and isolation. State schools dot the landscape of our countrysides, and day schools for the handicapped form part of the skyline of our cities. These represent great financial, as well as career and life, investments. Similarly, professional societies and professional schools have been organized in ways that may be detrimental to conversion, i.e., according to diagnostic categories. There is, for example, the American Association on Mental Deficiency. Special education departments have specific programs in emotional disturbance, mental retardation, learning disabilities, speech and hearing disorders, and so on.

Another barrier to conversion is the profession's insistence that special children need specially trained professional people to take care of them. While, to some extent, this is true, it is not wholly or always the case. A major challenge for the professional lies in demystifying himself and freely sharing some of his understanding with others, so that they too can join in helping the handicapped.

Bureaucratic Structures

As we have seen, deinstitutionalization means nothing more than the exodus of individuals from an institution. Usually, it has resulted in "dumping" and re-institutionalization (Conroy, 1976). But who is responsible for the failure of deinstitutionalization? Is it the institution that sends people into the community? Or the community that fails to provide local services? Or perhaps the private agencies that refuse to serve the formerly institutionalized? The institution points to the local community, the local community to the institution, the private agencies to both, and all to the legislature that balks at additional appropriations, in an endless display of buck-passing and rationalization (Biklen, 1974).

This brings us back to our original question. Who is responsible for the failure of deinstitutionalization? Perhaps everyone in general, yet no one specifically. The deinstitutionalization process has been based on faulty assumptions and models. In this section, we identify three major "deinstitutionalization" models and show how they have been doomed to failure (see also President's Committee on Mental Retardation, 1976). Most states have adopted one of these models with only slight variations. Some have combined two or more, to further complicate matters. Still others have adopted no model at all.

Institutional Expansion   In many states, the same agencies that operate institutions have been expected to develop community-based programs. However, whether for ideological, economic, or pragmatic reasons, these agencies remain committed to the institutional model. As a matter of ideology, many state and institutional officials believe in segregation. As a matter of economics, they strive to meet minimal standards of institutional care in order to obtain federal monies. As a matter of pragmatism, they wish to avoid scandal and exposés. "We can only have community programs," these officials state, "after we have good institutions." Thus, they may continue to pour resources into the institution endlessly even though this may drain away funds necessary for community services. Or they may alleviate institutional overcrowding and understaffing through the haphazard release of people into the community, as though small warehouses were better than large ones. In the context of an institutional system, then, resources for the community-based services, like minorities in the job market, are the last to be employed and the first to be cut.

Dual Systems Of Services   Some states have turned to local governments or regions to develop community programs, while themselves maintaining a state institutional system (Goldman, 1975). Typically, these states offer to reimburse localities if they allot a certain proportion of their expenditures for community services. For example, a state may underwrite one-half to three-fourths of the net operating expenses of programs in the community. As currently established, such schemes are certain to fail. In times of fiscal austerity, which is almost always, localities will hesitate to pay even a part of the costs of services as long as the state will pay the full cost of institutionalization. Thus, even the mildly retarded will be labelled as "the state's problem," being "too retarded to live in the community," or "in need of specialized services only the institution can offer." Under a dual system of services, the local government's incentive to institutionalize people all too often offsets its incentive to serve those people in the community.

Laissez-faire   Finally, some states have adopted a laissez-faire system, based on the assumption that private agencies will develop a range of services if sufficient funds are allocated for that purpose. Yet a continuum of services cannot evolve through the voluntary actions of service providers. In the absence of proper planning and coordination, small agencies will flounder, because they lack the expertise to obtain funds and to establish programs; large agencies will operate mini-institutions, with little accountability; and services will be congregated in low income areas of the community. Under a laissez-faire system, service providers also tend to engage in "creaming" (Miller et al., 1970; Bogdan, 1976) and "bounty hunting" (Bogdan, 1976). That is, they serve those who are the easiest to serve and those who may not require services at all, rather than those with the most severe disabilities. In short, laissez-faire guarantees neither quality services, nor services for all who need them.

Unlike these deinstitutionalization models, the conversion model implies an orderly and planned transition from an institutional to a community-based system of services. As such, it requires administrative structures with fixed lines of responsibility to prevent bureaucratic buck-passing. In a later section of this paper, we describe the administrative precondition to conversion.

The Institutions

We have seen how handicapism and school exclusion policies act as obstacles to conversion. Because of their disabilities, the institutionalized are discriminated against by society and excluded from typical school programs. They face further discrimination as well, for institutions foster the very behaviors which society and the schools find least acceptable.

In response to progressive ideologies, the custodial institutions of the past have gradually become "training schools" and "developmental centers." However, today's institutions, like yesterday's custodial asylums, foster dependence and incompetence among their residents (Blatt, 1970; Butterfield, 1967). At institutions, both new and old, residents' meals are selected, prepared, and served at specific times; the inmates' clothes are laundered; their routines and activities are planned by others (Biklen, 1973; Bogdan et al., 1974). They are told what to do and when to do it. As a staff member at one institution we have studied put it:

> The staff has a lot of power here and they do use it. The staff tells them when to get up in the morning, when to go to bed at night, when to eat, when to brush their teeth . . . . The residents are virtually completely dependent on the staff for everything.

In some instances, the brutal realities of institutional life have even more dramatic implications. For the sake of convenience, staff members feed residents, rather than teach them to feed themselves, or change the children's diapers, rather than toilet-train them (Bogdan et al., 1974). Thus, residents are denied opportunities to develop the skills needed for adjustment to the community.

Institutions also tend to accentuate the behaviors they claim to treat (Blatt, 1970). As a response to boredom or lack of stimulation, many residents develop habits such as head-banging, rocking, and self-abuse. In the absence of proper exercise, their limbs may atrophy and wither away (deGrandpré, 1973). Because they have never known privacy, residential inmates urinate, defecate, or masturbate in public. Since they have had to fight for social-psychological rewards at the institution, residents and former residents attempt to ingratiate themselves with strangers by such inappropriate remarks as "I love you," or "You're my friend." Ironically, institutional staff members often cite such behaviors as the reason why "the community will never accept this kind of person." So they breathe life into handicapism and provide school officials with rationales for exclusion and segregation.

Institutionalization itself is therefore a major barrier to the integration of the formerly institutionalized into society. In deinstitutionalizing the residents of state schools and centers, we must take the institution out of the people, as well as the people out of the institution.

RELEVANCE FOR TEACHERS

The transition from institution to community is a complex process. Deinstitutionalization has failed because its proponents have ignored this reality. Such factors as societal discrimination; funding mechanisms and construction costs; school exclusion; professionalism; bureaucratic structures; and institutional dependence have acted as barriers to the movement of individuals from the institution.

We have discussed a different way of thinking about deinstitutionalization: in the context of the larger society, and in terms of specific elements of the conversion system. We must now articulate the relevance of conversion to teachers and to schools.

1. Teachers cannot control the course of deinstitutionalization. The process of bringing children from institutions back into the community involves many groups, and interests other than those connected with the schools. For example, in a handicapist society, a teacher cannot pretend to overcome prejudice toward children with disabilities by using a new curriculum that emphasizes positive attitudes toward the disabled.

2. However, if the teacher wishes to do more than add a new curriculum or subtract an old one, his actions can surely influence society's treatment of disabled children. How?

3. The answer is found in the term itself: conversion means societal efforts to eradicate handicapist attitudes and practices. Obviously, teachers, as members of a larger society, can play a role in such efforts. Conversion means rechannelling funds to support community placements for the handicapped. This process will ultimately provide resources for the schools. Conversion means retraining institutional staffs and community personnel. Teachers can play major roles in such programs. Conversion means creating noncategorical systems of educational treatment. Such policies will eventually affect the design, the appearance, and the functioning of all school classrooms and curricula. Conversion means changing attitudes of school administrators toward acceptance of zero reject policies. Conversion means planning community services, of which education is a major component. Conversion means the appointment of professional and consumer advocates for community programming. Finally, conversion means developing classroom strategies that focus on promoting integration of disabled children into regular school programs. This implies efforts to increase awareness, understanding, and acceptance of disabled students by non-disabled students and, obviously, acceptance by teachers, principals, and other school officials.

Teachers and their colleagues can promote new understanding and positive values about individuals with special needs. They can learn, and teach others to learn, to recognize handicapist assumptions and to work to eliminate them. If conversion is to succeed, the schools must change. For the schools to change, and for children to change, teachers must change.

REFERENCES

Abeson, A. Movement and momentum: Government and the education of handicapped children—II. *Exceptional Children*, 1974, *41*, 109–115.

Abeson, A., Bolick, N., & Hass, J. *A primer on due process*. Reston, Va.: The Council for Exceptional Children, 1975.

Allport, G. W. *The nature of prejudice*. Boston: Beacon Press, 1954.

Biklen, D. Exclusion. *The Peabody Journal of Education*, 1973, *50* (3), 226–234.

Biklen, D. Human Report: I. In B. Blatt (Ed.), *Souls in extremis: An anthology on victims and victimizers*. Boston: Allyn & Bacon, 1973.

Biklen, D. *Let our children go*. Syracuse, N.Y.: Human Policy Press 1974.

Biklen, D. Advocacy comes of age. *Exceptional Children*. 1976, *42*, 308–313.

Biklen, D., & Bogdan, R. *Handicapism*. Syracuse, N.Y: Human Policy Press, 1976 (slide show with script).

Blatt, B. *Exodus from pandemonium: Human abuse and a reformation of public policy*. Boston: Allyn & Bacon, 1970.

Blatt, B. Instruments of change—the executive. In R. B. Kugel (Ed.), *Changing patterns in residential services for the mentally retarded* (2nd ed.). Washington, D.C: President's Committee on Mental Retardation, 1976.

Blatt, B., & Blank, H. D. *Children with special needs in New York State: A report for the New York State Commission on the Quality, Cost and Financing of Elementary and Secondary Education.* Syracuse, N.Y: Syracuse University, Center on Human Policy, 1971.

Blatt, B., & Garfunkel, F. *The educability of intelligence.* Washington, D.C: Council for Exceptional Children, 1969.

Bogdan, R. National policy and situated meaning: Head Start and the handicapped. *American Journal of Orthopsychiatry*, 1976, *46* (2).

Bogdan, R., Taylor, S., deGrandpré, B., & Haynes, S. Let them eat programs. *Journal of Health and Social Behavior*, 1974, *15*.

Butterfield, E. C. The role of environmental factors in the treatment of institutionalized mental retardates. In A. A. Baumeister (Ed.), *Mental retardation: Appraisal, education, and rehabilitation.* Chicago: Aldine, 1967.

Conroy, J. *A review of trends in deinstitutionalization of the mentally retarded.* Unpublished manuscript, Temple University, Developmental Disabilities Center, 1976.

Construction of mental hygiene facilities. New York Legislative Commission on Expenditure Review, October 3, 1973.

Children's Defense Fund. *Children out of school in America.* Cambridge: Washington Research Project, 1974.

deGrandpré, B. *The culture of a state school ward.* Unpublished doctoral dissertation, Syracuse University, 1973.

DesJardins, C. *How to organize an effective parent group and move bureaucracies.* Chicago: Co-ordinating Council for Handicapped Children, 1971.

Dexter, L. *The tyranny of schooling.* New York: Basic Books, 1964.

Ensher, G. E. (Ed.). *Final report on assessment of the handicapped effort in experimental and selected other programs serving the handicapped.* Syracuse, N.Y: Report to the Office of Child Development, Department of Health, Education, and Welfare, October 1974, 199–230.

Estimates of current manpower needs in education for the handicapped 1968–69. Washington, D. C: United States Office of Education, 1968.

Fleischman, M. *The Fleischman report on the quality, cost, and financing of elementary and secondary education in New York State* (Vol. II). New York: Viking Press, 1972.

Gellman, W. Roots of prejudice against the handicapped. *Journal of Rehabilitation*, 1959, *25*, 4–6.

Gilhool, T. An inalienable right. *Exceptional Children*, 1973, *39*, 597–609.

Goffman, E. *Stigma.* Englewood Cliffs, N.J: Prentice-Hall, 1963.

Goldman, E. R. A state model for community services. *Mental Retardation*, 1975, *13* (5),33–36.

Kakalik, J. S. *Services for handicapped youth: A program overview.* Santa Monica: The Rand Corporation, 1973–74.

Mackie, R. P. & Dunn, L. M. *College university programs for the preparation of teachers of exceptional children.* USOE Bulletin No. 13. Washington, D.C: U.S. Government Printing Office, 1954.

Merton, R. *Social theory and social structure.* New York: Free Press, 1957.

Miller, S. M., Roby, P., & de Vos van Steewijk, A. Creaming the poor. *Trans-Action*, 1970, *7* (8), 38–45.

New York State Department of Mental Hygiene. Governor Carey recommends $924 million DMH budget. *Mental Hygiene News*, January 30, 1976, p. 1.

Persons released from state developmental centers. New York Legislative Commission on Expenditure Review, December 18, 1975.

President's Committee on Mental Retardation. *Mental retardation: Trends in state services.* Washington, D.C: U.S. Government Printing Office, 1976.

Rossmiller, R. A., Hale, J. A., & Frohreich, L. E. *Educational programs for exceptional children: Resource configurations and costs.* Madison: University of Wisconsin, Department of Educational Administration, 1970.

Ruskin, M. *Parent power.* New York: Walker, 1975.

Scheff, T. J. *Being mentally ill: A sociological theory.* Chicago: Aldine, 1966.

Scott, R. *The making of blind men.* New York: Russell Sage Foundation, 1969.

Swift, S., & Melby, R. *A report to Speaker Stanley Steingut.* Albany: The Assembly Joint Committee to Study the Department of Mental Hygiene, March, 1976.

Task Force on Children Out of School. *The way we go to school.* Boston: Beacon Press, 1971.

Wolfensberger, W. *The principle of normalization in human services.* Toronto: National Institute of Mental Retardation, 1972.

Wolfensberger, W. *The origin and nature of our institutional models.* Syracuse, N.Y: Human Policy Press, 1975.

Wright, B. *Physical disability: A psychological approach.* New York: Harper, 1960.

Yinker, M. *A minority group in American society.* New York: McGraw-Hill, 1965.

Yuker, H. Attitudes as determinants of behavior. *Journal of Rehabilitation*, 1965, *31*, 15–16.

CHAPTER 10

The Family Papers: A Return to Purgatory

This chapter retraces and extends a journey which Fred Kaplan, a freelance photographer, and I took about a decade ago. On that journey, we visited five institutions for mentally retarded people, four of which presented scenes of unmitigated horror and cruelty. Those four institutions, as well as countless others across the nation, represented a secret world of torment which was vigilantly protected from public scrutiny. Getting into such a world was difficult; photographing it, unheard of. The direct approach was blocked by regulations, forbidden by "professional ethics," and feared as a threat to a bureaucracy which perpetrated the atrocities committed within its citadels. Yet, by forcing, bluffing or wheedling our way, we did get in, with a concealed camera on Fred Kaplan's belt, and we gathered the material which was published in 1966 as *Christmas In Purgatory, A Photographic Essay on Mental Retardation*.

While America busied itself with the space race, with flower children, with the "new freedom," and with Super Bowls, we witnessed a world that stood apart from it all, suspended in dark and eternal despair. Thousands of human beings spent their lives in conditions which would be deplorable for animals; the smell of filth was unbearable; the sound of screaming, moaning, crying and shouting echoed throughout the tiled chambers. Care was virtually non-existent, and education was entirely "non-existent"—although these places were called "State Schools." In many "dayrooms," that is, large rooms which in institutions presumably serve the same function as living rooms in homes, excrement covered the floors, the walls, even the ceilings. People were ill-clothed, if they were clothed at all. Even toward children, the heart of the institution was hardened, for without playthings, without friendship, attention, or stim-

This essay, co-authored with Andrejs Ozolins and Joseph McNally, was originally published in *The New Renaissance*, 1978, *3* (2), 16–34. It summarizes a book of the same title published by Longman, Inc., 1979. Because so much here juxtaposes my past experiences with our present study, it is written in the first person singular.

ulation from other human beings, the institutionalized children were as ignored or forgotten as the institutionalized adults. In each of the depressing four, there was the occasional ray of hope, the occasional rare person who treated the residents with love, and who worked to help them. But a benefit to the few could not mitigate the betrayal of the many.

The fifth institution, The Seaside Regional Center in Connecticut, was an example of what genuine and practiced respect for people could produce. Seaside was a place where the staff at all levels acted on the belief that each person is valuable, capable of growth, deserving of attention. And the response of the residents justified this belief. The experience of Seaside gave us courage to hope that the other institutions could be changed, that from their desolation a world could be built that wouldn't have to be a secret.

That was *Christmas In Purgatory* ten years ago. Today, we have a different hope and a different conviction.

This chapter is an indiscretion and many people will be angry at our having committed it, for we are exposing to the public the sordid side of The Family's institutions. The sordid side of some personal families can remain hidden because of their very ordinariness. But with other families, it is not just permissible to reveal secrets, but necessary to do so. Such a family is the large group of men and women who have protected the hidden world of mental retardation from public scrutiny. It is a family which—whether wittingly or unwittingly, by deception or self-deception—has prevented thousands of mentally retarded people from participating in the sort of life Americans are entitled to.

Who is this family? It is all who work, or say they work, with the problems of retarded people in institutionalized settings. It is the supervisors and superintendents and commissioners. It is the professional societies such as the American Association on Mental Deficiency and the Council for Exceptional Children. The Family includes government agencies, such as the National Institute of Mental Health, the Office of Education, even groups such as the Associations for Retarded Citizens. From the attendants who show up every day to do an impossible job to the prestigious professionals who often don't bother to show up at all, the Family consists of everyone who should know better than to allow this hidden world to continue in existence. The academic community, which legitimates it by issuing so-called credentials and generating so-called expertise, is also part of the Family. Some of our readers are probably Family members as are two of the three of us who worked in this study. In spite of professed intentions, ideals, and commitments to reform, we in the Family have preserved this abhorrent abuse of our fellow man.

The Family still protects itself through concealment and secrecy but 10 years ago, to bring the horrors of institutionalization to public awareness, we had to photograph with a concealed camera. The secrecy was strict, then, and one could visit institutions only by stealth, arm-twisting, or string-pulling. Today, the barricades are less formidable but they still exist. The institutions are still hard to get into and taking photographs in them remains difficult for everyone and next to impossible for most people. Some institutions refused us access altogether; one admitted us for a tour but locked our cameras in the superintendent's office. The change from a decade ago is that we were able, in five of the big traditional institutions, to take pictures openly. The cameras caused nervous suspicion; we were often admonished not to photograph anyone's face (why not?) but, still, today we were able to finish our work and to leave with film.

Only later did we discover that the institutions had yet another way to preserve secrecy: by controlling permission to publish the photographs. This permission is of course not theirs to give; the recognition of human rights of retarded people has advanced far enough that only the people photographed or their legal guardians can authorize or prohibit publication. But the institutions can, and do, obstruct the process of requesting permission. They can determine that a person is not competent to give permission; they can have records so confused or out-dated that family or guardians cannot be located; they can decide a request is "not in the best interests of the client" and refuse to approach the patient; they can put the matter off indefinitely by having it considered at various meetings and then referred to committees or still other meetings. These obstructions are the more reprehensible because they are not necessary, not even considering the bureaucratic nature of institutions. We know this because one institution—and not the best one, either—chose to be cooperative and obtained most of our permission forms promptly.

More impenetrable and more sinister than overt secrecy is the misleading publicity by which the Family defends its dominions. The first thing one discovers in these places is that the official description of what goes on gives no clue to what actually happens. The hypnotic language of humanitarian concern encapsulates the victims of institutionalization and seals off their world from examination, understanding or hope. An elaborate camouflage of benign vocabulary—rehabilitation, treatment programs, normalization, therapy, modularized privacy—is thrown over the reality of idleness, segregation, neglect, and loneliness.

We are used to condemning secrecy and camouflage when we see it elsewhere: if the Soviet Union locks up political dissidents in psychiatric hospitals on the pretext of looking after their mental health, we are quick to protest. Yet in our own institutions for mentally retarded people, thousands of Americans are locked up on the pretext of receiving care, training, and education, and by speaking as though that pretext were a reality, we are able to call for more money and more resources to implement the pretext rather than confessing that none of it works.

In seeking to understand human rights in the Soviet Union, we ask the victims, not the victimizers, for their experiences. We take the reports of the dissidents seriously and dismiss as propaganda the authorized version of the state officials and psychiatrists. But when it comes to examining the mentally retarded, we dismiss the opinions of the incarcerated and turn instead to the Family—psychiatrists, social workers, educators, all the professionals—to tell us what the truth is and we accept their reports even, perhaps especially, when they contradict the reports of the victims. The Family tells us about innovative new treatments and the need for more research money where the most minimal human sympathy is enough to know that the treatments are brutal or heartless; the Family says that each resident is served by an individualized program when we can observe that countless residents are sitting or standing or lying aimlessly around; the Family says that the institutions are in compliance with all the Federal standards though we see little but barren environments and wasted lives. The Family discourages taking photographs with the explanation that it is simply protecting the privacy of the residents *though the residents are confined to controlled environments in which there is no privacy.* The Family talks piously about healing the wounds of the mentally retarded but we can see they have not yet stopped inflicting those wounds.

Our indiscretion is that we are ignoring the rhetoric of the Family to make public the actions of the Family. We believe with our minds and hearts that these Family Papers are as vital to know about as any governmental treaty. The malaise in our culture stems not from doubts about our forefathers but from doubts about ourselves. There is little here that challenges the idea of America but there are grave concerns about what we have made of America—and what we are making of ourselves. The only hopeful sign we've seen is that, while 10 years ago, and for generations before, where these institutions had been run by one happy family, they are now run by an unhappy one. If the Family must become unhappier still before it changes, then we are willing to contribute to that unhappiness.

Hour after hour we trudged from building to building, classroom to classroom, living unit to dying unit, and I looked for the changes that 10 years and a budget of $70 million have made in this institution. Was it significant that along the rows of unstalled toilets there now appeared an occasional roll of toilet paper? A cynical member of our tour remarked that this was the first time she had ever seen toilet paper, that it might have been set out for our benefit. "Not for your benefit to *use*," she explained, noticing my uneasiness at the total lack of privacy, "but to *see*." An occasional toilet now even has a seat to protect the user from the cold of the porcelain. Hardly ever was there both a seat *and* paper, however.

The buildings were less crowded, less dirty, less foul-smelling, but the same. In Building 8, more people wore clothes, though not in a way that makes much difference: no inmate has clothes of his own—each day brings its chance at the grab bag, the pool of common garments. One might turn up a nice flannel shirt with buttons one day but the next day is apt to bring an ill-fitting, torn one. There may or may not be socks or underwear and the odds are that on any given day the shoes will be the wrong size or have no laces or that a brown shoe will be the mate to a white sneaker.

For most of the inmates there are no activities, no recreation, no education, no deviation from the routine of loneliness and despair. After 10 years of promises, resolutions, and increased funding, the people trapped in institutions are reduced to the same collection of head-bangers, shit-kickers, vomiters, sore-pickers, screechers, assaulters, sleepers, and weepers; and, on the other side, armed with their authoritative rings of keys, is the same collection of understaffed, untrained attendants sitting or standing around, watching, chatting, drowsing. In this world of agony and chaos, the attendants are always ready to swing into action should anything "unusual" happen. Otherwise, it is rare that any one of them reaches out to make contact with the enveloping turmoil of humanity that surrounds them.

I have seen it all too many times. A gust of fresh, clean air rushed around us as the front door was unlocked, but the relief at regaining my freedom was shattered by a scream from above, "Good-bye, you fuckin' doctors!" A shirtless man, his face twisted in anger, was waving his fist from the second-story window. I smiled and waved to him. He waved back and, as anger gave way to a smile, he waved again, this time with open palm. This was Building 8, a "custodial dormitory" for people the institution has labelled "severely mentally retarded" and for people who label their keepers "you fuckin' doctors."

The tour took us through other dormitories, to rows and rows of beds where, now and then, a huddled figure with blanket drawn over head was moaning; past the very small and very large or totally naked people, past those who don't look different from us. The twisted and gnarled bodies are not to be found in this sea of beds—these special among the special are kept together in places reserved for them only, the "crib cases" or "bed cases." In due course, my tour passed through those special places too.

In the school building, the teachers seem to have given up to the daze of purposelessness that pervades the dormitories. "There is no progress here, most of the children regress," they say, speaking calmly of what once might have made them angry or fired their dedication. "If you complain to get changes or more support, it goes on your record, a mark against you." The teachers spoke about their lesson plans, their curriculum, their planning conferences. There is no actual planning, only plan books; there is no curriculum development, though plenty of curricula are around. Individual planning conferences? There is a lot of talk, mostly complaints, about the children.

This hopelessness in the face of $30,000 per year per resident is puzzling. Why shouldn't things be better? The supervisors are human beings; they know that the institution has a $70 million budget yet know they can't equip a classroom; they know the institution has been permitted to hire hundreds of additional staff yet they still see only one or two attendants for a whole group of residents; they know that specialized doctors, psychologists and other professionals have been made available for consultation yet they wonder why these "colleagues" are so seldom on the premises. These supervisors lack the vision or courage to put an end to institutionalization but they have the humanity to recognize that deinstitutionalization is the only answer to the horror which they are implicated in, where they are as imprisoned and as isolated as the residents. "I wish I could convince myself to speak out. I wish there were others who would speak out with me," they confide. It is good to be convinced of their humanity; we only wish we could decide whether their anguish and good intentions excuse their lack of courage.

Flying thousands of feet above the ground, I pass the time by reading the *New York Times* and see that the director of the institution I'm headed for has been transferred to a new position while maintaining his previous salary of $42,000 a year. Another story in the same edition tells of people suing to get residents out of the institutions to "new positions"—with their families, in foster homes, or halfway houses, anywhere so long as *they are out of the institution.* I happen to know something about the economics of that particular institution; it costs $30,000 a year to keep each resident there and I can't help wondering if the residents would also maintain their previous salaries if they were transferred back to their homes. The rules for the mentally retarded people are different from the rules of their keepers. But there is no story in the *Times* on this difference; maybe it isn't fit to print.

The day-long training session for the institution's staff featured several films on sex education. We didn't stay to watch them but we were tempted: one was for "trainables," one for "educables," and one on "fertility regulation for persons with learning disabilities." We were curious about what "fertility regulation" would mean; there seemed to be an important point made by the fact that the mentally retarded were merely "trainables" and "educables" while those with learning disabilities were elevated to "persons."

The institution was small (for an institution), clean (as institutions go), more homelike than the traditionally large places and expensive beyond belief. The building, which could hold about 140 residents, cost more than $11 million which works out to about $80,000 per bed. The yearly cost of running it, with its current 120 residents, was $8 million or about $65,000 per resident. It was the most expensive program for retarded people I had ever seen—yet there wasn't anything exceptional about it though the quality of life here was certainly above the institutional average. Throughout my tour, I couldn't take my mind off the costs. Institutionalized people, sleeping in $80,000 beds and with "incomes" of $65,000 a year, yet they were still ostracized, still isolated, still stagnating; their lives were hopelessly but inevitably wasted. The more I saw the more clearly I was driven to a harsh conclusion which I am beginning to find inescapable: people are not institutionalized for their good but for their money. Yet, over and over again, I find economics at the foundation of the edifice that well-meaning people have tried to treat as educational, philosophical or therapeutic problems. Indeed, several weeks after my visit, the Director of this institution confirmed my conclusion for me.

I had given a talk on the economics of mental retardation and used his institution as an example. The gist of the talk was this: most states finance institutions the same way people finance their homes—by mortgaging the property. To pay off the mortgage, the states count on receiving the money to which mentally retarded people are entitled—much of it through social security payments. But such payments can be applied to construction debts only if those mentally retarded people occupy the buildings. Thus, if we remove them from new institutions to community accommodations, the problem would then arise: Who would pay off the bond holders? The Director had been irritated by my using his institution as an example of the tremendous expenses which can only be met by keeping people locked up. He pointed out that the institution was not full and that if it were, the *per capita* cost would fall from $65,000 to $40,000 or perhaps as low as $30,000 a year.

If only I could be amused by such logic. Even in finding fault with my presentation, he was illustrating my point: the institution needs more inmates to defray the cost. If only one person were left, it would cost $8 million a year to serve that person; if there were no one, it would still cost $8 million for the state is committed to paying off its bond holders. That is why we can't evacuate institutions. To challenge the institutional approach to the problems of mental retardation is to threaten the solvency of the state; it is to endanger the state's economic structure by raising the specter of an unemployable army of civil servants who now service the institutions; and, ultimately, it is to attack the stability of political powers which rest on the continuation of present financial and employment patterns.

Years ago, but long after the horrors had ceased, I forced myself to visit the Dachau Concentration Camp, now a memorial park bordered by attractive garden apartments and other commonplace scenes. But within that still dreaded death camp remnants of the holocaust linger. On hundreds of pictures in dozens of languages, embedded in every grain of dirt, written even on the shiny walls of the new facsimile barracks, there is a message: *do not forget, remember what happened, remember us, remember I once lived.* But the Jews were The People of the Book. They expressed their anguish and pleas the way all literate people express themselves, through language. And because they knew that voices are eventually silenced, theirs especially, they scrawled their messages on the walls of the barracks: *Do not forget us.*

Today, in institutions across the United States, one can see the scrawlings of the anguished. But the words are not in English, Yiddish, Polish, or Russian. Because these inmates can't write, because many of them can't talk, because there is no one willing to listen, because no one wants to understand, these inmates—our American shame—use their fingers instead of pens, feces instead of ink. But whether it was the fine hand of a former professor at the University of Heidelberg or the ugly smear of a drooling mute, the message is the same: *Why are we forsaken?*

We have seen happy faces and normal-looking rooms. We have seen good times and friendship in the institutions. But the good news doesn't go very far. Walking from cottage to schoolhouse, we passed buildings where the screaming does not begin to subside. Yes, compared to the past, there is talk of the rights of the retarded; they are represented now in various organizations; there is more advocacy by and for retarded people. Yet there remain places where human beings are herded like animals day after day, year after year, places where photographs are forbidden. "It would serve no useful purpose," we were told, "to publicize such conditions." And between the best and the worst, there are the countless "dayrooms" in which time just passes, where the retarded people just sit around, lie around, mill around.

What is needed to understand these settings is not objective research but merely the recognition that these people are human beings. With the recognition must come an awareness that *their plight is our plight*. The objective and scientific questions lose their force in a place where time is suspended in a monotony of waiting. It doesn't matter how many people pass their lives this way; no one should have to. It doesn't matter what their mental handicap may be or whether they have one at all: they should have a home that they are part of. It doesn't matter what reasons we have for keeping them there; these reasons are no excuse.

But have we been objective? Wouldn't a systematic inquiry find places where things are not so bad? Surely there are improvements to be noted, bright spots that a scientific study should document. It is true we haven't focused on the whole picture. Our study is not scientific in that sense. But it is not clear that anything would be gained if we adopted a more "rigorous" stance. We could have cast our observations in a more objective—less painful—form; we might have expressed the suffering we witnessed as a percentage or calculated its probability. In the name of objectivity we could have specified the degree to which the hopelessness was a representative sample of institutional life. But such precision would not have added anything to our understanding.

The question is not whether our reporting is representative or typical of traditional institutions, but rather why such places exist at all. If only one child were withering in front of a television set, if only one woman were locked into eternal dejection or if only one man were huddled against the tiles in endless despair, it would still be one person too many. And the fact is we saw hundreds of such people—they were the rule, not the exception.

Our reportage reflects our belief that the cruelty and injustices of these institutions demand both human and scientific attention. Of course it is not impossible to discover a measure of good news from these institutions; for example, all were much cleaner, less crowded, less fetid than a decade ago. Also, at each institution we visited, we encountered a few residents who seemed to be living relatively free and satisfying lives. Outside the strictly supervised buildings and the buildings for non-ambulatory people, we met residents who stopped to chat with us or with our guides. Some asked to have their pictures taken; some wanted to show us their prized possessions, from radios to motorized golf-carts. We even met a few whom the institution's staff had encouraged to return to the community but who refused to do so. Despite their being able to hold a job and be self-sufficient, they presumably find it preferable to remain in a state facility where the risks and responsibilities of daily living were borne for them by others. Such stories are clearly good news but, like the bad news, they illustrate a failure to foster strength and self-reliance. Those who can laugh and enjoy friendship together have escaped what is most dreadful in the institutions but they have not escaped the institutions themselves.

A decade ago, though we found little to give us hope, we were reluctant to admit that the concept of the institution was hopeless. Today, we find more hope but are now unable to see any way to save the institutions. Ten years ago, with the single exception of Seaside Regional Center in Waterford, Connecticut, every institution was terrible, hopeless. We then concluded that the way to improve those too large, too crowded, too ugly places was to make them smaller, provide more resources, develop ways to ensure proper inspection and accountability. The subsequent years and this, our most recent round of visits, convince us that those were foolish ideas. *We must evacuate the institutions for the mentally retarded.* There is no longer any time for new task forces and new evaluation teams; the time is long past such nonsense. Joint accreditation commissions are doing no good; we are already buried in reports and studies. *We need to empty the institutions—now.* The quicker we can accomplish this, the quicker we will repair the damage done to generations of innocents. The quicker we convert our ideologies and our resources into community models, the quicker we will forget the evil we have perpetrated in the name of humanity. The quicker we demolish the institutional monolith to diversified community life, the quicker we will be able to forgive ourselves for our contribution to human suffering.

A decade ago, we reported the need for a Board of Institutional Visitors appointed by the Governor of every state, a Board of Advisors for each institution for the mentally retarded, a comprehensive inservice training-and-consultation program for *all* institutional employees, and, of course, more money to do the job. Today we don't ask for any of those things. Although we have no authority to do so, *we demand that every institution for the mentally retarded in the United States be closed.* We insist that a society which claims to be civilized find other ways and means to re-locate institutional inmates to decent and more personal community environments. The inmates have suffered enough. Let us do no more damage. Those who fear that community placements will cause problems are quite right. To live with our retarded children, our handicapped friends, our aging parents, *does* place burdens on all of us, but what we must learn from the nightmare of institutionalization is that these burdens cannot be avoided or delegated, for to have a decent society we must first behave as decent individuals. Ultimately our society will discover that it is easier to meet the responsibilities to our fellow men than it is to avoid them.

The Family uses such terms as "normalization," "deinstitutionalization," "advocacy," with as much frequency and with more zeal than those who call for simple evacuation of the premises. Since the Family never lived by any principles, they consequently will live by any lie. The Family's eventual demise is known to everyone, especially to its members. They have lost their pride, their status, and every purpose they once had. The Family is dying but it is a lingering terminal illness. Although we are impatient to be rid of them, our concern is not with them but with the 200,000 inmates whose degradation and suffering should not be allowed to continue for even a few more months. So while it is true that nothing has changed in Purgatory, it is also true that everything has changed. While the institutions have endured until now, they are certain to close in our lifetime. And although we can't count on it, we expect to be around when the last rotten detention camp shuts down and the last inmate is set free. Only then can we, as a nation, be free of the world's censure.

PART III
HUMAN POLICY

CHAPTER 11

Man Through a Turned Lens

It has been said that artists distort reality to present reality. Most of us must distort reality to preserve it. For things aren't what they are, but how they appear to a man. He views his world in his own way, and each perception is a special perception. If, in this chapter, you believe my lens has taken a wrong turn, please attempt to adjust your focus, not my vision. In this special way permit me to behave as though things are how I see them.

My thesis is that society will not eradicate institutional back wards, will not guarantee human rights, and will not eliminate hunger by tearing down back wards or "guaranteeing" human rights or feeding hungry people. Mankind must change if we are to reduce inhumanity, if humanity is to survive.

You and I have experienced too much. We observe and record the devastation and consequences of mankind's mad excesses and, in bewilderment, we grope to comprehend this sickness infecting normal people. In despair, we must conclude that, while humanity is imperiled, life continues to flourish heedlessly. In anger, we realize that, as man perseveres, his soul dies. In frustration, we observe that, during our evolution, we have camouflaged the body but accomplished little on behalf of the spirit. We have smoothed the skin but not the conscience, brought dignity to the carriage, but scant any to the carrier.

In humility, and with knowledge that I am no better qualified as accuser than those to whom I speak, I seek redress for certain acts committed by and against mankind.

I am a collector of injustices. Is there a profession as villified, held more in contempt? I appear as a modern-day Pharisee, and enjoy my role less than those upon whom I intrude. I cringe with embarrassment, pre-

This essay originally appeared in the author's book, *Souls in extremis: An anthology on victims and victimizers.* It was also published in D. L. Walker & D. P. Howard (Eds.), *Special education: Instrument of change in education for the 70's.* Charlottesville, Va.: University of Virginia, 1972. (Also published as Human treatment and public policy, in G. J. Williams & S. Gordon (Eds.), *Clinical child psychology*, New York: Behavioral Publications, 1973; and in part as Man through a turned lens, in N. J. Long, W. C. Morse, & R. G. Newman (Eds.), *Conflict in the classroom* (3rd ed.), Belmont, Ca.: Wadsworth Publishing, 1976.)

suming to tell you what you must become. Yet I abandon caution, not to save my brothers, but to preserve myself. And, to preserve myself, I ask you to please hear this review of a small segment of human history.

Have you been to Dachau? Can you add all of the Dachaus to all of the Siberias? Is there a man willing to catalogue our own Southern history, life in demented mental hospitals, Vietnam, and the world of man-made subhumans some call state institutions? In his own manner, each man thinks about evil. And, in his curious mind, there are times and situations where he is comforted by its presence. But is there a man who will tolerate a flood that is endless and fathomless and senseless?

In his own manner, each man dreams about clean, happy, laughing people. And, watching a lively girl stroll the avenue on a clear morning, a day that is perfect for mankind, is there a soul who can think about beaten and made-ugly humanity? Yet I am driven to remind you that the moon does have its dark side; the human spirit does entice the inhuman act; man does not always please. Without credentials for these responsibilities, I seek to preserve the precarious thread between each of us and the humanness that we are fast losing. Without credentials, I make demands—yet prefer to follow. I am forced to enjoin my betters, for you have rejected the wisdom of your betters. While the time is long past when mankind ceased its climb upward, there is yet a chance to revive that destined goal and divert ourselves from this faithless journey to nowhere. And, today at least, I believe our one chance lies not in extolling the glories and virtues of that dreamed-of ascendancy, but in describing, dissecting, and comprehending our debasements and agonies. We may save ourselves, not with promises of a new good life to goad us, but with plain accounts of the real-unreal world we have fashioned for ourselves and now must either change or eternally wallow in its slime.

What must we change? Where shall we do battle? Who are the people responsible for Dachau and Song My, for Hitler and Stalin, for some now nameless forgotten German officer and for our own, for the Cancer Ward and the State School, for bloated starving Biafran children, and too many of our children, for wars and killings and hunger and slavery and avarice and dehumanization and inhumanity? Who are the people responsible? You are the only person and I am the only person responsible and accountable. If you do not change, all is lost, and if I do not change, nothing will change. If I blame an evil world, a stupid system, blind leaders, or man's obvious imperfections, I may be right. But if it means I do not have to change, I contribute to the evil.

You and I are all that is needed to change the world. Our necessary confrontation is not social. It is personal. The battle is not against society but with oneself. It is not political, but psychological; not within the group, but in the mind; not to safeguard one's civilization, but oneself;

not legal, but moral. The final confrontation will not be among groups of men such as those seated at the United Nations, but within the depths and images and mazes that comprise and consume the substance of each man. The race to eternity will be between a civilization moving toward its infamy and each man weighing his belief in its glory or his worship of its obscenity. In whatever way the race concludes—win or lose, the survival of humanhood or the triumph of savagery—individual man will determine the outcome.

My thesis is, and must be, expressed with repeated use of such terms as *I* and *my*. This can not be an objective discourse concerning ambiguous Man. It must be the subjective revelation of someone who is forced to flee the safety and comfort of dispassionate exchange. Both this report and whatever you and I do in reaction to it must be personal—in the profound sense—not social.

During my travels through Germany, I had often wondered,
          "Was *he* guilty? Was *she* involved?"
Having never encountered one who was guilty or involved,
I realized that I had been asking the wrong questions.
Can a man be guilty just because he is not involved?

Where were those 50 million uninvolved Germans?
Where are the 150 million (175 million?) unbigoted Americans?
Were the good Germans innocent?
Is liberal America racist?

They were guilty.
We are racists,
          not because we abuse and destroy,
          but because our voices are silent.
The silent Americans are guilty!

The racist tells the coon joke and the kike joke and
The racist listens without rancor.
The racist does not rent to blacks and
The racist does not protest.

Every German who lived unharmed was guilty.
Every American—white and black—who is comfortable in his society
          is racist.
All who have experienced or know of Purgatory, asylums, and totalization—
          and are untroubled—
Dehumanize their brothers.

To observe sorrow untouched is to cause it to continue.

I ask you to change humanity by changing yourself, to solve the riddle *I* before you attempt to solve the human puzzle, to commit yourself before you commit mankind. I ask you to think of yourself, not society, and how you must evolve, not what civilization must endure. And for he who concludes that I ask the chicken to change the egg when I say that the individual must change himself first, and then society, does he still doubt that man one day will change his genes?

It is clear that, ultimately, each man must account for his personal behavior and the behavior of those he influences. And it is clear that each point has its counterpoint. For each deed there is another deed or a misdeed. And all these fulfill a grand design for man to alter and improve. As man comprehends his mission and destiny, the design for each of us will reveal as much as he wishes. Man is able to judge and determine his future, and the condition in which he will achieve it. Man is capable of understanding *how* the human world is the complex parts, the sum, and the substance of infinite points and counterpoints.

As each point has its counterpoint, each paradox can unfold understanding. To study human behavior is to study apparent paradoxes—as it is to seek truth. If to know all is to accept all, to know people is to bring one closer to understanding and accepting them—and their weaknesses as well as that which makes them unique and marvelous. In the profound sense, there is no paradox to:

> the thief who is honest,
> the harlot who is virtuous,
> the noble man who is ignoble,
> the wait for Godot that is the wait for God.

> And knowing that to be comfortable in a mad universe one must
> operate in a state of discomfort.

In the profound sense, it may not be paradoxical that, as we grope toward an understanding of dehumanization, we may be led to accept the puzzle of humanity. In the process, we may learn that, while living is a paradox, life is a simple and self-revealing truth.

Since time immemorial, man has heard—and done little—about starving and tortured children. However, even the cleverest among us is unable to conceal or justify mankind's historical denial of fundamental human rights to some among his brothers. There is a difference between truth and fantasy, and he who doesn't appreciate this difference can be dangerous. Such a person finds his truth as it conveniences him and as it fits his behavior. To that man truth is operational belief, a kind of functionalism; if I do it or believe it, by my definition of the infinite it is the correct thing to do or to believe. Even such a person is unable to conceal or justify our sorrowful heritage.

Despite my belief that we in America no more—or less—than other nations sanction human indignities, what I have to report draws its reference from the historical antecedents and the contemporary character of life in America. For we must admit that the *Zeitgeist* of our obese society is menacing:

Fat, indolent, oppressive
America, America
God shed thee of your waste
Plunder and spoil
You destroy
And that which you destroy
Destroys
And much that you conserve
Destroys

Busy, ingenious, submissive
America, America
Your crown has thorns
With paradoxes that have paradoxes
Our days are better
As they grow worse
We become more affluent
As we sink
Lower

Our obese and hungry together average where we should be
Not where we were or what we are
All of our wars have been righteous and we fight mental illness
As we continue to kill and be killed
In foreign lands and at home
We are confused and inept with the Blacks
The Reds, The Yellow (not Yellows?)
No not Yellows, never Yellows
Always the Yellow Menace, the Yellow Horde

And in our crises with the Blacks
And the Yellow Horde
We lose what we know of ourselves
And what man can make of himself.
While bright young Ph.D.s and other D.s engage themselves
And prove to us
That ants are elephants
That the world is a marvel
That society brings me happiness

That I cannot change the world
That I am not responsible

Our pioneering forefathers carved out a great and mighty civilization from an indomitable wilderness that required billions of years to form and but a mere hundred or so to conquer. And the price of that wondrous achievement was destroyed Indian civilizations, exploited and brutalized Oriental field workers, victimized Italian railroad laborers, hollow-eyed children working in Manhattan sweat shops, and probably the longest and most continuous and most systematic dehumanization program known to mankind—American slavery. Through some quirk, we are as careful to record for posterity our sicknesses as well as our spiritual victories. There has never been a scarcity of injustice collectors, and in view of our behavior through the years they should have been kept quite busy. It would benefit each of us to review recorded descriptions of the auction block. Read about men, fighting and crying, begging not to be separated from wives and children; a girl, no more than fifteen, her dress torn away to show that she has no whiplash scars, to demonstrate she isn't a "mean nigger." Slaves branded on the thigh, head, breasts, or back—chained together and marched from one state to another—and those too old or too tired or not caring to live anymore, left by the wayside to die. Generations of blacks, engulfed and mired in a culture so inhumane that only now can some appreciate the myth of their inferiority and natural subservience. And although there will always be the rebel leader and heroic freedom fighter, America's humanscape will long bear the scars of a system that taught human beings to believe they were not human while they were taught to pray to, and believe in, a merciful God. From the beginning, our history is not unspoiled.

In New York, recently, the papers reported the arrest of a man and his wife for murdering the woman's daughter. The child was starved and beaten and eventually thrown into a river and anchored to forty-five pounds of rocks. However, it is not child beaters, insane killers, pathological rapists, and humanity gone berserk that I seek to write about here. Horrifying and painful as those situations are, for thousands and thousands of years civilization has upheld the illegality of such behavior, and thus society has recognized and accepted its responsibility to exact an "eye for an eye" or to impose whatever punishment or retribution it finds necessary to protect itself. Rather, I ask you here to consider our legal, or quasi-legal, sanctioned policies and practices that lead to and encourage the denial of human rights to human beings. I ask you to consider the public's will, not the criminal's code; society's ethics, not its prohibitions.

I ask you to reflect upon the consequences of our unique American slave system, injustice in our schools, and the evil perpetrated within our mental hospitals and state schools for the mentally retarded. I ask you to view contemporary American life and your personal activities and convictions with the same diligence and remorselessness we in America judged Hitler's policies in the Warsaw ghetto, Stalin's at Lubyanka, and Mussolini's. As—to our misfortune—the American list is not unlike most other nations', this review will focus particularly on children and their treatment in institutions.

As I exhort you to change, and as I remind myself that reform will not come unless I change, I am compelled again to seek a form more personal than prose to communicate beliefs concerning man and his interrelatedness.

For mankind must believe that:

> *Each man's life means everything,*
> *Or it means nothing.*
> *He is the only man,*
> *Or no man exists.*
> *Each life and each death*
> *Is a profound event,*
> *Or no life—not a single life ever—*
> *Was of any consequence.*
> *Everything matters or nothing has mattered.*

But to account for oneself as one accounts for his brother, to speak of personal anguish so as to deal better with the anguish of others, is a severe test. To do this and to be optimistic in the face of reality—in spite of reality—is *the* test of poets.

> *For who can describe beauty in institutions*
> *Who can pay honest tributes to their bucolic scenes*
>   *of lush fields and clear streams*
> *Who can so reduce the terror inside*
>   *to permit its physical appreciation outside*
> *Who can view the scatological in relation to its*
>   *tautological—not its villainy*
>
> *Who will attempt to discuss the humanitarian ethos*
>   *in terms of:*
>   *asylums*
>   *custody*
>   *totalization*
> *Who is so capable that he may bring dignity to such*
>   *words as:*
>   *inmate*
>   *patient*
>   *material*
> *Who is so sensitive, and insensitive, as to drive from*
>   *his mind:*
>   *the back ward*
>   *the day room*
>   *the nonschool school*
>
> *Is there a poet—has there ever been one—so brave or*
>   *wise that he dared:*
>   *to squeeze out the truth until it appeared as a lie*
>   *to be so objective as to be beyond reality*
>   *to stare down evil and find goodness*
>
> *Are there men—is there a human being—who can*
>   *detach themselves from passion and prejudice*
> *Who can write a true account of life in the institution*
>   *who can write about:*
>   *the good as well as the evil*
>   *the beauty with the horror*
>   *the profound asylum and the vivid confinement*

Is there one person not of the establishment—
   and not of the reformists—whose axes are ground and whose
   battles are won:
   who can take distance and yet have compassion
   who is neither frightened of evil nor awed by goodness
   who can forgive everything and nothing

Is there a poet with words so true, with a mind so clear
   and soul so deep that:
   he comprehends the incomprehensibility of asylums
   his language permits new understandings
   we accept his words as deeds

If there is such a poet
   he would appear

Some day, a man will be known
   Who will teach us of life, of beauty, and evil
   Who will help us unfold the meanings of things
   And will cause us to learn that there is a design

He will teach us that:
   in spite of the back wards
   in spite of the inmates
   in spite of the evil
The design for each of us holds nothing but good

In Paris, on December 10, 1948, the United Nations General Assembly adopted a Universal Declaration of Human Rights. Its preamble spoke of dignity and equality and freedom, once revered concepts that—in recent years—have fallen upon evil days. I am compelled today, more than two decades after adoption of the Universal Declaration, to review some of the Articles—thereby assessing the state of humanity as I have experienced it and as I judge it to be.

If "All human beings are born free and equal in dignity and rights," then why have I seen, in dormitories for the severely mentally retarded, solitary confinement cells that are continuously filled and with waiting lists for their use?

If "Everyone has the right to life, liberty and security of person," then why have I seen a female resident at the state school for the mentally retarded who has been in a solitary cell for five years, never leaving— not for food or toileting or sleep?

If "No one shall be held in slavery or servitude," then why have I seen men who have been held in state school custody for twenty or thirty years, neither having been granted a review of their cases nor genuine consideration of the possibility that they may be capable of discharge and community placement?

If "No one shall be subjected to torture or to cruel, inhuman, or degrading treatment or punishment," then why have I seen two young women in one solitary cell at the state school, lying nude in a corner, their feces smeared on the walls, ceiling, and floor—two bodies huddled in the darkness, without understanding the wrongs they have committed or those committed against them?

If "Everyone has the right to recognition everywhere as a person before the law," then why have I seen another young woman, in solitary confinement, day after day and year after year, nude and assaultive, incontinent and nonverbal—except for one day each month when her parents call for her, and when she is washed and dressed and then taken home or for a ride in the country—except for one day each month when her clothes remain on her, when she communicates, when she is a human being?

If "No one shall be subjected to arbitrary arrest, detention or exile," then why have I seen men and women—residents of state schools for half a century—never knowing why they were placed originally, no longer caring to experience the outside world, and with no possibility that anyone outside is either interested in them or knows that they exist as human beings?

If "Everyone is entitled in full equality to a fair and public hearing by an independent and impartial tribunal in the determination of his rights and obligations and of any criminal charge against him," then why have I seen a boy at a state school in continuous seclusion twenty-four hours a day, described by the dormitory physician as a "monster"?

If "No one shall be subjected to arbitrary interference with his privacy, family, home or correspondence, nor to attacks upon his honour and reputation," then why have I seen incoming mail to state school residents, and their outgoing mail, read and censored by institutional supervisors?

If "Everyone has the right to freedom of movement and residence within the borders of each state. [If] Everyone has the right to leave any country, including his own, and to return to his country," then why have I seen human beings who have never—in ten or twenty or thirty or seventy years—left the one hundred or two hundred or a thousand acres of the state school—they who were delivered there at birth, whose souls only will leave?

If "Men and women of full age, without any limitation due to race, nationality or religion, have the right to marry and to found a family," then why have I seen the mentally retarded, the epileptic, and others denied such rights by state statutes; why have I seen young women sterilized as a condition for their release from the state school?

If "Everyone has the right to own property alone as well as in association with others. [If] No one shall be arbitrarily deprived of his property," then why have I seen residents of the state school deprived of their personal possessions and their entitlements under public assistance?

If "Everyone has the right to freedom of thought, conscience and religion," then why have I seen some residents at the state school required to attend church services and other residents prohibited from such attendance?

If "Everyone has the right to freedom of opinion and expression," then why have I seen a child berated by his state school teacher because of the opinions he expressed and why did I hear her tell him how ungrateful, how wicked he was, in light of the bountiful state that had given this unwanted child everything and expected only loyalty and gratitude in return?

If "Everyone, as a member of society, has the right to social security," then why have I seen more securing than security, more solitary than social, more indignity than dignity, more enchainment than freedom?

If "Everyone has the right to work, to free choice of employment, to just and favourable conditions of work and to protection against unemployment," then why have I seen residents of state schools in custody long beyond that time when they merited community placement, in custody because they were performing essential and unpaid work at the institution?

If "Everyone has the right to education," then why have I seen children at state schools for the mentally retarded permanently denied any semblance of education, treatment, or training?

If "Nothing in this Declaration may be interpreted as implying for any state, group or person any right to engage in any activity or to perform any act aimed at the destruction of any of the rights and freedoms set forth herein," then why have I seen human beings who have been given nothing, who have nothing and who, tomorrow, will have less?

Why have I seen a state school superintendent who did not call for a postmortem, an inquiry, or even a staff conference to determine the possibility of negligence or other unusual circumstances surrounding the death of a severely retarded child who choked when an attendant fed her a whole hard-boiled egg?

Why have I seen a state school director of nursing leave suddenly for a three-day vacation, without assigning additional staff or someone to succeed him in his absence, during the midst of a hepatitis epidemic where in one building alone twenty-seven of seventy-one patients were diagnosed as having this dreaded disease?

Why have I seen a severely retarded ambulatory resident, stabbed in the testicles by an unknown assailant while he slept, who almost died because the night attendant bandaged him as best she could, with no one doing anything else for the wound until ten hours later?

Why have I seen children at the state school go to bed each night wearing dungarees instead of pajamas, on mattresses without sheets, without pillows, and not one child "owning" even a single article of clothing?

Why have I seen children nude and bruised, sitting, sleeping, and eating with moist or dried feces covering them and their surroundings?

Why have I seen children lying on filthy beds, uncovered, flies crawling all over them?

Why have I seen children playing in and eating garbage?

Why have I been forced to view my brothers, and the world in which they live, as if I were standing in garbage, as if it were to consume *me*?

Form in your mind's eye this scene, this continuation, this last vulgar ounce of value squeezed from those least valued. Visualize this short true story.[1]

Fine grains of snow fall gently on the roughly hewn gray stone fort. Inside, amid the harsh lives and broken thoughts, a procession silently and fleetingly mourns. Those who comprehend learn that one has passed and they mourn, not for him, but for themselves and for each other.

They mourn for lives lived without hope, that end without meaning.

They mourn for a soul used in his lifetime as material, whose bones and meat continue to serve science.

They mourn for those deadly years and now this restless death, swirling in gleaming vats in Boston and Syracuse, waiting for bright lively boys in white to perform one final necessary obscenity.

They mourn for their wasted lives that shall end as this one ends, not cleanly, neither in sympathy for the living survivors nor with respect for the immortal spirit.

But they mourn more for the creations of God and obstetricians than the final indignities imposed by chairmen of medical school cadaver committees.

For the law requires that their bloated, mutilated, and sewn flesh must be scooped together, someday, and returned to the earth they long

---

[1] Based on infrequent involvements with medical school cadaver committees, experiences the reader may wish to forego. I have observed that certain deceased state school residents are selected for medical study as they were selected for institutionalization, and are treated in death as they were treated in life. On the average, each selected corpse involuntarily contributes one year of his eternal life to society before he is permitted his rest; he, of all people, who owes so little to society, from whom society has exacted so much, and from whom society has made his entire life—and now his death—a sacrifice.

for, the earth that will treat them more gently than the world that spawned them.

For is there a law, is there an authority that can do for one—in life—what all beings achieve in death?

Is there a mundane justice that, however infinitesimally, compares with the equality and brotherhood of the ground?

Dare we believe that there is a faithful conclusion, even for one whose life is as faithless as his mortal mission is senseless, as it is a violation of his right to be faithful?

Dare we hope that dead people bear no grudges, even as the living remorselessly pursue the unforgiven, unblessed departed?

I have brought up the past and now the deceased. What of the living and how may we predict the future? For the living confound as we are drawn to them. Can there be a better world for the mentally retarded? Asking the question implied that, indeed, there can be a better world, that, in retrospect, this is a better world. Asking the question denies the inevitable answer.

Some among you may conclude that an insuperable chasm lies between this discourse and evidence. Some may claim that I bring the softest data to support these words. In truth, I need no data, for everything reported here is well known to those who know about such matters; and anyone who requires data is unlikely to put such evidence to useful purposes. We need no data to conclude that there never was, there isn't now, there will not be a better world for the mentally retarded.

There cannot be a better world for the mentally retarded, or a poorer world, or any world. Worlds and futures are for the living, not for labels and nomenclatures and retards or defectives. Worlds are for lives, not for things or prejudices or administrative configurations. The mentally retarded are no more people than is the photograph a person. To understand this permits one to appreciate the beauty of a Helen Keller and to realize that—while she was not mentally retarded—before she was not mentally retarded, and before Anne Sullivan, she was mentally retarded.

We are trapped. Now that man has created the "mentally retarded" (and the "mentally ill") he must label and catagorize him, not only as he seeks to help him—irony of ironies—even as he struggles to wipe away the effects of his evil taxonomy, even as he strives to erase forever the taxonomy itself. As I entreat you to destroy the concept "mental retardation," I find myself using the term as you use it, adding to the layers of inhumanity heaped upon those souls so foully designated. As I tell you there is no future for the mentally retarded, there will not be any until they are returned to their brothers as men and women; as I tell you these things, I meander about human beings as "mentally retarded." We are trapped by civilization's penchant for creating insane problems. And our brothers and we will not be rescued by psychologists or sociologists or special educators—and, although they will better describe and teach us about the benchmarks of civilization, not even by poets or historians. We have a modest chance to permit the now-retarded, the now-disturbed, the now-abused to enter our world—albeit an imperfect world—and, I believe, that chance depends upon a decision society must take, but only insofar as each man must make his personal decision.

Men can no longer hide their faith and their souls in the United Nations or with any other group. What we have done to each other no nation and no group can rectify. What I have done to you, only I can repay and correct. Before each man seeks to change the world, he must change. Before these words become more than just words, I must become more than I am now. As I lament on the plight of mankind, I must account for my own plight:

For, who can tell a man, "We will make up to you for the lost years?"
Who can return to a man the sweet pleasures of a summer day,
His wife and carefree children at his side—
To a man destroyed before his marriage,
With children never to be conceived?
Who can describe the fragrant sensation of a pine-covered hill in May,
Backdropping a neat farmhouse overlooking fields and streams,
And living things—
To one who had hardly lived and had barely been given time to stop,
And gather in these wonders?
Is there a man who can claim, "I have seen these times restored,
I have been given back the years that were taken,
The flesh that was ravaged,
The being that once ceased to be"?
Who will unfold the years that are gone,
The times that are past,
The moments that are wasted,
This instant that will never again be?
When a man thinks about these questions, he cries.
He doesn't cry for mankind, nor for you.
He cries for himself and for the wasted times in a
Desolate and plundered
Cosmos.

Man is a wise fool and a sentimental sadist. Is this his natural manner? The fundamental question is whether man is able—and if, as I believe, he is able, is he willing—to change. Both fearfully and hopefully I conclude that if he doesn't change, nothing will matter. And if he doesn't, all of our past could not have mattered. If he doesn't, he will have become an example of the Rabbis' ancient saying that God gives wisdom only to those who have wisdom.

Further, I believe that what each man does—and how his every act causes and effects—is more than a reflection of his selfhood. It is a re-creation of it. But what has he fashioned?

Man differentiates himself from other beings.
He has speech.
He can protect himself from the elements.
He can leave the old and adapt to a new environment.

Man's speech, his clothing, and the ingenious ways he travels and migrates,
Allow him to be freer than:
     The Eagle
     The Jungle Beast and
     Even
     The Wind.

Man is capable of controlling the forces of nature more than they are
     capable of controlling him.
But man has not demonstrated his capability to control himself.
And that which permits him to fly, to build, to shape his destiny,
Causes him to impede and destroy other men.
That which gives some men their freedom, gives enslavement to others.
That which makes man uniquely free,
Makes him uniquely harassed.

Our gifts are our demons.
Never having spoken, the lion rules with a roar.
Hardly moving, the snail endures.
In his pond, the fish is free.

But man, prideful and eloquent man!
He disdains the mute and struggles against a relationship with them.
He binds the crippled and increases their spasticity.
He restrains the weak and incompetent and guarantees their infirmity.
He envelopes the old and feeble and ensures their loneliness.
He segregates the ill and re-creates their mental and spiritual disabilities.

Man enforces his retribution on those who do not speak by incarcerating them.
On those who do not think by enchaining them.
On those who do not conform by denuding them.
On those who will not be broken by breaking them.

The animals have fewer gifts than man but
     fewer imperatives
     fewer options but
     fewer requirements
     fewer accomplishments but
     fewer needs.

Animals are less civilized than man but have more civilization.
Animals have less freedom.
But the animal world has more freedom.

Mankind has enslaved his brothers and himself.

Some may wonder why I wrote this paper. There is a compelling Israeli dialogue wherein a visitor asks, "Why did you come here?" The Israeli replies, "I came to Israel to forget." "To forget what?" "I forgot."

I wrote this paper to remind those who have forgotten and to help instruct those who claim not to know. For there are other compelling words, born and nurtured and forevermore carved in the soil of Dachau: "Remember us. Do not forget."

Our Jerusalem will be the back ward. And we must not forget its existence—and all of mankind's ideological back wards—until civilization makes it unnecessary for us to remember.

Most of all, I wrote this paper to remind myself. I must not forget.

CHAPTER 12

On the Bill of
Rights and Related Matters

THE ORIGINAL PAPERS

Why the United States? As you know, on July 4, 1776, the Declaration of Independence set down reasons. Entitled by the laws of nature and God, we are a nation equal to other nations. As individuals, we are created equal and we have certain inalienable rights. No foreign government may set aside this country's equality among the family of nations and each individual's equality within the human family. Independence had to be declared when once loyal colonists refused to tolerate a King of Great Britain who would deny us that most valuable of all freedoms, free will. Free will, which even God does not intrude upon, formed the core of the idea we call America. School children know all of this, but too few adults do.

Signed on September 17, 1787, and ratified by the States a year later, the Constitution described that more perfect union in terms of justice, common welfare, and liberty. The first ten amendments to the Constitution were enacted on December 15, 1791. Eight of these are known as the Bill of Rights. And for good reason. As the Declaration of Independence proclaimed that all men have the right to life, liberty, and the pursuit of happiness, these and later amendments enlarged and deepened such guarantees. It's all there: the form of our government, the freedoms, due process, equal protection, and equal rights.

But if it's all in the Constitution and its amendments, how did the Founding Fathers explain the treatment of certain "different" people? Why, despite constitutional guarantees, did many people have to fight for their rights? You may not like their answer, but here it is. The idea of equal treatment is based on the premise that people are equally valuable as human beings. Otherwise, such a claim doesn't work. As for a relevant example, in the Virginia Declaration of Rights, which served as the basis

---

This essay was originally published in R. Heinich (Ed.), *Educating All Handicapped Children*. Englewood Cliffs, N.J.: Educational Technology Publications, 1978.

of our Bill of Rights, slaves were not considered constituents of society; the principle, "all men are equally free" did not apply to them. The fact of slavery produced the "fact" of inhumanness about that oppressed group. And that fact was "necessary," else how could slavery have been tolerated by a civilized state? How indeed? So the Blacks were specifically excluded from enjoyment of supposedly inalienable rights until, of course, the Emancipation Proclamation and the 13th, 14th, and 15th amendments. And as most everyone knows, until enactment of the 19th amendment, women were denied the franchise and even today are denied a great deal more than could ever be articulated in the laws. Obviously, there are other examples that come to mind.

Tradition takes almost forever to die, especially unjust tradition. Therefore, although Blacks and women have come a long way, it's only within recent years that they have attained the semblance of true equality. Now we must examine another oppressed group, the so-called handicapped, and redress violations of their inalienable rights; the law is a human instrument that requires constant surveillance and tinkering sometimes.

The handicapped have always been a paradox to Americans. And in America. In this Land of Opportunity, they seem unable to seize opportunities. In the Land of the Free, they are enchained. In the Land of Plenty, they are in need. In America the Bountiful, they are treated meanly. For them, the idea of America is little different than the idea of the Totalitarian State. But that which was denied Blacks and women by statutes, has more often been denied the handicapped by the handshakes and winks of ladies and gentlemen. What was legislated and implemented in the guise of friendship and compassion for the handicapped—sterilization codes, marriage prohibitions, even euthanasia—did not free but further restricted them or denied them their very lives. Especially here, the flight to legalism reflected the weakness rather than the strength of our society and what was not *legislated* was *perpetrated*, in the name of treatment or protection but often with negative consequences. What has been done to those human beings does not make for a pleasant story. What we have done does not make our lives pleasant.

Like the Blacks, the severely handicapped especially were not considered to be persons as you and I are persons. Unlike the Blacks, the founding laws of our land were silent about them. Unlike the Blacks, the handicapped were not considered to be valuable merchandise and, thus, were not a political issue. Times have changed. For whatever reasons—compassion, votes, humanism, dollars—the handicapped are big business today, are political factors not to be taken lightly. My thesis is that, had the original Constitution and Bill of Rights included the handicapped, the new Bill of Rights would be unnecessary. Furthermore, this new Bill of

Rights is necessary for exactly the same reasons that the 13th, 14th, 15th and 19th amendments had become necessary. However, because the Constitution was silent on the handicapped, there is nothing now to amend. So public Law 94-142, the Bill of Rights for Handicapped Children.

I once wrote that, while a person may thrill to the words chiseled on the lintel of the courthouse entrance that a commonwealth must have a government of laws and not of men, it is difficult to live with that belief unshaken. There are times when one has the strong feeling that, while our government may be of laws for men, in the ultimate dimension it must be *of* men *with* laws. There have always been people who worried about governments ruled by laws but not by the people. But that's so much theory, and, for many years, "all" the handicapped seemed to have had were the laws of the land; theory. There was little in the way of action on their behalf. One purpose to my writing this chapter is to examine the heresy that once there was a lot of theory and little action while today there is much action and little theory.

EDUCATION OF ALL HANDICAPPED CHILDREN

There should be something called "The Law of Inertia." With seeming inevitability, when action on an important issue is indicated, it is either too early or too late to do anything at the moment. Furthermore, the predominant theme of the day is "business as usual." And nowhere are these two motivations—"inertia"and "business as usual"—observed with more regularity than in government. If forming this nation had been contemplated during our time, the Founding Fathers might have waited so long to declare its independence that it never would have happened; people would have surely become bored with the whole thing. Research on an important issue doesn't seem to matter either, such as the research on exercise. If you don't exercise, you will experience 25% increased danger to your vital system. If you do exercise, you will also experience 25% increased danger because of something that has to do with shock to a flabby and indolent body. It seems that today we can't get a school bus to go on an agreed route much less create a country—or an educational mandate. Of course, school busing is an important and complex issue. But that's the point; we can't seem to deal with important and complex issues. Maybe technology itself is part of the fault as well as the solution. A computer mistake gets multiplied, its effects influencing the lives of thousands of people. Maybe the telephone is partially to blame; a lie is transmitted all too quickly. Maybe the tube; the mistake is immediately made known to the world (the living room bore offers almost instantaneous knowledge of what were once the dark secrets of kings and king makers). Maybe as it now seeks to come to our rescue, technology itself must bear some responsibility for the many leaders today who lead so few and for the many advocates in a culture that is characterized by such weak advocacy. Maybe with the magnification of mistakes today, few in government will take responsibility to act. Of course, there is another explanation of the notion that governments change slowly. There's something to the belief that organizations are most successful when they deal vigorously on behalf of individuals but conservatively on issues related to complex systems. Nevertheless, the point remains that governments respond reluctantly to the demand for major systems change, however powerful a case for change may be.

Hence, "everyone's" surprise with the passage of PL 94-142. It catches us unprepared, still stunned and still unbelieving. And who's to blame us? Who's to believe that by 1982 the federal government will invest 3.1 billion dollars a year in this program? I don't. But that's my problem more than it need be your reality. So I'll act as if my cynicism is but another of my aberrations. And I'll not appear as if I'm searching for the likely perversions of the legislation. Yet admit it, isn't it a surprise that our government enacted this law and scheduled its full implementation by fiscal year 1978? Didn't most of us merely go through the motions of trying to give support to the bill that eventually became the law? Weren't there only a zealous few who believed in its inevitability? Of course. And who ever believes zealots?

As Goodman (1976) noted, the law is a blockbuster. Not only will the handicapped feel its influence, not only will the schools feel its influence, but the entire nation will feel it. Overwhelmingly passed by the Congress, it puts the nation's stamp on the claim that the handicapped child is entitled to a first rate education, thus making the claim for all children. But why did the Congress pass what's believed to be the most significant federal legislation relating to the schools since the enactment of Title I of the Elementary and Secondary Act of 1965? And why now?

As reported to the Congress, the situation is alarming. There are reputed to be more than 8,000,000 handicapped children in the United States, but more than half of them do not receive appropriate educational services. A million of these children are excluded or exempted from any public school opportunities, appropriate or otherwise. Because of the unavailability of adequate programs within the public schools, many families are forced to look elsewhere for services, and at their own expense. It seems that teacher training institutions are in better positions than ever before to provide sufficient instruction for regular and special education teachers to serve this group. It seems that now, more than ever before, state and local agencies accept responsibility to provide services to the handicapped, but inadequate resources prevent them from fulfilling such responsibilities. Simply, it was the conclusion of the Congress that it will be in the best interest of our nation if the government sought to engage more directly and vigorously in educational programs on behalf of the handicapped. The law became the exception to the Law of Inertia.

PL 94-142 has been written about to the point of saturation. However, it may be well to briefly note some of the major elements comprising this Law (Gettings, 1976):

1. A new entitlement formula goes into effect in fiscal year 1978. Under it, states will be able to receive amounts equal to the number of handicapped children between ages 3 and 21 receiving special education services multiplied by a specified percentage of the average per pupil expenditure in public schools in the United States. Federal aid will increase from 5% in fiscal year 1978 to 10% in fiscal year 1979. In fiscal year 1982 and in succeeding fiscal years, federal aid will have grown to 40%.

2. To discourage states from including non-handicapped children in the program, the law provides limitations on the numbers who may be counted (to a maximum of 12% of total school age population between the ages of 5 and 17) and also limits to no more than 2% the percentage of children who may be counted because of specific learning disabilities.

3. To qualify for participation, the state must establish policies for all handicapped children between the ages of 3 and 18 by 1978, and between the ages of 3 and 21 by 1980. Such policies will not apply to children between the ages of 3 to 5 and 18 to 21 where mandatory services are inconsistent with state law or court order.

4. The states each will receive up to $300 for each child between the age of 3 and 5 who will receive special education services.

5. The law requires that an individualized educational program must be developed for each handicapped child. First priority must be given to unserved children. The severely handicapped who are not receiving adequate services will be given second priority.

6. To qualify, a state must submit a plan which: guarantees that federal funds will be used in a manner consistent with the law's requirement; includes a program for personnel development; provides free services for children placed by local educational agencies in private schools; guarantees that federal funds will supplement and increase rather than supplant state and local funds; prescribes a program evaluation system; provides for an advisory panel on unmet needs; and includes specific procedures for record keeping and accountability. Each participating local educational agency must submit a plan similar to the aforementioned.

7. Due process safeguards have been incorporated into the requirement for state and local participation. Federal and state monitoring procedures are included. All participants must include affirmative measures to employ qualified handicapped individuals (which may raise the issue of "deviant" staff serving "deviant" clients). Lastly, the legislation requires the Commissioner of Education to conduct whatever studies are necessary to adequately report to the Congress on progress achieved as a result of this legislation.

Obviously, there are and will be problems, some quite serious. For example, while on the one hand many parents are pleased with the "mainstreaming" thrust of legislation, others worry about the effects of general as contrasted with specialized programming. Teachers too have their concerns. Regular teachers express anxiety about their unpreparedness to assume responsibilities for children with problems unfamiliar to them. Special educators worry about the "least restrictive environment" as another way of saying "removal of intensive specialized services." Both groups of teachers keenly feel the need for major efforts to prepare regular teachers and administrators to assume the new responsibilities demanded of them if the legislation is to work. Of course, institutions that prepare teachers have those concerns magnified in light of their direct responsibilities for preparing teachers. It seems that everyone's worried, but it also seems that everyone thinks this was good legislation and it's a fine thing that it happened at last.

Most of us are uncertain about the consequences of "Child Find." We've had too many experiences where such efforts led less to finding children in need of special services than "capturing" children in order to receive bounties (reimbursements). Nevertheless, while we worry about the bounty hunters, we're also looking forward to a day when every child in America goes to school, and in an environment that is there to serve rather than to discriminate.

INSTRUCTIONAL TECHNOLOGY AND THIS LAW

Others are so much more erudite about instructional technology itself that I feel a little like the child who is taught to speak only when given permission, and hoping for it not to be offered on this occasion. But no such luck, and therefore this section. To guide my writing, I was given a definition of instructional technology, no doubt necessitated by the editor's conviction that this term is only slightly less metaphorical than the term "handicap" itself, champion of metaphors. Essentially, I was told that instructional technology is a systematic approach to the total learning-teaching interaction, encompassing the best that's known about enhancement of human development and its evaluation. That's a large umbrella. But to be asked about virtually everything connected with what's good about education in relationship to its facilitation of the most sweeping educational reform in years may be asking too much for the reader to digest and certainly too much for this writer to deliver. I think it will be quite enough if I comment upon what I think might be helpful in serving the goals of this legislation. And of course, the good editor of this volume appreciates my limitations and, I'm certain, will be quite satisfied with my modest interpretation of the charge.

First off, it is good that this law enunciates that the handicapped are entitled to full access to the best that technology has to contribute to their education. While one might argue that people don't have the inherent right to chickens in their pots or TVs in their living rooms, this law nails down the principle that if the TV set is good for instructing all children it must be made available to instruct disabled children. What may be a costly unattainable gadget on the outside must also be a basic necessity inside the schoolhouse.

Now for the debate, which is really war disguised. I don't believe that technology can replace teaching, nor can it make poor teachers into good teachers. Those who believe that have been oversold on a pretty good thing. The probable truth is that instructional technology neither offers as much assistance as its enthusiasts claim nor is it as trivial as its detractors make out. Look at the definition itself. Exactly because it's supposed to be virtually everything connected with learning and teaching, instructional technology can't be viewed as *the* answer, except as a summary of many answers. Of course, beware of those who assign unnatural powers to teachers, but also be aware of those who assign such power to technologies. Mystique in any form is usually a mistake. But frankly, if I were to make such a mistake, I think it would be about the former lie and not about the latter. "Teachers" who can't organize and implement a classroom program without a great deal of technological assistance shouldn't be called teachers. The title should be reserved for those who are capable of creating as well as technically managing educational environments. Call the others what they are, technicians or aides. To be sure, instructional technology can offer enormous help to teachers, but not every user need be a teacher and not every teacher need be a user.

The problem with understanding instructional technology is that people don't ask the right questions about the area. It's like the SST. Almost daily, there's an article in the newspapers about the SST. But the questions asked about the SST have to do with whether it pollutes, whether it's too expensive, or whether it's safe. The real question, the question to ask first, is whether anyone needs to travel between London and New York City in three hours.

Take Camphill Village in Copake, New York. Camphill is a community for people some would call "mentally retarded." But to those who live there, Camphill is a self-sustaining village whose citizens *choose* to be there. When I visited Camphill I found it easy to believe that the people there *choose* to remain together, the so-called retarded and the others. You will be hard pressed to locate another community that offers more of the good life. For example, the farmers at Camphill milk by hand. Why? A basic principle of the village is that every member must be given opportunities to make contributions to the welfare of the community. Everyone works. Hence the hand milking. However, from the point where milk has been delivered from cow to pail, technology takes over. Pasteurization, refrigeration, storage, and transportation of the milk is accomplished in the cleanest, safest, speediest, and most efficient manner known to the dairy industry. Camphill Village represents the utilization of technology in a manner which truly serves people rather than makes them useless or unnecessary.

Instructional technology offers us opportunities to help great teachers extend their influence, and to help good teachers become better teachers, and to help all teachers better understand what they are doing. But, left to its own devices, instructional technology is silent on the "why" questions. Instructional technology is silent on objectives; and while having an objective doesn't solve a problem, it gives one a reason to work to solve a problem. And what happens when technologies are implemented without reason shouldn't happen in education. The consequence of such mindlessness is often as if you would save the bottle and pour the Johnny Walker down the drain, buying the real goods to get the by-product on the container. If one isn't careful, he becomes too fond of the panel of flashing lights that tell him the machine is working, so he buys the jazziest model for the sake of its flashing lights or its bells and whistles. Or, he installs an instructional system that is designed to solve a problem he doesn't have and ignore a problem he does have. For example, oftentimes the problem is not that one hasn't been able to get a computer printout of information, but he hasn't been able to get accurate data to feed the computer. So the mechanisms and reforms of data gathering that would make the computer feasible might also make it unnecessary. And furthermore, until the data gathering system improves, it would be valueless. Certainly, instructional technology offers opportunities that can't be spurned. Nevertheless, we should recognize that so much of instructional technology has yet to be controlled, to be used intelligently and to help solve our problems to serve us and not be our masters. The dog has to wag the tail.

Technology should extend the capabilities of people rather than limit or subvert human talents and accomplishments. Prescribing technology without thoughtfulness and applying it without limitation is like love-making without love, a bodily function, not human. Instructional technology is a powerful beast that demands taming. At what better time and in what better context could it appear than today as we embark on a visionary and crucial educational experiment?

THEORY AND PRACTICE

In the same manner that the Emancipation Proclamation was not only about Black people, this law is not only about handicapped people. In one way, *The* problem in special education is simple. In a way, there is virtually no problem. Yet, special education has proved to be not only a problem but a monumental one. I mean by the above that society has it within its capabilities to include the handicapped not only in its regular school programs but everywhere. If we but thought differently about certain things, we would behave differently. It is not that we can't, but we choose not to. And indeed, because we choose not to, we have the seemingly insurmountable problem.

There's another point of view from a different mountain, the idea of those who would enjoin us to simply change ourselves and stop the foolishness of creating legislation and bigger opportunities for people in the business of special education and its derivative occupations. That point of view will not argue against the wisdom that society can change and, thus, *The* problem could be solved by us merely changing ourselves. However, they do indeed argue that, because there must be laws about something and somebody, there should be such a law as we have before us. They argue that while PL 94-142 may not have been necessary had we not made it necessary, the way things are today it's a godsend, or at least the best we know how to do. Therefore, irrespective of agreement that we would all be better off if we stopped the foolishness around special education, there is also agreement that this law has been long overdue.

We should now turn to the claim that *The* problem is quite simple. All serious human problems are simple. Simple to avoid and simple to end. For example, ending pollution of the environment is simple to achieve. That kind of problem is not like such complex affairs as finding a cure for cancer or eradicating heart disease. In the former, it seems as if we don't want the problem to go away. In the latter, we can't make the problem go away. Obviously, the situation is different for the individual. The person deals better with his own than with society's problems, be they simple or complex. That's a truism that only the ignorant would argue about.

What needed to be done was done. For the first time since I entered this field years ago, I witnessed the passage of legislation that contained the best thinking in our field, imperfect as it is, and a plan for the most vigorous action. Earlier, I suggested that what is wrong with so much of society, for example the university, is that it's all theory and no action. Others have suggested that what's wrong with society, for example the government, is that it's all action and no theory. Here we have a law based on the best theory available, funded at a higher level than any previous legislation, and which promises to deliver the goods fairly quickly. That's impressive.

THE RIGHT BILL FOR THE RIGHT TIME

I once said something like, "People should be judged by what's best about them, but governments must be judged by what's worst." If there were such an understanding, the capacity of an individual would be determined less by the averaging of his scores and more by the highest score he received. However, with governments, which in principle should be distrusted, there would be an element of disbelief, of knowing that someone somewhere among the politicians or the bureaucracy is trying to pull the wool over our eyes. Therefore, where governments are concerned, the rule should be that if the behavior is rotten, it's to be expected and incurable. And if the behavior is exemplary, it's an accident or a mirage.

Applying the above law to judgment of our nation's efforts on behalf of so-called handicapped children, we score poorly. The children aren't getting their due. Too many are in inadequate or no classrooms. Too many are growing up without the proper tools they will need to serve society and themselves as well as they might have otherwise.

The early bird catches the worm. But had the worm been late, he wouldn't have been caught. Being early can be good. Being late can be good too. Forget those arguments and recriminations. Today and tomorrow are all that matter now. So what better time than now is there to correct the errors of those who misinterpreted the original Bill of Rights, of those who had unfortunately concluded that the handicapped were to be held exempt from many of the rights and opportunities enjoyed by other citizens? What better time than now is there to proclaim to the world, but most of all to proclaim to ourselves, that each human being counts for something, that merely to be a human being entitles one to a privileged place within society? Probably today more than ever before, we must live as if a decision to deny a person any right enjoyed by others is to be made only after proof is given that the person is a serious threat to the public's good, and only under the most carefully supervised equal protection and due process guarantees, and only after all other means have been exhausted. PL 94-142 may become the instrument to correct the errors of the past.

Sure, there will be problems attendant to this legislation. Certainly, there is a definitional issue and, consequently, an epidemiological issue. Are there 8,000,000 handicapped children in the United States? Some say there are more and others say there are less. That's what happens when subjects determined by metaphors are counted. What will be the effects of categorical labeling? Of zero reject? Such questions are not unrelated to ones concerning voting rights for people with severe limitations. Some people do not approve of the extension of the right to vote to severely mentally retarded people, and such sentiment is not merely the voice of prejudiced people venting their meanness. Similarly, there may be problems when the handicapped themselves participate in the development of their educational programs. There may be problems if the demand that evaluation instruments not be racially or culturally discriminating is taken seriously. Will they be intellectually discriminating? Will new norms to be developed from the guidelines be useful in separating children who learn well from those who can't or don't learn well? Undoubtedly, there will be problems arising from the intensification of efforts to locate and identify youngsters with handicaps. If such efforts are weak, we will not do well in locating unserved children. On the other hand, if efforts are strenuous, certain children may be unnecessarily labeled or unnecessarily separated from the mainstream.

What I'm trying to indicate is that there must be a prudent balance between discovery and creation, between what needs to be changed and what should be preserved. And because so little of our society is prudent or balanced today, we should expect problems. We should expect that public involvement in the adoption of policies is a real plus, but such involvement raises the specter of confusion and indecision. Does democracy work in the clinic? We'll find out. And employment of the handicapped themselves in order to implement the legislation may offer new opportunities, but also problems. Is it better to make a special effort to employ the handicapped or a special effort to employ the best workers? You know the arguments, both ways. And, of course, some current supporters—some of those who led the way to passage of this legislation—may be the same people who will eventually resist implementation. When implementation begins to rock one's own domain, or future, the friend sometimes becomes the foe.

Surely, there will be problems. But there will also be opportunities never before possible. There can be a day when historians and your children's children will look back on this period and say, "That was the time when our ancestors finally learned that, while all humanity is a wonderful and awesome creation, each individual is fragile and dependent. While our people are strong and free, each person needs the protection of the total society. That was the time when our forebears learned that each human being is an irreplaceable link to the past and to the future. Each life is priceless.''

That's the message in Public Law 94-142. I pray we take it as seriously as if our very souls depend on it.

REFERENCES

Gettings, R. M. A summary of selected legislation relating to the handicapped: 1975 (Part I). *Programs for the Handicapped* (U.S. Department of Health, Education and Welfare), 1976, *6*, 2–15.

Goodman, L. V. A bill of rights for the handicapped. *American Education*, 1976, *12* (6), 6–8.

CHAPTER 13

On Competencies and Incompetencies, Instruction and Destruction, Individualization and Depersonalization: Reflections on the Now-Movement

BIASES

I was almost inclined to tiptoe onto the bandwagon, if not volunteer as its driver, until the state informed me that my presence was expected—in truth, demanded. Long ago I became convinced that, although I think of myself as a loyal citizen, the state (and the federal government) have ways of making it easy for one to separate the American Ideal from the American Experience. Therefore, when we were enjoined by the Regents of the State of New York to redesign our teacher preparation program in special education in such a manner as to reflect a "competency-based approach," I decided it would be a realistic reflection of past experiences to assume my locally famous conceptual fetal position and, as they say, stonewall it. If the state thought there was "something" in the competency-performance-accountability movement, then I suspected from past experiences that there might be nothing in it for me. I've given notice that this section sets out my biases, so I'm comfortable saying it: if government has an opportunity to screw something up, it will find a way. And, an all-time prize example now seems to be competency-based teacher education or, as the pro's say, CBTE.

This essay was originally published in *Behavioral Disorders*, 1976, *1*, 89–96, and in *Family Involvement*, 1976, *8*, 9–14. Reprinted by permission.

Fetal positions notwithstanding, the Regents made it clear that they will entertain no exceptions; each teacher preparation program in special education is to present a redesigned curriculum by February, 1975, else it will have to find other ways to serve humanity. What with deans, colleagues, primary and secondary constituents, I never had much of a chance in ignoring or stonewalling the mandate. Consequently, in self-defense, I did what I usually do in such circumstances; I applied for a grant to study the competency-based movement. Federal and state officials, joint benefactors, were thrilled with our proposal and showered us with the dollars needed to comprehend competency-based curriculum development in teacher education. Our proposal claimed it was a simple task confronting us: what was needed was a field-based curriculum designed to prepare special educators—a curriculum embracing relevant, clear and concise entrance and exit criteria for students.

One of the first things we attempted, after appointment of a project coordinator and small staff, was to define competency-based teacher education. I thought this would be a reasonable assignment, neither particularly difficult nor time consuming. It's always an amazement how wrong I am about certain things. Certainly, I should have remembered that definitions of metaphors are slippery things indeed. My very naive and gross understanding of CBTE was that it is very similar to what the schools call performance contracting. CBTE is concerned with what teachers do in their training, and what professors do with their students. Performance contracting is more concerned with what teachers do with the children. However, I thought of both as very much related, possibly aspects of but one general model for thinking about teachers, pupils, and teaching. In some fuzzy ways, I thought of CBTE as promising new opportunities to bring together diverse elements of a community—teachers, parents, consumers and the organizations they represent—to solve together problems confronting those who would educate our people. I thought that this movement would promise to confront the mindlessness of much of what is called teacher preparation, e.g., the idea that one should, or that anyone ever really tries to, teach curriculum and methods apart from the psychological-social settings of children, teachers, and community life.[1] As I noted earlier, I would have been interested in the

---

[1] If there is to be a debate about this, it should not be whether one can or can't but, rather, whether one should or shouldn't teach curriculum as if it can be separated from some describable reality. That there is not agreement with the above observation may account for, if not explain, the irresolution surrounding CBTE, i.e., the attempt to find can-type answers to should-type questions. That's the Yin and Yang of it all, the constant tension between prescription and discovery, creation and conservation, the difference between those who think in "can-can't" terms and those who are more concerned with "should we or shouldn't we."

problem had the Regents not told us we must be interested; in fact, had they not, I might have been even more interested, certainly less defensive.

Our search for a definition of CBTE led everywhere and, therefore, nowhere. Some colleagues asserted that a critical element of the model is the *individualization of instruction*. We bought that. Others added that, even more central, the program had to be *field-based*. We bought that too. Still others, not disagreeing with the aforementioned elements, added the idea of a wider sharing of program responsibility and authority to include not only university professors, but college students, public school teachers, administrators, and consumers; they claimed that such *parity* was a differentiating characteristic of CBTE. We thought this was entirely reasonable. There were those who described CBTE as programs that reify abstract concepts and artificial settings by bringing the *real world* to the college classroom and, even more so, the college classroom to the *real world*. We expected that this would be very desirable. An important factor in the movement was the intrusion of *Instructional Technology*, embedding hitherto untapped traditional facets of the curriculum. We agreed that teacher preparation might better embrace the wonders available in this scientific age. We were told that CBTE must utilize new instructional modes to deliver individualized real world stuff. Therefore, there would be new emphases on *modules, mini-courses,* and *team teaching*.

These new elements appeared to be propelling us to new, if not scary and sometimes uncontrollable, heights; so, somewhat scared and not in full control, we actually agreed to apply for provisional membership in the Society of CBTEers. One of the compelling reasons for the movement was the public's seeming disenchantment with traditional teacher preparation. The bits and pieces of their unhappiness were funneled through ideological loudspeakers—legislators, elected executives, and their appointees—and what we once thought were muted voices and timid whimpers became the roars of zealots and revolutionaries. Legislators leaned on Regents, who leaned on commissioners, who leaned on functionaries, who now lean on teacher educators. So, what else is new? Nothing is new, but how we wish something would be new, or different, anything not to have what we now have (writer's note: for reasons such as illustrated in the aforementioned, this section was clearly labeled). The problem with accountability (making public clear criteria for entrance to teacher preparation programs, success bench-marks, and criteria for program completion) is a simple one: we do not have either the evaluation skills or tools or interests, and some will claim that we have no need, to accurately measure what someone in the pedagogy business is doing, much less assess how successful or unsuccessful he is. It's a little like the Pompeian wishing for a seismograph.

After reading a great deal about the CBTE model, listening at more meetings than is my custom (something almost guaranteed to make me irritable), and indiscriminately buttonholing friends and those not so friendly, I had to conclude the CBTE is either a very large umbrella or a very fragile idea. Literally, it was impossible to find a single "expert" in that field willing to define CBTE in other than the most global manner, including in such a definition everything that seems to be virtuous and right-headed about training. Further, at least among the "experts" that I encountered, there was unwillingness to exclude from the category those who were less (or not at all) interested in modules or technology, those who were more (or singularly) interested in traditional formal courses, those who had hardly worked towards (or worked not at all for) an accountability model. I had to conclude that CBTE was either Mother Earth herself in pedagogical guise or just another school marm with another grandiose idea to save the world.

MORE BIASES

This section continues the first. However, even biases may be categorized; they appear to be more official that way, less like biases. I began with the implicit claim that CBTE is a metaphor, and if not that an inkblot, with many understandings, therefore many misunderstandings, about the concept. It is either something very important or very trivial, and my bias had led me to believe the latter. Now, in this section, I want to discuss several inconsistencies—non-sequiturs—observable to one who observes this movement with my biased eye. One of the unusually fascinating things about CBTE concerns its adherents, their past polemics, and their current nostrums. *Look it up if you doubt me, but those who advocate today that teacher preparation must be centered in children's schools rather than in the universities are, more often than by chance, those reformers who but a few years ago admonished us to evacuate the public schools.* First, some of our leaders told us that the public schools were dry and dead places, neither fit for learning or human congregation of any sort. Now, some of these same colleagues scold or shame us to entrust our university students to those dangerous and precarious environments. Exactly what do they mean? What's good and what's bad? How can a school be a dead place one year and the "only" place the next year? It's difficult to understand all of this—first the castigation, then the invasion, now the love affair. Possibly, those critics are like so many others today, those who have the idea that romatic love affairs outlast arranged marriages. Possibly, not until educational critics were able to fall in love with the schools would they consent to their value. And, now that there is love, possibly because it dawned upon the reformers that the schools are where the people are, it became obvious that children's schools are not only the best places for children but also for those who are preparing to be teachers.

I hope the reformers know what they are saying and doing. I hope they have studied the data. If they haven't, they may wish to begin with the data on marriages, real marriages, which indicate that arranged affairs appear to be at least as successful as waiting and working for romantic love; look it up in the divorce statistics. Or, better, reread the section of Genesis that tells us that Isaac took Rebekah for his wife, then he loved her. The point of all of this is simple, I think. If the reformers, or the conservators, would first make their commitment to principles, there would be less of this wishy-washiness in education, less of these on-again and off-again relationships, less of perennial searches for romantic love affairs, and more agreements or arrangements where people devote themselves to making things work because it's right, or decent, or necessary.

One of the advertised strengths of CBTE is connected with the "publication" of what is required to enter a program, to succeed in it, and to be certificated. It is claimed that, eventually, a "book" will be created which will include the explication of task analyses, teacher competencies, and evaluative criteria—preferably in a three column arrangement; or is it a four column arrangement, or four rows? Even now, today, we have available to us the catalogs of "this" State Department of Education, and "that" University, and growing numbers of catalogs from other state department and university groups, each detailing four hundred, or four thousand, or forty thousand competencies that teachers have, or should have, or would have if the colleges would but use this model, or that model, or this and that model. Where is it written that the "book" is really very helpful, either in pedagogy or in other spheres of human struggle? How many times do we hear someone plead, or do we plead ourselves, that the "book" be set aside? How many times do we hear, or say, or think that the "book" is a roadblock to justice, to thoughtfulness, to parity, to understanding the views of the people, to doing the "right" thing?

It appears so ironic, yet so fitting, because we've been on this road so many times before, that the very problems that the competency-based movement were created to attenuate may actually become more worrisome because of the movement. Going by the "book" seems more certain to lead us to normative (what's good for the group is good for the person), not individualized, approaches to education, seems to be less rather than more humanistic, seems to promote thoughtlessness and not thoughtfulness, seems to be connected more with technical than with professional preparation.

AND MORE BIASES

What is the purpose of the university? What is education? What is learning? What is culture? What is the objective of it all, or the objectives, or the idea of the educated life? I have written so much about these matters in past years that I fret now, worried that this chapter will divert from conviction to parody. So, I shut out the memory of past shibboleths and slogans; that is, if I can. I try to say things as plainly and simply as possible, which for me is not very plain or simple. Possibly to invigorate myself, probably to escape this task, I stop for a bit to read Alfred North Whitehead's, *The Aims of Education* (1964). I am invigorated. Whitehead had the right ideas, my ideas. He reminds me of an old French proverb, "To understand all is to forgive all." Where did I see it before? Was it on the entrance way to Hull House, Jane Addams community center in Chicago? Did I read that proverb there during a visit to the Chicage Circle Campus of the University of Illinois, now surrounding Hull House, once a place for weary but education-hungry immigrants and their children, now a museum of sorts extolling what we were and lamenting what we are? Isn't it strange, or coincidental, that Whitehead would quote this proverb, when there were so many others he could have chosen? Strange, because it's one of my favorites, yet I'm not certain that I understand it; but why should I understand, I'm not always forgiving; I guess it's all very complicated. Yet, as I reread Whitehead's book, I think again of some of the ideas I had written about, ideas dealing with clinical and normative teaching and the educational supermarkets that serve the pedagogical enterprise. I think about the promises that the CBTEers are making: teachers will be prepared better to utilize relevant curricula; teacher competencies can be identified, measured; teacher competencies can be validated against the measurement of change in children; there are better curricula than others and better methods than others and these too can be identified, particularized, measured, and reproduced at will. All nonsense, sheer nonsense! There is nothing, absolutely nothing, in our literature that supports adherence to any one method, curriculum or administrative design over any other method, curriculum, or administrative design. What we really have are lots of competing insights and prejudices. Some methods work under certain circumstances and not under others, and what works is often dependent upon how one stipulates criteria for what does or doesn't work.

Then, why have all this curriculum and methodological development, this search for new procedures? It's part of the need to do something and record the history of our efforts. Disseminating summaries of our curricula, or methods, or designs is very important work, not because such dissemination offers better prescriptions for treating subsequent clients, but because it's by common definition a method to understand the ways in which educational problems were once viewed, and measured, and dealt with. It's all so clear to me, yet I feel that the curriculum makers and the methodologists either don't understand what I'm getting at or have reasons of their own for ignoring what I'm getting at.

Permit me to deal with the curriculum-methodology question another way. Let's look specifically at the colleges and universities. Who should inhabit, or matriculate at, colleges and universities? Everyone, anyone, only some? For many generations, the colleges and universities were ruled by so-called scholars, that is, those individuals who had procedures to collect data, who were skilled in the reliable reduction of data, and who did not dare proceed beyond their data. Essentially, scholars are a conservative and very valuable lot. More and more today, intellectuals and "unhinged scholars" are inhabiting places of higher education, and some have gained considerable support there. Intellectuals are willing to go beyond the scope of what is known, beyond data and facts. Intellectuals are less bound by science and scholarship, although the better ones are much more than dilettantes or merely facile and witty verbalizers. Now, so it seems to me, not only will the intellectual, but the scholar himself— he who once owned the university—be forced to move aside for the technician. What the CBTEers are saying is that we probably never had and certainly don't need creators of educational environments. Teachers are not bright enough, inquisitive enough, or talented enough to create learning environments; we must help them more that we have, we must provide them with the technical supports necessary for them to manage good learning environments; we must make them more competent, as we define competency, as we who are competent can now dictate the competencies they must have before they can be certificated. I think that, if Education was a Monolith before CBTE, it will become a monstrous Monolith once the movement gains final control, if it does.

AND YET MORE BIASES

While this new Monolith is developed, one wonders about the thousands (millions?) of person hours now devoted to the identification and parsing of competencies. Where will these professors find time for their scholarship, for the development of their clinical skills, or their research? Is it so urgent that education be standardized more than it is today? Enough already! How much standardization do we want, or need? In fact, there are some who would claim that teacher preparation is much more standardized than it should be. There are some who have observed that the teachers' college in one state is little different from the teachers' college in another, which is little different from the teachers' college in a third, which is little different from the teachers' college in a fourth, or fifth, or sixth. There are some who would claim that, whatever differences exist in teacher education, the Educational Monolith is such that in three or four months after initial appointments, all teachers behave alike, and think alike, and are alike. Some will say it's enough already, what is needed is not more standardization but more exceptions, more unique-ness, more diversification, more idiosyncracy. Some will say that what we need, more desperately than standardization and catalogs of compe-tencies, is an effusion of creative people passionately interested in their own educations and in opportunities to help others develop. That, some will say, would be Utopia, more so than the S, Y, or Z State University catalog of competencies, three columns, four columns, or whatever.

AFTER BIASES, WHAT REMAINS? BIASES

I once wrote that the teacher—not the book, not machines, not curricula, not hardware, not software, not procedures, not even the "methods"— is the method, as the pupil and the teacher are the purposes of it all. Good methods are good teachers and poor methods are poor teachers. Since that time, I have seen a lot and I read and heard a lot about competency-based teacher education (CBTE). And, from what I've seen and heard, from what the literature on CBTE informs us about, I have not been dissuaded that what there is within the teacher contributes more to dif-ferentiate teaching than whatever variance exists between and among the various methods, curricula, and administrative designs. And, further, the CBTE literature cannot offer adequate contradiction to this belief. The CBTE literature, in fact, explains very little; rather, it defends its position and, almost in an instant, rolls it out for our approval. But, hardly any-where, in psychology, education, and social policy, will one find justifi-cation for adherence to a competency-based model, either on theoretical grounds or because of widespread agreement with its principles and values espoused. There are available enormous catalogs on competencies, but how many contain substantive discussions, and how many contain data? What we need from the CBTEers is fewer of those catalogs and more of what they claim is important, facts. After all, isn't this why they're cashing in on tradition?

How much of the CBTE position is based on the implicit belief that teachers are more often technicians than creators, both in the sense of what they do as well as what they are judged to be capable of doing? It is also based on the implicit belief that learning is more efficiently and effectively promoted when it is supervised in the context of small defin-able operations and tasks as on a factory assembly line, with the order of difficulty increasing in some lawful manner. Is there sufficient evidence in our literature or experience to support the idea that this is how most people, or some people, learn best, or more efficiently? I don't believe so. Can a stronger case, or any case, be made for anatomizing the learning of anything that is important to the individual, really important? What I am saying is that maybe, just maybe, one can learn syllables, or how to give an intelligence test, or how to administer a standardized reading test, as the result of some discrete competency-based modular experience. However, does the model have equal relevance with respect to teaching styles, values, whatever it is in the teacher that makes the teacher a teacher? Again, rather than read the various state catalogs, we might be better prepared to appreciate these issues were we to read Alfred North Whitehead. We might be less persuaded that learning should always evolve from a less difficult to a more difficult task, from concrete to abstract substance. We might better comprehend that, although antecedents always influence matters—learning tasks, competency attainment, anything—antecedents are not easily understood; they have a way of gumming up simplistic analyses. Great profit would accrue to those who read or write competency catalogs if they were to spend some time with Alfred North Whitehead.

In the context of this discussion, one cannot avoid raising the freedom issue. Certainly, citizens should have the right to choose their community's teachers. Long overdue, the principle of local determination must extend to teacher selection. In one sense, the competency-based movement adheres to this principle. At least in my state, New York, there will be the requirement for local participation in teacher preparation programs. However, in another sense, CBTE will only deepen national standardization, control, and certification of teachers. Local community representatives will be invited to participate in the design of college and university teacher preparation programs, but only as those designs do not deviate significantly from the state, or region, or wherever, mandated standards and models. Rather, communities should be given the plain right to choose their teachers in whatever manner they wish, utilizing whatever criteria they develop, competency-based or not, traditional or not, what you or I think is appropriate or not. For exactly the same reason, to safeguard their responsibilities to pursue their historic missions, colleges and universities must be equally protected. Communities are entitled to hire the teachers in their ways, and colleges are entitled to prepare teachers in theirs. Our representation should be *Caveat Emptor*, let the buyer beware, not "thou shalt not" or "thou must," or whatever it is that state departments and certifying agencies often choose as a slogan.

All of the above is related to things I have thought about and read about for a number of years, matters connected with our desire to protect people more than to guarantee their freedom. These concerns also relate to one's fundamental conception of how development unfolds—not for ambiguous children but for oneself. Such interests also relate to concepts of teaching, normative and clinical styles, process and substance, alchemy, the efficacy studies, slot machine teacher preparation, centralization and decentralization, certifying bodies, local prerogatives and national interests, who the schools are for, what schools do, what they should do, what we do, you do, and the inevitable me, what I do.

Possibly, it is not too late to reverse or impede the tide, to inhibit adding a new layer to the Educational Monolith. It may have been because of some of these concerns that the Attorney General of Texas ruled recently that:

> . . . it is not within the authority of the State Board of Education or the State Commissioner of Education to stipulate that institutions seeking approval for teacher education programs must present performance-based applications, but the Board, with the advice of the Commissioner, may promulgate rules and regulations whereby institutions seeking such approval could choose between alternative plans for program approval (one or more of which might be 'performance-based') and submit applications accordingly. (Memorandum by J. W. Edgar, Commissioner of Education, Texas Education Agency, to the Presidents of Teacher Preparation Colleges/Universities and Deans of Education, January 15, 1974.)

I think about lighting candles in the dark, and that the Attorney General's opinion may be no more than the flicker of a firefly as summer wanes. On the other hand, it may be the beginning of something and, to continue but redirect and mix the metaphor, an example of when it is better to curse and extinguish a misbegotten light than to be led in frivolous or cynical paths.

AND, LAST BIASES

Enough, already, with the threat to force colleges and universities to kneel before the power of the state, or its commissioners, or its regents. By what right does a state claim authority to demand not only the substances of a credentialing program but, also, the manner in which that substance is to be transmitted? It's enough, probably too much, to have to live with the state bent on credentialing almost everyone from teachers, to barbers, to doctors, to lawyers, to real estate salesmen, you name it. Now, it would even tell us how we are to transmit those facts, values, and skills. If such nonsense is constitutional, then the constitution isn't as constitutional as I thought it to be, and Santa Claus is dead—but everyone knew those things anyway.

I wish I could understand all so I could forgive the CBTEers. Or, better, I wish they understood all so they could forgive those poor professors who are more interested in learning for its own sake, scholarship for the thrill of it all, and creating rather than implementing environments. I wish somebody in authority, really in authority, agreed with me that the universities are places for students—intellectuals and scholars—and not for technicians, memorizers, cultists, or thoughtless applicators. I wish those in charge would understand better the difference between reverence for life (which is very important), reverence for competency (which is probably what built America so quickly and powerfully), and reverence for freedom (which is what America is really about, or supposed to have been about). That is, I wish that those in charge would understand better that competency involves mainly technical matters, but freedom concerns itself with not only the means to achieve competency but the stuff at the end, if we get there. I wish that those in charge would better appreciate the difference between individualizing programs and individualizing goals; the competency-based movement is great at accomplishing the former, and a dismal disaster in even recognizing the importance of the latter. I wish those in charge would appreciate the distinction offered by one of my colleagues, the difference between a teacher who has developed various competencies and a competent teacher. I wish that those in charge would truly believe that, when all else fails, or succeeds—when everything, or nothing, matters—one must do something for himself, not for the state, not even for the client, but just for himself; and, could someone in charge truly believe that the learner always learns just for himself?

I wish, once or twice in a generation, somebody right at the top—in charge of those in charge—would have listened when his grandma told him stories with important lessons to be learned, maybe a story like this:

An animal once asked a centipede how he managed to walk with those hundred legs. The centipede thought hard and long about the question and finally said, "I take the right front leg, then the. . ." And he thought more about the matter, and more, and he never walked again.

What happened to the centipede could well happen to our most gifted teachers.

REFERENCE

Whitehead, Alfred North, *The Aims of Education*, New York: The New American Library, 1964.

CHAPTER 14

Life with the Decision Makers

It is within and around 15 Ashburton Place that many of the long-range and long-lasting decisions are made relating to the care and treatment of the mentally retarded in our Commonwealth. This is where the "action" is. The Massachusetts Department of Mental Health, centered at 15 Ashburton Place, together with the State House, is a complex of authority, action and inaction, good deeds and bad deeds—but always power and influence. Life in this complex is always strange to the newly initiated, especially to one whose previous professional life was almost solely academic. The following is my attempt to bring some illumination to those who haven't experienced "government from the inside."

Admittedly, I take a very narrow view of things and have had very limited experience. To the degree that the reader finds me fair or unfair to certain kinds of individuals or operations, he will better understand that in a system such as I am describing it is not unusual to be both fair and unfair and to be treated both fairly and unfairly. Therefore, at the outset, I want to share my conviction that, in this particular system, decision-making is a reflection of the System and its capacity to initiate good deeds or poor deeds, rather than of individuals and their attributes. It is my impression that the System does more to change individuals than individuals do toward changing the system. Yet it is not possible for me to discuss the System other than in terms of individuals. In this regard, I must maintain that whatever is expressed in this chapter and whatever approaches the reader uses to evaluate the origins of the pandemonium described elsewhere in the book, it would be erroneous in the extreme to place primary responsibility for these evils on certain individuals or types of individuals. We could continuously replace people or add new people or create new positions and not—in any but trivial ways—change the conditions we agree must be changed. For, in fact, it is very probable that the people replaced were as anxious to change conditions as those

This essay was originally published in the author's book, *Exodus From Pandemonium: Human Abuse and a Reformation of Public Policy*. Boston: Allyn & Bacon, Inc. 1970.

who had been pressing for their replacement. Adding new "good" people
to a sick System does not make the System appreciably healthier, but it
does infect the "good" people and they, eventually, behave in much the
same way as those they've replaced. Our goal, then, should be to change
a System which promotes inadequate and inhuman care and treatment.
Whereas, till now, our goal has been to change the people and, thus,
rescue a System which is, in fact, without hope.

THE DEFENSIVE MOAT: SOPHISTS' PARADISE

A man can get along, quite adequately and for many years, on the elegance
of his language and the passion and conviction of his speech. One would
suppose that this is the hallmark of the university professor, and so it
may be. However, I have observed sophistry and pedantries much more
frequently in 15 Ashburton Place and its tentacles than in the halls of ivy.
Very few people at 15 Ashburton Place *must* make decisions, if they do
not wish to make them. The Commissioner of Mental Health must, as he
is the Appointed Authority over all programs sponsored by the Department. The Business Office must, because they are responsible for both
payrolls and hardware, items that are quickly missed if they are not
delivered on time. Most other people—some high-ranking professionals
included—do not have to make decisions, if they do not wish to. Obviously, many choose to make decisions, but they elect to decide and are
not required to decide. For some, departmental activities are one grand
round of debating, discussion, more debating, and more discussion. The
payoff for sophistry is rather good, considering the investment. Men have
been promoted on the passion of their verbal convictions, rarely having
been required to influence the life of one child, but having persuasively
proclaimed their regard for the lives of all children. Further, the System
is such that one learns quickly of the peril of making certain decisions
and the impossibility of making others. Rather than torment oneself with
the uselessness of trying to "buck the System" (and one hears this time
and time again), many men make their peace with it. They give expression
to their good intentions, good training, and anger in activities that appear
vigorous and dynamic but are empty repetitions, which are heard by no
one of any importance or influence, but reassure the speaker that he is
doing his job and that he is on the side of the "good" people. (We should
not discount the cathartic effect such activities provide the speaker.)

DECISION-MAKING AND ACCOUNTABILITY

Few people are forced to make decisions because few people are accountable for specific programs or activities. Obviously, those people

who are accountable for specific activities must make decisions. How are these decisions made? A better question might be, "What causes an individual to make one decision rather than another?" For many months, my experiences at 15 Ashburton Place puzzled me because I was completely unable to "read" the System vis-à-vis decision-making. For example, several of what I considered to be very reasonable requests were denied by various business offices without explanation or apparent reason. Other requests were ignored. Still others were quickly and categorically honored to our complete satisfaction. There was no apparent logic to these responses. It seemed as if some mad table of random numbers was at work here, approving one thing, denying another, and ignoring the third. It must be admitted that, in each instance when I did require an explanation for a decision, there was some law or regulation or policy that seemed to lend credulity and wisdom to the decision. However, on other occasions, similar requests—in equal violation of the regulation or policy—would be granted. All one can do is speculate about the basis for decision-making at 15 Ashburton Place—as, obviously, one can't read the decision-maker's mind and there seems no logical pattern to his activities. My speculations have led me to three insecure and tentative conclusions: 1) It is thought much simpler and less perilous to make no decision, or to decide negatively, than to decide positively. 2) The System makes it more satisfying to decide negatively than to decide positively. 3) The process of working with laws, regulations, and policies encourages their utilization to prohibit activities and developments rather than to promulgate such activities and developments.

Because so few people have accountability and, consequently, so few people may make a final decision about a matter, most requests for one thing or another pass through several hands if, eventually, they are to be approved. With the exception of upper echelon business office personnel, there are few so-called "middle management" professionals who make final *positive* decisions. In innumerable situations, these individuals may make final *negative* decisions, i.e., they have the authority to ignore or deny a request but do not have the authority (or do not believe they have the authority) to approve it. Further, to approve a request for funds, personnel, a specific program, a transfer of personnel, or some other change from the "usual" is to—in effect—approve the wisdom of that action and certify the legality of that action. To ignore or deny the request permits the decision-maker freedom from accountability for his decision, yet permits him to make a decision. Inasmuch as the laws, the regulations, and the policies are not always without ambiguity and discrepancies and are, in fact, frequently open to multiple interpretations, one can more easily find his safety in that part of the law or policy that permits the decision-maker to ignore or deny than in that part that permits him to approve and, thus, requires him to stand behind his decision.

Whatever the central cause or causes are, there are many more negative than positive decisions made at 15 Ashburton Place.

As the decision-maker rarely has the authority to approve, he is caught continuously in the frustration of "shuffling papers" from his desk to a higher desk, and of getting entangled in the red tape, bureaucracy, and inertia that are companion to such activities. It appears to be so much "cleaner," manly, and authoritative to deny a request than to involve oneself in the frustrations implicit in passing on the request to higher authority. It is, therefore, not difficult to surmise that there are negative decisions made whose sole purpose is to "satisfy" the decision-maker. And further, this narcissistic behavior is understandable, if not completely forgivable, in light of the untenable position most decision-makers are forced into. That is to say, most decision-makers may make *no* decision or *a* "no" decision but very infrequently have the option to make a positive decision. It is this set of circumstances that, I believe, causes more unhappiness and job dissatisfaction, frustration, and mutual ill will at 15 Ashburton Place than any other—including problems involving salaries, working conditions, job pensions, and the enormousness and complexity of the departmental mission.

Lastly, the innumerable frustrations and roadblocks one encounters in the decision-making process must eventually wear down a man's will to move things along in the proper direction and to make the proper decisions. From my limited observations, it appears that the Commonwealth laws and the Departmental regulations and policies are used—not to facilitate or permit positive decisions to be made—but to determine if it is legally possible or departmentally justifiable if a positive decision should be made. Essentially, and I know there is a fine line of distinction here between what may be and may not be legal or prudent, the departmental *modus operandi* is to, first, find something in the laws or regulations or policies that prohibit one from doing something rather than view these statutes for the purpose of finding justification for doing something. I have observed that departmental officials do not comb the statutes to find new opportunities to offer services and facilities, but they do comb the statutes for any prohibitions or incumbrances to a request that has been presented to them. Laws and regulations and policies being what they are—and Massachusetts being a Commonwealth long in the mental health business—it is often very difficult to "get something done" in the face of governmental and departmental restrictions, precedents, and inertia. I do not wish to communicate the impression that I am advocating flagrant violation of laws or regulations. Nor do I believe it unwise to proceed carefully and thoughtfully before decisions are made that affect the lives of patients, or the careers of personnel. However, if a System is based on convictions and standards and precedents that make it easier, less perilous, and more satisfying to make negative decisions than to make positive decisions, to the degree that this assumption is true laws, regulations and policies will be interpreted in the light of their prohibitionary powers rather than in the light of their enabling powers.

THE "WE-THEY" SYNDROME

There are a good many "we-they" dichotomies emanating from and funneling to 15 Ashburton Place. My observations lead me to believe that these dichotomies are always pragmatically real yet, in essence, artificial, more destructive than constructive, and usually based on various forms of bigotry, ignorance, and disrespect for particular "types" of individuals, their jobs or training, or their location of employment. To illustrate the "We-They" Syndrome, it may be helpful to discuss some of the common distinctions, or labels, used in the department, like: "Across the Street," "Professional Staff–Business Staff," "Unions," "Central Office–The Field," "Mental Health–Mental Retardation," "Parents–Professionals," "Physicians–Non-Physicians," and "Ethnic Mafias."

At 15 Ashburton Place, "Across the Street" *always* refers to the State House, the executive government, and employees in the executive branch. The people "Across the Street" include everyone from the governor to individual legislators to personnel in the various divisions of the executive branch. In one form or another, I suspect that every department of state or federal government has its "Across the Street." In some state capitols, "Across the Street" may be cross town and, obviously, the term used at 15 Ashburton Place would not be appropriate. However, it is unlikely that a "We-They" feeling does not exist between every department of state government and those in the executive branch who guide the legislation, promulgate the budgets, and make other vital executive decisions. There are various ways staff members of state departments attempt to deal with the people "Across the Street." Some spend a great deal of time "Across the Street," many of these on official business representing the commissioner or on request to appear before a legislative committee or at an executive office. Others, however, spend a good deal of time "Across the Street," doing errands for legislators or executive personnel, establishing and confirming their "ins," and currying one kind of favor or another. Still other members of a state department avoid "Crossing the Street," almost at any cost. They have learned that the risks are greater than the possible benefits. No doubt as a reflection of my own personality and style of behavior, during my year with the Department of Mental Health, not once did I walk "Across the Street" without either being asked by "them" or sent by "us." Rightly or wrongly, I concluded that a state official who is responsible for the place-ment of citizens in state institutions—where the waiting lists are inter-minably long and, therefore, there are no waiting lists—should not be-come too friendly with legislators and should never be in their debt. I entered state service with the impression (from the many stories I had heard) that the "only way" to receive approval for the placement of a person in a state school for the mentally retarded was to enlist the support of a prominent legislator who, in turn, would request such placement through his friends at the Department of Mental Health. Although, during the year, I had numerous such requests from legislators and other state officials, I can honestly claim that *no* person was placed during that year *because* a legislator requested or demanded such placement. Further, at no time did I receive abuse or any form of argumentation from a legislator after we explained to him why an individual should not be placed in the state school or why it was not possible to place that person at that par-ticular time. After it was clearly established how people were to be placed and what the situation was in each state school, we were never confronted with unreasonable demands or requests for special services or special considerations for constituents of specific legislators. I learned that most legislators are very reasonable people and, once the facts of a situation are explained to them and they are satisfied that every possible effort has been or will be extended in behalf of their constituents, they are satisfied to permit the Department to do what is can—whatever that might be—for those for whom they are seeking help. Lastly, I have found that if legislators or other state officials are guaranteed (by your own behavior and reputation) that your office will treat *everyone* equally and without special advantage, they will not press you with demands for unfair con-sideration. All of the above is to suggest, at least from my viewpoint, that whatever ill will and mistrust exists between one side of our street and the other, much of it is due to a prejudice and ignorance about the other side. My infrequent contacts with the people "Across the Street" found them surprisingly like those on our side of the street, just as reasonable and equally concerned with the distressful conditions confronting us.

It's possible that our office was able to achieve this "state of things" because, not only did we not give special favors, we never asked for them. However, I truly believe that we did achieve this condition—which I believe to have been one of our important achievements that year—because, essentially, executive officers and people in the legislature are, as human beings, no better or worse than other state employees. There is such a complex as "Across the Street" because, I think, people huddle in their own little worlds afraid of the unknown other person and not daring to discover that he is, just, another person.

There exists a dichotomy between the professional staff and the business staff of the department. It is not an "Across the Street" dichotomy but it is an "Upstairs-Downstairs" one. The "Boys Upstairs" are the business office people and "Downstairs"–anywhere or everywhere or "never to be found"–are the "Doctors," the professional people. The differences between these two groups are many and very subtle, and it is neither possible to understand all of these nor possible to adequately discuss the few I do understand. However, it is well known that most professional staff members are on higher salary levels than the business staff and, on the other hand, the business staff have major control of such items as purchasing, new positions, and the interpretation of state and departmental laws and regulations. Many central office professional staff are not "tied down" to a nine-to-five office schedule and, consequently, their whereabouts or activities are varied—some comment, "to say the least." Undoubtedly, suspicion exists among those people who are required to spend most of their working hours at 15 Ashburton Place that some professional staff do not spend all of their required working hours on behalf of the Department of Mental Health and in discharging their responsibilities as state employees. Every now and then, one hears such terms as "private practice," "consulting," "salary supplementation," and "goofing off." At least equally, professional staff members distrust business staff. However, their criticisms run along different directions. Mainly, the professionals whisper or rage about "favoritism," "capriciousness," "unilateral decisions," "high-handedness," "bureaucracy," "paper shuffling," and on and on it goes. To be sure, there are some professional staff (as there are such people everywhere) who abuse their privileges and shamefully neglect their responsibilities. Also, the department has its share (but no more than its share) of bureaucrats, paper shufflers, and those who are plainly unfair. However, I believe that the important controversy (if there is one, and I should hasten to add that there are some who do not believe there is) between professional and business staff in the department revolves about the superior job status of the one group and the superior decision-making authority of the other. I do not know how to go about developing better relationships between these two groups. However, I do believe that, if such relationships are to be developed, the first step is to find more adequate ways to encourage individuals from downstairs and upstairs to interact.

Mental health is an industry and, as with all industries today, it has its unions and union problems. If it would serve a clear purpose, one could relate story after story—true stories that I witnessed or was, in some way, a participant in—concerning the evil influence of unions and union members on our mental health and mental retardation programs. It would be grist for those who buy from the anti-union mill to hear about malfeasance or misfeasance or nonfeasance that was attributable directly to union influence or union members. On the other hand, one can relate equally compelling anecdotes about management and management staff in mental health. Albeit very interesting and extraordinarily entertaining, such stories rarely do any good or shed any light on a situation. It is enough for me to say that I do not view the development of unions in the field of mental health as unmixed blessings; on the other hand, I neither view all of our management or management practices as unmixed blessings. My conviction about the union-management dichotomy is that to the degree unions have taken advantage of management in mental health, management bodies have taken equal advantage of unions. Whether one group is more right or more wrong is both a specious and senseless question. Certainly, there are differences between the two groups. However, I do not believe that these are so much differences between people as they are differences in objectives and, to some extent, differences in means to attain objectives. Certainly, as a group, management is better educated, more highly trained, and better compensated than labor. Certainly, as a group, labor provides more direct resident care and has more resident contact than management. These, and innumerable other differences, we can agree upon. However, I don't believe these are the differences that cause the deep undercurrent of labor unhappiness and distrust and management hostility and fearfulness. On two occasions, I invited the chief state union executive, members of his staff, and union representatives to meet with our central office staff and our superintendents and directors of facilities for the mentally retarded. What was confirmed for me, during these and other meetings, was the continuing theme in all dialogues I've participated in with union members. It isn't higher salaries that they are asking for, not because they don't want (or deserve) higher salaries; salaries are fixed by the legislature, and state departments have absolutely no control of this matter. What union members ask for—continuously—in one way or another, using one type of verbiage or another, is: respect, fair treatment, and honesty in mutual dealings. Time and time again, I listened to union members asking only to be treated with dignity, as human beings, and with appreciation for their efforts and accomplishments. Ironically—possibly, predictably—management is asking for exactly the same things: respect, fair treatment, and honesty in mutual dealings. I have met some union members and local union officials who offend or annoy me. However, so do a few of the so-called management team. While, on the one hand, I have been aghast at certain union stances and practices, I developed, on the other hand, after but one or two meetings a deep respect and trust for the highest state union official in our Commonwealth. I imagine that management will always resist labor and vice versa—and, further, some believe that this is the way things should be in the best of all worlds—but this resistance should be limited to single issues and not be fed by some false image that the other side is "different" and must be treated as an enemy.

In our department, as in all departments that have both consultative and direct service responsibilities, a dichotomy exists between the central office (or regional office) and the field. There are those of us who are responsible for overall supervision, coordination, interdepartmental liaison, and statewide planning. There are others among us who have direct supervisory responsibility for clients or patients. The dichotomy is strong and often heated. Sometimes differences are put in terms of line-staff authority. Less charitably, they are discussed in terms of those who coordinate versus those who do things for people. Superintendents have complained to me that they are on duty seven days a week for 24 hours a day (which, in reality, is impossible) while central office or regional staff are on duty five days a week for eight hours a day. Central office staff claim they must administer and supervise all state programs and all facets of these programs that they are responsible for (which, in reality, is impossible) while superintendents have responsibility for only very limited programs and areas. Essentially, this dichotomy is very similar to the problem continuously facing the researcher with a limited (however generous) budget and resources. To the degree he restricts his sample, he may study more variables and, to the degree he restricts his variables, he may increase his sample. However, there must always be a compromise between the size of the sample one is studying or treating and the extent of involvement with those he is studying or treating. It became clear to me that the true dichotomy between the so-called field and the central office was not one involving different degrees of dedication, responsibility, or hours worked, but one involving small samples versus the entire population, on the one hand, and intensive involvement versus superficial or indirect involvement, on the other hand. If we, in the central office and in the field, could but make our peace with, and understand, the inevitable need to either restrict samples or restrict variables—much as the researcher has made his peace—we might learn that the central office–field dichotomy is, at best, a trivial one and, sometimes, a destructive one. Insofar as I understand the dichotomy of central office–field or staff-line, the important difference is not that one group does "better than" or "more" than does the other group. The important difference is that one group works a little bit for everyone and the other a great deal for a few. There is but a finite amount of time, energy, and talent each man can bring to his work and to his mission. It would seem that, by this time, we could agree that the world is a big place and there should be enough room for anyone who has a serious purpose and a dedication to that purpose.

There are other dichotomies that flow from or to the Department of Mental Health. The separation of the field of mental health from the field of mental retardation is a serious one and, often, causes many problems. A similar separation involves the distinction between those who are physicians and those who aren't. It might be sufficient to relate an illuminating incident. Several years ago, before assuming my position with the department, I was asked by the then Commissioner of Mental Health to serve on a "blue ribbon" committee charged with the development of a plan for a diagnostic and research center in mental retardation for the city of Boston. A member of the committee was one of the most distinguished psychologists in the world, a man whose work I have admired for many, many years. The one contribution he made to our joint effort that I will always remember was the recommendation that this center be constructed adjacent to a medical school and that ramps be built leading from the medical school to the center. Our colleague attempted to impress upon us that, without this contiguity, we could not (nor should not) expect any involvement by medical faculty in this program. He indicated that it was not terribly important whether the center was constructed within easy commuting distance of graduate schools or schools of education or schools of social work. It *had* to be constructed contiguous to a medical center. I do not want to belabor this dichotomy between physicians and non-physicians; nor do I consider myself prejudiced against the medical profession. Having been brought up in a culture that reveres medicine, if anything, I am usually blind to the imperfections in this field that are continuously pointed out to me by much more jaundiced colleagues. Yet I am uneasy sometimes, especially when faced with the kind of situation that occurred recently. In a program quite apart from mental health and mental retardation, several colleagues and I have been studying the education of psychiatrists. As part of this project, we arranged for the supervision of psychiatry residents in a program preparing them to teach. For reasons that are not important to this discussion, it was necessary for a distinguished professor of education to meet with one of the psychiatry residents. The professor of psychiatry suggested to the professor of education that *he* come to the medical school to meet with this student, in view of the student's heavy schedule.

I have heard, time and time again, about differences between parents and professionals. Again, this is undoubtedly a reflection of my own personality and experiences, but I can say very truthfully that during this past year and—in fact—during my twenty-year career in mental retardation, I have never been confronted by parents' groups with unreasonable requests and I have rarely been confronted by individual parents with unreasonable requests. My experience has been that there are no more—and no fewer—unreasonable parents than there are unreasonable professionals or unreasonable any other group of people.

The most interesting "we-they" phenomenon that I observed during the past year was the "Insider-Outsider" division that is associated with ethnic power. In every large city where great numbers of immigrant families settled, particular ethnic groups sought opportunities and developed strength in certain professions and with certain departments of civil government or sectors of private industry. As such groups broke down the barriers of discrimination and hostility, their co-religionists or national brethren followed in the footsteps of those who led the way. Thus, in New York City, most of the school teachers and most of the school principals and administrators are Jewish—first, because there are many Jews living in New York City and, second, because the school department was a receptive and "upward mobility" type of organization that the children in the ghetto would predictably aspire toward. In a similar fashion, the Irish came to dominate politics and state civil service in Massachusetts. The Pole has his "bag" in Chicago and the Japanese his in San Francisco. And, yet, saying these words so rationally, and truly believing that we understand them, does not prevent men from discussing the New York City school crisis in terms of Jewish domination and control and does not prevent men from setting black against Jew (lunatic as that sounds) and Jewish teachers against blacks (after the evidence, still absolutely unbelievable). In Massachusetts, we are reputed to have our "Irish Mafia." I believe it exists to the degree that Jewish teachers control the public schools in New York and Japanese grape growers control the valleys of the west coast. In fact or not, however, believing that such an Irish Mafia exists causes the same kinds of difficulty—on both sides of the ethnic fence—as believing Jews control the New York City schools.

It will be no surprise to those who are acquainted with my work to read again that I do not believe men are very different, one from another. I believe that we are different to the degree that living with each other is interesting, more than that, necessary, but not so different that living with each other should ever lead to irreconcilable conflict. Possibly, the following letter, received by me in January of 1969 illustrates the essential interdependence of man and the essential goodness that is found in man—in both the most commonly expected and surprisingly unpredictable places. Possibly, men such as Jim C_____ will, in our generations, teach us the fallacy of the "we-they" syndrome:

> Dear Sir:
> I am writing to you in response to your most anguishing article. That you published it incomplete, when you obviously had more information should be causing great concern and torment among the mothers, fathers, brothers,

and sisters. You have told of and shown me a spectre of horror almost beyond the average person's grasp. I wonder how many people asked, was that my Tommy he saw, was that him cowed and neglected in that cell. Was that my boy that he stood and watched being kicked repeatedly or do they ask as I do, did you see my brother sitting on those bleachers staring at a blank T.V. waiting. . . . It's entirely possible, for my brother is in an institution for the mentally retarded in _____. What is it like there, Doctor. When you, or I should say, when I ask them how he is doing, they assure me that he is getting the best possible care. Just what is the best "possible" care that the State of _____ affords as to the following: hygiene, pleasant surroundings, schools, and training facilities with recreation areas with abundant equipment, competence of the staff as opposed to their position, volunteer organizations, is the administrator politically appointed or the result of competitive examination by a Civil Service board, brutality or unusual "punishment" (i.e., restraint), ratio of staff actually involved directly with the care and supervision of patients to the number of patients. You see, sir, before he was placed or to put it more accurately, railroaded and abandoned for some nebulous reason that my parents are procrastinating about, well, anyway, they put him in _____ Mental Hospital, _____ and I still don't know why. He wasn't violent or hard to handle, although you had to watch him pretty close or he would be into something which would be normal for a child of his mentality. Well I suppose that you are familiar with _____'s mental health program. It's the best going. How do you think of moving him from a known pleasant and healthy environment to _____? I think that if it is not a progressive institution where he will be loved and cared for properly I can put enough pressure on my parents to get him out. I'm in a pretty bad place myself, and I'll be here for a long time, but as they say, I brought it on myself. But any hell that my brother is going through is because of my parents and not because he did anything wrong. Obviously I'm not in any position to demand anything, though I am a criminal and must live behind walls of stone and steel, I still have feelings. I still believe in justice. I still believe in helping those who can't help themselves. I laugh, I cry, I feel compassion, tenderness, hurt and shame though I am a crook, a criminal, and the scum of the earth in the eyes of God and common man. I guess I'm still human too. For I want to help my brother if he needs help, but not only him, but the tens of thousands of others less fortunate than myself. I can't do much, I suppose, compared to others, but I can do something. Thank you for reading my letter. Let me know what I can do to help.

Respectfully yours,
Jim C_____

THE MERETRICIOUS SYSTEM AND UNCIVIL SERVICE

The beautiful concepts of the merit system and the civil service, concepts that are basic to our fundamental form of democratic government, have fallen on evil days. There is not very much I want to, or can, say about merit in state government and the civil service system. However, I do believe that we must find a better way to recruit, select, promote, and encourage state civil servants—from the most unskilled level to positions requiring highest attainments in education and experience. We must face squarely the knowledge that time is always on the side of the mediocre and a system based on "putting in one's time" for promotion, more favorable assignments and duties, and other benefits is a system that promotes mediocrity; it is a system that programs for and reinforces slothfulness and inefficiency and, consequently, these are the products it deserves. Why should having served in the military for 25 years have anything to do with one's standing on a civil service list for chief social worker or chief psychologist? Does a system make sense that requires all new attendant employees to work every weekend, every holiday, and the least attractive "shifts" so that employees with seniority may receive all weekends and holidays off and may work the most desirable shifts? Especially, in the face of severe staff shortages at our state schools, can such a system be justified when prospective employees are eager to accept positions but not under conditions they deem intolerable? Yet, we continue to permit these policies, on the one hand, and decry the sixty vacancies for attendants at the state school, on the other hand. I don't have any better answers to these problems than other people have proposed. Further, in principle, I support a merit system and the concepts of civil service. However, I do not believe that our system today has merit—both as a system and as a way to reward deserving employees. Nor do I believe that the civil service is anything but another kind of spoils system, one that's different from Boss Tweed's but one that is now based on similar operating principles for the purpose of achieving similar objectives.

DEFINING GOVERNMENTAL UTOPIA

I worry for planners who plan for a livelihood, that is, those whose major assignments are to plan. All too often, I have observed and participated with them in planning changes in our state programs for the mentally retarded, and found they are given neither the resources nor encouragement to implement these changes. As a result, we have a great many thoughtful, oftentimes exquisite, plans that lie fallow gathering dust on administrators' bookshelves or on desks buried under avalanches of reports of commissions and reports of advisory boards. The lives of decisionmakers would be happier and more productive if they had environments at their disposal that permitted both planning *and* implementation. All organizations are in a constant flux and, at any one time, represent a balance between the stability of the System and the pressure for change. To me, governmental utopia would provide a System that is stable—i.e., a System that is reliable and tested, one that can be counted upon to deliver goods and services—while it would always have at its command options to change parts of the System radically or the entire structure of the System evolutionally. For me, governmental utopia means stability and comfort and reliance, on the one hand, and options and dynamism, on the other hand. While it is quite understandable that we have not achieved utopia, it is regrettable, to the extreme, that we are barely on the right road. Our optimism must lie in the knowledge that now, at least, we may have stumbled onto that road. I believe we have, or people such as myself would never have been permitted to study the things we have studied and say the things we are saying.

CHAPTER 15

Bureaucratizing Values

Since the beginning of human experience, man has behaved as if freedom means more to him than his life. Yet, even more important to him has been the need to belong to his community, to be part of a fabric larger and more enduring than his fragile self. This is why, among the ancient Greeks, to be banished was a punishment more severe than death. Only recently have we come to realize that many recipients of our human services have been punished by *both* banishment and loss of freedom in socially and often physically restrictive environments. As a result, uncounted commissions and agencies, bureaus and bureaucrats are today engaged in righting the wrongs under the flag of the "least restrictive alternative."

I too have grieved for those we punished in the name of kindness; and I am glad that at last some of our official bureaus have taken human rights as an official concern. Yet, the term "least restrictive alternative" is one I have misgivings about. Though better than outright banishment or imprisonment, it nevertheless implies an environment and conditions which I would not want for myself. So long as we speak of "least restrictive," we are speaking of "restrictive"; and no "alternative" could be my "first choice." Certainly, we must work at minimizing the harm our society does, but in this chapter I would also like to look past this task to a society that maximizes good.

There is, however, a more immediate—less utopian—concern I wish to explore in this chapter. The issue we confront in human services is one of very fundamental human values—freedom and community. Yet, our hopes and plans for securing these values for everyone are invested in government agencies and public laws, in an attempt to codify and mechanize the "delivery" of values. In this, I'm afraid, we have seriously overestimated the power of bureaucracy. That's why, in the last analysis, the concept of "least restrictive alternative" will remain, even in its most precise definition, no better than an exactly specified degree of banishment.

This essay will appear in J. Joffee & G. Albee (Eds.), *Prevention Through Political Action and Social Change* (Vol. 5), Hanover, N.H.: University Press of New England, in press.

UNDERSTANDING TRANSITIONS

In the past 30 years, the mission of the mental retardation field has changed in crucial ways. In the 1950s, it was to provide expertise and professional treatment to those afflicted with retardation. Our plea was to the nation, but our focus was clinical. To the extent that we addressed society at large, it was only to ask for support of our professional efforts— that is, to provide funding. Today, our primary work seems to be one of transforming not mentally retarded people but the society in which they live. Certainly we are still concerned with special applications of, for example, medicine and education. But the pivotal concerns of our field are now societal—gaining community acceptance of mentally retarded people, changing the attitudes of typical children toward handicapped children, securing for mentally retarded people the legal and human rights which the rest of us enjoy. Our major benchmark of this century was created with the passage by Congress of Public Law 94-142. In short, our activities have assumed a significant political thrust.

One of the characteristics of political activity is that it can seldom expect to succeed by boldly seeking its final goal. A program must be broken down into politically feasible steps. In part, this is necessary because society would repel any attempt at wholesale change—it must be urged and lured by small, often circuitous, steps toward the larger goal. But in still larger part, this is necessary because the goals of social change are invariably unclear. Not only is it difficult to specify what we would wish, it is usually impossible to anticipate what the achievement of our wish would bring in actual practice. History is replete with political visions turned to nightmare by success; and even "successful" social experiments more often than not turn out rather different from what their authors initially had as their objectives. For example, today's "bad guys," the segregators, were our heroes of the 1940s, the 1950s, and the 1960s, and can well be heroes again if society says it's had its fill of mainstreaming, normalization, and PL 94-142. And who knows, psychoanalysis could make a comeback, behavior modification can be declared unworkable, and the trains could again be made to run on time. Almost anything tried with enthusiasm works well for awhile. Then there are unexpected consequences, then disillusionment, then nothing seems to work.

Though our goals may be unclear, we in this field know enough about them to specify some essential elements of the future we have in mind. Mentally retarded persons will have to have certain legal rights which have been denied them—public education, public standards of health care, a fair chance at economic self-support, and the incidental rewards of self-support. Because most of us don't have serious doubt that a society which grants these and other basic rights to everyone will be a better society, we don't worry about what that society will be like in detail. But it should be apparent to us that, although we needn't worry, we *really don't* know what that society will be like—except that it will be different, and that there will be many points of great strain for all of us in the change. Whatever the price may be, we are committed to pay it for the sake of a better world.

However, not only is the future obscure, the present as well is often hard to assess. One of the lessons implied by the suddenness with which the rights of handicapped people emerged as a social issue is that we haven't understood the nature of society as it is presently constituted. If we had understood the social implications of labeling, institutional segregation, and devaluing stereotypes, most of us would have acted quite differently 15 or 20 or 30 years ago. Thus, the political and social process in which PL 94-142 is but one step is a powerful thrust from a world we don't understand very well toward a world we can't predict and, quite probably, won't ever understand well.

This is certainly not to say we shouldn't continue that thrust. In the real world, the "facts" are never all in and analyses and understandings are always imperfect. This is why action has to be based on judgment rather than deduction. This is also why there is often so much disagreement among people who share similar goals; their judgments of what should be the next step toward the goal can vary widely. But though we all know these things—that our understanding is imperfect, that the consequences of what we passionately advocate today may be unanticipated or even undesirable—nevertheless, we must act as though there could be no doubt about what we do. The success of any program of social reform depends too much on decisiveness and confidence to permit the awareness of our human condition to dampen it. Thus, PL 94-142 has its enthusiastic advocates not because the law is "the" answer, but because it is perceived to be an important step in the right direction; and those who feel that the next urgent order of business is to create jobs for handicapped adults have their eyes on the immediate benefits to the economic and social status of handicapped people rather than on global economic factors. Obviously, these and other programs have merit. Each nudges us closer to the Good Society. But also obviously, each of them is in a sense irrelevant to what we want as a goal. PL 94-142 is quite clearly a transitional device; no one could suppose that its reimbursement incentives and formulas should constitute a lasting form of justice for all citizens. Like affirmative action, it can be justified, if at all, only as a part of the remedy, not as a state of health. And providing jobs for handicapped people is also important as a step, but hardly begins to address the factors which have heretofore oppressed mentally retarded people. At this time, when the mentally retarded are excluded almost entirely from job opportunities, we are justified in demanding the creation of those opportunities. Yet, in the long run we will have to reconcile this demand with the fact of widespread unemployment in society as a whole, and even with our nation's uncertain fortune in the economy of the world.

It would be foolish of me to offer solutions to such complicated and long range problems. But neither can I bring myself to concentrate on the daily business of our current programs. Just like those we were enthusiastically promoting 20 years ago, it seems all too likely that these programs contain new prejudices and misunderstandings. We should begin to look for them and clarify them now, before they become too firmly established in our thinking, our practice, and even in our laws— that is, before they become a new set of intransigent institutions for us to evacuate.

The temptation is to take the easy way and write about PL 94-142, to discuss the various ingredients of that law: individual educational plan, mainstreaming, zero reject, and of course the topic of the day, least restrictive alternative. The problem with these terms and others like them is that, at present, they are little more than shibboleths and slogans. We simply don't have an adequate understanding of what they mean. That may be a harsh conclusion but there aren't many people around who would deny that there are lots of different definitions for each of the aforementioned concepts, some of them in conflict with one another. So I will take the hard road, which is for me the easy way out, which is to get to ideas that go beyond the current law or, indeed, beyond the issue of the handicapped themselves. If we are going to offer mentally retarded people the freedoms and benefits of our society, we should look at what it is we have to offer. To protect a person in spite of himself is to sometimes protect him from living. To avoid potential dangers is sometimes to avoid life. Even for the retarded, possibly especially for the retarded, the rule should not be to reduce risk taking. Rather, it should encourage certain reasonable risk taking. Risk taking is unavoidable for those who would develop well. To legislate prohibition of virtually any potential hazard is to also inhibit one's opportunity to mature. Anybody who ever mattered took risks. Consequently, anybody who matters, that is, any human being, is entitled to as few restrictions as society can restrain itself to impose. Equally, as educators, we must be committed to the belief that people can learn and mature in their judgment and that, when all is said and done, this is the only protection from the dangers of life.

WHAT'S A LEAST RESTRICTIVE ENVIRONMENT?

What's going on in the United States? How free are we? Never mind the mentally retarded, how free are you? Let's take a look, a "once over lightly" look at the businesses, the schools, the arts, the religions, and the government. The Talmudists have the luxury—the divine responsibility—to read word by word, letter by letter, a tiny mark compared to an even tinier mark. Because they no longer have legal power over the people, they could be legalists of the narrowest variety. Contrast the founding fathers of this country who needed a Supreme Court to interpret the law in the context of the times. To appreciate the concept of "Least Restrictiveness" requires, I think, a long arm's look at the whole of society's institutions, and not the Talmudist's, nor the scientist's nor compulsive's special talents. That is, I think this concept should be understood as a whole and not by its parts. Of course, the Catch-22 is that the concept is too complex to be understood that way. And, of course, there is too much to know about all of those institutions to get it all down here. But you live here as well as I do, and you know what's going on as well as I do. Consequently, these remarks are intended to do no more than to make us want to think about what we already know.

First of all, it seems to be as true today as it was when Calvin Coolidge said it years ago, that "business is the business of America." That's why we needed stock exchanges and antitrust laws. That's why we need law schools, corporations, and Madison Avenue and much of what's on television and much of what is on people's minds. That's what explains General Electric's claim that progress is their most important product, though nobody believes them. And it's in the name of business that DuPont can bellow from today to doomsday that chemistry makes better things for better living, but nobody will believe DuPont. Because it's good for business, Nestle's can get away with building powdered milk factories in third world countries which will be as lethal to babies there as uncontrolled asbestos plants are here.

It seems impossible to conjure up the march of American business without its accompaniment of nonsense and outright harm. Our system and its freedoms have been designed to foster the creation of wealth and power, not to control them when they are used or pursued irresponsibly. And all of that is why Ralph Nader is now inevitable as well as necessary, though terribly wrong. He is incontestably right that "they" are bastards (my interpretation). "They" couldn't be anything else because the profit-motive and the free market are utterly indifferent to human values—unless those values affect sales. However, Nader begins to be wrong when he suggests that what "they" are doing, from price-fixing to exploding gas tanks, represents some sort of aberration that could be corrected without attacking the business of America at its heart. And Nader is quite wrong in his avalanche of proposed laws for us to control the bastards. (Again, my interpretation). The effect of those regulations is likely to be as destructive as "their" lawlessness. We betray the human race and, in the final accounting, the individual as well, when we deny that the world must necessarily be a dangerous place—or when we don't deny it but prohibit people from making potentially dangerous decisions. I started all of this out by saying that most of us would pay high prices for our freedom, and I'm claiming now that Nader exacts more than I'm willing to pay for my safety.

American business has given us the four-day week and the two-home and three-car family, while it's given us the choice of either destroying our health or our freedoms. Seizing upon the wonders of American technology, big business has made us free, but within narrower than ever confines. And it's given us the time to pursue virtually any hobby or interest we have, but it's also enticed us to sit in drugged stupors watching a lighted box. In America, only the truly brave, strong-willed, innovative person exploits the genius of the American system while he or she rejects that part which gums everything up, which makes us less well off than our grandparents.

Why is it so difficult for one parent to gain permission to teach his child at home, and for another parent to gain permission to help the teacher teach his child in school? Schools seem to be unnecessarily restrictive. Schools today teach bad attitudes about what was once a national activity which most parents accepted as their parental responsibility: teaching their young. After all, schools only became necessary because society accumulated too much knowledge for parents to handle both their vocations and their teaching functions. But there remained important things for parents to teach. But they've been excluded from sharing that responsibility. With technology being what it is today, and with so many people spending their time sitting around doing nothing, society may not need the kinds of schools and teachers it now has. What I am getting at is that most everybody today has the time and the potential competence to teach something to somebody. And one would think that most people would enjoy the opportunity to teach if they could believe in themselves sufficiently to enter into such activity. Teaching could be like jury duty, although if it were like jury duty practically everyone would ask to be excused. Most people would feel they have nothing to teach. Today, even teachers ask to be excused. They too have nothing to teach, except in their specializations. The French teacher seems to be able only to teach French, and the science teacher will only teach chemistry, not even biology. Everybody seems to have excuses when it comes to teaching something outside of their narrow ranges of interest and preparation. All of this is another way of saying that, with the exception of a few genuine professors, virtually everybody in America lives in a very restricted intellectual environment. And furthermore, virtually everyone seems to be content in claiming that they know hardly anything that other people might find worthwhile.

Things could be different. A friend of mine has the idea that a person should learn the names of trees in his neighborhood, that when he walks to work it's good to be able to distinguish the sycamore maple from the sycamore. It helps one better know where he is going, and even why. Knowing what to call things makes all the difference in life. Ask Noah. This friend of mine studies bees. He knows what most of us forgot, that they're absolutely essential for our lives to continue, and that in no sense are they in competition with humans. But while he and the bee know that, we don't. As we shoo bees away, we shoo life away. Humans seem to behave strangely at times. There are millions and millions of potentially excellent teachers around, people who could interest us in trees, and bees, and aerodynamics, and how the body works, and how to make a kite or bait a hook. And yet, in spite of this knowledge which everyone really knows, our "best minds" have come to the conclusion that the only people who may teach must be certified and suitably degreed. There is more to this problem before us than what's the least restrictive environment for the mentally retarded!

There was once a time—admittedly a dangerous time—when learning and living weren't governed by certification and regulation and legislation. It was the time when our idea of freedom started its development toward its present shape. From "Sweet Land of Liberty" to "Born Free," from Tchaikovsky to Tin Pan Alley, we have been sung to, entranced, and bombarded with cannon in the name of liberty. If musicians thought like lawyers and spoke like legislators, they would serenade us in the names of least restrictive environment, zero reject, and mainstreaming. And if the prophets and the psalmists had thought like bureaucrats, they too would have told stories about zero reject rather than about strangers in the land of Canaan. But what was once one—religion and the law—is now, by law, separate. And so what was once the predominating influence, our religion, today predominates only on Sunday, and even then for a minority in our society. Today, the law prevails over all beings and institutions, over religion itself, and our freedom must live between its lines.

The law is concerned with who is and who isn't restricted. There are forced restrictions (of convicted felons, people dangerous to themselves or others, people committed for this or that reason) and voluntary restrictions (by monks, recluses, and by the family who knows what's best for the child or other relative). There are those restricted by prejudices (Blacks and those with certain physical conditions are restricted). The law and our customs have a lot to say about who shall be and who shall not be restricted, and in what ways. In our "let it all hang out" culture today, "least" is best. But the Puritans thought differently. The mode today is the less restriction the better. But also, the mode today is concerned more with the body than with the soul. Today, the mode is about what we do rather than about what we think. It seems that most people today would be satisfied with being physically unrestricted although mentally enchained. So today, what looks like a nearly completely unrestricted, unfettered, unhampered, "doing your own thing" society is, in another view, a culture that works by rote response to the members and by communication through intermediaries. It may be fair to say that ours is at once the most unrestricted and restricted society ever created. *So what's a least restrictive environment?*

PRIVILEGED EXTENSIONS OF FREEDOM

Least restrictive alternatives cannot be understood out of the context of a particular culture under examination. Whether an environment is restricted or free depends on where that environment is, who is in it, and how we look at it.

Certainly, the least restrictive alternative in Nazi Germany was not at all the same as the least restrictive alternative in the United States. And the least restrictive alternative in the United States of 1800 was not at all the same as the least restrictive alternative in the United States in 1979. Within the context of any of these settings, moreover, we find privileged extensions of freedom, the unchallenged special considerations which certain people or groups enjoy. Certainly, Nixon not only wanted the privileges awarded to the President of the United States but he took for himself privileges that earlier office holders did not have. Certainly, a Rockefeller, a United States Senator, a "super star," and other individuals and groups (such as priests and rabbis) enjoy specific and sometimes general unchallenged special privileges. Such privileges as those which are the right of clergy and celebrities are not what we have in mind when we advocate the least restrictive alternative for mentally retarded people, but they are part of the context in which our definition will have to work.

For a year once, I was on leave from my university responsibilities in order to direct a new Division of Mental Retardation in a State Department of Mental Health. It was my responsibility to oversee all of the state's institutional programs for the mentally retarded, which were many, as well as their community programs, which at that time constituted a handful of nursery school classes. Soon after assuming this position, I visited one of those state schools and, accompanied by the superintendent, toured the entire facility. It was payday and lines were queued up at the cashier. Off to the side was a large table on which were piled hundreds of dozens of eggs. And as the workers left the cashier's cage, many of them stopped at the egg stand and purchased one or more boxes of eggs from a man who seemed to be very familiar with the situation. I went over to ask him what the jumbo eggs cost. "Twenty cents a dozen," was the reply. I identified myself and expressed surprise that the state was selling its eggs in this manner and at such a low price. He informed me that these weren't the state's eggs, but his. He also informed me that he was the manager of the state school's farm and that the chickens who laid these eggs were his chickens. After probing, I learned that the state indeed owned thousands of chickens, but so did he. I also learned that this man had the unusual ability to know for sure which were the state's chickens and which were his. And he repeated that these, indeed, were his eggs, laid by his chickens.

Anyone who can look at a field of thousands of chickens and know which are his and, furthermore, know for sure that his chickens would not eat the state's feed, is indeed a special person. But I think it's not coincidental to find such special people who enjoy omnipotent characteristics and unusual privileges in places where most of the other people are exempt from virtually all privilege. And certainly, a home for the mentally retarded is just the place for a bright state employee to learn to be better than most other people, not only better but different, possessed with rare powers.

There are many reasons why people lust for privileges, but I think the main reason—in a way the only reason—why a person wants more than he deserves is because he has a rotten memory. People who don't remember that they are going to die seem to engage in more than their share of silly business as they take more than their share of the common wealth. Of course, everyone is greedy and everyone is silly, and therefore greed and privilege are relative terms. And so their definitions must be relative, with greed meaning to want more than one's share, and privilege determined by who's above and who's below you. Consequently, in one sense I am talking about all of us, myself included; but in another sense I am trying to concentrate on those among us who never have enough, may have more than what's good for them, and always seem to need to be told what's real and what's artificial.

Nixon is a prominent example of forgetful and silly greed. Why did he buy a million dollar house here and another one there, while all the time he had a big free White House in Washington and a free camp in Maryland? He may have expected to live forever. Not really, but really!

But there are other examples to recall. I want to believe that at least some of the people who enjoyed extended freedoms once felt a sense of duty attached to their privilege or, at least, they appeared to pay back something to society. For whatever harm he did to the Greek Culture, Lord Elgin served his government, the British Museum, and indeed the future culture as well when he brought the rubble of the Acropolis to England. The Elgin marbles, and other grand gestures of the privileged, seem to share a common trait: service to their people. And when we see the monuments of ancient times, we realize that they were so grandiose that they couldn't possibly have been offered to man, that they surely must have been created wholly for God. The monuments today are too puny for God, but too much for any one man. San Clemente doesn't even measure up to King George's summer palace, but is too much for Mr. Nixon.

There are infinite anomalies in *our* thinking and not thinking about death, perhaps because we tend to think about death only in terms of human beings. We assume animals are not concerned with their impending deaths. But it's the human being who's anomalous and not death. As everyone really knows, death is the most invariant of phenomena to which there is no less restrictive alternative. But how do the mentally retarded think about death? They do, of course, but do *we* remember that they do? It seems that it's difficult enough to remember our own deaths, much less whether the mentally retarded remember theirs. Of course, we think a lot about what will happen when we go, and what will happen to Billy or Mary, our retarded son or daughter. Or that Billy is one of God's innocents and he'll therefore surely go to heaven. But do we ever think about whether Billy thinks about his death? Of course not! In the same way we don't think (or is it care?) about what our pet canary thinks about his death, it is difficult for us to think that retarded people have the same thoughts and worries that we have. As a matter of fact, in all the years I've been in this work, I found but one article in the literature that deals with this question; and that forty-year-old report restricts itself to the mildly retarded, those who are most nearly like the rest of us.

What does death have to do with privileged extensions of freedom? Maybe almost everything. The privileged "need" a San Clemente to counteract the often dim but always disquieting knowledge of their fate. A mentally retarded person isn't even thought about as a person who knows he's going to die. Consequently, what difference could it make what else he may be thinking about, what he may like to have in terms of the world's extras? After all, *we* deserve that car, that cruise, that cashmere, that special privilege. *We* have something to worry about; not the retard! He gets life's subsistence rations, not merely because he hasn't earned more, but because he won't appreciate more, and because he won't suffer the way we suffer during our mortal life. He doesn't need diversions to make him forget his mortality.

Well, it may not be true. The mentally retarded person may know an awful lot more than we think he knows. The mentally retarded person may know more about the underprivileged than most anyone around, even those who live in the ghetto. He's an expert on the most restrictive environment. The mentally retarded person and Mr. Nixon should write the definitive book on the least restrictive environment. They represent the range and the expertise.

LOOPHOLES

Perhaps the most important point I want to make is that the issues and solutions in our field can appear clear and simple only as long as we wear the blinders of specialization. It isn't hard to think we know exactly what a least restrictive environment is if we think of it as a contrast to a dreary, segregated, and educationally counterproductive special class. It's even easier to think we know what it means in contrast to the locked back ward of an antiquated institution. Yet, life does not derive its meaning or dignity from contrasts; people don't remain cheerful from being told that things could be or used to be worse. Though in the end we may be unable to articulate precise definitions, we must try to provide mentally retarded people with opportunities that are not merely better but good. It should be a sobering reminder to us that, when the pioneers in our field undertook this task, despite the greatest good will and thoughtful deliberation they led to the development of modern institutional settings. In offering enormous benefits, their work led to the loss of everything important to their beneficiaries.

If the line between love and hate is at times indistinct, the line between privilege and restriction may be at times nonexistent. How can we distinguish between people who are very rich and people in the most restrictive institutions? To be provided with all possible services, to have them at hand and receive them free is to enjoy enormous privilege. The very rich can have tutors instruct them or their children in their own homes. So can the mentally retarded—although their homes are called state schools. The very rich and the mentally retarded have swimming pools, parks, playgrounds on the premises where they live; doctors make house calls; paid staff cook meals, wash clothes, clean and straighten up their rooms.

And the difference between the very rich and the mentally retarded is not to be found in the attitudes of the public. Both are viewed in stereotyped, often dehumanizing, ways by "typical" members of society. They are frequently assumed to be unable and unwilling to perform meaningful work. They are assumed to prefer to be "with their own kind," apart from general society. Neither group is supposed to have an understanding of "real life" sufficient to make them independent and viable members of society. And finally, both the very rich and the mentally retarded are often regarded as unpredictable and potentially dangerous.

Of course in making these comparisons, which could be extended even further, I am in no uncertainty as to which structure is the mansion and which is a state school. Their important similarity is only in the fact that most of us can tell instantly which is which. I have constructed the ridiculous parallel only in order to point out that, in practice, we distinguish between the conditions of wealth and mental retardation not on the basis of the objective criteria—in which they are similar—but by means of an intuitive grasp of countless unspecified subtleties. Precise criteria only work in these matters when we know the conclusion ahead of time. We know that, despite the restrictiveness of the trappings of wealth, the life of the wealthy is the freest possible; and that despite the privileges of institutionalized life, it is a life restricted to the point of extinction.

In the past, when policy was guided by the supposedly dangerous mechanism of judgment, this intuitive understanding of differences was enough. Today, because we have grown impatient with our history of cruelly mistaken judgments, our policy must be in the precise and objective form of a federal law. So, what *is* a restrictive environment today?

QUASI-LEGAL PRACTICES

Part of the reason we are now in need of legal definitions for the field is that so much of what has been reprehensible in the past has been quasi-legal. I'm no lawyer, and a good lawyer would surely discuss this less clumsily than I am about to, but most good lawyers probably don't know as much about the quasi-legal practices in the field of mental retardation as I do. So you will have to settle for the inevitable trade-off. Discussing quasi-anything usually requires one to walk a fine line, because while "it" isn't quite kosher, "it" isn't exactly out of bounds. While there may not be a law or regulation allowing the practice, there doesn't seem to be very much precedent forbidding it. Or conversely, while there may not be something on the books forbidding the practice, it doesn't seem to be in good taste, the kind of thing that ladies and gentlemen would condone. Some examples of quasi-legal practices in the field of mental retardation must certainly include the continued approval of sterilization, inmate employment without compensation, and assignment of the recently deceased as medical school cadavers.

For many years, I've written about all of the above and more. Indeed, I have spent the last 20 years cataloguing virtually every type of legal, illegal, and quasi-legal abuse perpetrated on the mentally retarded. I've described the work of the cadaver committee in a New England city, sterilization practices at various state schools, the pulling of teeth of inmates who bite themselves or others, the pulling of plugs at distinguished medical centers, other premature or strange deaths, even stranger autopsy investigations, peonage in its almost-infinite forms, a severe spastic choking to death on a whole hard boiled egg, a severely retarded bed patient nearly bleeding to death after his groin was ripped open by a night assailant—yet he was not seen by a doctor until morning infirmary call, inmates involuntarily volunteered for dangerous experiments at Ivy League medical schools, children raped by older inmates, and older inmates brutalized by marauding adolescents. And of course, although many of these atrocities could have been classified as illegal and the perpetraters could have been prosecuted, they hardly ever were; there is hardly a disruption of institutional routine when such situations occur.

I rummaged through my files, but there seemed nothing new to say about quasi-legal practices. Yet, I knew that I must say something. The very idea of "least restrictive environment" was born out of a history of quasi-legal practices applied to people. I then went to my diary, which is used, if anything, as a last resort. I usually think about the diary as "the desperation book." It contains hundreds and hundreds of pages of observations never published, ideas never fully developed, and lots and lots of things that can't be published until I and/or some people are gone, or I am too old to care about the consequences. The diary is my "money in the bank" book, because most of it can be published any time—this year or in 10 years—not because it's so good but because it represents timeless problems. I knew exactly what I was looking for, the raw notes and descriptions that provided the background for a book I started alone in late 1975 and, luckily for me, finished in 1978 with Andrejs Ozolins and Joe McNally. I found pages and pages of description of institutional observations and stories about inmates and keepers.

Now I've read all of those pages and I want to tell you about Sophie, poor Sophie, who was a resident of the state school for the retarded and died at a local hospital, and may have died of neglect. To this day, the only consequence of Sophie's quasi-legal demise was the withdrawal of medical services to the state school by the group of physicians in the community who had then been serving that place. There have been other inadequately explained deaths since Sophie's, and there have been other medical groups attending residents of the state school. (Life goes on. And death.) What follows was written at the time it happened in late 1975. I am sure that somebody somewhere in America today has just seen an inmate die needlessly, or has just learned that a medical group is withdrawing its favors from the state's bughouse, or has just attended a meeting where promises were made to finally fix up the state school, or is right now reading in the evening paper that the state has finally found a way to serve the residential needs of the mentally retarded. But the deaths continue, nearly unnoticed and sufficiently legal. I'm not surprised. If everything about Sophie's life was legal, why shouldn't everything about her death be legal?

This has been a strange week, very strange indeed. While I write this, we are flying thousands of feet above the earth (stewardesses and pilots have told me exactly how high these planes go, but I seem never able to remember). I try to read yesterday's local paper, but my mind wanders to thoughts about last evening's meeting of our Advocacy Board. I could kick myself for getting so angry, not really for getting angry but for showing my anger. Why can't these good people realize, as I realize, that case-by-case advocacy will consume us, will play into the hands of those who want to maintain the status quo, or regress further toward a segregated and bureaucratized society? We "win" victory after victory on behalf of this family or that one, no mean achievements, and I am not knocking those accomplishments. However, while we win those skirmishes, the city breaks ground for a new segregated facility, this one to contain the so-called "trainables." Case by case, we advocate for children and their families. Some we win, some we lose; the record is fairly impressive. But, we are losing too many; too many children are still denied educations; too many people sit in back rooms receiving little or nothing of society's interest or services; too many are in locked institutions, not because they must be locked up but, rather, because there is no other "place" to be, because others are presumed to need locked institutions and *the* (only) "place" was created for them. And, with most of those clients whom we cannot help, the problem is exacerbated because of a paucity of resources, and an absence of community interest in them. How could it be any different, when the major policy decisions have been, and continue to be, anchored to institutional development and support? So I battled with my friends, decent people torn between what they want for their own children and what they want for society. The debate wore me out, driving me eventually to leave the meeting, not because of my anger— though I was angry—but because I was weary, and wanted to go home, and remove those stale clothes and drive out of my head the morbid thoughts of practical people.

Indeed, it has been a strange week. I force myself to think about Sophie, but not to cheer myself up. Last Monday was scheduled to be a low keyed routine day: a few appointments, the return of a few calls, some letters to write and, if I were really lucky, a stolen hour or two to write some prose or verse for myself. Nobody knew very much earlier than Monday, therefore nobody told me, that Sophie was to be buried on Monday. And, even had they known it would happen she needed to be buried on Monday, nobody would have suspected then that I would have been asked to attend the funeral, or that I would have accepted the invitation had the offer come. You see, the very first time I ever laid eyes on Sophie was this past Monday at the Garfield Funeral Home. I saw her, but she didn't see me.

Sophie was a resident at the State Developmental Center, nee the State School, nee the Asylum for Idiots. She had been there for many, many years, leading what I was told was an uneventful and unhappy life. She became ill, very ill, so ill that she was removed to the Community General

Hospital. There she died, approximately one week later. All of the afore-mentioned doesn't appear very interesting, even to me. But what was more than interesting, quite inflammatory in this community, concerned the allegation that Sophie did not die of natural causes. There were charges, confused and contradictory but strong charges, that—as we have lately learned to say—the plugs were pulled; Sophie was euthanized: she was rewarded with a dignified death. A big cheer for Death With Dignity, and the Happy Angel that supervises it all. Rejoice, some told us. Sophie has left this vale of misery to an eternal peace and happiness that she did not find on earth. So we gathered together at the funeral home, the priest gave his blessings and read from the Scriptures, some said their Hail Mary's or Hail whatevers, we signed the guest's book—guests?—and went our own ways.

The local Death With Dignity Society, and there really is one here, should be pleased. The crazy thing about it all is that, in the Cosmos, there may be some explanation for all of this; and, it would not surprise me if such an explanation agrees with the death wishers. Yet, there is also something evil here, something that would tell a human being that it is time for her to die; but if we were in your shoes, sister, we would live! It's best that you die now, first because you're sick. If you were not sick, we would not kill you. Yet, not only are you sick, you are old (is 63 really that old?), and not only are you sick and old, you are defective. Sickness we sometimes tolerate if it's not too much sickness. The aged are sometimes revered, if they are lucky and not sick. And, even the defectives need not be marked early or, especially, with the Terrible Decree. But, Sophie, even you must agree that you gave us no choice. Being sick, old, and defective necessarily must strip you of the rights other people have guaranteed to them. Don't blame us, Sophie, this is all your fault. Besides, you'll be happier up there than down here. You're really very lucky. It's all over for you, and we have yet to face the terror that is now behind you. What we have done for you is the stuff that causes ordinary people to become true humanitarians.

My thoughts continue to wander, focusing now on Tuesday evening. It is the day after Sophie's funeral. It is 8:00 p.m., then 9, then the hour approaches midnight. We are in Room 407 of the County Courthouse. The County Legislative Commission to investigate Mental Health and Mental Retardation is holding its last formal hearing prior to the creation of its report to the citizens. I am a member of the Commission and, just before termination of the long evening's discussions, I ask the Superintendent of the State Developmental Center to reflect upon the future, "In the best of all possible worlds, what do you envision for the Developmental Center in 10 years?"

"In 10 years things will not be very much different than they are today. Can I speculate about the world in 50 years?"

"Will the people wait 50 years? There are people who desperately need help, not even in 10 years, tomorrow."

"Don't misunderstand me. If I had my way, we would evacuate the Developmental Center in 10 years, five years, or sooner if we could. We would give it to the State, or to your University, to use as a dormitory, or for some other educational purpose."

I don't respond. I am embarrassed for him. I think about those times six years ago when it might not have been too late to stop the construction of this $25,000,000 monstrosity. I attempt to avoid remembering the pleadings and arguments, even the threats we made, anything to block construction of the new State School. I remember too much. With a parliamentary tactic, I influence my colleagues to adjourn. Enough is enough.

Quite early the next morning, I am back in my office returning calls again, answering mail, trying to see each of the people who want to see me. The phone rings. It's the Executive Director of the President's Committee on Mental Retardation. Not any president's committee, *The President's!* Would I do a study for them? Would I visit the institutions that continue to defy extinction? Would I expose the rottenness, the abuse, the mismanagement, the inhuman treatment?

"Sure," I reply, "what else do I have to do? As a matter of fact, I was just thinking about those problems today. Just coincidentally, the morning *Times* had an article summarizing the deliberations of the Select Legislative Committee Studying the Mentally and Physically Handicapped in our state. You wouldn't enjoy hearing this, but that Committee heard witness after witness berate the State Mental Health program for neglecting their clients, for the confusion it spawns, for its bureaucratic indifference and insensitivity. Sure, I'll study those state schools for you. I hope you don't think I've been sitting by this phone all morning waiting for you to call, though. You just happened to catch me in, between assignments, so to speak, between life and death. You caught me just as I was beginning to believe that Sophie was the lucky one."

I've been arguing that, as Robert Frost might have said if he had been a poet of the human service industry, "Something there is that doesn't love a definition." No sooner do we build a row of definitions—definitions of restrictiveness or abuse, freedom, or dignity—than it begins to crumble into loopholes, exceptions, and quasi-legal rubble. And I've been trying to show that this doesn't happen so much because we don't build good definitions but because life simply won't be captured in definitions.

Yet, even as I describe our failure to define things better, even as I read my notes on Sophie, whose life slipped away over the edge of a definition of human rights, I too have to agree that we need better definitions. Perhaps, to burden Robert Frost a little more, "Good definitions make good neighbors." And though they fall down in the winter of our inattentiveness, each spring we must build them anew, as though they would stay.

VARIATIONS ON THE DEFINITION OF RESTRICTIVENESS

The courts and administrators, the hosts of professional fields involved—and of course everyday citizens too—all of those who have given it a serious try have had their difficulties defining restrictiveness. Consequently, I need not preface my suggestions with any elaborate disclaimer: I too will not provide the definitive statement. But for whatever it is worth, I think about a "restrictive environment" as one in which, if placed there himself, the superintendent of a state mental institution would feel insulted and threatened. Conversely, I think about a "least restrictive environment" as one in which, if placed there, the inmate of a state mental hospital would sense that he is now living somewhere that is quite different from and much more pleasant than, the hospital. Certainly, these definitions will not escape the need to be rebuilt. And certainly, they don't provide anything but the shape to our thinking for purposes of developing a continuum. But in some situations, they may offer useful analogies, and analogies may be the strongest definitions we can get.

A golden rule of the Old Testament and all human discourse since the beginning of civilization, has been, is, and most surely continues to be that, "You shall love your neighbor as yourself." It's found as the cornerstone of the faith and strivings of all decent people. It's the fundamental rule of the Torah and has been reiterated again and again by Christ, His disciples, and people everywhere in the world. "Love your neighbor as yourself" is easy to recall, so easy that everyone seems to know this law; yet it seems even easier to forget.

The term, "least restrictive environment" is also easy to recall, but it is the wrong term. It lets us all off the hook, speaking about those at risk in such a way as to deny this golden rule, the "agreement" that we must love our neighbors as ourselves. Suppose "least restrictive environment" were termed "What I demand as my rights," and suppose "restrictiveness" was termed "that which is contemptible and inhumane," wouldn't the mentally retarded and the mentally ill and the elderly and other modern day pariahs be better represented than they are now? If we thought about restrictiveness in terms of this golden rule, would we be arguing anymore to defend small institutions as relatively less restrictive and, consequently, more acceptable? If we remember this golden rule, would we need to remember all of this folderol about per capita floor space, staff/patient ratios, standards for state and federal reimbursements, or accreditation?

I think that the reason such a big deal is made about the technical aspects of environments for the unwanted is because, first, people don't want to admit they are dealing with the unwanted and, second, people don't want to put themselves in the same category as those unwanted. I know that any loving son or father could never easily place his parents or child in one of our traditional state institutions, whether it has been designated most restrictive or least restrictive. Therefore, I also know that the term "least restrictive environment" ought to be reserved for places that, by definition, fall outside of the state's traditional mental institutions. If an environment is truly "least restrictive" it would have nothing to do with departments of mental health or with clients placed in their facilities *because* of mental incapacitation. In the world of mental health and mental retardation, people live only in large institutions or small institutions. If they are caught in the mental health-mental retardation net, by definition they shouldn't be thought about as living in a least restrictive environment.

In my mind, I see many variations of the definition of restrictiveness. How can we be satisfied with single one-dimensional definitions? Is that really what science is all about? Or is it really what blind professionalism is all about? I am dissatisfied with the official definitions, so dissatisfied that I am unable even to merely note them for the record here. Maybe it is my idiosyncrasy, but I think I would better understand the situation a person is in if I knew how many mistakes he was entitled to make before he was yanked from the game. Robert Frost defined my idea of the least restrictive life very satisfactorily when he wrote:

> But yield who will to their separation,
> My object in living is to unite
> My avocation and my vocation
> As my two eyes make one in sight.

Two Tramps in Mudtime, 1967

Getting yanked after one mistake or two seems to illustrate what a terribly restrictive situation might be like. And being in a position where a man's job and his interests are part of one life, where what he wants to do is what he has to do, seems to be an example of what a least restrictive environment might be.

Why is it that artists seem to describe life so much better than the rest of us do? Of course, that's the *one* thing that artists do so much better than the rest of us. Then why is it that the rest of us don't turn more to artists to explain what we are unable to explain for ourselves? It hasn't always been this way. In the old days, artists were used exactly that way, from Victorian painters who described street urchins and fallen women, to Dickens who wrote about them, to journalists who reported it all, artists were once society's definers. What got in the way were the universities and their professors, and the professionals they eventually trained, and the disciples of the professionals, the gullible public. Unnecessary science became a mischievous nuisance.

This discourse sounds more conspiratorial and menacing than I want it to be. To be sure, professionalism in America wasn't created to close out the artist and do in the consumer. To be sure, the country had its fill of barber surgeons, patent medicines laced with dope, and not only quack doctors and quack patients but quack ministers, teachers, and scientists. Abraham Flexner had a point to make just as Ralph Nader had virtually the same point to make half a century later. But while Flexner's point was that amateurs were running things and it is about time that professionals got their various acts together and monitored the world, Nader's point is that we better beware of the professionals, who are greedy louts running things for their own benefit. Abraham Flexner once saw the enemy embedded within the suspicion, the prejudice, and ignorance of the 19th century. Ralph Nader sees the enemy embedded within the firm pillars of status and respectability created out of the Flexner Revolution. And while it is not difficult to find many among us today who see the shortsightedness of Flexner's vision, there are too few here who see the catastrophe of Nader's Revolution. Flexner created a professionalized society. Nader seems to want to overcome that evil by a bureaucratized society, one to be controlled by the people to be sure but, nevertheless, people who would weigh everything, test everything, define everything, and be suspicious about anything. Possibly, at this time what is needed more than either Flexner or Nader is a good poet who would give us some hints on how to live better with each other. Maybe we once needed Flexner. Maybe we needed Nader when he came along. But I'll take Frost.

CONCLUSION

In the real world, people die for their freedoms. In the field of mental retardation, they hold conventions or invite each other to conferences. In the real world, people learn from each other, help each other, and protect each other. In the field of mental retardation, one must be licensed to teach, certified to treat, and commissioned to protect. That which is considered to be good about the real world naturally unfolds. That which is considered to be good about the field of mental retardation is professionally controlled. What's least restrictive about the real world derives from thousands of years of human discourse under such diverse leaders as Attilla and Lincoln, Pharaoh and Moses, George III and George Washington, Martin Luther and Martin Luther King. What's most restrictive about the world of mental retardation derives from 200 years of professional interest in the pathology rather than in the universality of people. Professionals have created much of the need to do something about the problem of too restrictive environments forced upon the mentally retarded. We have created or been much of the problem, and now we seem anxious to do something about our unholy work. Indeed, we must do something, but less to rescue the mentally retarded than to redeem ourselves, less to obtain their freedoms than to establish ours, less because they need us than because we need them.

　　When I was a little boy, I would jump out of bed most mornings barely able to wait for what lay ahead. And there were days when I couldn't sleep because of eagerness to push aside the darkness for a time when people were allowed to take advantage of all the wonders there. Frost said he had a lover's quarrel with the world. Of course, I didn't know about Frost then and I surely didn't know the world on those terms, but I too have had an affair with the world, with the air and the birds, but also with the movement of people on hot steamy sidewalks, and even with the institutions, with everything we think of as life. From the start, I was lucky I was born and lived as a free person. I never needed to learn what it is to be alone in an alien land. I never needed to know what it is to be without advocates, what it means to need advocates. I never needed protection against my brothers. I never needed protection against my government. I never needed protection against God. What harm befell me, I usually did to myself. What grief occurred was the grief done to any fragile human being, usually more by accident than by design. Thank God I was born free and now live free. But I am very sad that not everyone shares such good fortune.

We have listened to neither the inner heart nor the call for the common good, to neither God nor fellow man. We have made swords into guns. We've done unto others. We will believe only the poets who confirm what we have believed. We want to believe that literal fences do indeed make good neighbors, and that tough attitudes characterize practical and wise men of the world. We seem convinced that stone is good for fences, and hearts, and ideas. Our faith is more in ourselves than in mankind, but little in ourselves. We have created an unnecessarily restricted society. To free ourselves, we must free the old, the weak, and the handicapped because, in truth, they *are* us. And we resist that kind of world. Our problem is not one of merely defining what represents the least restrictive environment in an unjust society, but rather one of changing that society for everyone. This is not a local or professional issue, but a world issue. We should stop confusing ourselves. We should try to better understand that we are not dealing here only with the problem of the mentally retarded, but with our common problem, yours and mine, the problem of facing our lives as if it will end, and in believing in the hereafter as if it might be there.

Perhaps the reason I kept returning to poets in this paper, the reason I believe they can give us better guidance in life than bureaucrats or scientists, is that when we read poetry we *know* that we are dealing with metaphors, analogies, ways of thinking rather than list of facts. Surely there can be no doubt that if 'Love thy neighbor' were a federal regulation, it would become meaningless and useless. Emerson nailed down one part of our common problem when he said that, "All our science lacks is a human side." A more serious part of our common problem is that too much of humanism has gone scientific. And too much of our science makes it easier to banish our brothers from our lives.

REFERENCE

Frost, Robert, "Two Tramps in Mudtime." In E. C. Lathem (Ed.), *The Poetry of Robert Frost*. New York: Holt, Rinehart, & Winston, 1969.

Annotated Readings

These suggested readings do not include all of the books, monographs and other references which you may find helpful in your study of mental retardation. However, it's a start, formidable enough to require you to make judgments concerning what you should and need not read, and extensive enough to cover much if not all of the field's literature. A special effort was made to suggest readings that would particularly complement essays appearing in this book.

This book's author is grateful to Kathleen O'Brien Ganley, a graduate student in the Syracuse University School of Information Studies and a former special education teacher, for accomplishing the major work on the development of this reading guide, culled from a lengthy bibliography created during the many years the author has taught the basic course in mental retardation.

Begab, M. J., & Richardson, S. A. *The Mentally Retarded and Society.* Baltimore: University Park Press, 1975.

The proceedings of the joint conference of the National Institute of Child Health Services and Human Development of the U.S. Public Health Services are presented in this collection of papers. The intent of the conference was to join the two diverse areas within the field of mental retardation, the biological aspect and the behavioral aspect, in the hope of developing a biosocial approach to research.

Braginsky, D. D., & Braginsky, B. M. *Hansels and Gretels.* New York: Holt, Rinehart and Winston, 1971.

The authors report on a study conducted to examine the inmates of state training schools. They report that many children labeled cultural-familial retarded or educable mentally retarded are placed in institutions solely because they could not or would not function 'normally' in society. The authors propose that these institutions are merely society's holding areas for unwanted children. Their findings call for reevaluation of placement procedures and recognize the need for special programs for these children.

Carver, J. N., & Carver, N. *The Family of the Retarded Child*. Syracuse: Center on Human Policy and Syracuse University Press, 1972.

A group of families, each with a severely retarded child, were interviewed for this study. The effects of the retarded child on the family and social relationships are reviewed. The attempts of the family to cope with rearing the retarded child and the eventual decisions concerning her/his care are discussed.

Clarke, A. M., and Clarke, A. D. B. *Mental Deficiency: The Changing Outlook*. New York: The Free Press, 1974.

This is the expanded and revised edition of a major work in the field of mental deficiency. Study in this field has undergone many changes in recent years; it is no longer being neglected as it once was. Major advances in research in the prevention and treatment of mental deficiency are presented. The authors also discuss assessment and educational services.

Conley, R. W. *The Economics of Mental Retardation*. Baltimore: Johns Hopkins University Press, 1973.

Numerous aspects of mental retardation are covered in this work, from epidemiology to examination of various programs intended to introduce the retarded into the community. Included is a lengthy, important cost-benefit analysis that compares the cost of various treatment programs to their effectiveness.

Foster, H. *Ribbin', Jivin' and Playin' the Dozens*. Cambridge: Ballinger Publishers, 1974.

Many educators in inner city classrooms are ill equipped to relate to the urban black culture. This creates a serious obstacle to effective education. The cultural and communication barrier between teachers and ghetto youths often results in the child being misinterpreted as mentally retarded or learning disabled. The author discusses tactics educators may employ to increase their understanding of black culture and jargon.

Gerbner, G., Ross, C., & Zigler, E. *Child Abuse Reconsidered: An Analysis and Agenda for Action*. New York: Oxford University Press, 1980.

This collection of essays examines child abuse and its causes, defines abuse more carefully, and restudies the role of the United States in preventing child abuse. The abuse of children in both legally and socially sanctioned contexts is studied. The authors close with an "agenda for action" that calls on public organizations and the private citizen to aid in abolishing child abuse.

Ginzburg, E., & Bray, D. W. *The Uneducated.* New York: Columbia University Press, 1953.

A major study to examine the poorly educated in military and civilian life is reported in this book. The authors examine the progressive changes in American educational systems, noting a high rate of poorly educated and semi-literate persons in certain geographic areas. A presentation of case studies concerning poorly educated military personnel provided with special training shows that people can learn given adequate motivation. A need for additional federal aid and programming is recognized in order to alleviate regional deficiencies in basic education.

Goffman, E. *Asylums.* New York: Doubleday, 1961.

Contained within this work is a collection of four essays that deal with various aspects of inmate life in institutions. Topics discussed include examination of social life within institutions, the effects of institutionalization on prior social relationships, the efforts of inmates to retain self-esteem and independence, and the professional's role in inmate adjustment. This book has become the definitive work in understanding the impact of institutionalization on people.

Grossman, F. K. *Brothers and Sisters of Retarded Children.* Syracuse: Syracuse University Press, 1972.

The impact of a mentally retarded sibling within the family is examined. The author's report on this previously unstudied problem presents the siblings' attitudes and feelings about mental retardation and the effect of having a mentally retarded sibling on their self-image, home environment, and social situations.

Grossman, H. J. (Ed.). *Manual on Terminology and Classification in Mental Retardation.* Washington D.C.: American Association on Mental Deficiency, 1975.

The American Association on Mental Deficiency has recognized the need for a systematic, well-designed scheme for classifying the mentally retarded in order to meet individual needs. The Association first published its official manual on terminology in 1921, and it has been revised periodically to reflect current professional thinking. The manual is composed of charts and tables for classification and an extensive glossary of terms useful for the layman as well as the professional.

Hausserman, E. *Developmental Potential of Preschool Children: An Evaluation of Intellectual, Sensory and Emotional Functioning.* New York: Grune and Stratton, 1958.

Professionals dealing with handicapped children have long recognized the inappropriateness of using standardized tests for measuring the abilities of these children. The author has developed a series of examinations pertinent to the special child and her/his abilities. The results of these examinations provide a profile of the child's abilities and developmental potential. Lengthy directions for the administration and interpretation of the tests are provided.

Hobbs, N. *The Future of Children*. San Francisco: Jossey-Bass, 1974.

The inappropriate classification and labeling of exceptional children led to the Department of Health, Education and Welfare project summarized in this book. The goals of the project were to identify the best services available for the exceptional child and the means for providing these services.

Hurley, R. *Poverty and Mental Retardation*. New York: Random House, 1969.

The relationship between mental retardation and poverty is examined. Public ignorance and apathy toward the poor have created a continually deteriorating condition. Poverty leads to cultural deprivation, often resulting in mental retardation that subsequently breeds further poverty. Poor-quality education and substandard health care, both common to the poor, increase the potential for cultural-familial retardation. Two vivid case studies representative of this syndrome are presented.

Jenkins, J. J., & Paterson, D. G. (Eds.). *Studies in Individual Differences*. New York: Appleton-Century-Crofts, 1961.

The meaning and measurement of intelligence are the focus of this selected collection of readings. The editors have attempted to present a representative historical sampling of major contributions to this field.

Lippman, L., & Goldberg, I. I. *Right to Education*. New York: Teachers College Press, 1973.

This book chronicles the Pennsylvania Right to Education case of 1971. This landmark decision found that all children, regardless of their handicap, are entitled to educational opportunities equal to their ability. Many aspects of the case, the history and development of the suit, and the court's decision and its repercussions, including its effects on similiar litigation in other states, are examined.

Sarason, S. B. *The Creation of Settings and the Future Society*. San Francisco: Jossey-Bass, 1972.

An examination of human settings, their creation, and their failure is presented. The author labels a setting as any instance in which two or more people come together in a new relationship over a sustained period of time in order to achieve certain goals. He examines the formation of new settings and the reasons why so many of them fail. He suggests a series of preconditions for creating successful settings consistent with their purpose.

Sarason, S. B., & Doris, J. E. *Psychological Problems in Mental Deficiency*. New York: Harper and Brothers, 1969.

Many aspects of the study of mental deficiency are discussed. A brief historical presentation of the field is developed. Examination of the use of labels and classification in dealing with the mentally retarded, the institutionalization of mentally retarded persons and the associated problems, as well as various specific types of mental deficiency such as phenylketonuria (PKU), mongolism, and autism, are discussed.

Sarason, S. B. & Doris, J. E. *Educational Handicap, Public Policy and Society History: A Broadened Perspective on Mental Retardation*. New York: The Free Press, 1979.

The premise that mental retardation is a convenient label invented by culture and society rather than a definable concept is presented. Historical research and an overview of present-day issues such as deinstitutionalization, professional training, and mainstreaming are discussed.

Scott, R. A., *The Making of Blind Men*. New York: Russell Sage Foundation, 1969.

Presented in this text is the theory that blindness is a social role created by society and played out by the blind. Sighted people have specific expectations of acceptable blind behavior and blind people have learned to play these roles. The effectiveness of programs and agencies for the blind are examined and suggestions for needed improvements are given. Although the author discusses only blindness, this analysis has applications to other disabilities, including mental retardation.

Seagoe, M. V. *Yesterday Was Tuesday, All Day, All Night*. Boston: Little, Brown, 1964.

This interesting book traces the life of a "mongoloid" boy from birth to death. The boy, Paul, raised by his wealthy father, is provided with intensive tutoring and training. He learns to read and write—the major part of the book is composed of excerpts from the diary he kept. The book raises the question of just how much mentally retarded persons are capable of learning given proper stimulation and training.

Shelley, M. *Frankenstein*. New York: The New American Library, 1965.

Unlike Hollywood's interpretation, *Frankenstein* is the story of a thinking, feeling, caring being rejected by his creator, Doctor Frankenstein, and society, solely because of his "different" appearance. Subtle analogies can be identified between the so-called monster and the mentally retarded. The being's eventual violent retaliation is a result of society's scornful rejection. Passages concerning the being's development of language and his unsuccessful attempts at friendship are very moving.

Smith, E. W., and Smith, A. M. *Minamata*. New York: Holt, Rinehart and Winston, 1975.

This photographic essay employs graphic illustrations to depict the human suffering arising from unregulated industrial pollution. The people of Minamata, Japan, were subject to deformity and untimely death as a result of the unchecked methyl-mercury poisoning of their bay. This work identifies the injustice done to these people, their struggle to correct the situation through legal channels, and the eventual outcome of their efforts. This book underscores the unintended consequences of industrialization and illuminates the importance of an ecological approach to the study of human problems.

Sontag, E., Smith, J., & Certo, N. (Eds.). *Educational Programming for the Severely and Profoundly Handicapped*. Reston, Va.: Division on Mental Retardation, Council for Exceptional Children, 1977.

The need for a more scientific approach to the educational programming of the severely and profoundly retarded is brought forth in this book. The editors present a threefold concept for effective educational programming. The presentation of educational models and teaching strategies should be useful for educators of retarded children.

Szasz, T. *The Manufacture of Madness*. New York: Harper and Row, 1970.

The author presents the position that the term mental illness is a fabricated label for people who do not fit society's norms, just as the term witches was a fabricated label in the past. He calls for the termination of "institutional psychiatry" in which the patient loses his individual rights and is subjected to treatment and control without his consent. The use of "controlled psychiatry," in which the patient retains control over himself and treatment methods, is advocated. The author's position has been later applied in reconceptualizing mental retardation.

Task Force on Children Out of School. *Suffer the Children: The Politics of Health in Massachusetts*. Boston: Beacon Press, 1970.

The Task Force on Children Out of School conducted a study into the lack of concern and outright neglect shown by the Department of Mental

Health in Massachusetts for children with special needs. The Task Force blames this condition on seriously misguided priorities and inappropriate use of funds by the Department. The Task Force aims to increase the awareness of Massachusetts citizens in an effort to enlist their assistance in correcting this situation.

Turnbull, A. P., & Turnbull, H. R. *Parents Speak Out*. Columbus, Ohio: Charles E. Merrill Publishing Company, 1978.

The authors have compiled an interesting collection, written by professionals in the field of special education who themselves have raised a handicapped child. The inability of some to find satisfactory answers to their questions or aid for their children, and their efforts to erase community ignorance, are reported. The frustrations encountered while learning to cope with a handicapped child are vividly presented in these frank and revealing chapters.

Wolfensberger, W. *The Origin and Nature of Our Institutional Models*. Syracuse: Human Policy Press, 1975.

The conceptual models used for designing institutions and caring for the mentally retarded come under close scrutiny in this report. The author examines various models of retarded behavior that are imposed in part by the architectural design of buildings. He calls for a more careful examination of the needs of the mentally retarded in order to establish services free of imposed models.

Wolfensberger, W. *The Principle of Normalization in Human Services*. Toronto: National Institute on Mental Retardation, 1972.

The author states that the goals of his work are to explain, clarify, and elaborate on the principle of normalization as a system of "human management." Normalization is defined as utilization of means that are as culturally normative as possible in order to establish and/or maintain personal behaviors and characteristics that are as culturally normative as possible. Strategies and mechanisms for implementing the normalization process are presented.

Wright, B. *Physical Disability—A Psychological Approach*. New York: Harper and Brothers, 1960.

It is a commonly held belief that a person's physical characteristics are an indication of the person's inner nature. The physically handicapped must deal with a society filled with such prejudices. The author examines the social relationships of disabled persons and how they attempt to cope with life and their handicaps.

Index